Dutch New York

Dutch New York

The Roots *of* HUDSON VALLEY CULTURE

EDITED BY ROGER PANETTA

with a foreword by Russell Shorto

HUDSON RIVER MUSEUM / FORDHAM UNIVERSITY PRESS

This book is being published in conjunction with the exhibition *Dutch New York: The Roots of Hudson Valley Culture*, organized by the Hudson River Museum, Yonkers, June 13, 2009 through January 10, 2010.

The exhibition was made possible, in part, through the support of the Office of the Westchester County Executive and the Westchester County Board of Legislators.

The catalog for *Dutch New York: The Roots of Hudson Valley Culture* was made possible, in part, by a grant from Furthermore: a program of the J.M. Kaplan Fund.

The exhibition and catalog for *Dutch New York: The Roots of Hudson Valley Culture* is supported by a grant from the New York Council for the Humanities.
Any views, findings, and conclusions expressed in this exhibition and catalog do not necessarily represent those of the National Endowment for the Humanities.

"The Days of the Patriarchs: Washington Irving's *A History of New York*" by Phillip Lopate was originally published in *Boulevard*, Winter 1997, 204–222.

Library of Congress Cataloging in Publication Data
Dutch New York : the roots of Hudson Valley culture / edited by Roger Panetta.
    p. cm.
Includes bibliographical references and index.
ISBN 978-0-8232-3039-6 (cloth : alk. paper) — ISBN 978-0-8232-3040-2 (pbk. : alk. paper)
1. Hudson River Valley (N.Y. and N.J.)—History. 2. Hudson River Valley (N.Y. and N.J.)—Social life and customs. 3. Dutch—Hudson River Valley (N.Y. and N.J.)—History. 4. Dutch Americans—Hudson River Valley (N.Y. and N.J.)—History. I. Panetta, Roger G., 1939–
F127.H8D88 2009
974.7'30043931—dc22   2009008804

12 11 10 09   10 9 8 7 6 5 4 3 2

Frontispiece
CHARLES E. PONT
The Becalmed Half Moon 1609, 1937
Wood engraving, sheet: 11¼ x 9¾ in., image: 8 x 6 in.
Franklin D. Roosevelt Presidential Library and Museum, Hyde Park, New York, Gift of Franklin D. Roosevelt, 2005-13-40-8

Contents

Foreword *Russell Shorto vii*

Acknowledgments *xiii*

Introduction *Michael Botwinick 1*

PART ONE: 1609—THE PLANTING

1. Seafarers and Businessmen:
   The Growth of Dutch Commerce in the Lower Hudson River Valley *7*
   Oliver A. Rink

2. Encounters: Slavery and the Philipse Family: 1680–1751 *35*
   Dennis J. Maika

3. American Indian Villages to Dutch Farms:
   The Settling of Settled Lands in the Hudson Valley *73*
   William A. Starna

PART TWO: 1709—THE PERSISTENCE OF DUTCH INFLUENCE

4. Constructing the Tradition of Dutch American Architecture, 1609–2009 *93*
   Sean E. Sawyer

5. The Reformed Dutch Church and the Persistence of Dutchness
   in New York and New Jersey *137*
   Firth Haring Fabend

6. "I could not guess what she intended to do with it":
   Colonial American–Dutch Material Culture *159*
   Ruth Piwonka

PART THREE: 1809—ROMANTICIZING THE DUTCH

7. The Days of the Patriarchs: Washington Irving's *A History of New York* *191*
   Phillip Lopate

8. Imagining Dutch New York: John Quidor and the Romantic Tradition *223*
   Bartholomew F. Bland

9. Return in Glory: The Holland Society Visits "The Fatherland" *257*
   Laura Vookles

PART FOUR: 1909—SEARCHING FOR DUTCH HERITAGE

10. The Hudson-Fulton Celebration of 1909 *301*
   Roger Panetta

11. Franklin Roosevelt's "Dutchness": At Home in the Hudson Valley *339*
   Cynthia Koch

12. Displaying the Dutch: The Dyckman Farmhouse Museum
   and the Dutch Colonial Revival *377*
   Laura M. Chmielewski

CONCLUSION: 2009—WHAT DOES DUTCH HERITAGE MEAN TODAY?

13. The Dutch Legacy in America *411*
   David William Voorhees

Contributor Biographies *433*

Index *437*

Foreword

RUSSELL SHORTO

What is "Dutch"? What does the syllable signify? I remember the appearance, in 1999, of Edmund Morris's infamous biography of Ronald Reagan (infamous because Morris bizarrely fictionalized parts). It was called *Dutch* because that was Reagan's nickname, given to him at birth after his father pronounced that he looked like "a little bit of a fat Dutchman." It was striking that, amid all the coverage of the book, no one seemed to be confused about the topic; the word was just a word, just a title, signifying not a people or a language or a culture but, improbably, Ronald Reagan. In Amsterdam, where I currently live, I will sometimes be asked what Americans think of "the Dutch." I respond, gently or moderately aggressively, depending on the circumstances, that, in point of fact, by and large, they don't.

In the colonial history of North America, and in particular of the Hudson Valley, "Dutch" and "English" are clear, sometimes fierce, counterpoints. So it's interesting, mildly amusing even, to note that in the earliest written record of the word "Dutch," in 786, it is used to refer to the English. ("Dutch," of course, relates to *Deutsch*, and for part of the Middle Ages the term covered variations of German, including Old English.) "Dutch" is so very specific, yet it's ephemeral enough that the Dutch don't use the word to refer to themselves (except of course when they are speaking English, which is somehow a very Dutch thing to do).

All of this is to suggest that in American culture, and for that matter globally—in the Netherlands, the Low Countries, Holland (the very multiplicity of designations reinforces the point)—these people maintain, shall we say, a modest profile.

And yet, the Dutch have made an undeniably outsized contribution to world history. Their empire, their art, their ships. The stock market. Santa Claus. Cookies. The scope of Dutch innovations and influence beggars the imagination. The development of the concept of tolerance as a social glue to bind disparate peoples into one society, which the Dutch of the seventeenth century crafted, by itself calls for some reverberation, some recognition. Instead of which, you are more likely to get in response other, bastardized referents to tolerance: legalized prostitution, soft drugs.

And what does "Dutch New York" signify? While the term probably has little resonance in the broadest popular reckoning, it does carry various mean-

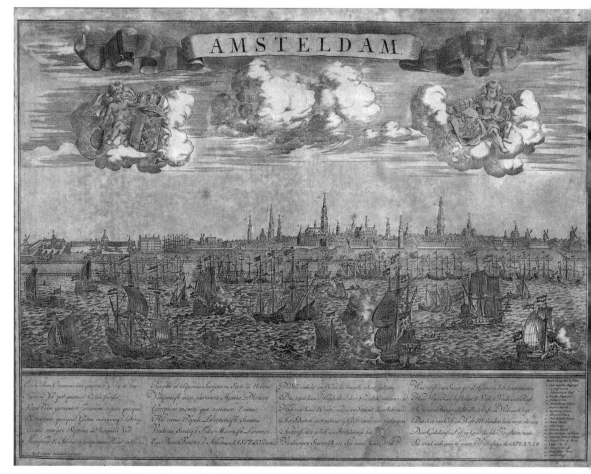

JACOB LOOTS
View of Amsterdam, c. 1660
Ink on paper with hand coloring, 20 x 28 in.
Van Cortlandt House Museum/The National Society
of Colonial Dames in the State of New York

ings, which have wended their way through the societal imagination over the past couple of centuries. In large part this is the legacy of Washington Irving's writings. Irving knew his history, but he chose, in his so-called Knickerbocker stories (that is, *Knickerbocker's History of New York*), to render it into fictional comic caricature. The historian Edwin Burrows has argued that it was the ubiquity of newspaper cartoons in the nineteenth century—and the need of cartoonists for stock characters to carry messages—that helped give the waddling, pink-faced Dutchmen Irving portrayed a place in the American popular imagination, and in so doing obscured the actual history.

But Irving's stories are mostly forgotten today. In the course of giving hundreds of talks about Dutch New York over the past four years, I came to con-

ALBERT BIERSTADT, American, 1830–1902
Discovery of the Hudson River, 1874
Oil on canvas, 72 x 122 in.
U.S. House of Representatives, Washington, D.C.

clude that for anyone under the age of sixty, I didn't need to dismantle the Irving myth because it was never a piece of their mental furniture in the first place.

The problem, then, for anyone interested in exploring and disseminating the history of the Dutch in New York and the surrounding area, is that of the blank slate, which is in a way a better problem to have, just as it's easier to build a house on an empty lot than to tear down a preexisting one first. But the blank slate has its own difficulties. Americans don't know a lot about the topic, but then again, they may not much care. If the topic is hopelessly twee and parochial, *should* they care?

But it isn't a small subject. The Dutch colony of New Netherland, founded in the wake of Henry Hudson's voyage of 400 years ago, proved to be remarkably fertile soil in which were planted several features of Dutch culture. These included the concept of tolerance, which the United Provinces had fashioned not as some grand ideal but as a practicality, a way to yoke together a society of immigrants, many of whom had streamed with relative ease into the aptly

HOWARD PYLE (1853–1911)
Arrival of Stuyvesant in New Amsterdam, 1901
Oil on canvas, 24 x 18 in.
Neville Public Museum of Brown County and Green Bay & De Pere Antiquarian Society
Painted for "Colonies and Nation" by Woodrow Wilson, *Harpers Monthly Magazine*,
February 1901.

Much of the seventeenth-century imagery on this book is actually from the nineteenth
and early twentieth centuries. The intense interest in colonial history inspired many later
American painters and illustrators, who looked to historical images and artifacts as
references.

JUSTUS DANCKERTS
Novi Belgii Novaeque Angliae—detail: cartouche
(New Netherland and New England), mid-1650s
Hand-colored engraving, 21¾ x 18¼ in.
Bert Twaalthoven Collection of Antiquarian Maps of New Amsterdam,
New York and New England, Fordham University Library, Bronx, New York

This cartouche of New Amsterdam is one of the earliest images of the settlement.

named Low Countries as they escaped persecution or war. Also transplanted was free trade, the Dutch form of which was particularly vigorous, allowing the tiny country virtually to explode into one of history's great empires in a very short time.

Both of these elements helped Manhattan—the island on which the capital city of New Amsterdam sat—grow into a remarkably fluid, mixed, aggressive, acquisitive, vibrant, expansive city. New York—when it became New York, after the English adopted the role of invaders—became the immigrant center of the American colonies. Over the centuries, as droves of Europeans sailed into its harbor and took their first timorous steps into its mean streets, they experienced the turbid churn of cultures, the dense stew comprising distinct elements but somehow with its own flavor, and they called this new experience "American." Then many of them continued farther west and brought this notion with them: the idea that a mixed society, undergirded by faith and mercantile principles and somehow opening doors to hitherto unimagined possibilities, was the gem of the New World, the precious reason they had left behind all they knew.

So "Dutch New York" is not a parochial subject, any more than "America" is. But it is a smaller story, comprised of clusters of finely etched meanings. The slope of a barn roof, or of a woman's bonnet. A turn of phrase. A Bible. The odor of food cooking. A certain way of coddling or holding a child. Culture is so very intimate, so very precise. You can tell by a flicker of eyebrows that someone hails from your hometown. Meaning is transferred in the most delicate ways. That fact, as much as the larger history, is what this volume conveys. Who came to these shores 400 years ago? What were they after? What did they find instead, and what did they make of it? In what formations of blood, bone,

CHARLES BALTHAZAR JULIEN FEVRET DE SAINT-MÉMIN (1770–1852)
View of the City and Harbour of New York, 1796
Etching with hand coloring
Van Cortlandt House Museum/The National Society
of Colonial Dames in the State of New York

Inscription in cartouche: View of the City and Harbour of New York,
taken from Mount Pitt, the Seat of John R. Livingston, Esq.

and sweat did they interlock with the native peoples, and with the Africans who were brought here? How did they build, speak, write, love? Into what did they evolve? What part did they play in the weaving of the American fabric? How did Americans centuries later look back upon them, lampoon and valorize them? And what does all of this mean for us, in 2009, four centuries after this chapter in the history of humanity's presence on the planet dawned?

Answers to all of those questions are offered in what follows. What you, the reader, choose to make of this information that is laid before you, how you react to news that may alter your previous perceptions: that is where the authors of these essays and I, their introducer, bow out of the picture. The role of the historian is to deliver the past into the present. The reader takes it from there.

Acknowledgments

It is easy enough to have an idea for a book and an exhibition and a whole other matter to translate that into reality. So many colleagues gave generously of their time and energy to make this a truly collaborative effort. Hudson River Museum Director Michael Botwinick encouraged this publication from the start, championing its scholarly possibilities. The earliest discussions drew on the expertise of Martha Shattuck, who guided me through the world of New Netherland historiography and connected me to many of the leading scholars who are represented in this volume. The professional and expeditious manner in which they completed their essays was admirable.

At the Hudson River Museum, Laura Vookles and Bartholomew F. Bland were heroic in their pursuit of images, approvals, and research materials while staying engaged in the intellectual development of the project. As co-curators of the exhibition that accompanies this book, their persistence and engagement with *Dutch New York* in the face of multiple responsibilities earned my deepest respect. They are wonderful and gifted colleagues.

Susan Callanan, the museum's former registrar, worked diligently in coordinating images, captions, and loans, and complemented the efforts of previous registrars Erica Blumenfeld and Annette Van Aken in laying the groundwork for success. Registrar Takako Hara provided invaluable support in the final months of preparation leading up to the mounting of the exhibition and Senior Art Technician Jason Weller oversaw the handsome installation.

Jean-Paul Maitinsky, Assistant Director of Exhibitions and Programs; Maria Dembrowsky, Manager of Public Programs; Linda Locke; Director of Public Relations; and Kimberly Woodward, Assistant Director, Advancement contributed key pieces to the project over the past three years.

At Fordham, James P. McCabe, University Librarian; Michael Considine, Director of Information Technology Services; and Patrice M. Kane, Head, Archives and Special Collections provided access to the map collection and scanning services with a generous and warm spirit typical of the library staff. My fall 2008 honors class at Fordham University's Lincoln Center campus studied, debated, and researched the 1909 Hudson–Fulton Celebration, developing a Web site for the public. This would not have been possible without the encouragement and support of Anne Mannion, Director of the Honors

Program at Lincoln Center, and Robert R. Grimes, S.J., Dean of Fordham College at Lincoln Center.

For Fordham University Press, Leslie Kriesel provided invaluable copyediting; Richard Hendel created the attractive design; and Loomis Mayer served as the production manager. Robert Oppedisano, the previous Director of Fordham University Press, was a longtime champion of this project, as has been the new director, Frederic W. Nachbaur. All of them have been true partners in this publication.

At the Westchester County Historical Society, Director Katie Hite and librarians Elizabeth Fuller and Diana Deichert, along with Patricia Dohrenwend, Director of Westchester County Archives, provided images and sound historical advice throughout the project.

My wife, Eileen Panetta, shared in and debated many of the issues of Dutch New York with her usual incisive comments and patience. She was my intellectual companion throughout this journey.

Many individuals provided invaluable assistance in completing this book, and it is a pleasure to offer my thanks:

James M. Sousa, Associate Registrar for Collections and Archives, Addison Gallery of American Art, Phillips Academy, Andover, MA; Allison Munsell, Rights, Reproduction and Digitization Coordinator, Albany Institute of History and Art, NY; Christine Shannon, American Illustrators Gallery, New York, NY; Emily McKenney and W. Graham Arader III, Arader Gallery, New York, NY; Janet Parks, Curator of Drawings and Archives, Avery Architectural and Fine Arts Library, Columbia University; Deborah Powell, President, Bergen County Historical Society, River Edge, NJ; Leanne Hayden, Collections Manager, Berkshire Museum, Pittsfield, MA; Ryan Grover, Curator, Biggs Museum of American Art, Dover, DE; Christine B. Podmaniczky, Associate Curator, and Bethany Engel, Assistant Registrar and Rights and Reproductions Coordinator, Brandywine River Museum, Chadds Ford, PA; Ruth Janson, Coordinator Rights and Reproductions, Brooklyn Museum, NY; Rebecca A. Davis, Registrar, The Butler Institute of American Art, Youngstown, OH; Jennifer M. Holl, Collections Registrar, Delaware Art Museum, Wilmington; Sylvia Davis, Manager, Rights and Reproductions, The Detroit Institute of Arts, MI; Susan De Vries, Director, Dyckman Farmhouse Museum, New York, NY; Glenn Linsenbardt, Assistant Registrar, Fenimore Art Museum, Cooperstown, NY; Michelle M. Frauenberger, Museum Specialist/Registrar, Franklin D. Roosevelt Presidential Library and Museum, Hyde Park, NY; Christopher Wm. Linnane, Rights and Licensing Specialist, Harvard Art Museum, Fogg Art Museum, Cambridge, MA; Isabel Silva, Assistant to the Head of Retail and Visitor Services, The Frick Collection, New York; Jonathan Z. Friedman; Abby Lootens, Director of Communications, Historic House Trust of New York City; Kate E. Johnson, Curator, and Anne Goslin, Collections Manager, Historic Hudson Valley, Tarrytown, NY; Sara Mascia, Curator, The Historical Society, Serving Sleepy Hollow and Tarrytown, NY; Jessica Kuhnen, Curator of Collections, Historical Society of Rockland County, New City, NY; Andrea McCutcheon, Archives Assistant, Special Media, Hudson's Bay Company Archives, Manitoba; Theresa Slowikowski, Registrar, Hunter Museum of American Art, Chattanooga, TN; Gary Spanier, James Dart Architects, New York, NY; Library of Congress, Prints and Photographs Division, Washington, DC; Inga Stevens, Assistant Collections Manager, Mead Art Museum, Amherst College, Amherst, MA; Neal Stimler, Associate Coordinator of Images, The Metropolitan Museum of Art, New York, NY; Lori Eurto, Assistant Registrar, Munson-Williams-Proctor Arts Institute, Museum of Art, Utica, NY; Erin M.A. Schleigh, Digital Image Resources, Museum of Fine Arts, Boston, MA; Wendy Stayman, Director of Collections Management, and Joanna Hanna, Collections Data and Rights and Reproductions Specialist, Museum of Fine Arts, Springfield, MA; Chris Murtha, Rights and Reproductions, Museum of the City of New York, NY; Barbara C.G. Wood, Images and Permissions Coordinator, National Gallery of Art, Washington, DC; Pat Magnani, Registrar, Neuberger Museum of Art, Purchase College, State University of New York; Lindsy Parrot, Collections Manager and Associate Curator, The Neustadt Collection of Tiffany Glass; Louise Pfotenhauer, Curator of Collections, and Marilyn Stasiak, Curator of Art, Neville Public Museum of Brown County and Green Bay and De Pere Antiquarian Society, WI; John DeFeo, Collections Assistant, Rights and Reproductions, New Britain Museum of American Art, CT; Jill Slaight, Rights and Reproductions, The New-York Historical Society, NY; Thomas Lisanti, Manager, Photographic Services and Permissions, The New York Public Library, NY; John MacDonald, President, Ossining Historical Society Museum, Ossining, NY; S. Victor Burgos, Accountant/Accounts Manager, Photofest, Inc., New York, NY; Tara C. Craig, M.L.S., Reference Services Supervisor, Rare Book and Manuscript Library, Columbia University; Margaret Tamulonis, Manager, Collections and Exhibitions, Robert Hull Fleming Museum, University of Vermont, Burlington; Julie B. Sopher, Rights and Reproductions Manager, Shelburne Museum, Shelburne, VT; Richard H. Sorensen, Rights and Reproductions, Smithsonian American Art Museum, Washington, DC; Maxine Friedman, Chief Curator, and Sarah Clark, Associate Curator, Staten Island Historical Society, NY; Stephanie Standish, Collections Manager, and Elizabeth Petrulis, Curator of Collections and Exhibits, Swope Art Museum, Terra Haute, IN; Jeanne C. Pardee, Digitization Services in Scholarly Resources, and Gayle Cooper, Special Collections Cataloger, Tracy W. McGregor Library of American History, Special Collections, University of Virginia Library; Lorraine C. Miller, Deputy Clerk, U.S. House of Representatives, Washington, DC; Laura Carpenter, Director, Van Cortlandt House Museum/The National Society of Colonial Dames in the State of New York, Bronx, NY; George Way; Patrick Raftery, Assistant Librarian, Westchester County Historical Society, Elmsford, NY; Douglas W. Evans, Registrar, Westmoreland Museum of American Art, Greensburg, PA; Kirk A. Eck, Wichita Art Museum, Wichita, KS; David Whaples, Rights and Reproductions, Yale University Art Gallery, New Haven, CT; Clifford W. Zink, NJ.

Roger Panetta
New York

Introduction

MICHAEL BOTWINICK

As we at the Hudson River Museum were thinking about 2009 and the Hudson–Fulton–Champlain quadricentennial, it was always clear that the museum's commemoration would somehow take its cue from Adriaen van der Donck, the young lawyer who played an important role in New Netherland. His land grant lay along the river north of Manhattan Island, encompassing much of the Bronx and southern Westchester. He was known as the young squire or "Jonker," and his land was often referred to as the "Jonker's" land, shortened to "Yonkers" under the British. Russell Shorto's book *The Island at the Center of the World* gave broad access, via the story of van der Donck, to the academic world's evolving view of the true place of New Netherland in the construction of American identity. Looking at the brief period of Dutch rule in a broader perspective than the Anglophone view that had held sway, Shorto found the template for contemporary New York in the formative years of seventeenth-century New Amsterdam. His work, with its popular appeal should be considered the opening of the 2009 Hudson–Fulton–Champlain quadricentennial celebration, in which we ask anew about the sources of our political ideals and our economic life.

Centennials of all kinds (bi, tri, or quad) are occasions to reexamine legacy and the relationship of our perception of the past to the present and future. We should have that ambition for this 400th anniversary of Henry Hudson's arrival. However brief the Dutch rule in the Hudson River Valley was, aspects of that settlement persisted throughout the following centuries. And while it is enjoyable to look at things like Dutch gables and biscuits and quaint place names as the substance of this influence, a great deal more evidence suggests that the true impact of that Dutch period has been more profound. As Shorto notes in this volume, "the development of the concept of tolerance as a social glue to bind disparate peoples into one society, which the Dutch of the seventeenth century crafted, by itself calls for some reverberation, some recognition." The American self-image that we revere is more closely tied to the open, entrepreneurial, self-reliant, tolerant, immigrant-driven colony that was New Netherland than to any of the other mythic forbearer colonies from Massachusetts Bay to Jamestown.

That Dutch colony provided many of the essentials of what we understand to be the American character. And the geography in which this story played

UNKNOWN ARTIST
Attack on House of Adriaen Van Der Donck, 1655, n.d.
Reproduction image courtesy of Westchester County Historical Society, M-3156

out lies almost entirely within sight of the Hudson River. The act of discovery was an act of entrepreneurship, and Oliver Rink shows how, from the first, this was a mercantile empire with the river as its central artery. William Starna describes how the river was at the center of a complex Indian economic system that was modified and displaced by the Dutch, an important reminder that the Dutch did not come into a primeval world. And as history has so often forgotten the Native Americans who lived throughout the Hudson River Valley, it often forgets that slavery played a role in the economy of New Netherland. Dennis Maika's research gives us access to the actions of real people and a sense of a community that he shows was both "grim" and unique.

In this book and the exhibition it accompanies, we have adopted the conceit of the '09s, using 1609, 1709, 1809, and 1909 as symbolic moments to give form to the waxing and waning of Dutch influence. The year 1709 picks up the thread of the persistence of Dutch influence in the Hudson River Valley, despite the Netherlands having been ousted by the British in 1674. Sean Sawyer, Firth Fabend, and Ruth Piwonka examine some of the material aspects of Dutch influence and the ways they were carried forward. Conversely, Philip Lopate, Bartholomew Bland, and Laura Vookles illuminate ways that the nineteenth century romanticized the Dutch tradition. Roger Panetta's examination of the 1909 Hudson-Fulton Celebration brings us full circle, considering the ways

Westchester Year of History
Displays of Hudson River Museum
and Yonkers Historical Society, at
the County Center, *Yonkers Herald
Statesman*, Dec. 3, 1959.
Hudson River Museum
(institutional scrapbook)

HALF MOON model draws attention of Bernard Condon, representing the Hudson River Museum, and Miss Isabel Scotland for the Yonkers Historical Society, at the Westchester Year of History exhibit last night at the County Center in White Plains. The model of Henry Hudson's ship is part of the display provided by the Yonkers Historical Society and the Hudson River Museum. — Staff Photo by Ray Hoover.

"Dutch girls" and "Indians" at the
Hudson River Museum chat with
Helen C. Hutton, teacher and author
of a citizenship education unit on New
York State's "Year of History," *Yonkers
Herald Statesman*, Dec. 3, 1959.
Hudson River Museum (institutional
scrapbook)

SHARING her personal collection relative to the Hudson River valley, Mrs. Helen C. Clutton, teacher of a second grade at School Thirteen, chats with "Indians" and "Dutch girls" at the Hudson River Museum at Trevor Park. The children are, left to right Roberta Lasko, Maureen Rogers, Alan Barasch and Leslie Browne. Mrs. Clutton is the author of a citizenship education unit on New York State's "Year of History," copies of which have been distributed to elementary schools throughout the city. Her collection has been on display at the museum.— Staff Photo by Jerry Sarno.

historical reexamination becomes a vehicle for the transmission of cultural values. Laura Chmielewski examines Dutch influence during the colonial revival and Cynthia Koch shows how a quintessential American figure, Franklin Delano Roosevelt, consciously grounded his actions and his persona in his own understanding of persistent Dutch themes and with them gave

JAN JANSZ
Belgii Novi, Angliae Novae et Partis Virginiae
(New Netherland, New England, and parts of Virginia), 1650
Engraving and watercolor on paper, 20¼ x 17¼ in.
Bert Twaalthoven Collection of Antiquarian Maps of New Amsterdam, New York
and New England, Fordham University Library, Bronx, New York

This map is based on a 1648 manuscript map that accompanied a 1649 petition
on the New Netherland Commonalty delivered by Adriaen van der Donck to the
States General.

shape to a historic presidency. Finally, David Voorhees shows how essential
seventeenth-century Dutch characteristics, from freedom of conscience to
political parties, are so firmly embedded in the American character that they
will continue to influence us as we move forward toward 2109.

PART ONE 1609 — The Planting

LAMBERT DOOMER (baptized 1624, died 1700)
Couple with a Globe, 1658. Oil on panel, 28½ x 21½ in.
Robert Hull Fleming Museum, University of Vermont, Gift of Prentis Cobb Hale Jr.
1957.21.1

Seafarers and Businessmen

1

THE GROWTH OF DUTCH COMMERCE IN
THE LOWER HUDSON RIVER VALLEY

OLIVER A. RINK

When Dutch explorers and traders arrived in the lower Hudson River Valley after Henry Hudson's voyage of 1609, a complex Native economy already existed. Although linguistic and ethnic differences persisted, the Algonquian tribes of the area shared many common cultural practices.[1] Farming was the core activity for most, but the regional economy also included hunting, gathering, manufacturing, and trade. To cite but one example: the largest cultural group, the Lenape (Delaware Indians to the English), engaged in manufacturing and participated in a thriving Native American trade system.[2] Excellent farmers, who consistently produced surpluses of maize that sustained a population estimated to have been nearly 20,000, the Lenape were also renowned producers of fine baskets, some of which were treated with pitch to produce watertight conveyances. Many of these baskets entered the Native trading system, as did Lenapi cooking pottery, which appears to have been particularly prized. A great variety of these pots, some large enough to cook a deer, have been found in archaeological sites throughout the region. Regional specialization thus encouraged trade across a vast network of trails and waterways. Other manufactured goods were twine, dressed deerskins, moccasins, birch- or elm-bark canoes, eagle feathers, and furs. European accounts of the early seventeenth century describe a trade in agricultural products including corn, beans (both fresh and dried), dried meat, squash, berries, and tobacco. Virtually all the Native American inhabitants of the lower Hudson estuary participated in this exchange as producers or consumers. European colonists did not so much invent an American economy as they stimulated and modified an economy already in existence.

By the second decade of the seventeenth century, Europe's demand for animal skins and furs was insatiable. The religious wars of the age drove a thriving international trade in hides to make protective covers for musketeers and pikemen, saddles, tackle, gloves and sword scabbards for cavalry, and bandoliers, belts, and shoes for the common soldier. The European leather market was expanding rapidly when Dutch ships began to frequent the area of Hudson's discovery.

HOWARD PYLE (1853–1911)
Dutch and Indians Trading Goods, 1884
Oil en grisaille, 14¼ x 17 in.
Published in Horace E. Scudder, *A History of the United States of America*
(Taintor Brothers & Co.), 1884, p. 58
Image courtesy Archives of American Illustrators Gallery, New York, New York

Civilian fashion drove the market for furs. The felt hat craze alone created
such a demand for beaver pelts that by the second decade of the seventeenth
century European beaver species were nearing extinction. The closest source
for thick furs before the discovery of North American supplies was Muscovy.
That trade created fortunes for merchants in England and the Netherlands and
had financed Hudson's earlier Arctic voyages, but beaver prices continued to
rise. On the eve of Hudson's voyage to America, European hat makers were
already substituting rabbit fur for beaver in the manufacture of felt hats. Affluent Europeans preferred beaver and other luxury furs such as mink, otter, fox,
and sable. And thanks to the commercial revolution then under way, they were

JOHANNES VERMEER (1632–1675)
Officer and Laughing Girl, c. 1657
Oil on canvas (lined), 19⅞ in. x 18⅛ in. (50.48 cm x 46.04 cm)
The Frick Collection, New York, Henry Clay Frick Bequest. 1911.1.127
Image copyright The Frick Collection, New York.

Perhaps the most famous beaver felt hat of the Dutch Golden Age. This painting by
Jan Vermeer is known as *The Soldier and the Laughing Girl* (*de Soldaat en het Lachende
Meisje*) and was painted between 1655 and 1660 at the height of the fur trade.

Modifications
of the Beaver Hat, in
H. T. Martin, *Castorologia*,
London: 1892, p. 125.
6¾ x 4⅛ in.
Hudson's Bay Company
Archives, Archives of Manitoba,
HBCA
1987/363-C-308/2 (N8318)

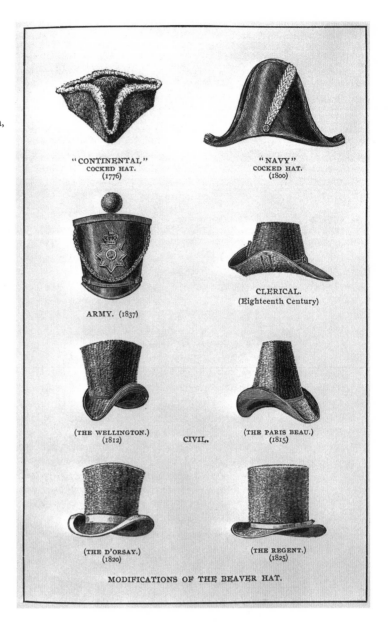

MODIFICATIONS OF THE BEAVER HAT.

able to pay high prices. Unfortunately for the American beaver populations, felt hats rode the crest of fashion for nearly three centuries.[3]

Initially both sides saw the exchange as beneficial. Europeans could trade cheap surplus manufactured goods for highly valuable furs and hides, and Native Americans could obtain a wide range of items that not only improved their lives but also added to their prestige and, with the introduction of firearms, metal knives, and swords, significantly enhanced their war-making abilities. The Native peoples of the lower Hudson estuary desired metal tools, metal wire (good for binding and the making of fish hooks), bladed implements,

WILLEM BLAEU
North American animals, detail from *Nova Belgica et Anglia Nova*
(New Netherland and New England), Amsterdam, 1635
Engraving and watercolor on paper, 19½ x 15 in.
Bert Twaalthoven Collection of Antiquarian Maps of New Amsterdam,
New York and New England, Fordham University Library, Bronx, New York
Map collection #2

Many maps included illustrated details such as Native American and North American
animals of interest to traders.

pots and containers, cooking utensils, cloth, clothing, blankets, beads, looking
glasses, silver jewelry and ornaments, liquor, firearms, and ammunition. They
competed with one another to acquire European goods and were willing to
form political alliances with Europeans to maintain the supply. Dutch traders
rushed to exploit the abundant supplies of furs and hides reported by Hudson's crew. Within two years of the English explorer's return, merchants from
Amsterdam, Hoorn, and Monnikendam were vying for the furs of the Hudson River area. Given the value of the pelts and the premium to be earned by
being the first to offload them in the fatherland, competition was not friendly.

By 1614 a number of incidents, some of them violent, drove the merchants to file dozens of claims, counterclaims, and statements of grievances before Amsterdam notaries.[4] The controversy eventually required the intervention of the States General, the national parliament of the United Provinces.

On March 27, 1614, the States General passed a resolution calling "diverse merchants, wishing to discover New Unknown Rivers, Countries, and Places" to apply for the exclusive right to make four voyages to the region of Hudson's discovery. The resolution stipulated that merchants had to provide a detailed report, including charts and maps, within fourteen days of the return of their ships to the fatherland.

Seven months later, most of the merchants who had competed so fiercely in the Hudson River fur trade formed the New Netherland Company. The "Figurative Map" submitted by the company directors was the first to refer to the area as New Netherland. Its boundaries extended as far east as the Connecticut River Valley and as far north as the confluence of the Mohawk and North

GERRIT ADRIAENSZ BERCKHEYDE (1638–1698)
The Dam and Damrak, Amsterdam, 1665–1669
Oil on canvas, 24⅜ x 28 in.
Harvard Art Museum, Fogg Art Museum, Gift of Mr. and Mrs. Samuel B. Grimson, 1968.65
Photo: Imaging Department © President and Fellows of Harvard College

This image depicts an important site of early capitalistic commodities trading.

(Hudson) rivers.[5] Some time later these same merchants attempted to acquire exclusive patent rights to the territory between the 38th and 40th parallels (Delaware Bay), but the States General rejected their claim. In October 1618, the New Netherland Company asked for an extension of its patent to the area of Hudson's River, but this too was denied. The Twelve Year Truce with Spain was due to expire in 1621, and already plans were afoot for a national West India Company. The States General was reluctant to extend patents to territory likely to fall within the domain of the planned national monopoly.

The New Netherland Company achieved much in its few years of operation. The elimination of competition permitted the partners to coordinate annual voyages with the cycle of the fur trade. The traditional Indian hunting season occurred in the winter months, when the fur of the animals (primarily beaver) was thickest. Therefore, the exchange of European goods for furs had to begin in late winter or early spring. Since ships were routinely icebound in Holland during the months of January and February, most departed Amsterdam in the fall to assure their presence in New Netherland in March or April. Timing was everything in the transoceanic fur trade, but time was running out for the private merchants.

The founding of the West India Company (WIC) ended the era of private trading in the Hudson River area.[6] As a national monopoly, the WIC was intended to reduce the competition among private merchants while simultaneously organizing the trade of the Atlantic world so as to further the collective aims of the United Provinces. The company's most important national task was to serve as the point of the spear in the renewed war with Spain. The WIC provided the means to direct the maritime resources of the provinces against Spanish holdings in the New World.

By the terms of the charter, no citizen of the Netherlands could trade at any point on the African coast between the Tropic of Cancer and the Cape of Good Hope or on the American coast between Newfoundland and the Straits of Magellan without the company's permission. However, such bold language paid little heed to the realities of politics, financial resources, and the company's complex corporate structure. Across the WIC's domain stretched the immense Spanish-Portuguese empire. Areas untouched by the Catholic enemy were claimed and in some cases already settled by the United Provinces' erstwhile allies, England and France. The most sought-after prizes, the mines and sugar-growing regions, were already occupied or claimed by the Iberians. The struggling tobacco plantations of English Virginia and the fur trade of New France were only beginning to return profits, while New Netherland's rich bounty of furs was a promising but minor source of wealth. Company directors, many of whom were motivated by Calvinistic zeal and nationalism, believed war against Spain offered the best hope for profit.

Although the WIC was a national joint-stock company, the charter approved by the States General in 1621 institutionalized the provincialism and particularities of Dutch politics. The administration of the West India Company was divided into five chambers, each representing not only a specified amount of the subscribed capital but also a distinct political and geographic constituency. The chambers met separately, maintained their own books and operations, and frequently competed with one another for trade.

The Amsterdam chamber, whose share of the company's operations included New Netherland, was the most powerful, but it could not act without the consent of the other chambers that represented the Maas cities (Rotterdam, Delft, and Dordrecht), Middleburg, the Noorderkwartier (Northern Quarter or North Holland), and Groningen and Friesland.

Overall authority was vested in a "general assembly of directors," known in Dutch as the *Heeren XIX*. The *Heeren XIX*, or simply the Nineteen (in Dutch, *Negentien*), included representatives from all the chambers; each received two representatives for each one-ninth part of the capital it administered. Within

HOWARD PYLE (1853–1911)
Slaves at Jamestown Being Unloaded from a Dutch Man-of-War, 1901
Oil on canvas, 24 x 18 in.
Neville Public Museum of Brown County and Green Bay & De Pere Antiquarian Society

The network of seventeenth-century trade established by the Dutch included English colonies and depended on slavery as well as fur trading.

the Nineteen, however, power followed capital. The Amsterdam chamber, with the largest subscribed capital, elected eight directors, while Zeeland, the second most powerful, had only four. Each of the remaining chambers elected two. The nineteenth director was appointed by the States General. This complex and unwieldy corporate structure may have reassured wary investors, but it made the company ponderous and slow to respond to local needs.

SETTLEMENT AND COMMERCE

The company that began as an instrument of war became over time a reluctant and sometimes befuddled government of thousands of European colonists in North America. As late as 1623, the WIC had only twenty ships, far too few to undertake hemispherewide operations, and although Article Thirty-Nine of the charter provided a government subsidy of one million guilders, the initial capitalization was slow to come in. While the company was engaged in organizing stock sales and establishing the infrastructure for transatlantic operations, it conducted no business in New Netherland. Dutch merchants continued to trade in the area. Some of these were the "*particuliere kooplieden*" (private traders) who had participated in the operations of the New Netherland Company. Others appear to have been new traders hoping to clear a profit before the WIC takeover.[7] In the meantime, the English government registered its official protest of Dutch operations in the Hudson River area.

In a carefully worded letter, Sir Dudley Carleton, English ambassador to The Hague, defended English rights to the entire North American seaboard, noting that

> Subjects of the English Lords to their honor and quality have, for a long time past, been in possession of the precincts of Virginia and have planted there their habitation, and [also] in certain new quarters of Nova Anglica, desired by their Majesty . . . for the advancement of religion and enlargement of commerce. [Furthermore,] the king's government has lately been informed that the Hollanders have planted a colony in these regions, and renamed the ports and harbors, as is their fashion, and are of the intention to continue trafficking there.[8]

Years of diplomatic wrangling and eventually war settled the matter in favor of the English. When Carleton filed his protest in 1622, however, the rival claims to the area of Hudson's discovery had yet to be studied. As relative newcomers in the race for colonies, the Dutch could not base their colonial claims on first discovery. Instead, the Nineteen, with the approbation of the States General, worked out a different justification.

In a report requested by the States General on the possibility of a commercial alliance with English and French joint-stock companies to further the war with Spain, the Nineteen made clear that the simple fact of discovery did not grant rights of ownership. Occupation and effective use of disputed territories were the only practical bases for colonial claims. "Any nation who for itself possesses such places, harbors, and rivers…and already occupies the same with colonists, cities or forts, containing at least 50 persons from the respective kingdoms and countries sent there, does possess and therefore has exclusive rights to said districts."[9] Nothing came of the proposed merger of joint-stock companies, but the report sheds light on the first colonization attempt in New Netherland the same year and may partly explain its timing.[10]

In 1624 the 260-ton *Nieu Nederlandt* dropped anchor in the roadstead before Manhattan Island. Aboard were seeds and seedlings, livestock and farming tools, and other accoutrements for the establishment of an agricultural colony. It also carried the vanguard of New Netherland's European colonists.[11]

The voyage of the *Nieu Nederlandt* was the culmination of years of planning and countless negotiations between the directors of the WIC's Amsterdam chamber and the heads of thirty Walloon families seeking refuge in America. As early as 1622 the families had petitioned the provincial States of Holland and West Friesland "to be employed by the West India Company." The states turned the matter over to the directors of the Amsterdam chamber for consideration. The directors responded quickly, characterizing the petition as "very serviceable to the company."

United by language and their immigrant status, the Walloons were defined by more than their religion. Their goals in emigrating were more diverse than those of the English separatists who were preparing to board the *Mayflower* at about the same time. Traditionally employed in the cloth and dye industries of Antwerp, they lost nearly everything in their trek north. In the United Provinces they became surplus labor and suffered frequent unemployment. Consequently, the Walloons were not particular where they were sent as long as they were employed. In July 1623, ten families departed for Guiana as part of the WIC's effort to establish a colony on the mainland of South America. The conditions proved brutal, and by January 1624, most of them were back in Amsterdam. The colony was eventually abandoned when company plans changed.

Some of these returnees were probably among the group of thirty families aboard the *Nieu Nederlandt*. Thus New Netherland's first colonists were a wary lot, inured to the folly of good intentions and well aware of the dangers of colonization. In their negotiations with the Amsterdam chamber, they were careful

PETER SCHENK
Nieu Amsterdam, een stedeken in Noord Amerikaes Nieu Hollant, op het
eilant Mankattan: Namaels Nieu Jork genaemt, toen het geraekte in't gebiet
der Engelschen (New Amsterdam, a Small Town in New Holland in North America,
on the Island of Manhattan, Renamed New York When it Became Part of the Territory
of the English), published in Schenk's *Hecatompolis*, 1702
Hand-colored engraving, 10¼ x 7¾ in.
Bert Twaalthoven Collection of Antiquarian Maps of New Amsterdam, New York
and New England, Fordham University Library, Bronx, New York
Map collection #20

New Amsterdam is shown as it appeared in 1673.

not to bargain away their rights before they sailed. On March 29, 1624, shortly
before boarding ship for the Atlantic crossing, the families listened to a public
reading of the "Provisional Orders."

Intended as both a recruiting device and a set of regulations delineating
company authority and the colonists' realm of personal freedom, the Provisional Orders were a curious mixture of incentives and responsibilities. For
example, while the colonists were obligated "to obey and to carry out without
any contradiction the orders of the company," they were encouraged to seek

out "mines of gold, silver, copper or any other metals, as well as of precious stones, such as diamonds, rubies and the like, together with pearl fisheries." The company offered to pay the discoverer 10 percent of the net proceeds for a period of six years.

For those without ready cash, the company provided interest-free loans to buy livestock, farm tools, and the like. The greatest incentive, however, was land. The Provisional Orders directed the company commander to assign farms according to family size, but the location of the farms was his alone to choose, as were the crops to be grown.

The fur trade received special consideration in the Provisional Orders. The Amsterdam chamber was particularly interested in protecting and expanding the one known source of profit in the colony. Thus the colonists were expected to assist the other company employees in gathering furs, as either trappers or traders. The company promised to buy all pelts for "reasonable" prices. As in other matters, the Walloons served as free colonists and company employees simultaneously. By seeking their own fortunes, they assisted the company in its efforts to expand profits.

Cornelis Jacobsz May, the skipper of the *Nieu Nederlandt* and interim commander of the colony, was a former employee of the New Netherland Company and a seasoned explorer. Upon arrival in the roadstead before Manhattan

UNIDENTIFIED ARTIST *Proposed Coat-of-Arms for New Amsterdam, New Netherlands*, c. 1630 Watercolor, gouache and red chalk on paper with mat, 14 x 18 in. The New-York Historical Society, Gift of Carson Brevoort, 1885.5

in the late spring of 1624, he dispatched a sloop with two families and eight single men to Delaware Bay to set up a garrison. The intent of the directors was to make the Delaware garrison on High Island (present-day Burlington Island, near Burlington, New Jersey) the center of company operations for all New Netherland. Other families and single male company employees were sent to establish a trading post on the Connecticut River, and eight men were left on *Noten* or Nut Island (present-day Governors Island) to set up facilities for storing furs and transferring them to ships. The remaining eighteen families were taken up the Hudson to a site near present-day Albany. On the west bank of the Hudson River, opposite the main base of operations for the old New Netherland Company on Castle Island, May ordered the ship's carpenter to build a small shelter and redoubt, christened Fort Orange in honor of the Prince of Orange.

The scattering of colonists from one end of New Netherland to the other was part of a plan to improve the fur trade by establishing agricultural support communities near the three major river systems in the colony: the Hudson, the Connecticut, and the Delaware. The dispersed settlements thus served to stake out the most vital sites of the water-dependent fur trade. Moreover, since the entire area was under a jurisdictional cloud, the presence of permanent settlers in these areas met the company's definition of "occupation and effective use."

Meanwhile, the Amsterdam chamber prepared a massive expedition to bring even more people to New Netherland. This represented the largest investment yet in the fledgling colony on the Hudson: six ships carrying dozens of families, farm tools, seeds, provisions, and livestock. The 150-ton *Oranje Boom*, the lead vessel of the fleet, sailed into a violent storm in the English Channel and nearly sank. English customs agents seized the ship when her captain sought shelter at Plymouth. In Plymouth a "plague" broke out, killing some passengers and crew. Fearing further contagion, English authorities released the vessel. It made the crossing without further mishap and arrived in New Netherland after the rest of the fleet.

The detention of the *Oranje Boom* disrupted the entire timetable. The ship with farming tools, seeds, and live plants was supposed to be waiting in New Netherland when the main body of the fleet arrived in spring. Instead, the four-ship squadron under the command of Willem Verhulst arrived first, and time was lost in establishing the colonists on their farms. Moorish pirates off the coast of Africa captured the sixth ship, the *Ruijter*.

Willem Verhulst, leader of the expedition and the first of New Netherland's commanders, had explicit orders to transport to the colony "divers trees, vines, and all sorts of seeds" and to have them "planted and sown in their proper season." His tenure in New Netherland was brief, for he was removed from office by his council. His efforts to curb the smuggling of furs seem to have angered some of the company employees, and he was reported to have berated some of the colonists for failing to work their requisite hours on the company farms. Whatever the case, Verhulst's removal was only the first of many abrupt administrative changes in New Netherland. Pieter Minuit replaced Verhulst in the spring of 1626.

One of Minuit's first acts was to dismantle the vulnerable outlying settlements set up by Captain May. An Indian war near Fort Orange may have brought about this decision. Daniel van Crieckenbeeck, the company agent and commander of the garrison, had disobeyed explicit orders by taking the side of the Mahicans in a war with the powerful Mohawks. While accompanying a Mahican war party, Van Crieckenbeeck and three of his soldiers were killed in an ambush a short distance from the fort. The Mohawks, incensed to see the Dutch commander aiding their enemy, threatened to annihilate the Europeans at the fort and shut down the fur trade.

When this news reached Minuit, he sailed immediately to Fort Orange. To appease the Mohawk sachems, he agreed to remove the families to Manhattan Island. With the permission of the Mohawks, he left behind a handful of company employees to carry on the fur trade. In the meantime, probably between May 4 and June 26, he purchased Manhattan from local sachems for 60 guilders' worth of trade goods.

The families on Manhattan Island were soon joined by the families evacuated from the trading posts on the Connecticut and Delaware rivers. The company eventually reestablished its presence in the Delaware River Valley by building a new trading post, Fort Nassau, on the eastern bank near present-day Gloucester, New Jersey. In the 1630s, the Dutch returned to the Connecticut River Valley, establishing a trading post near present-day Hartford. In 1626, however, the dispersed settlements were too vulnerable to Indian attack. Henceforth, Fort New Amsterdam, on the southern tip of Manhattan Island, would be the economic and administrative center of New Netherland. With its protected deepwater harbor, it proved to be the finest port in colonial America.

Furs and hides remained the "cash crops" of the lower Hudson estuary for at least a decade following the arrival of the Walloons. By the 1630s, however, the population of beaver and deer in the area was already in decline. The leading edge of the Dutch fur trade frontier moved steadily north and west from 1640 on. Nonetheless, the lower Hudson region remained at the crossroads of this trade. The fur trade connected the region to large-scale capitalism that employed thousands as traders, merchants, recluse and solitary hunters, shippers, bankers, furriers, hatters, tanners, cobblers, and saddlers. Great profits were possible, but only to those who mastered the details of the exchange.

E. ROSCOE SHRADER, *"Henry Hudson got many furs from the Indians and made them all his friends,"* in *The Men Who Found America* by Frederick Winthrop Hutchinson (New York: Barse & Hopkins, Publishers, © E. Stern & Co., Inc., 1909), opp. p. 120 Hudson River Museum

The title of this romanticized scene is indicative of the narrow historical perspective of many late nineteenth- and early twentieth-century artists and writers.

Native Americans also approached the trade from self-interested motives. While European traders considered the Indians gullible for accepting cheap trade goods in return for fine pelts and hides, the Indians were equally astounded to see the wealth Europeans were willing to squander on items that, to them, seemed common. One item highly valued by Dutch traders seemed to confirm in Indian minds that Europeans were dupes. The most desirable pelts for the making of hats were what the French dubbed *Castor gras*. These were pelts that had been worn by Indian trappers for the hunting season and, as a result of the sweat and body oil, were more pliable and easier to felt. Dutch traders were willing to pay premiums for what Indians considered dirty garments.[12]

The profit potential in the fur trade thwarted the WIC's efforts to maintain its monopoly. The centripetal forces of a virtually open market constantly challenged the company's authority and drove its officials to rail against it. At the height of the fur trade in the lower Hudson estuary, even the Walloons could not resist the call of Mammon.

In 1626, some months after the arrival of Minuit, Isaack de Rasieres took up residence in New Netherland as the chief commercial agent of the WIC. Described as "a man of a fair and genteel behavior" by New Plymouth's William Bradford, he also served as the secretary of the province. Shortly after de Rasieres' return to Amsterdam in 1628, he delivered a letter describing conditions in the colony to a West India Company director. For the most part it glowed with optimism. On the island of Manhattan he noted the existence of "six farms, four of which lie along the Hellgate [East River], stretching to the south side of the island."[13] From a Hollander's perspective, these were large farms, about 60 *morgens* or 120 acres. He was pleased to report that the land was ready to be sown with winter wheat, but appeared to suffer from the inattention of the managers of the farms, who were hired men. Nicholaes van Wassenaer, the famed Dutch chronicler, described a different scene. "Everyone there who fills no public office is busy about his own affairs. Men work there as in Holland; one trades . . . another builds houses, the third farms."[14] Such entrepreneurial ambition drove up the cost of furs and made some Walloons unwilling to accept company prices. A lively clandestine trade in furs developed among Walloon women. Isaack de Rasieres related the following incident. "It happened one day that the wife of Wolfert Gerritsz came to me with two otters, for which I offered her three guilders, ten stuivers. She refused this and asked for five guilders, whereupon I let her go, this being too much. The wife of Jacob Laurissz, the smith, knowing this, went to her and offered her five guilders. . . . Thereupon to prevent the otters from being purloined, I was obliged to give her five guilders."[15]

In the late 1620s the WIC decided on a different approach. Instead of settling colonists at company expense, influential directors in the Amsterdam chamber convinced the board to experiment with a manorial system. The intrigues involved in this giveaway of resources and power are too complex to deal with here, but the end result profoundly changed the commercial history of the region.[16]

In 1629 the Amsterdam chamber adopted the new colonization scheme. Known as the Patroonship Plan, it clearly favored the wealthiest and most influential shareholders in the Amsterdam chamber. Much has been written of the feudal rights granted the patroons, of their right to hold manor courts and their princely domains.[17] Of greater concern to those in the chamber who opposed the plan were the provisions that allowed patroons to outfit their own ships and conduct trade along the entire coast of North America. For these

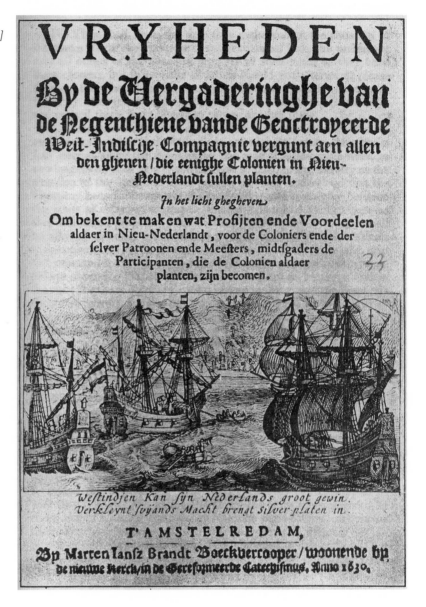

VR.YHEDEN

By de Uergaderinghe van
de Negenthiene vande Geoctroyeerde
Weſt-Indiſche Compagnie vergunt aen allen
den ghenen / die eenighe Colonien in Nieu-
Nederlandt ſullen planten.

In het licht ghegheven

Om bekent te maken wat Profijten ende Voordeelen
aldaer in Nieu-Nederlandt, voor de Coloniers ende der
ſelver Patroonen ende Meeſters, midtſgaders de
Participanten, die de Colonien aldaer
planten, zijn becomen.

Weſtindjen Kan ſyn Nederlands groot gewin,
Verkleynt ſvyands Macht brengt ſilver-platen in.

T'AMSTELREDAM,

By Marten Ianſz Brandt Boeckvercooper / woonende by
de nieuwe Kerck / in de Gereformeerde Catechiſmus, Anno 1630,

"contrary-minded" shareholders, the requirement that each ship must carry a company supercargo on board seemed little defense against the violations of the company charter likely to occur.

The "Freedoms and Exemptions for the patrons, masters, or private persons who will plant any colonies in, and send cattle to New Netherland" granted extraordinary privileges to the patroons.[18] Among the most important was the right to participate in the fur trade. The company's decision to abandon its lucrative monopoly on furs may have been a realization that it was no longer enforceable. Isaack de Rasieres had suspected widespread smuggling among the colonists and reported the same in his 1626 report to the directors of the

Amsterdam chamber.[19] One well-documented incident in 1630 involved the smuggling of 300 florins' (fl.) worth of pelts aboard the company ship *Eendracht*. An investigation produced several depositions before an Amsterdam notary that confirmed widespread smuggling of beaver pelts in the private sea chests of company employees. The testimony suggested that this clandestine trade had been going on for some time.[20]

New Netherland's furs, however, continued to generate significant company profits in the late 1620s. Johannes de Laet, a WIC director and important advocate for Dutch overseas colonization, reported that the colony had exported 31,024 beaver pelts and 3,097 other pelts, mostly otter, between 1624 and 1628. The total value of these pelts in Amsterdam was 225,495 fl. New Netherland's imports during the same period were valued at only 110,895 fl.[21] Of course these figures did not take into account the expense of settling the Walloons, nor could such sums offset the costs of war in other parts of the WIC domain.[22]

The effect of the Freedoms and Exemptions was to encourage private trade throughout the area. By legalizing the trade in furs and allowing patroons to build and outfit their own ships, the Dutch developed a lucrative intercolonial tobacco trade with Virginia over the next decade. By 1637 this was important enough to draw European tobacco merchants to the colony,[23] and over the next two decades, until the passage of the English Navigation Acts, the tobacco trade grew steadily. It offered another avenue to wealth for the citizens of New Netherland, and tobacco joined pelts and hides as a valuable commodity in the expanding commerce of the lower Hudson River Valley.

The decline of the beaver population in the lower Hudson estuary drove up the cost of the furs. A survey of the notarial records in the Municipal Archives of Amsterdam bears testimony to a sharp inflation that forced company agents to raise the price per pelt from 5.77 to 8.21 guilders. Even this was not enough to reduce the thriving "black market" in pelts, although the development of the wampum trade may have been one of the factors sustaining company profits in the 1630s.

Piece of Wampum, illustrated in *The History of Yonkers from the Earliest times to the Present* . . . , by the Rev. Charles Elmer Allison (New York: Wilbur B. Ketcham, 1896), p. 16.

Although a number of his facts and opinions, reflecting the prejudices of his day, are outdated, Allison was greatly interested in the original residents of the Hudson Valley and devoted the lengthy second chapter of his book to the Native Americans who lived in Nappeckamack, the future site of Yonkers.

The first mention of wampum, or *sewant* as it was called in Dutch, comes from 1622. In that year, a Dutch trader on the Connecticut River extorted a ransom of nearly 35,000 beads for a Pequot sachem he had kidnapped and later murdered.[24] Four years later, Isaack de Rasieres recommended that the company set up a secondary trade in wampum by exchanging cheap cloth, called duffel, for the polished shells. If the company could control the sources of supply (the inlets and bays of Long Island and the Connecticut River Valley), it could carry the product to the wampum-poor areas around Fort Orange and there exchange it for furs. So valuable was this commodity among Native Americans that de Rasieres believed it might even be possible to draw the "French Indians" south to trade their luxuriant winter pelts with the Dutch. Other motives were also evident. The company could use its access to the most desirable wampum to spoil the fur trade of the "Brownists at New Plymouth" by enabling its agents to outbid them "with duffels or hatchets."[25]

De Rasieres recommended the company outfit two or three large sloops for the wampum trade and station them more or less permanently in the sound. The WIC does not appear to have followed through on de Rasieres' recommendation, but the private traders of New Netherland did so almost immediately. By the late 1640s poor-quality and counterfeit wampum flooded the free market and significantly added to the inflationary pressures on commodity prices.

While Europeans considered wampum to be the equivalent of money, to Native Americans it was much more. Its uses included ornamentation and tribute, ransom for captives and compensation for crimes, presents between friends and prizes for victory in games or sport. It could be used to exact fines for deviant behavior or given as incentive to maintain peace. Its more mundane uses included payments for services of shamanism, for memorial gifts to accompany a marriage proposal, and for bribes and rewards. It was also used in burials and as the insignia of sachems. Its transformation into a simple and corruptible medium of exchange was but one of many cultural shocks brought about by the fur trade.[26]

In 1650 the director-general and council at New Amsterdam issued an ordinance to stop "the decline and daily depreciation of the loose wampum, among which are circulating many without holes and half finished; also some of Stone, Bone, Glass, Muscle-shells, Horn, yea even of Wood and Broken beads." Wampum had become such a vital currency in the colony's economy that the decline in its value and quality had caused "manifold complaints of the Inhabitants that they cannot go to market with such Wampum, nor obtain any commodities, not even a small loaf of white Bread or pot of Beer from the Traders, Bakers or tapsters." In an effort to stem the inflation in prices of commodities purchased with wampum, the council outlawed loose beads and required legal tender wampum "to be strung on a cord, as has been the common custom heretofore." In addition, the council established an official exchange rate of one stuiver (1/20th of a guilder) for six white beads or three black beads. Two categories of wampum were sanctioned as currency in the colony: good wampum that traded at the above rate and bad wampum that traded at the rate of eight white or four black beads for one stuiver. The effort was apparently unsuccessful, because eight years later the council officially devalued wampum again, noting that "the high, excessive and intolerable dearness of needful commodities and family necessaries" required a new exchange rate of eight white or four black beads per stuiver.[27]

New Netherland's domestic economy suffered from a chronic specie shortage. The guilder or florin (expressed as fl.), the national coin of the United Provinces, was one of the most stable currencies in the seventeenth century, because its metallic content was standardized and remain unchanged for nearly two centuries.[28] Unfortunately for the merchants and traders of New Netherland, it remained in short supply throughout the colony's history. Colonists had no choice but to use furs, wampum, and in some cases, tobacco, maize, fish, and timber as currency.

High prices and inflation remained a fact of life for colonists of the lower Hudson estuary. Most had access to food they grew themselves, and high food prices encouraged production for market. The WIC soldiers and merchant marines, as well as the hundreds of contract workers who came to the colony to work on company projects, suffered the most from the inflation. The steady drop in the value of *sewant* hit this sector of New Netherland's population especially hard. In 1658 company directors in Amsterdam were persuaded by the widening gap in the value of *sewantstivers* and *beverstivers* to permit the company fiscal officer to keep two separate cash accounts, one in each denomination. By 1662 the price of a beaver pelt, even at the artificially low 7 fl. set by the company, sold for as much as 24 guilders' worth of *sewant*. WIC employees often drew their monthly pay in beaver pelts, if available, or *sewant* if not. More often than not it was the latter, calculated at the official exchange rate. Petrus Stuyvesant and his council tried to make it clear to their bosses in Amsterdam that "*sewant* before it is reduced to beaver value and is reckoned at seven guilder per beaver, suffers a loss of 50 percent, as the beaver calculated at the usual rate of eight guilders is bartered and estimated in public sales at fifteen or sixteen guilders in *sewant*."[29] Company employees, in effect, suffered a 50 percent loss in purchasing power when forced to take their pay at company exchange rates.

Although local farmers and free artisans benefited from the rising prices, New Netherland's merchants, who engaged in the transatlantic trade, did not.

ARNOLDUS MONTANUS
Novum Amsterodamum. (New Amsterdam), as it looked in 1651.
Cartouche from map first published in Arnoldus Montanus, *De Nieuwe en Onbekende Weereld* (The New and Unknown World), 1671. Possibly based on a drawing by Augustine Herrman made in 1656 or 1657.
Hand-colored engraving, 6½ x 5 in.
Bert Twaalthoven Collection of Antiquarian Maps of New Amsterdam, New York and New England, Fordham University Library, Bronx, New York
Map Collection #11

The notarial records of Amsterdam contain numerous references to high prices in the colony and complaints about the sharp practices of the Amsterdam merchants to whom colonial products were sold.[30] In a particularly revealing deposition given before an Amsterdam notary, Cornelis de Grijp, Dirck Kroon, 40 years old, and Jan van Baal, 30 years old, both merchants in New Netherland, testified that goods worth 100 fl. in New Netherland *sewant* could fetch only 25 fl. in Amsterdam, while 100 fl. worth of beaver pelts, reckoned at 8 fl. apiece, obtained only a little over 56 fl.[31]

Financial difficulties in the 1630s forced the WIC to eventually abandon most of its monopolistic privileges throughout its chartered territory.[32] The company continued to ease its restraint on the economic activities of the colonists. In 1639, after the failure of all but one of the patroonships, the company opened up the fur trade to everyone and dispersed large tracts of land to attract colonists. The last two decades of New Netherland's existence witnessed a substantial population growth of Europeans. On Long Island alone five new Dutch towns were founded after 1640: Breuckelen (Brooklyn), Amersfoort (Flatlands), Midwout (Flatbush/Midwood), Boswijck (Bushwick), and Nieuw Utrecht (New Utrecht). Colonists from New England also poured into the Dutch colony and settled five towns of their own under Dutch authority: Heemstede (Hempstead), Vlissingen (Flushing), Mespath/Middleburgh (Maspeth/Elmhurst), Gravesande (Gravesend), and Rustdorp (Jamaica). The growing population of colonists pushed hard against the territories of the Algonquian tribes of the estuary, sparking Indian rebellions and prompting genocidal military campaigns that largely succeeded in removing the human obstacles to the expansion of Dutch farms. The population boom also stimulated a thriving trade in provisions for new colonists and encouraged the growth of a Dutch merchant community. Operating in partnership with the wealthy Amsterdam cartels to extract furs, tobacco, and other colonial products for the transatlantic trade, the merchants gained the important financial connections that allowed them to flourish in the last days of the Dutch colony.

The commercial evolution of the lower Hudson River Valley reflected the mixed goals and often-contradictory aspirations of the West India Company and the thousands of colonists who came to the colony to carve out new lives. The company sought to control the commerce, to channel it, and to profit from it. The colonists sought more personal goals and inevitably found themselves at odds with the colonial administration. This tension between company profits and settlers' entrepreneurial energy dominated New Netherland's politics. But always at the center of the conflict stood trade, the ubiquitous buying and selling, bartering, and bargaining of exchange. The commerce of the river was the commerce of the colony. Whether wheat from Esopus, oysters from Long Island, furs from Fort Orange, manufactured goods from the fatherland, or a mundane assortment of ropes, canvas, milled lumber, bricks, cloth, beer, and brandy, the river moved the goods from buyer to seller.

If we could time travel to a summer in the early 1660s and board a yacht in modern Westchester County for a day's voyage to New Amsterdam, we would find ourselves in a surprisingly crowded waterway. Our skipper would have to be constantly alert to maneuver around and through a daunting array of vessels: small barks carrying cattle and grain; schooners and ketches returning from the South River (Delaware Bay) with cargoes of furs, timber, whale oil, salted fish, and summer peaches; undecked sloops, loaded with passen-

HET WEST INDISCH HUYS.

UNIDENTIFIED ARTIST
Het West Indisch Huys (West India Company House), Amsterdam, the Netherlands, c. 1685
Published in T. Van Domslaer, *Beschryvinge van Amsterdam*
Engraving, 7¾ x 11¾ in.
Museum of the City of New York, Gift of G.C.J. Boissevain, 33.225

The offices and storage facility for the Dutch West India Company in Amsterdam
were built around 1641.

gers and livestock; and, as we neared the roadstead before New Amsterdam,
the oceangoing *fluyts* and company frigates, their decks bristling with cannon.
Dutch sailors, skippers, farmers, and merchants built this vibrant trade system by adapting and ultimately transforming the preexisting Native American economy. The ecological costs were high: the virtual extinction of the
beaver, the decimation of Native Americans through virgin-soil epidemics
and warfare, and the reconstruction of the landscape as old-growth forests
were cut down to supply wood for construction and fuel and to make way for
farms. As the land changed, so too did the people who inhabited it. By the
end of the Dutch period both Indians and Europeans had been transformed.
Native Americans had to adapt to the presence of the invaders, and in doing

so they were Europeanized in their material culture. The demand for European trade goods challenged traditions associated with the hunt, generated a maldistribution of wealth, and exacerbated intertribal divisions. The Dutch too were profoundly changed by the experience. Of the crops that formed the basis of colonial agriculture—maize, beans, squash, and tobacco—not one was of European provenance. For the Dutch to survive, they had to grow crops domesticated by Indians and incorporate hunting into their way of life. From the standpoint of those who remained in Holland, a New Netherlander was a person considerably Indianized in culture and habits.

By the mid-point of the seventeenth century, the lower Hudson River estuary had become a vital part of the Atlantic trading empire of the United Provinces of the Netherlands, and it would remain so until the English conquest of 1664. From the date of the estuary's discovery by Henry Hudson to the end of Director General Petrus Stuyvesant's administration, the lower Hudson River was mapped, sounded, and sailed by hundreds of Dutch ship captains. They noted its dangerous eddies and shoals, its wind sheers and ventures. For two generations, seamen who had honed their skills in the deadly waters of the Zuider Zee and the North Sea made the lower Hudson River their workplace. This "beautiful and fruitful place" must have seemed both exotic and familiar to the sailors, traders, company men, and swashbuckling adventurers who sailed its waters.[33] Exotic because it remained a verdant wilderness of primeval forest, teeming with thickly furred animals that were gold on the run for fur traders. Exotic too because it was densely inhabited by *wilden* (savages) whose strange tongues and bloodthirsty rituals conjured up the image of devil worshippers. And yet it was familiar, so much like the fatherland with its navigable rivers and deep-water bays, its islands suitable for farming, washed by the brackish mixture of rivers and sea. Here a Netherlander could feel at home working a farm, hawking goods at market, manning the deck of a ship, or grasping the tiller of a yacht.

NOTES

1. Algonquian Indians of the lower Hudson Valley were linguistically related to the Algonquin tribe of Canada. The Algonquians occupied a larger geographical area than any other group in North America: from the east shore of Newfoundland to the Rocky Mountains and from the Churchill River to Pamlico Sound. Iroquoia, the region controlled by Iroquoian-speaking peoples, bisected this territory along the Hudson River corridor from just south of Albany, New York to the Huron territory of Canada. The eastern Algonquian tribes, of which the Indians of the lower Hudson River Valley were part, occupied a thin slice of the Atlantic seaboard from Newfoundland to the Neuse River. They were the first Native Americans to have contact with Europeans in virtually every colony.

2. Native Americans considered the Lenape the root stock of the Algonquian people. In the first half of the seventeenth century they still occupied the central home territory

from which most of the cognate tribes had diverged. Other Algonquian tribes called them "grandfather." Even the Iroquoian Huron accorded them this honorific title of priority among their people. They inhabited more than 100 villages throughout the entire basin of the Delaware River, eastern Pennsylvania, southern New York, and most of New Jersey and Delaware. The English knew them as the Delaware, following the English practice of naming Native American bands after the nearest important geographical point. The Dutch made a greater effort to distinguish individual bands and to phonetically reproduce what they thought to be the names used by the Indians themselves. Johannes de Laet listed seven different tribal names in the Delaware Valley alone. J Franklin Jameson, ed., *Narratives of New Netherland, 1609-1664* (New York: Charles Scribner's Sons, 1909), 53.

3. Furs provided three primary materials used in hats and clothing: the full pelt (fur and skin), leather or suede (the skin with all fur removed), and felts (made of the fur scraped from the hide). The process known as felting involved the use of heat and pressure to form a piece of pliable material. Felts were used extensively in hat making. The physical structure of beaver fur made it particularly good for felting. The North American beaver (*Castor canadensis*) and the European beaver (*Castor fiber*) were, for the purposes of the pelt trade, nearly identical. The American beaver was thus an easy substitute for the near-extinct European species. J. F. Crean, "Hats and the Fur Trade," *The Canadian Journal of Economics and Political Science* 28 (August 1962): 373-386.

4. Simon Hart, *The Prehistory of the New Netherland Company: Amsterdam Notarial Records of the First Dutch Voyages to the Hudson* (Amsterdam: City of Amsterdam Press, 1959), *passim*.

5. John Romeyn Brodhead, comp., Edmund B. O'Callaghan and Berthold Fernow, eds. and trans., *Documents Relative to the Colonial History of the State of New York,* 15 vols. (New York, 1856-87), 1:plate opposite 13; hereafter cited as *DCHNY*.

6. The exact title was the Chartered West India Company, or in Dutch, *Geoctroyeerde Westindische Compagnie.*

7. Hart, *Prehistory*, 38n.

8. Algemeen Rijksarchief (National Archives), The Hague, Netherlands, "De eerste serie registers van ordinaries net-resolutiën van de Staten Generaal," 318:54-54v

9. Algemeen Rijksarchief, "De liassen West-Indische Compagnie," 5751: April 22, 1624.

10. The following discussion of the events of 1624 to 1626 is based on Arnold J.F. van Laer, ed. and trans., *Documents Relating to New Netherland, 1624-1626, in the Henry E. Huntington Library* (San Marino, Calif.: Henry E. Huntington Library and Art Gallery Press, 1924).

11. Debate over the exact date of the arrival of the first colonists in New Netherland has persisted since the publication of the *DCHNY*. This controversy was sparked by the affidavit of Catelina Trico. On February 14, 1685, Trico, then about eighty years of age, testified before Governor Thomas Dongan: "That she Came to this Province either in the yeare one thousand six hundred and twenty three or twenty four to the best of her remembrance." Three years later, in testimony before William Morris, justice of the peace, she confidently declared: "That in ye year 1623 she came into this Country with a Ship called ye *Unity* whereof was Commander Arien Jorise belonging to ye West India Company." Most scholars agree she must have been referring to the arrival of the ship *Nieu Nederlandt*, since there are no records of a ship named *Eendracht* (*Unity*) in this area. Nicholaes van Wassenaer noted the voyage of the sixty-ton *Mackereel*. To reconcile the known facts with Trico's testimony, we must assume that they relate to the sailing of the yacht *Mackerel* that returned to Amsterdam in August 1624. The famed archivist and translator Arnold J.F. van Laer suggested it may have been the same ship that Dutch historian Baudartius described as having "conveyed some families from Holland thither." A.J.F. van Laer, "The Essays of A.J.F. Laer,"

Annals of New Netherland (Albany, N.Y.: The New Netherland Project), http://www.nnp.org/nni/Annals/1999.pdf (accessed June 28, 2008).

12. Crean, "Hats and the Fur Trade," 381.

13. Jameson, *Narratives*, 104.

14. Jameson, *Narratives*, 84.

15. Van Laer, *Documents Relating to New Netherland*, 216-219. The Dutch florin contained 20 stuivers and was frequently referred to as a guilder. For the first half of the seventeenth century, 48 stuivers, or roughly 2½ fl., equaled a Spanish rial-of-eight. In New Netherland, a good-quality beaver pelt sold for about 8 fl. and a 240-pound hogshead of Virginia tobacco was worth about 114 fl.

16. Oliver A. Rink, "Company Management or Private Trade: The Two Patroonship Plans for New Netherland, " *New York History* 59 (1978): 5-26.

17. Ibid. For a discussion of this historiography, see Oliver A. Rink, *Holland on the Hudson: An Economic and Social History of Dutch New York* (Ithaca, N.Y.: Cornell University Press, 1986), 94-116.

18. Arnold J.F. van Laer, ed. and trans., *The Van Rensselaer-Bowier Manuscripts* (Albany, N.Y.: State University of New York Press, 1908), 136.

19. Van Laer, *Documents Relating to New Netherland*, 216-219.

20. Gemeentlijke Archief van Amsterdam (hereafter cited as GAA), Nicolaes Rooleeu, Notarial invoice 758 (April 3, 1631), 210.

21. Johannes de Laet, *Historie ofte Iaerlijck Verhael van de verrichtinghen der Geoctroyeerde West-Indische Compagnie, zedert haer begin, tot het eynde van 't jaer sesthien-hondert ses-en-dertich; begrepen in derthien boecken, ende met verscheyden koperen platen verciert* (Leyden, Netherlands: Abraham Elzevier, 1644), Appendix:29-30.

22. For an estimate of the total costs of settling the Walloons, see Rink, *Holland on the Hudson*, 89.

23. In that year four experienced tobacco merchants sailed out to "Virginies in Nieuw Nederlandt" aboard the *de Haring*. They carried 100 Carolus guilders' worth of knives to trade for tobacco. GAA, Cornelis Touw, Notarial invoice 1420 (September 3, 1637), 121.

24. For a discussion of this incident and the English bias of the documents, see Charles T. Gehring, "The Dutch Among the People of the Long River," *Annals of New Netherland* (Albany, N.Y.: The New Netherland Project), http://www.nnp.org/nni/Annals/1999.pdf (accessed June 29, 2008).

25. Van Laer, *Documents Relating to New Netherland*, 224.

26. Frank G. Speck, "The Functions of Wampum Among the Eastern Algonkian Indians," *American Anthropological Association Memoirs* VI (1919): 3-71. For the trade itself, see Kevin McBride, "The Source and Mother of the Fur Trade: Native-Dutch Relations in Eastern New Netherland," in *Enduring Traditions: The Native Peoples of New England,* ed. Laurie Weinstein (Westport, Conn.: Bergin and Garvey, 1994), 31-52; Lynn Ceci, "Native Wampum as a Peripheral Resource in the Seventeenth-Century World System," in *The Pequot in Southern New England: The Rise and Fall of an American Indian Nation*, ed. Laurence M. Hauptman and James D. Wherry (Norman: University of Oklahoma Press, 1987), 62.

27. Edmund B. O'Callaghan, ed. and trans., *Laws and Ordinances of New Netherland, 1638-1674* (Albany, N.Y.: Weed, Parsons and Company, 1868), 115-116, 357.

28. The guilder or florin contained 20 stuivers, and a stuiver contained 16 penning. A seventeenth-century guilder would be worth, depending on what calculation is used, between $15.07 and $22.85 in 2007 dollars. Several foreign coins were also in circulation, and among these the most sought-after was the Spanish "piece of eight," or *Pathienje* (expressed as P in colonial account books), worth about 2 fl., 8 stuivers. Other coins mentioned in the records of Amsterdam merchants were the Amsterdam ducat (3 fl., 3 stuivers), the *pond Vlaamsche*,

or "Flemish pound" (6 fl.), and English shillings and pounds sterling. The exchange rate among the various circulating specie fluctuated with the quality of the coin and the balance of payments in the transatlantic trade. The former was an especially vexing problem for New Netherland's merchant community because so many of the coins in circulation were shaved and clipped, forcing the merchants to eventually set prices by weight rather than face value. For colonial exchange rates, see John J. McCusker, *Money and Exchange in Europe and America, 1600-1775: A Handbook* (Chapel Hill, N.C.: University of North Carolina Press, 1978). Calculations for 2007 dollars were made using Measuringworth.com software available at http://www.measuringworth.com/index.html (accessed June 29, 2008).

29. DCHNY, 14:484.

30. Rink, *Holland on the Hudson*, 209-210n.

31. GAA, Cornelis de Grijp, Notarial invoice 2578 (November 16, 1662), 688-689.

32. R. Bijlsma, "Rotterdam's Amerika-Vaart in de eerste helft der zeventiende eeuw," *Bijdragen voor vaderlandsche geschiedenis en oudheidkunde*, 5th series, 3 (1916): 97-142.

33. The phrase "a beautiful and fruitful place" comes from Johannes de Laet's *Nieuwe Wereldt ofte Beschrijvinghe van West-Indien, uit veelerhande Schriften ende Aen-teekeningen van verscheyden Natien* (Leiden, 1625). De Laet used it to sum up a passage in Hudson's journal. See Nancy Anne McClure Zeller and Charles T. Gehring, eds., *"A Beautiful and Fruitful Place"*: *Selected Rensselaerswijck Seminar Papers* (Albany, N.Y.: New Netherland Publishing, 1991), x.

Encounters

SLAVERY AND THE
PHILIPSE FAMILY, 1680–1751

2

DENNIS J. MAIKA

In January 1697, Frederick Philipse wrote to two of his ship captains about to leave for Madagascar, asking their help in returning one of his slaves, a mulatto named Jack who had run away from Philipse's Upper Mills in Westchester County several years earlier. Philipse tracked him as far as Stratford, Connecticut, then assumed he'd traveled to Rhode Island "and perhaps is gon from (there) with Some of the Pryvateers that fitted out there for the Gulph of Persya," and could possibly be in Madagascar. Philipse asked his captains to look for Jack when they arrived, describing him as a "remarkable fellow, looks extreem Squint, Speaks verry good English & Dutch, and is of Stature Very Tall." The captains were either to capture him or, "if you think fitt to quit him for half or any other parts of the Share that hee has made."[1]

It is apparent that Philipse knew a great deal about Jack in addition to his physical attributes: he was resourceful, had sailing skills and even business acumen. Philipse was also interested in closing accounts; Jack was obviously valuable enough for his master to want him returned. He also knew that Jack possessed an understanding of local geography that would get him to a transatlantic seaport to facilitate his escape. Jack was probably aware that in wartime—King William's War (1689–1697) between England and France had been raging for several years—his maritime skills made him valuable to privateers. And clearly Jack had no desire to live at Philipsburg.

Encounters like this one between Frederick Philipse and Jack offer tantalizing images of early New York slavery. Each episode offers unique opportunities—for a glimpse of the intricate, kaleidoscopic relationships that existed between master and slave; for revelations about the nature of New York slavery, the lives of those who endured it, and the society that supported it. These relationships may be messy and fragmentary, but can nonetheless be suggestive and illuminating.[2] They encourage us to consider how the lives of slaves and their enslavers were intertwined.[3] This is particularly true of the Philipse family and the people they owned.

In colonial New York, the Philipses were a dominant force on the political, physical, and economic landscape from the time of Frederick Philipse

ARTIST UNKNOWN
Portrait of Adolphus Philipse, c. 1695
Oil on canvas
Museum of the City of New York,
Gift of Mrs. Frederick Grosvenor Goodridge, 33.45

JOHN WOLLASTON (active 1736–1775)
Margaret Philipse, c. 1750
Oil on canvas, 36 x 31⅜ in.
Historic Hudson Valley, Tarrytown, New York,
Gift of Mrs. John D. Rockefeller, Jr., PM.80.1 a-b

(1626–1702), the family patriarch in America, to his great-grandson Frederick Philipse III (1720–1786), who remained loyal to the British Crown during the American Revolution. From humble beginnings as a carpenter-builder for the Dutch West India Company, Frederick Philipse established himself as one of the colony's wealthiest men by the 1670s; with his wife, Margaret Hardenbroeck, he made a fortune from trade and commerce.[4] Their son, grandson, and great-grandson remained at the top of New York's socioeconomic pyramid for the next hundred years. The Philipse men held positions on the Governor's Council, in the New York Assembly, in the New York Supreme Court, and in New York City's Mayor's Court. The family owned land in Manhattan, New Jersey, and the Hudson Valley that included the Manor of Philipsburg (the Upper Mills in today's Sleepy Hollow and the Lower Mills in Yonkers—some 57,000 acres in today's Westchester County).[5] Like other prominent families in early New York, the Philipses were major slaveholders, employing slaves in urban, rural, and maritime environments and in a variety of occupations: as laborers in their city households and warehouses; as millers, craftsmen, and farmers at their rural farming centers; as boatmen on their Hudson River sloops; and as translators and cooks on their Atlantic voyages.

Most Americans, especially New Yorkers, are surprised to learn that slavery was important in the colonial North; images of American slavery are generally based on perceptions of the American South. Yet slavery was an integral component in colonial New York's development with roots in the earliest days of New Netherland.[6] The Dutch West India Company turned to slave labor when it had difficulty attracting free workers to its colony. The first enslaved people in New Amsterdam were a diverse ethnic mixture of Africans from the Guinea Coast, Brazil, the West Indies, and Spanish colonies. This heterogeneous group lived side by side with free Africans, reinforcing an ambiguous legal definition of slavery. Although essentially noncitizens and involuntary servants, West India Company slaves could hire themselves out for wages, raise their own crops, own moveable property, sue and be sued, and marry and raise children. A system of "half-freedom," offered to eleven Company slaves in 1644, reinforced the institutional ambiguity. After the English intrusion in 1664, the number of enslaved Africans in New York City increased, but slavery's legal structure remained uncertain. New York slavery became more rigid in response to the murder of a family by their two slaves in 1708. After the slave insurrection in New York City in 1712, provincial legislation effectively ended slavery's legal ambiguity and hardened the institution for the next forty years.[7]

It was during this transitional, ambivalent era that Frederick Philipse became an active slave trader and owner, relying on enslaved Africans to build and maintain his properties and man some of his transatlantic ventures. After his death, his son Adolph and grandson Frederick Philipse II continued to acquire and employ slaves but adjusted their perceptions to changing times. The experiences of the people they enslaved during this seventy-year period can never be fully known, but a careful examination of several noteworthy encounters between them and three generations of Philipses provides us with an appreciation of the lives they led and the nature of slavery in early New York.

BUILDING THE UPPER MILLS AT PHILIPSBURG

One of the earliest encounters between the Philipses and their slaves took place accidentally: the first permanent cohort of enslaved Africans arrived at the Upper Mills as an unplanned result of one of Frederick Philipse's first slave trading ventures. In 1685, Philipse's ship the *Charles* boarded 146 slaves from Soyo, a port on the Kongolese coast, and sailed to Barbados. Only 105 survived the voyage, 21 of whom were ill upon arrival. Nine of the infirm slaves were sent to New York, deemed "refuse cargo" unacceptable for sale in Barbados. Eight were delivered to Philipse's 19-year-old son Adolph near Rye, New York, who then took them approximately 15 miles across Westchester County to the confluence of the Hudson and Pocantico rivers, where the Upper Mills was under construction. The ninth, a Negro boy with one eye, was sent to New York City, perhaps to serve in Philipse's Manhattan household.[8]

This small, ethnically coherent group of Kongolese became the core of the Upper Mills enslaved community. The bonds that formed among them, forged during their journey from Kongo to Barbados to Westchester, were based securely on the Kongolese culture they shared.[9] As they built the Upper Mills and prepared the surrounding land for cultivation, to what extent did their heritage guide their experience and influence their adjustment to the Hudson Valley? Identifying and appreciating several unique elements in Kongolese culture allows us to speculate.

In the seventeenth century, Kongolese villages were essentially agricultural societies. Villagers cultivated manioc, yams, taro, groundnuts, maize, and palm and fruit trees, using the hoe as their primary tool. A variety of crops were usually planted in the same field, to maximize the soil's fertility as well as minimize crop loss due to pests.[10] Men cleared the new fields, tended the fruit and palm trees, fished, and hunted, while women did the daily agricultural work. Kongolese villagers also developed an effective practice of herbalism and mental healing.[11]

Kongolese had extensive experience with other cultures, facilitated by proximity to the Kongo River. They were regular river traders and developed

Map of
Philipsburg
Manor.
Map by Robert
Romagnoli,
courtesy
of Historic
Hudson Valley,
Tarrytown, New
York

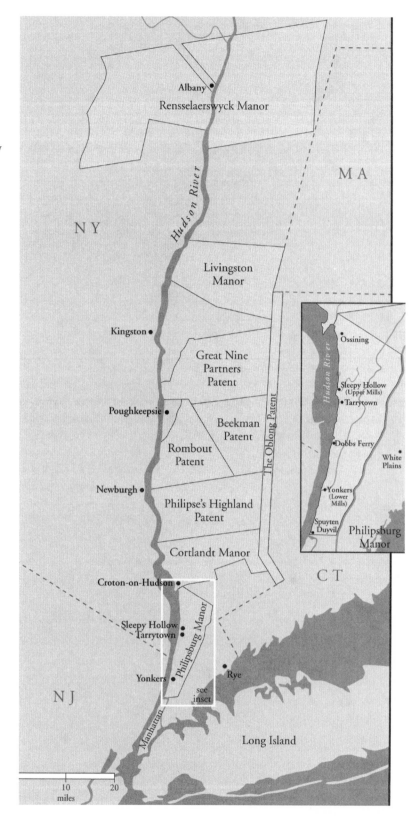

JOAN BLAEU (1596–1673)
Cartouche with African figures and animals
(detail from page: West and West Africa).
In [*Atlas maior*] *Geographia, quae est Cosmographia Blaviana . . .*
Amstelaedami, Labore et sumptibus Ioannis Blaev, 1662–1665 [v. 1, 1665]
Hand-colored engraving, image: 15½ x 22¾ in; sheet: 22 x 25½ in.
Tracy W. McGregor Library of American History, Special Collections,
University of Virginia Library (A1662.B53)

navigational expertise as they improved their commerce. Trade led to cultural exchange and made assimilation of different cultural traits part of the Kongolese milieu. No doubt the close linguistic association between Kongo's Bantu speakers and others who used Bantu language constructs encouraged interaction with ethnic groups from Loango to Luanda.[12]

Such interaction sometimes led to armed conflict, which stimulated the taking of slaves. Soyo, the point of departure for the Philipsburg cohort, had begun to export enslaved captives in the 1640s. By the late seventeenth century, this trade intensified as English and Dutch traders competed for slaves in the Soyo market.[13] The deteriorating political situation and persistent warfare resulted in frequent seizures of people, many of whom were moved quickly for sale, some to Soyo nobility and others to transatlantic agents.[14] Kongolese captives were held in high regard by European slave traders and buyers because of specific cultural traits that were valued by slave owners.[15]

When they arrived at Philipse's Upper Mills, the Kongolese cohort would have survived war and captivity at home, the cruelties of the Middle Passage, and illnesses that sent them from Barbados to New York. As they recovered

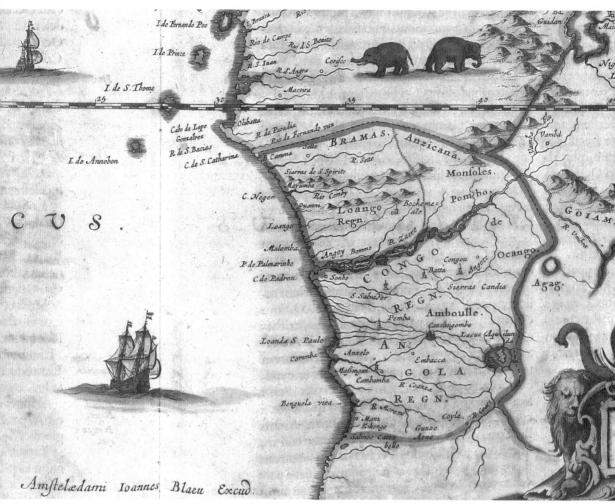

JOAN BLAEU (1596–1673)
Congo (detail from page: West and West Africa).
In [*Atlas maior*] *Geographia, quae est Cosmographia Blaviana . . .
Amstelaedami, Labore et sumptibus Ioannis Blaev, 1662-1665* [v. 1, 1665]
Hand-colored engraving, image: 15½ x 22¾ in; sheet: 22 x 25½ in.
Tracy W. McGregor Library of American History, Special Collections,
University of Virginia Library (A1662.B53)

The name of the port, "Sonho," is also spelled "Soyo," as on this map.

from their ordeal, they would have relied on Kongolese traditions to adjust
to enslavement. They most likely employed their agricultural skills to create a
garden to grow their own food, a common practice in rural areas in America
and the Caribbean. They would have adapted to foods suitable to their new
climate, finding tubers like Hudson Valley sweet potatoes similar to Kongolese
manioc and yams.[16] They would have applied their knowledge of herbalism to
the cultivation or collection of plants needed for remedies and medicines.

Philipsburg Manor from the air.
Photograph courtesy of Historic Hudson
Valley, Tarrytown, New York

Frederick Philipse (d. 1750) controlled his
commercial empire from Philipse Manor
and sold the agricultural production of his
European tenant farmers and slaves through
his Atlantic trading ventures.

Philipsburg Manor Garden, as it appeared c. 1750.
Photograph courtesy of Historic Hudson Valley, Tarrytown, New York

As they built the mill, mill dam, and manor house, their principal work, they interacted with other enslaved peoples, probably a mixture of Kongolese, Coromantines, Paw Paws, Malagasy people, and seasoned slaves from the West Indies who had been living in New York City, some of whom had become skilled craftsmen.[17] The Kongolese would have learned from them the skills of milling, coopering, and masonry, if they didn't already possess these talents. Finally, we should not be surprised to eventually find a Kongolese boatman at the helm of a Philipse sloop after his master recognized his navigational skill, derived from Kongo River experience.[18]

This early encounter between the Philipses and the Kongolese cohort suggests ways African culture may have influenced the lives of those new to the Hudson Valley and offers initial insight into Frederick Philipse's perception of the people he enslaved. As he responded to the portion of a slave cargo that was no longer saleable in Barbados, he was strongly influenced by a sense of functionalism and efficiency. Since he did not travel with the *Charles*, he would not have made the decision to send the nine infirm Kongolese to New York, but he certainly would have made his Barbados representative aware of his concern for maximizing profit; he may have even made these instructions more explicit, as was his practice in later voyages. A practical use was immediately found for all nine—eight were deemed worthy to work at the Upper Mills and the young boy with one eye fit to work in the Philipse New York City household.

BUILDING A RELIGIOUS COMMUNITY AT PHILIPSBURG

A story has often been told about the building of the Old Dutch Church at Philipsburg. While the church was under construction, a freshet washed out the mill dam at the neighboring Upper Mills. Labor, most likely of the recently enslaved Kongolese Africans, shifted away from the church to make repairs on the dam, but in spite of these efforts, it washed out two more times. At this point, one of Philipse's slaves, either Harry or Cuffy, told his master of a recurrent dream in which God expressed displeasure that the church had not yet been completed, and that it needed to be finished before the dam would hold. According to legend, this advice was followed—the church was completed and the dam held.[19]

Although the provenance and accuracy of such a tale are difficult to verify, it nevertheless raises questions worth considering. What religious knowledge did enslaved Africans bring to Philipsburg? How might Frederick Philipse's religious background have affected his response to a dream that suggested divine intervention? To what extent did the enslaved Africans who built the Old Dutch Church participate in the Reformed community it served?

WILLIAM RICKARBY MILLER (1818–1893)
Old Dutch Church at Sleepy Hollow, 1861
Oil on canvas, 15½ x 22⅛ in.
Historic Hudson Valley, Tarrytown, New York, SS79.3 a-b

The Kongolese who arrived at Philipsburg was probably familiar with Christianity and may have been Roman Catholic. Christianity was a fundamental part of religious practice in Kongo, dating back hundreds of years before the *Charles*'s arrival in 1685. In 1491, João I Nzinga a Nkuwu was baptized according to the Roman Catholic tradition and became Kongo's first Catholic king, and his successors further solidified the Church's influence.[20] Roman Catholic missionaries and priests, supported by an active laity made up of teachers and students, provided instruction in the rudiments of the Catholic faith for Kongolese villagers. Using an old catechism translated from Portuguese into Kikongo in 1624, teachers engaged children of all statuses and classes in a dialogue that began with the sign of the cross, offered lessons on Christian faith, and encouraged the memorization of standard prayers and the Ten Commandments.[21] For African Christians, basic principles of a proper Christian life, including divine intervention in daily affairs and the importance of a place of worship, were understood.

Traditional Kongolese culture supported adherence to Christianity. Kongolese Christians used Kikongo religious terminology—*Nzambi Mpungu* for God, *nkisi* for holy, and *moyo* for spirit or soul—as they articulated their belief in the resurrected Christ and an afterlife with God in heaven.[22] Kongolese tradition also held rivers as sacred places, as a "boundary between the everyday of This World and the spiritual realm of the Other World." Streams could be oracles of an *nkita* or local deity; turbulence might indicate a personal or communal failure. Furthermore, indigenous Kongo religion accepted the idea that revelations could be received from the "Other World," a belief shared with Roman Catholicism. Dreams were acceptable conduits for such revelations and, in Kongolese culture, special individuals known as *ngangas* served as interpreters of dreams.[23] Given his cultural heritage, we should not be surprised that an enslaved Kongolese at Philipsburg shared a dream suggesting divine intervention in building the church.

Frederick Philipse did not subscribe to Roman Catholic beliefs and was not well informed about traditional Kongolese cosmology. If he was aware of his slaves' Catholicism, he would have kept that knowledge a secret from his neighbors and associates. A deep fear of a Roman Catholic conspiracy and antipathy toward Catholics hung heavily over New York in the 1680s; as a prominent man, Philipse would have been reluctant to offer any cause for public scrutiny.[24]

But as a believer in the Dutch Reformed religion, Philipse might have given his slave's dream some credibility. It was common in seventeenth-century Dutch theology to believe that God often spoke to his people through omens, which were perceived as calls "to turn away from all sins by which people angered God." Thus, true Reformed believers were taught to fear God's wrath and be sensitive to signs of his displeasure. Aware of the coincidence of his mill dam's destruction with the building of his church, Philipse may have acted on an omen coming from both nature and a slave.[25]

Although Frederick Philipse and the enslaved Kongolese may have shared a belief in divine intervention, they never shared full membership in Philipsburg's Reformed community. There is no evidence that slaves were ever accepted as formal members; the surviving registers of members, baptisms, and marriages do not contain enslaved African names and the church minutes, which might have revealed a discussion about slaves, are missing from 1697 to 1785.[26]

Refusing to admit enslaved Africans as formal members of the Old Dutch Church community was consistent with practices that evolved from the earliest years of settlement in New Amsterdam. Although free and enslaved Africans were married and baptized in Manhattan's Dutch Reformed Church, this practice was discouraged by the 1660s primarily because of fear that baptized slaves could claim release based on their status as Christians. By the early eighteenth century, the Reformed churches in New York typically denied slaves full membership.[27]

It appears that enslaved Africans were nevertheless connected to the church they built—they were permitted to attend services. Dutch Reformed churches ordered the communities they served by providing a hierarchy of church membership. Clergy, elders, deacons, and communicants occupied the top three categories, while a fourth was reserved for the "unregenerate," an informal group admitted to church services. At the Tappan Reformed Church on the other side of the Hudson River, slaves were denied admission to communion and minister-performed marriages but were permitted to attend worship ceremonies seated apart from formal members in a separate gallery. Segregation continued even in death, as some slaves were buried on church property apart from white decedents.[28]

The Philipsburg Reformed community followed similar practices because Tappan's Pietist minister, Guiliam Bertholf, was also the itinerant minister serving the congregation up to the 1720s.[29] The Philipsburg church would have admitted enslaved Africans to worship services but denied them communion and other benefits of formal membership.[30] A description of a Sunday procession into the Old Dutch Church confirms this. The Philipse family, finely dressed and accompanied by the minister, entered first, followed by local tenant farmers, then by "negro slaves," poor whites, and a few "aboriginal landholders," who proceeded to the gallery where they were segregated from church members. Architectural evidence of a separate balcony in the Philipsburg Church supports the report of a separate gallery.[31]

The informal but nonetheless real connection between the free Reformed Church community and Philipsburg's enslaved Africans was manifested in specific religious celebrations. The Sabbath procession at the Old Dutch Church was similar to Sunday gatherings of New Amsterdam's slaves, which continued in New York City into the 1690s. What typically followed Sunday church service was a time of singing and dancing, a practice found in traditional African cultures.[32] The Pinkster celebration, originally the Dutch observance of Pentecost, became a time of "interracial celebration" in the Hudson Valley when enslaved Africans played on African-style drums and string instruments and danced to traditional African rhythms. The seasonal celebration offered a respite from labor as well as an opportunity to express traditional cultural practices within the new Hudson Valley environment.[33]

The possible encounter between Harry or Cuffy and Frederick Philipse allows us to imagine a rich and complex cultural interaction between Dutch and Africans in the Hudson Valley. Although Sabbath rituals would have been different, the enslaved Kongolese would have recognized Christian symbols like the cross and the Lord's Supper and found them meaningful as they attended services in the Old Dutch Church. As free tenants of Philipsburg par-

Kongo Crucifix, Africa,
Angola; early 17th century
Brass, 10 x 5½ x ¾ in.
The Metropolitan Museum of Art,
Gift of Ernst Anspach, 1999
(1999.295.4)
Image © The Metropolitan
Museum of Art

ticipated in Pinkster or in regular Sunday celebrations, they would have been
moved by African music and dance. Frederick Philipse and his family would
have expected to occupy an exalted position at the top of the local hierarchy,
but the community they surveyed was clearly multiracial.

Yet as their lives ended, enslaved Africans were segregated from white
Philipsburg residents. Evidence unearthed in the summer of 1905 points to a
separate African burial ground. As digging began for new homes near Pier-
son Avenue in the village of Sleepy Hollow, a large number of full and partial
skeletons were found clustered together. The discovery did not surprise some
local residents who remembered seeing old tombstones, one with the inscription HERE WAS BURIED CAESAR, WHO WORKED THE MOST OF HIS YEARS
AT THE MILL, AS WELL AS OTHER AFRICANS.[34] The existence of a slave
burial ground on the hillside behind the present Philipsburg Manor restoration opposite the Old Dutch Church would certainly have followed Reformed
practice in early New York.

HOWARD PYLE (1853–1911)
New York City Slave Auction, 1894
Oil on canvas board en grisaille,
16 x 12¼ in.
Published in Thomas A. Janvier,
"New York Slave Traders," *Harper's
Monthly*, January 1895, p. 299.

The caption under the printed
illustration in *Harper's Monthly*
reads: "The choicest pieces of her
cargo were sold at auction."
Image courtesy of Archives of
American Illustrators Gallery,
New York, New York

PHILIPSE'S MARITIME SLAVES

Frederick Philipse became a more active participant in the slave trade while the Upper Mills was being built. The *Charles*'s voyage that brought the Kongolese cohort to Philipsburg was probably his first slaving venture, but he quickly explored new opportunities. By the 1690s, he was actively trading in slaves from Madagascar.[35] In one of these voyages, he relied heavily upon one of his slaves, a man named Nicholas Cartagena.

His surname suggests he was an "Atlantic creole," one of a small group of Africans defined more by their active participation in maritime activities than by their enslavement experience.[36] Atlantic creoles served as intermediaries in early contact between Africans and Europeans and were later found in prominent Atlantic ports like Cartagena, Havana, Mexico City, and San Salvador. They spoke a variety of European and African languages, even a pidgin language that became the Atlantic world's lingua franca. Sometimes they were enslaved and shipped to Pernambuco, Barbados, or Martinique. They were especially prized by the Dutch, who valued their "gift for intercultural negotiation" as far back as the days of Jan Rodriguez, a free mulatto from San Domingo who came to the Hudson River Valley in 1612 and worked as an interpreter for Dutch trader Thijs Mossell.[37]

Nicholas Cartagena was either transported from Africa's west coast to South America or a second-generation slave living in Cartagena.[38] By the 1690s, he belonged to Frederick Philipse's oldest son, Philip Philipse, then living in Barbados. Although we do not know how Cartagena came into Philip's possession, we have some idea how he came to belong to his father. In poor health in 1690, Philip went to Spring Head Plantation in Barbados to recover from an injury or illness incurred while sailing as a privateer off eastern Long Island. Cartagena probably served Philip during this time and would have traveled with his master to Barbados. Since his obvious seafaring skills would have been wasted on a Barbados sugar plantation, Philip might have decided that Cartagena would be more usefully employed by his father. Perhaps Frederick himself made the request.[39]

Cartagena's experience was the reason Frederick Philipse selected him to serve on a venture into the Madagascar slave trade. In 1691, Adam Balldridge, a former New York mariner living in Madagascar, offered to supply Philipse with 200 slaves at a price of 30 shillings each, considerably less than the going rate for West African slaves.[40] Balldridge also suggested a market for whatever manufactured goods Philipse could send. Philipse responded by sending his ship the *Charles* to Madagascar in 1693, commanded by Captain John Thurber. Nicholas Cartagena was on board as "Linguistor" or interpreter. Unfortunately for Frederick Philipse, the voyage did not yield the promised number of slaves and Nicholas Cartagena never returned.

For unknown reasons, Captain Thurber sold Cartagena soon after the *Charles* reached Madagascar. Regretting the sale or simply trying to keep his wealthy partner happy, Adam Balldridge offered to compensate Philipse by sending the considerable sum of 100 pieces of eight. It is possible that Cartagena himself was involved in Thurber's "sale" and Balldridge's negotiation, hoping for his freedom. Given his experience, Cartagena certainly appreciated Madagascar's commercial opportunities and had no desire to remain enslaved. Philipse, aware of this as he tried to get him back, told his agents in Madagascar to keep their intentions secret since Cartagena would "give you or the Master the Slip." Ultimately, Cartagena himself purchased his freedom, paying a "valuable Sattisfaction" that Philipse was willing to accept.[41]

Understanding Nicholas Cartagena's story allows a deeper appreciation of the experience of Jack, the runaway described earlier. Like Cartagena, Jack was an Atlantic creole with readily recognizable maritime skills and abilities that led to Philipse's assumptions about where he would go. The timing of the two episodes coincides; Cartagena's departure with the *Charles* and Jack's departure from the Upper Mills both took place in the summer of 1693. Given that Philipse selected Cartagena for the maritime role, Jack's expertise in commerce was not needed and he was sent to the Upper Mills during a critical period in the farming cycle: harvesting of wheat and corn generally began in August, about the same time overseas voyages would have departed from New York.[42] We can imagine Jack arriving at the Upper Mills, disappointed not to have been sent abroad, unhappy with a future in the rural Hudson Valley, and deciding to escape—willing to risk capture and punishment rather than face a life away from the sea.

Philipse employed other slaves in maritime occupations. Marramita, one of Philipse's household cooks, was put on the *Margaret* to cook for the crew on a 1698 Madagascar voyage. She may have also supervised the feeding of slaves taken on board. On slaving voyages, food for slaves was generally similar to food for the crew—simple mixtures of what was acquired in various ports along the way, combined with provisions like biscuit (hard tack) that had been carried throughout the voyage. Slaves were fed ten at a time from a small, fat wooden tub, each eating with a wooden spoon.[43] The tubs were typically made and repaired by the ship's cooper, whose skills were also necessary on a transatlantic slave voyage. For this reason, Philipse added Frank or Francisco Domingo to the *Margaret*'s crew; he was a cooper owned by Jacobus Van Cortland, Philipse's son-in-law.[44]

Encounters with Nicholas Cartagena, Jack, Marramita, and Frank illustrate how some slaves applied their particular skills to the world of Atlantic commerce. Although Marramita and Frank apparently had no choice in their assignment, Cartagena and Jack demonstrated an ability to be agents of their own destiny—Cartagena negotiated his freedom, whereas Jack chose to emancipate himself by running away. Obviously, neither man was content with his situation and both ended their enslavement to Frederick Philipse.

Their stories also offer insight into the master-slave relationship. Philipse knew his slaves personally and chose their tasks deliberately to suit his advantage, making his decisions based on a functionalist approach.[45] Philipse's "personnel management" style was natural for a man intimately involved in supervising every aspect of his business interests. Yet his decisions did not go unchallenged. With Cartagena, he found it necessary to negotiate the relationship, a process that ultimately satisfied both parties. It is also clear that Philipse made mistakes as he assessed his slaves. It would appear that he trusted Cartagena to both serve and return to him. With Jack, Philipse made a serious error in thinking that a man with a maritime background would be content working at the Upper Mills.

THE LAST WILL AND TESTAMENT OF FREDERICK PHILIPSE I

In 1700, at the age of seventy-four, Frederick Philipse wrote his will.[46] After bequeathing his soul to the "merciful and Infinite God who gave it," he divided his substantial amount of real and personal property between his grandson Frederick Philipse II, his son Adolph, his stepdaughter Eva, and his daughter Annetjke. In addition to "ships, vessels, money, plate, goods, merchandize," he specified houses, lots, warehouses, a bolting house in Manhattan, the Manor of Philipsburg (the Lower Mills in Yonkers and the Upper Mills on the Pocantico River), his land in Tappan, Bergen, and Ulster, and a recently purchased saw mill in Mamaroneck. Also listed were people Philipse held as slaves—twenty-one living at the Upper Mills, unnamed "Negroes and Negro children" living on his Yonkers plantation, and at least six slaves working in his household in New York City. Ownership of some forty slaves made Frederick Philipse one of the largest slaveholders in the Hudson Valley, second only to Lewis Morris.[47]

Listing enslaved people along with landholdings and personal property may shock the sensibilities of those alive in the twenty-first century, but it was common practice in colonial New York and elsewhere in the Atlantic world.[48] What is unique and surprising about Philipse's list is that only the twenty-one Upper Mills slaves were personally identified: fifteen bequeathed to Adolph Philipse (who inherited the Upper Mills property), five others left to Frederick Philipse II (who inherited the Lower Mills on the Neperhan River), and Old Susan. Historians have often looked to slave names and naming patterns for insight into slave origins.[49] In this final encounter, Frederick Philipse left important clues about the origins and ethnic composition of Upper Mills slaves, and about himself as well.

We learn that Philipsburg's enslaved community was composed of a variety of ethnicities. A considerable number of the slaves were probably natives of Western Africa who had experienced slavery in the West Indies, specifically Barbados. Among the most common Anglo-European names among Barbadian slaves were names on the Philipse list: Mingo, Sampson, Billy, Charles, Peter, Mary, and Harry.[50]

Hannah, a common name among Barbados slaves, was identified as an "Indian." Her English name suggests that she was probably from North America, maybe from the Carolinas or another Southern colony. Perhaps she was a "Spanish Indian," sent to New York after being captured in New Spain. Hannah might also have been from the New York area, even though it was illegal

Will of Frederick Philipse (1626–1702), p. 4, 26 October 1700
Ink on paper
Philipse-Gouverneur Family Papers, part of seven-page manuscript,
Item 9, Rare Book & Manuscript Library, Columbia University

"I will and order that the Negroe woman Old Susan shall dwell and continue on the plantation at the Upper Mills so long as she lives."

to enslave native-born Indians after 1679. As a Western Hemisphere native, Hannah—and her child—helped create a racial mix at Philipseburg that was not uncommon in New York.[51]

Kongolese were part of Philipse's 1700 slave community, recognizable, as John Thornton has suggested, by their Christian names, some in Portuguese, others in an Anglicized form.[52] This may account for Peter and Symon among Philipse's slaves. Perhaps Mingo and Billy were also from west central Africa: Mingo is a shortened form of Domingo, a common slave name that also reflected Portuguese influence, and Billy is a rephrasing of Vili, indicating a Kikango-speaking non-Christian from Loango.[53]

Circumstantial evidence suggests that the slave called Wan may have been a recent arrival from Bermuda. The name Whan appears several times in one collection of Bermudian records, used by both "negroe" and "Indian" slaves. By the 1690s, as a result of the shift from agricultural to commercial labor in Bermuda's economy, a substantial number of blacks were sold off island. If Wan was part of this exodus, he may have been purchased by Philipse for his agricultural skills. It is also possible that Wan had seafaring experience; he may have been known as Juan while sailing on the Spanish Main.[54]

One is struck by the Dutch names Claes and Hendrick among the slaves in the 1700 will. Given the long tradition of slavery in both Dutch and English New York, it is possible that these two men were second-generation slaves from New York City, named after their parents who held Dutch names. As such, they may have been transferred from Philipse's city holdings to the Upper Mills.

It has not been possible to identify the origins of Baheynne, Touerhill, and Hector, though the latter name suggests origins in a Spanish possession in North America.[55] Given the breadth of Manhattan trade and Frederick Philipse's role in it, these slaves could have been from anywhere in the Atlantic world. They may have been Malagasy people, acquired through Philipse's trade with Madagascar that began in the 1690s.[56]

The name-holding patterns in Philipse's will also offer unique insights into the slave owner's character. The eclectic list suggests that Philipse did not rename his slaves, as was so often the practice of Southern slave owners and in Barbados, where many newly purchased Africans were given English names by their first owners.[57] His apparent willingness to accept the names the slaves brought with them suggests that Philipse held a very different attitude than that of Southern owners,[58] a functionalist relationship. He knew his slaves personally as valuable, individual properties that could be passed on to his heirs.

In a distinct section of his will, Frederick singled out Old Susan from the other slaves left to Adolph: "Item. I will and order that the Negroe Woman Old Susan shall dwell and continue on the plantation at the Upper Mills as long as she lives."[59] Who was Old Susan and why did she merit such special attention?

The woman's name gives clues to her identity. Susan was a common name for enslaved women. In Barbados, Susanna was a Christian name, and Sue is identified as a plantation name used among baptized slaves on the Codrington Plantation in 1741. Old Susan might have been from Barbados, given Philipse's commercial connections there.[60] But Susan was also a popular name in Kongo, derived from the Portuguese Suzanna, used by Kongolese Christians as a baptismal name and held by such royalty as Suzanne de Nóbrega, Queen of Kongo.[61]

Given the voyage of the *Charles* that brought enslaved Kongolese to Barbados and then to New York, might Old Susan have been part of that original "refuse cargo" sent to the Upper Mills?

It is unlikely that Philipse would have purchased an old slave woman. New Yorkers who imported new slaves generally preferred young adults. Jacobus van Cortlandt, Philipse's son-in-law, writing about a female slave to a partner in the West Indies, reported in 1698 that "our Country-people do not care to buy old slaves" and explained that the New York market favored slaves no older than twenty-five.[62] If Old Susan was not a recent purchase, how then would she have come to the Upper Mills?

Dutch New Yorkers showed a remarkable propensity to keep older slaves; several of Frederick Philipse's prominent contemporaries demonstrated this. When Derrick Ten Eyck, a New York City merchant, died in 1724, one of his slaves was an elderly black woman. Abraham de Peyster's 1726 inventory included an "extraordinarily ancient group of Negro slaves"—four of seven female slaves in de Peyster's inventory are ninety, forty-eight, forty-five, and thirty-four respectively.[63] In keeping with local custom, Frederick Philipse probably owned older slaves and Old Susan was one of them. If she was a member of the original Kongolese cohort and no more than twenty-five years old in 1685, she would have been approximately forty at the time of Philipse's will, an age considered "old" among enslaved women.[64] Recovered at the Upper Mills from any Middle Passage–induced illness, Old Susan spent the next fifteen years contributing to the manor's development. She would have participated in the early clearing and building, and could have tended to the needs of the master when he visited. Perhaps she associated the physical surroundings of the manor with her recuperation and, in spite of her enslaved status, had developed an attachment to place that he may have noticed.

Frederick Philipse was forming his own attachments to the Upper Mills at the same time. He began a series of land purchases in 1680 that ultimately became Philipsburg Manor. Construction on the Upper Mills began by 1682, and the manor house was built soon after. No doubt Philipse made regular visits to the site to supervise construction and to scout his new purchases.[65] He may have depended on Old Susan to prepare his meals and tend to other household needs. She and other house slaves lived in the original manor house, probably in the lower kitchen.

Personal attachments to people and places grow out of experiences over time. In fifteen years, Frederick Philipse's connection to his Westchester manor led him to request that he be buried at his Upper Mills Church instead of Manhattan, where he'd lived for most of his life. In the same fifteen years but for different reasons, Old Susan may have developed an attachment to the Upper Mills property. We can imagine a personal request being responsible for the special attention she received in her master's will. Perhaps that attention indicated a sense of paternalism in the master's attitude toward his slaves, a feeling that may have manifested itself in other ways to other slaves.[66]

By the time of Philipse's death in 1702, the enslaved community at the Upper Mills was a heterogeneous mix of races and ethnicities. Philipse knew them personally, and though he exhibited his own brand of personal kindness to Old Susan and perhaps others, he rarely saw beyond their functional contributions to his property and showed no interest in setting them free. The next generation of Philipse slave holders would respond differently to the people they enslaved both at the Upper Mills and in New York City.

REBELLIOUS SLAVES, AMBIVALENT MASTERS

It was called "The New York Conspiracy" and "The Great Negro Plot." A series of mysterious fires and robberies that began in New York City in March 1741 frightened white inhabitants, who perceived these events as evidence of a slave uprising. Some 152 enslaved and free black New Yorkers, along with several white allies, were accused of conspiracy to destroy the city and tried before New York's Supreme Court of Judicature sitting in Manhattan. The trial began

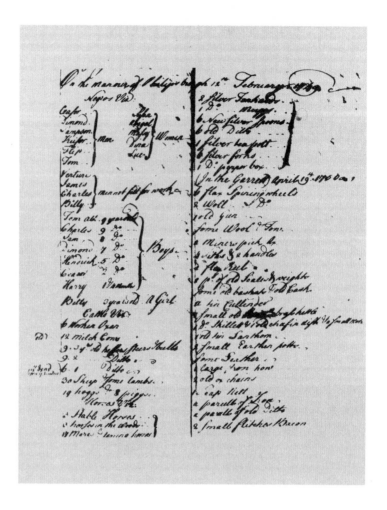

on April 21, 1741, presided over by Frederick Philipse II and Daniel Horsmanden. When the proceedings concluded, 13 blacks had been burned at the stake, 16 blacks and four whites were hanged, and 70 blacks and seven whites were banished from the colony.[67]

Among those burned was Cuffee, a slave owned by Adolph Philipse. Testimony recorded during the trial reveals something about Cuffee and his experience as an enslaved African in New York City. He lived in one of Adolph Philipse's houses in Manhattan and, with liberty to freely travel around the city, regularly associated with both free and enslaved city residents. Cuffee was reported to have had "a great deal of idle time, which, it seems, he employed to very ill purposes, and had acquired a general bad fame."[68] He was also known to speak both Spanish and English and was able to read.[69]

Cuffee was deeply involved in the conspiracy. He was accused and found guilty of setting fire to Justice Frederick Philipse's warehouse. Testimony revealed that the plot was discussed at a cock-fighting match held at Adolph

Philipse's city house, an event that was apparently attended by both blacks and whites.[70] On May 30, 1741, Cuffee and Quack, a slave belonging to John Roosevelt, reportedly confessed to the crime just before they were burned at the stake.

With all this activity taking place under his roof, what did Adolph Philipse know about Cuffee? Apparently, very little. When asked about him, Philipse replied that on the afternoon Cuffee was allegedly burning down Frederick Philipse's warehouse, Adolph Philipse had seen him at home "sewing a vane upon a board for his boat." Curiously, he could say nothing about the slave's character. This response must have surprised Cuffee, who had requested Philipse's testimony at the trial.[71]

Adolph Philipse's indifference stands in stark contrast to comments made by Justice Frederick Philipse II during the trial. In his initial charge to the grand jury, Justice Philipse stated his suspicion that excessive rum consumption was partly responsible for the slaves' criminal behavior.[72] When sentencing two other convicted slaves to their deaths, the judge railed against the "monstrous ingratitude of this black tribe" who were happier and better cared for in New York "than in the midst of the continual cruelty, and rapine of their native countries." But although he referred to the convicted conspirators as monsters, Philipse tempered his virulence with concern for their immortal souls, reflecting what historian Thelma Foote has identified as an ambivalent attitude toward blacks.[73]

Justice Philipse's ambivalence and Adolph Philipse's ignorance or deliberate indifference contrast sharply with Frederick Philipse's functional awareness of and knowledgeable acquaintance with Nicholas Cartagena, Jack, Old Susan, and the slaves named in his will. Thus, the Philipses' encounters with Cuffee and other slaves during the conspiracy suggest that second-generation slave owners perceived their slaves differently, reflecting the new environment in which eighteenth-century slavery existed.

Slave importation had increased significantly in New York. Estimates are that by the 1730s, the number of slaves in New York City alone rose to almost 1,600, a dramatic increase from the 1712 total of 970.[74] By 1737, approximately one in five New Yorkers was black and enslaved. That rough percentage persisted for the next 20 years. The vast majority of new slaves came from the West Indies, usually in small shipments and often as payment for debts owed to New York merchants.[75]

The increased number of slaves altered the ways black labor was perceived by New York's white population. Given the limited amount of white immigration into New York in the early eighteenth century, city residents relied more heavily on enslaved Africans. The resulting tension between white and black workers accelerated the "racialization" of black labor as slaves were increasingly assigned the least skilled, more physically demanding work in a more segregated domain.[76] Other local practices denigrated the personal worth of African labor. Perhaps most insidious was the trend among masters to rent out their slaves, claiming possession of their "idle (personal) time."[77] This new racialized perspective of black labor was reflected in the ever-tightening vise of regulations segregating whites from blacks and reinforcing chattel slavery.[78]

That Adolph Philipse was influenced by New York's changing culture of slavery is demonstrated not only in his response to Cuffee but also in his relationship to his Upper Mills slaves; Adolph began to distance himself from them, limiting the personal contact that had been his father's practice. In the early 1700s, he appointed Elbert Aertse as his overseer at the Upper Mills. From his room in the manor house, Aertse was responsible for the smooth operation of the grist mill, the transportation of Philipsburg products to Manhattan, and the daily supervision of slaves. Adolph also built separate slave quarters on the Upper Mills property. Archaeological evidence identified the foundation of a "Negroe House," probably built in the 1720s. Located 90 feet from the southeast corner of the manor house, the structure was almost 1,024 square feet (32 by 32 feet), large enough to accommodate all the manor's slaves and their families. In other parts of the middle colonies, building a "Negroe house" reinforced psychological as well as physical separation from owners. Thus Adolph's physical distance from his slaves contributed to or reflected his indifference or lack of attentiveness.[79]

Naming practices also suggest a widening gap between master and slave. Diamond regularly sailed the mill boat up and down the Hudson River, bringing foodstuffs both to market and to Adolph Philipse's New York City household.[80] Although the origins of the name Diamond are obscure, it is interesting to note that it was also used for one of Adolph's vessels that regularly sailed to and from Barbados, Curaçao, and other ports in the Caribbean, sometimes returning with small cargoes of slaves.[81] Diamond's assigned occupation may have prompted Adolph to give him the same name as that of his ship. This would signal a departure in naming patterns from his father, perhaps indicating the same lack of respect and desire to belittle the enslaved, a practice noted in the way Southern masters named their slaves.[82]

The ambivalence reflected in Frederick II's comments is echoed in the actions of Catherine Philipse, Frederick I's second wife and widow: she was the only family member willing to free her slaves. In her will, written in 1731, she requested that her two "Indian or Mustee" slaves, Sarah and Molly, be freed one month after her death; Molly's children were to be freed when they reached the age of twenty-one.[83] We do not know what motivated her actions.

Clearly she felt a closeness to her household companions and, given that she was the last of the first generation of Philipse slaveholders, she may have been reacting to New York's new, more restrictive slaveholding environment. But did she truly intend to free these slaves? In 1730, the year before Catherine's death, the law required a £200 security fee for slaves freed in New York. Her will contained no instructions for the payment of security money.[84]

DISMANTLING THE ENSLAVED COMMUNITY
AT PHILIPSBURG MANOR UPPER MILLS

Adolph Philipse died in New York City on January 24, 1750. His nephew Frederick Philipse II inherited his property in Manhattan and Westchester, rejoining Philipsburg Manor's Upper and Lower Mills. Within several months, Frederick II began by selling several of his uncle's slaves and putting others up for auction. When he died on July 26, 1751, some twenty-one men, women, and children were sold away.[85] Frederick III continued this process soon after his father's death, advertising the sale of Philipse slaves in the local newspaper and leasing the mill to Josiah Martin.[86] Within eighteen months, the lives of slaves at the Upper Mills were thrown into turmoil and their community fractured.

Two important documents—Adolph Philipse's inventory and Frederick II's will—offer clues as to how these combined Philipse deaths affected the people they considered property.[87] Since Adolph died without a will, the inventory taken after his death contains a full and complete listing of all his slaves. Frederick II's will offers a detailed list of forty-eight slaves at the Upper Mills, at the Lower Mills, and in Manhattan, an extraordinary number for the Hudson Valley. From close examination of the inventory and will, we learn much about the experiences of the 1750 Upper Mills enslaved community before the final encounter that changed their lives forever.

Adolph Philipse's inventory of twenty-three enslaved individuals reveals the existence of a stable, established slave community at the Upper Mills. Slave families are evidenced by the presence of eight children; a ninth child was soon to be born to Dina, who was seven and a half months pregnant.[88] Children were apparently named after their kin, a common practice among enslaved Africans, suggesting that some families were at least three generations old. The inventory's Susan may have been the daughter of Old Susan from the 1702 will; Sue may have been Old Susan's granddaughter. Similarly, Hendrick, the son of Massy, could have been the grandson of the 1702 Hendrick, and Charles could have been the grandson of the 1702 Charles. Repetition of other names hints at family relationships: Caesar the Miller—the father of two-year-old Caesar; Diamond, the boatman—the father of seven-year-old Diamond; and Tom a farmer—the father of nine-year-old Tom.[89] The similarity in names indicates decisions made by the slaves themselves, a conscious choice that reflected family solidarity.[90]

When the names on these two lists are compared with a 1755 census, it is clear that the Upper Mills slave community was broken up. Families were sold and separated. Caesar the Miller, young Caesar, and the two Toms were together at the Upper Mills in Frederick II's will but after his death were sold to different owners living on the manor lands.[91] Soon after Adolph's death, Massy and Dina were sold with their young children but without an identified husband or father.[92] Older members of the enslaved community were gone. All four considered to be "Men Not Fitt To Work" in Adolph's will—Venture, James, Charles, and Billy—were probably dead by 1751.[93]

The community was further dispersed as slaves were sold separately. Five slaves owned by tenant farmers on Philipsburg Manor and listed on the 1755 census are most likely the same individuals included in Adolph's inventory. Especially telling is that Caesar, the miller at the Upper Mills, was newly owned by Josiah Martin, the man who leased the property from Frederick III.[94]

This sale points to occupation as a reason for purchasing Philipsburg slaves and allows us to consider what Philipse's slaves were doing at the Upper Mills in 1750. The site was a vibrant economic center integrally connected to the region and the Atlantic world. Mill slaves, supervised by Caesar, ground wheat, bolted flour, packed barrels, and loaded them on ships at the wharf adjoining the mill. Flour from the mill was also taken to the nearby bake house where an enslaved baker made hard tack or biscuit, a basic provision for ocean voyages. Barrels of biscuit were loaded at the wharf, together with agricultural produce, and taken down the river by an enslaved boatman. Those slaves not working at the mill were involved in agricultural tasks. Production of foodstuffs, which the Philipses sold to overseas and local markets, required different activities that changed with the season. Livestock required tending, then finally slaughtering and curing. Wood had to be cut, fences built and mended, limestone hauled and crushed. There was a daily need for the skills of a blacksmith, a cooper, a carpenter, and a farrier. Slaves were expected to perform a "vast array of chores efficiently and well" and were valued for their versatility.[95] Each of these skills would have been attractive to potential buyers.

Female slaves performed other tasks. They cleaned, cooked, and preserved foodstuffs; they also tended the garden, ran the dairy, and spun wool and flax. They cared for domestic fowl and maintained a pigeon cote on the property. These women exhibited the same versatility that was a "hallmark of women in most African societies."[96]

While most names add to our understanding of enslaved life at the Upper

Office of the Overseer, Philipsburg Manor, as it appeared c. 1750
Historic Hudson Valley, Tarrytown, New York

Philipsburg Manor's furnishing plan is based on the probate inventory made after
Adolph Philipse's death, 1750, and with objects uncovered in a dig at the site, 1959–61.

Mills, other names raise interesting questions. The presence of Kofe, Coo
(perhaps short for Coobah), and others with Barbadian names indicates that
the Philipses continued to add to their holdings, but were these slaves purchased on the local market or directly from the West Indies? Does the presence of Maria and Issabella hint at Spanish origins for some slaves or were
they acquired from Spanish wartime prizes? Was Batavia chosen as a name
for a Philipse slave because of a fondness for the family's origins? If so, what
characteristics account for his/her name? Do Braveboy and Squire, names that
suggest a personality trait and occupation, offer evidence of new naming practices employed by Frederick II? And what of Philip or Flip? Is this name an
indication of a close, perhaps paternal, relationship with a family member?
And is there anything to the coincidence that Philip was the only slave belonging to Elbert Aertse, the overseer appointed by Adolph?[97]

The inventory and will confirm that Philipse family slaves continued to be

JOHN WOLLASTON (active 1736–1775)
Mary Philipse, c. 1750
Oil on canvas, 36⅞ x 32¾ in.
Historic Hudson Valley, Tarrytown, New York,
Gift of Mrs. John D. Rockefeller, Jr., PM.80.2 a-b

held in urban areas as well as on rural sites. The slaves bequeathed to Frederick II's daughters, son Philip, and wife Joanna probably represented the city cohort. It is likely that Sarah (bequeathed to Mary Philipse) and John (bequeathed to Joanna Philipse) were the same two slaves that had been part of Adolph Philipse's Manhattan household two years earlier. That the beneficiaries were city residents suggests that their new slaves were known to be useful in the urban environment. And although some Upper Mills slaves were sold at auction in Manhattan, probably for labor there, there is no evidence that the Philipses used their urban slaves for rural labor or vice versa.

The disbursement of the Upper Mills slaves signaled the end of an era for the Philipse family but offered a new beginning for the enslaved. Although they would continue to toil for their new tenant or urban masters, many may have lived to become the next generation of Westchester County's African Americans who ultimately gained their freedom in the early nineteenth century.

CONCLUSIONS

Set against the broad contours of New York slavery from 1680 until 1751, encounters between enslaved Africans and the Philipse family confirm the grim realities of slavery in colonial New York and illuminate many of its distinctive features. Slaves arrived with strong cultural ties to their African homelands and applied many of these traits to their experiences. They labored in urban, rural, and maritime settings and performed a variety of skilled and unskilled tasks. In some instances, slaves were agents of their own destiny as they ran away, bought their freedom, or rebelled. Owners increased their reliance on enslaved labor and supported the tightening of legal constrictions on their slaves. They treated some of their slaves with sensitivity and compassion and others with cruelty, condescension, or indifference.

In many ways, the experiences of the Philipses and their slaves were unique. The Upper Mills at Philipsburg Manor was not a typical Hudson Valley environment since most slaves were owned in much smaller numbers and on smaller landholdings. Although in some ways the work the Philipse slaves did mirrored what was happening in smaller situations around them, the mill's centrality to the economic life of white tenants on the manor assured a regularized interaction with free people that was reflected in religious life and seasonal celebrations. The ethnically coherent cohort of Kongolese that arrived in the 1680s provided a cultural core for a community that continued for generations, supported by an established family life. The regular admission of new members of different ethnicities confirms its unique heterogeneity. Although the ultimate dispersal of many slave families was not unique in colonial New York, the community that was destroyed most certainly was.

NOTES

1. "Letter to Capt. Cornelis Jacobs and Capt. Samuel Burgess from Frederick Philipse, New York, 11 January 1696/97," High Court of Admiralty Records, 1-98, Public Record Office, Kew Gardens, UK (copy in Historic Hudson Valley Library, Sleepy Hollow, NY). "Squint" may refer to the medical condition known as strabismus, "a visual defect in which one eye cannot focus with the other on an objective because of imbalance of the eye muscles." William Morris, ed., *The American Heritage Dictionary of the English Language* (New York: American Heritage Co., Inc. and Houghton Mifflin Co., 1973), 1272.

2. On the importance of "encounters," see Philip D. Morgan, *Slave Counterpoint: Black Culture in the Eighteenth-Century Chesapeake and Low Country* (Chapel Hill: University of North Carolina Press, 1998), 257-258. A different approach to the master-slave relationship is offered by Christopher Morris, "The Articulation of Two Worlds: The Master-Slave Relationship Reconsidered," *The Journal of American History* 85, no. 3 (December 1998): 982-1007.

3. On the need to "fuse the stories of enslaved and enslavers," see Joyce D. Goodfriend, "Slavery in Colonial New York City," *Urban History* 35, no. 3 (2008): 491.

4. The most recent examination of Margaret Hardenbroeck is found in Jean Zimmerman, *The Women of the House: How a Colonial She-Merchants Built a Mansion, a Fortune, and a Dynasty* (New York: Harcourt, 2006). See also Miriam Schneer, "She Merchants in Seventeenth-Century Holland and New Netherland," paper presented at a seminar of the Program in Sex Roles and Social Change, Center for the Social Sciences, Columbia University, April 1980.

5. For a brief overview, see "Philipsburg Manor" and "Philipse family" in Peter Eisenstadt, ed., *The Encyclopedia of New York State* (Syracuse, N.Y.: Syracuse University Press, 2005), 1199-1200. A recent guidebook to Philipsburg Manor is Margaret L. Vetare, *Philipsburg Manor Upper Mills* (Tarrytown, N.Y.: Historic Hudson Valley Press, 2004). The actual size of Philipsburg Manor has long been in dispute, but the most recent estimate has been made by an agency within the Westchester County government (60 n. 8).

6. For many years, the standard work on New York slavery was Edgar J. McManus, *A History of Negro Slavery in New York* (Syracuse, N.Y.: Syracuse University Press, 1966). The new standard has become Graham Russell Hodges, *Root and Branch: African Americans in New York and East Jersey, 1613-1863* (Chapel Hill: University of North Carolina Press, 1999). A new examination of slavery in New York City began with Joyce D. Goodfriend, *Before the Melting Pot: Society and Culture in Colonial New York City, 1664-1730* (Princeton: Princeton University Press, 1992) and, most recently, has been followed by Thelma Wills Foote, *Black and White Manhattan: The History of Racial Formation in Colonial New York City* (New York: Oxford University Press, 2004) and Leslie M. Harris, *In the Shadow of Slavery: African Americans in New York City, 1626-1863* (Chicago: University of Chicago Press, 2003). Major exhibitions on New York slavery at the New-York Historical Society were accompanied by an important volume—Ira Berlin and Leslie M. Harris, eds., *Slavery in New York* (New York: The New Press, 2005). The discovery of New York City's African Burial Ground in 1991 has yielded, among other works, Joyce Hansen and Gary McGowan, *Breaking Ground, Breaking Silence: The Story of New York's African Burial Ground* (New York: Henry Holt, 1998). Important work on slavery in the Hudson Valley include: A. J. Williams-Myers, *Long Hammering: Essays on the Forging of an African American Presence in the Hudson River Valley to the Early Twentieth Century* (Trenton, N.J.: Africa World Press, 1994) and more recently, Myra B. Young Armstead, ed., *Mighty Change, Tall Within: Black Identity in the Hudson Valley* (Albany: State University of New York Press, 2003). See also Graham Russell Hodges,

Slavery and Freedom in the Rural North: African Americans in Monmouth County, New Jersey, 1665-1865 (Madison, Wisc.: Madison House,1997). New York slavery has recently been included in more general studies of American slavery. See, for example, Ira Berlin, *Many Thousands Gone: The First Two Centuries of Slavery in North America* (Cambridge, Mass.: Belknap—Harvard University Press, 1998).

7. This brief summary is drawn from Dennis J. Maika, "Slavery, Race, and Culture in Early New York," *de Halve Maen* 73, no. 2 (Summer 2000): 27-33.

8. "Deposition of Seaman William Johnson and Peter Lochcourt Concerning the Voyage of the Pink *Charles*," 4 August 1685, in Peter Christoph and Florence Christoph, eds., *The Dongan Papers, 1683-1688* (Syracuse, N.Y.: Syracuse University Press, 1993), 171-172. See also "A Deposition by Charles Barnham and John Wilson," 271.

9. John K. Thornton, *The Kongolese Saint Anthony: Don Beatrix Kimpa Vita and the Antonian Movement, 1684-1706* (Cambridge: Cambridge University Press, 1998), 13; John Thornton, "The Africans Experience of the '20. And Odd Negroes' Arriving in Virginia in 1619," *The William and Mary Quarterly*, 3rd Ser., 60, no. 3 (July 1998): 421-422; Sidney W. Mintz and Richard Price, *The Birth of African-American Culture: An Anthropological Perspective* (1976; reprint, Boston: Beacon Press, 1992), 43.

10. Michael A. Gomez, *Exchanging Our Country Marks: The Transformation of African Identities in the Colonial and Antebellum South* (Chapel Hill: University of North Carolina Press, 1998), 144; Thornton, *The Kongolese Saint Anthony*, 15.

11. The Kongo-Angolan influence in herbalism and mental healing has been found in other parts of colonial America; the West Central African practice of *minkisi* (sacred medicines) is the basis for what has been called "hoodoo" in the American South. Gomez, *Exchanging Our Country Marks*, 148.

12. Thornton, "The Africans Experience of the '20. And Odd Negroes' Arriving in Virginia in 1619," 422; Gomez, *Exchanging Our Country Marks*, 141.

13. Soyo (Nsoyo or Sonyo), the point of departure for the Philipsburg cohort, was one of six provinces in the Kingdom of Kongo located on the coast and bordered in the north by the Kongo or Zaire River. David Birmingham, *Trade and Conflict in Angola: The Mbundu and Their Neighbors Under the Influence of the Portuguese, 1483-1790* (Oxford: Clarendon Press, 1966), 2; Anne Hilton, *The Kingdom of Kongo* (Oxford: Oxford University Press, 1985), 114.

14. John Thornton, *The Kingdom of Kongo: Civil War and Transition, 1641-1718* (Madison: University of Wisconsin Press, 1983), 87, 95; John Thornton, "From the General to the Particular: Ethnicity and History of the Slave Trade," paper presented at the "Conference on Transatlantic Slaving and the African Diaspora: Using the W.E.B. Du Bois Institute Dataset of Slaving Voyages," Williamsburg, Va., September 1998, 5. Paper cited with permission of the author.

15. It was reported that Angolans (Kongolese) were "docile, comely, not especially strong, possessed of a peculiar predisposition towards the mechanics but inclined to run away." These traits suited slave owners in Barbados, where "Angolans" were preferred. Gomez, *Exchanging Our Country Marks*, 136. The Europeans were correct in assuming a connection between Angola and Kongo. As both were parts of the West Central African region, many cultural similarities and continuities have been identified, and much is known about the culture of the people who lived there. In fact, a majority of Angolans were Kongolese. And the name Angola is derived from *ngola*, meaning ruler of Ndongo on Luanda, south of Soyo. Gomez, *Exchanging Our Country Marks*, 131, 134, 142.

16. Vetare, *Philipsburg Manor Upper Mills*, 51-52.

17. Goodfriend, *Before The Melting Pot*, 114.

18. Thornton, "The Africans Experience of the '20. And Odd Negroes' Arriving in Virginia in 1619."

19. Harold Dean Carter, "The Old Dutch Church of Sleepy Hollow: A Study Prepared by the Staff of Sleepy Hollow Restorations for the Consideration of Its Trustees, September 1, 1956," unpublished ms., 13; Robert Bolton, *History of The County of Westchester from Its First Settlement to the Present Time*, 2nd ed. (New York: Chas. F. Roper, 1848, 1881), I:527. That it was Harry's dream is cited in "Historical Address by the Rev. David Cole, D.D." in *Two Hundredth Anniversary of the Old Dutch Church of Sleepy Hollow, 1697-1897, Printed by the DeVinne Press for the Consistory of the First Reformed Church of Tarrytown, N.Y.*, 1898, 125. That it was Cuffy's dream is cited in Lucille and Theodore Hutchinson, *The Centennial History of North Tarrytown* (Cambridge, Md.: Western Publication Co., 1974), 18.

20. Thornton, *Kongolese Saint Anthony*, 86, 33-34. Michael A. Gomez disagrees with Thornton over the extent of Christian influence. Gomez, *Exchanging Our Country Marks*, 145-146.

21. Thornton, *Kongolese Saint Anthony*, 27-29.

22. John Thornton, "The Development of an African Catholic Church in the Kingdom of Kongo, 1491-1750," *The Journal of African American History* 25, no. 2 (1984): 152.

23. Thornton, *Kongolese Saint Anthony*, 12, 54.

24. At one point, Philipse was accused of "papist leanings," but he ultimately escaped any direct attack against his person or property in what soon developed into Leisler's Rebellion. David William Voorhees, "'In Behalf of the True Protestants Religion': The Glorious Revolution in New York" (Ph.D. diss., New York University, 1988), 77-78, 472; Robert C. Ritchie, *The Dukes Province: A Study of New York Politics and Society, 1664-1691* (Chapel Hill: University of North Carolina Press, 1977), 200.

25. A. Th. Van Deursen, *Plain Lives in a Golden Age: Popular Culture, Religion, and Society in Seventeeth-Century Holland* (New York: Cambridge University Press, 1981), 254. More dramatic omens from nature were a traditional feature of Dutch culture. See Simon Schama, *The Embarrassment of Riches: An Interpretation of Dutch Culture in the Golden Age* (New York: Knopf, 1987), 130-150.

26. David Cole, ed., *First Record Book of the "Old Dutch Church of Sleepy Hollow" Organized in 1697 and Now the First Reformed Church of Tarrytown, N.Y.* (Yonkers, 1901). There is a suggestion that manor slaves made an indirect contribution to the church: the Deacon's Account of March 23, 1709 records a payment to Catherine Philipse of 21 guilders 5 stivers for Communion Bread, probably made by the slaves. "Records from the Year 1697 to the Year 1818 of the Reformed Dutch Church of the Manor of Philipsburgh, Called Later the Old Dutch Church of Sleepy Hollow, Tarrytown, Westchester County, New York, Translated from the Original Dutch by Jacob Brinkerhoff of Brooklyn, Long Island, 1876," Manuscript Collection, Reformed Church of Tarrytown, Tarrytown, N.Y.

27. Writing from New Amsterdam in 1664, Dominie Selijns informed the Classis that efforts to teach the catechism to slaves were generally unsuccessful. He further remarked that, "as to baptisms, the negroes occasionally request, that we should baptize their children, but we have refused to do so, partly on account of their lack of knowledge and of faith, and partly because of the worldly and perverse aims on the part of the said negroes. They wanted nothing else than to deliver their children from bodily slavery, without striving for piety or Christian virtues." Edward T. Corwin, ed., *Ecclesiastical Records, State of New York* (Albany: State of New York, 1901-1916), I:548; Maika, "Slavery, Race and Culture in Early New York," 29-30; Eric Nooter, "Between Heaven and Earth: Church and Society in Pre-Revolutionary Flatbush, Long Island" (Ph.D. diss., University of Amsterdam, 1994), 101;

Goodfriend, *Beyond the Melting Pot*, 125, 126; Hodges, *Root and Branch*, 63; Berlin, *Many Thousands Gone*, 51.

28. Firth Haring Fabend, *A Dutch Family in the Middle Colonies, 1660-1800* (New Brunswick, N.J.: Rutgers University Press, 1991), 145, 160, 164. See also Fabend, *Zion on the Hudson: Dutch New York and New Jersey in the Age of Revivals* (New Brunswick, N.J.: Rutgers University Press, 2000), 9.

29. Fabend, *A Dutch Family in the Middle Colonies*, 157.

30. Although there were a few reported slave baptisms in the Tappan Church (Fabend, *A Dutch Family in the Middle Colonies*, 60), there was only one slave baptism in the Old Dutch Church from 1697 to 1761: Susanna Decks, a "negro woman" belonging to a John Harmse, was baptized on March 29, 1729. Rev. Cole, *First Record Book of the Old Dutch Church,* Fourth Division, Baptisms, 1725-1732. See *The Van Tassel Family History Homepage,* http://:freepages.genealogy.rootsweb.ancestry.com/~vantasselfamilyhistoryhomepage/ Dutchchurchhomepage.html.

31. Edgar Matthew Bacon, *Chronicles of Tarrytown and Sleepy Hollow* (New York: Putnam, 1919), 40.

32. Graham Russell Hodges, "The Emergence of a New Black Religious Identity in New York City and Eastern New Jersey, 1624-1807," in Armstead, *Mighty Change, Tall Within*, 15-16.

33. Ibid.; Willams-Myers, *Long Hammering*, 85-97; Vetare, *Philipsburg Manor Upper Mills*, 25-26.

34. "Philipse Manor Improvement," *Tarrytown Argus*, August 5, 1905. These same memories surfaced in 1958 when skeletal remains were found in an excavation on Merlin Avenue. "Skeleton Found In Excavation," *Tarrytown News*, November 18, 1958.

35. In 1688, Philipse's ship *Margaret* was given a pass by the Governor of Jamaica for 140 slaves from Madagascar. Christoph and Christoph, *The Dongan Papers*, I:xvii, 230-231, 244-247, 250-251. For more on Philipse's involvement in Madagascar, see Jacob Judd, "Frederick Philipse and the Madagascar Trade," *The New-York Historical Society Quarterly* 55, no. 4 (October 1971): 354-374.

36. Ira Berlin, "From Creole to African: Atlantic Creoles and the Origins of African-American Society in Mainland North America" (April 1996), *William and Mary Quarterly*, 3rd Series, 53, No. 2, 251-288. More on Atlantic Creoles is found in Berlin, *Many Thousands Gone*.

37. Berlin, *Many Thousands Gone*, 275, 257, 265. On Jan Rodriguez, see Peter Bakker, "First African into New Netherland, 1613-1614," *de Halve Maen* 67, no. 3 (Fall 1995): 50-52; Willie F. Page, "The African Slave During the Early English Period, 1664 to 1700," *The Journal of the Afro-American Historical and Genealogical Society* 5, nos. 3 and 4 (Fall and Winter, 1984): 125; Van Cleaf Bachman, *Peltries or Plantations: The Economic Policies of the Dutch West India Company in New Netherland, 1623-1639* (Baltimore: Johns Hopkins University Press, 1969), 6-7, 13.

38. Other slaves from Cartagena were known to live in New York. Stephen Domingo claimed to be a free man from Cartagena though his status was questioned. It is also likely that he was involved in trade. See "Deposition of Captain Charles Pinkethman," September 7, 1713, in Edmund B. O'Callaghan, *Calendar of British Historical Manuscripts in the Office of the Secretary of State, Albany, New York, 1664-1776* (Albany, 1866), 416. In 1754, Joseph de la Cruz also claimed to be a native of Cartagena in the Spanish West Indies. See "Affidavit of Joseph de la Cruz," October 7, 1754, in O'Callaghan, *Calendar of British Historical Manuscripts*, 661.

39. Jacquetta M. Haley, "The Slaves of Philipsburg Manor, Upper Mills," in *Encounters*

with *Living History: Activity-Based Lessons on the Enslaved Africans of the North* (Tarry-town, N.Y.: Historic Hudson Valley, 1996), 43-44. For Philip's permission to be a privateer, see "Commission to Philip Philipse," July 23, 1690, New York Colonial Manuscripts, Vol. 36, 142, the New York State Library (HHV Card File). Philip lived in Barbados until 1698, when he died at the age of 26. His son, Frederick Philipse II, was born that same year. "Extracts from Wills Relating to the West Indies Recorded in England," *The Journal of Barbados Museum and Historical Society* 12, no. 1 (November 1944): 67. Philip Philipse married Mary Sparkes of Barbados, part owner of Springhead Plantation, on November 6, 1694. Joanne McCree Sanders, ed., *Barbados Records: Marriages 1643-1800,* Vol. I (1982), 85. A listing of the 166 enslaved individuals on the Springhead Plantation does not include Nicholas Carte-gena or any other slave who might have had similar maritime skills. Thus, if he was not enslaved by the Sparkes family and since Philip himself had no need of and was not in any condition to purchase slaves, it is more likely that Nicholas arrived in Barbados with Philip Philipse and was subsequently "reassigned." The listing of slaves held at the Springhead Plantation is found in "Lease for the Springhead Plantation, 23 November 1693" (Deeds, RB3/19/425), "Hughes/Queree Abstracts in Queree Notebook #367," Barbados Department of Archives, Black Rock, St. James, Barbados. Jean Zimmerman suggests that Spring Head Plantation may at one time have been owned by Frederick Philipse and Margarer Harden-broeck. Zimmerman, *The Women of the House*, 148.

40. Jacob Judd, "Frederick Philipse and the Madagascar Trade," *The New-York Historical Society Quarterly* 55, no. 4 (October 1971): 357-358.

41. "Frederick Philipse to Captain Balldridge," February 25, 1695/1696 (Until 1752, the English used the Old Style Julian Calendar with the year beginning in March. Other European countries followed the New Style Gregorian calendar with the year beginning in January. Mindful of these differences, the English used both annual dates in January and February.) "Letter of Freedom from Frederick Philipse to Nicholas Cartagena," December 31, 1696. HCA 1-98, Public Record Office (PRO), London, England. Data from the Public Record Office was collected by Dr. Jacob Judd for Historic Hudson Valley and recorded in the Historic Hudson Valley Card File. References to the PRO data used in this essay are from the HHV Card File unless otherwise indicated. The Public Record Office (the national archives for the United Kingdom) is now in Kew Gardens, outside central London.

42. Farming cycles for Monmouth County, New Jersey, a geographic area relatively close to those for the Upper Mills, are described in Hodges, *Slavery and Freedom in the Rural North*, 46.

43. Hugh Thomas, *The Slave Trade: The Story of the Atlantic Slave Trade, 1440-1870* (New York: Simon and Schuster, 1997), 419.

44. "Account of Seaman's Wages of the ship *Margaret*, Samuel Burgess, commander, bound to Madagascar the Second Voyage, New York, 1698" HCA 1-98, PRO, 357 (HHV Card File).

45. On "functional relationships," see Williams-Myers, *Long Hammering*, 49.

46. "Last Will and Testament of Frederick Philipse, 26 October 1700," February 1768 copy in Collections of Historic Hudson Valley, The Rockefeller Archives, Pocantico Hills, N.Y., PA 815. Hereafter Philipse I Will. Among the Hudson Valley Dutch, who relied on traditional inheritance customs to settle their estates, it was not uncommon to wait until late in life to write a will. Fabend, *A Dutch Family in the Middle Colonies, 1660-1800*, 105. For Philipse, it is more likely that he was revising an earlier will to accommodate new circumstances: the recent death of his firstborn son, Philip, and his desire to care for his grandson, Frederick II, born in 1695, who would bear his name and title.

47. Philipse I Will. Philipse's 1702 inventory mentions 40 slaves. Frederic Shonnard and

W. W. Spooner, *History of Westchester County, New York From Its Earliest Settlement to the Year 1900* (1900; reprint, Harrison, N.Y.: Harbor Hill Books, 1974), 194. Only Lewis Morris owned more slaves than Frederick Philipse, perhaps as many as 66 on his Morrisania property. Ibid., 153. See also Eugene R. Sheridan, *Lewis Morris, 1671-1746: A Study in Early American Politics* (Syracuse, N.Y.: Syracuse University Press, 1981), 6. Among the other large estates in the immediate Hudson Valley vicinity at the time were Pelham Manor, Fordham Manor, Scarsdale Manor, Cortlandt Manor. Overall, slaveholding was broadly based in New York c. 1700. In the city itself, about 40 percent of households owned slaves. Thelma Wills Foote, "Black Life in Colonial Manhattan, 1664-1786" (Ph.D. diss., Harvard University, 1991), 91. This number is reaffirmed by David E. Narrett in *Inheritance and Family Life in Colonial New York City* (Ithaca, N.Y.: Cornell University Press, 1992), 186 n. 57. The number of slaves per household was small, usually between one and two. McManus, *A History of Negro Slavery in New York*, 47. Wealthier New Yorkers held more slaves. For example, Derrick Ten Eyck held 13 slaves in New York City in 1703. Foote, "Black Life in Colonial Manhattan," 105, 101; Goodfriend, *Before the Melting Pot*, 117-118. The number of slaves held by Philipse in New York City is unknown.

48. However, identifying specific slaves by name in a will was rare for New Yorkers. From 1696 to 1725, only 8 percent of men referred to slaves in their wills. Narrett, *Inheritance and Family Life in Colonial New York City*, 186.

49. Several historians recognize certain weaknesses in simple "lexical analysis," i.e., focus on a single list of names. Jerome S. Handler and JoAnn Jacoby, "Slave Names and Naming in Barbados, 1650-1830," *The William and Mary Quarterly*, 3rd Ser., 53, no. 4 (October 1996): 686; Herbert S. Gutman, *The Black Family in Slavery and Freedom, 1750-1925* (New York: Pantheon, 1976), 186.

50. Handler and Jacoby, "Slave Names and Naming in Barbados, 1650-1830," especially "Table III: Most Common Anglo-European Names Among Barbados Slaves," 704-705.

51. On Indian slaves in New York, see Goodfriend, *Before the Melting Pot*, 114-115. In spite of this regulation, there are frequent references to Indian slaves in the court records, and Philipse's position on the Governor's Council and his economic prominence would surely have permitted him continued ownership.

52. John Thornton, "Central African Names and African-American Naming Patterns," *The William and Mary Quarterly*, 3rd Ser., 50, no. 4 (October 1993): 727-742.

53. Ibid., 739. It is also possible that Mingo was the diminutive of Domingo, a West African day name for Sunday. Handler and Jacoby, "Slave Names and Naming in Barbados, 1650-1830," 699 n. 4.

54. Bill of Sale for Whan (Negro), 4 Sept. 1665, #506; Bill of Sale for Whan (Indian), 12 August 1668, #537; Certificate for the Indian boy Whan, 5 May 1670, #566, in Peter D. Garrod, ed., "A Calendar of Early Bermuda Deeds and Other Entries in Bermuda Colonial Records, Vol. 5A, 1618-1680," Bermuda Archives, Hamilton, Bermuda. One of every seven Bermudian sailors were slaves c. 1700. Michael Jarvis, "Maritime Revolution and the Transformation of Bermudian Slavery, 1680-1775," paper presented to the Omohundro Institute of Early American History and Culture, March 18, 1997, 6-7.

55. Hector was also a name found among New York City slaves belonging to innkeeper Roger Baker in 1704. Goodfriend, *Before the Melting Pot*, 117-118.

56. Jacquetta M. Haley, "Philipsburg Manor Tricentennial, 1693-1993." Prepared for Historic Hudson Valley, June 1992, 27-39. On Philipse Madagascar trade, see Jacob Judd, "Frederick Philipse and the Madagascar Trade," *The New-York Historical Society Quarterly* 55 (October 1971).

57. On the Chesapeake, see Allan Kulikoff, *Tobacco and Slaves: The Development of*

Southern Cultures in the Chesapeake, 1680-1800 (Chapel Hill: University of North Carolina Press, 1986), 326; on Barbados, see Handler and Jacoby, "Slave Names and Naming in Barbados, 1650-1830," 693.

58. Berlin, "From Creole to African," 251. Compare Philipse to Virginian Robert "King" Carter, for example, who sought to both separate them from their African inheritance and diminish their dignity.

59. Philipse I Will.

60. Handler and Jacoby, "Slave Names and Naming in Barbados, 1650-1830," 695. Sue was also a name found among Maryland slaves from the early eighteenth century. Kulikoff, *Tobacco and Slaves*, 378, 380. From 1664 to 1737, 70 percent (1,412) of slaves imported into New York were from the West Indies and 25 percent (504) were from Barbados. Foote, "Black Life in Colonial Manhattan," Table 1, 31.

61. On Portugese names in Kongo, see Thornton, "Central African Names and African-American Naming Patterns," 729. On Queen Suzanne de Nóbrega, see Thornton, *Kongolese Saint Anthony*, 39; Thornton, *The Kingdom of Kongo*, 50-53. Also see Thornton, "From the General to the Particular," 5-6.

62. Foote, *Black and White Manhattan*, 63.

63. Slaves were generally priced according to their age. In Abraham de Peyster's 1726 inventory, a 90-year-old Negro woman was of "no value," a Negro woman age 48 was valued at £45, age 34 at £55, age 18 at £60. The list includes as total of eight slaves, including males, an 18-year-old female, and a blind slave of "no value." The elderly woman included in Ten Eyck's holdings was valued at £9. Foote, *Black and White Manhattan*, 103, 105. Frederick Philipse's son Adolph also kept slaves for a long period of time, perhaps as long as 50 years. Haley, "The Slaves of Philipsburg Manor, Upper Mills," 42 n. 9.

64. Enslaved women in their late thirties or early forties were usually categorized as "old," as was the case for female slaves in Middlesex County, Virginia at approximately the same time period. Darrett B. and Anita H. Rutman, *A Place in Time: Explicatus* (New York: Norton, 1984), 173-176.

65. A discussion of Philipse's land purchases is found in Haley, "Philipsburg Manor Tricentennial," 9-13. That the manor house was begun around 1685 is suggested in Mary Ostrander, "Archaeologist's Report and Summary," Historic Hudson Valley Library (pamphlet file 974.727724, AP 1979 0).

66. For evidence of a "paternalistic ethos" among certain New York slave owners, see Foote, "Black Life in Colonial Manhattan," 138-158. A broader view of "paternalism" is discussed in Peter Kolchin, *American Slavery, 1619-1877* (New York: Hill and Wang, 1993), 59-60.

67. The original account of the conspiracy was made by Daniel Horsmanden in 1744. See Thomas J. Davis, ed., *The New York Conspiracy By Daniel Horsmanden* (Boston: Beacon Press, 1971). The results of the trial are from page vii. The most recent account is by Jill Lepore, *New York Burning: Liberty, Slavery, and Conspiracy in Eighteenth-Century Manhattan* (New York: Vintage, 2005), 9, 50. See also Foote, *Black and White Manhattan*, 159-186.

68. Horsmanden, *The New York Conspiracy*, 29.

69. Lepore, *New York Burning*, 37, 110.

70. E. B. O'Callaghan, *Calendar of Historical Manuscripts in the Office of the Secretary of State, Albany, NY* Part II, English Manuscripts (Albany, 1866), 553, 554, 556, 557, 561-562; "Mrs. Peter De Lancy to Cadwallader Colden," June 1, 1741, *New-York Historical Society Collections*, 1934 (New York, 1937), 265. See also HHV card files. Michael Kammen questions the actual nature of slave confessions in *Colonial New York: A History* (Millwood, N.Y.: KTO Press, 1975), 213-214.

71. Horsmanden, *The New York Conspiracy*, 101.

72. Horsmanden, *The New York Conspiracy*, 36.

73. Foote, *Black and White Manhattan*, 177, 176.

74. Harris, *In the Shadow of Slavery*, 28, 29; Goodfriend, *Before the Melting Pot*, 113.

75. Jill Lepore, "The Tightening Vise: Slavery and Freedom in British New York," in Berlin and Harris, eds., *Slavery in New York*, 60, 63.

76. Harris, *In the Shadow of Slavery*, 27; Simon Middleton, *From Privileges to Rights: Work and Politics in Colonial New York City* (Philadelphia: University of Pennsylvania Press, 2006), 133, 139.

77. Maika, "Slavery, Race, and Culture in Early New York," 31.

78. Lepore, "The Tightening Vise."

79. On Aertse, see Haley, "Slaves of Philipsburg Manor, Upper Mills," 41 n. 5, 43 n. 10; Mary Ostrander, "Archaeological Report and Summary," 11. The study was done in the late 1950s. The Upper Mills Negro house was considerably larger than the standard "diminutive" slave house more typical in the rural Hudson Valley. Berlin and Harris, eds., *Slavery in New York*, 72-73; Hodges, *Slavery and Freedom in the Rural North*, 53; on Adolph's personality, see Haley, "Slaves of Philipsburg Manor, Upper Mills," 47.

80. Haley suggests that Diamond was the boatman for the manor. "Slaves of Philipsburg Manor, Upper Mills," 56.

81. The *Diamond*, along with the *Abigail* and the *Philipsburg*, made annual trips to the Caribbean from 1715 to 1718 and later (PRO 609 CO5/1222 HHV file). When the *Diamond* returned from Curaçao in May 1717, it carried 3 slaves as cargo. Elizabeth Donnan, *Documents Illustrative of the History of the Slave Trade to America* (New York: Octagon Books, 1969), III:463. The *Philipsburg* also sailed to Africa from New York and returned with a cargo of 5 slaves (466).

82. Berlin, "From Creole to African," 251. Also, see previous discussion of Frederick I's slaves.

83. "Will of Catherine Philipse," January 7, 1730/31. Coll. of Dr. John G. Broughton, Albany, N.Y. Copy in PX 447, HHV File.

84. Haley, "The Slaves of Philipsburg Manor, Upper Mills," 52.

85. Haley, "The Slaves of Philipsburg Manor, Upper Mills," 52.

86. Vetare, *Philipsburg Manor Upper Mills*, 55.

87. "An Account of the Estate of Mr. Adolph Philipse, Deceased, New York, 24 January 1749/50" (HHV File); "Will and Codicil of Frederick Philipse II," June 6, 1751, June 22, 1751, PX 1567 (HHV File).

88. Haley, "The Slaves of Philipsburg Manor, Upper Mills," 54.

89. For a short, individual description of each of the twenty-three slaves at the Upper Mills, see Haley, "The Slaves of Philipsburg Manor, Upper Mills," 55-60.

90. Handler and Jacoby, "Slave Names and Naming in Barbados, 1650-1830," 694.

91. "A List of the Negro Slaves in the Mannor of Philips Burgh In the upper Part where William Hamman is Capt.," E. B. O'Callaghan, *The Documentary History of The State of New York* (Albany, 1850), III:852. Hereafter referred to as the 1755 Census.

92. Vetare, *Philipsburg Manor Upper Mills*, 55.

93. Haley, "The Slaves of Philipsburg Manor, Upper Mills," 57-58.

94. Haley, "The Slaves of Philipsburg Manor, Upper Mills," 57-58; 1755 Census.

95. For a description of slave labor in the North, see Hodges, *Slavery and Freedom in the Rural North*, 45-47.

96. Haley, "The Slaves of Philipsburg Manor, Upper Mills," 49-51; on the existence of a pigeon cote, see Ostrander, "Archaeological Report and Summary," 10; Hodges, *Slavery and Freedom in the Rural North*, 50.

97. Frederick. II Will, Adolph Inventory, 1755 Census.

3

American Indian Villages to Dutch Farms

THE SETTLING OF SETTLED LANDS

IN THE HUDSON VALLEY

WILLIAM A. STARNA

Of the many issues that give form to the encounter between Europeans and the native people of North America, none has garnered as much attention as land. For Indians land historically was, and often still is, a life force, a source of sustenance, a place for home and community, a domain over which some degree of control might be exercised, and not least of all, a core element of identity. It must be said that the same holds for Europeans and their equally ancient relationship to land. Yet these distinct people attended to and presided over land in different ways, some assumed to have long existed, others more readily discoverable, and some that remain unexamined.

American Indian land tenure for New England and much of the mid-Atlantic region is generally said to have taken two forms: communal and individualistic. These are in no way mutually exclusive means of holding and making use of land, but they are, by and large, associated with the requirements of fully committed horticulturalists as contrasted with those of foragers and fishermen, whose efforts were only occasionally supplemented by farming. Intimately related to and emerging from these patterns of subsistence was the design and distribution of native communities. Early in the seventeenth century, Iroquois farmers, situated west of the Hudson Valley, lived in large, densely populated, often fortified towns composed of multifamily longhouses surrounded, in season, by fields of corn, beans, and squash. Mohawk towns, close by the Mahicans, the Munsees, and the citizens of a bourgeoning Dutch colony, were strung along the Mohawk River and the fertile soils of its floodplains on an east-west axis that never exceeded a straight-line distance of twenty-five miles. Arguably the most intensely studied of any of the five Iroquois nations, the Mohawks also drew the interest of Dutch officials, who early on recognized the pivotal position these Indians occupied in the fur trade and in native–native, native–European diplomacy.[1]

The Hudson Valley, however, was home to a different sort of native people whose livelihoods were more firmly tied to the abundant resources of the river and of the region's forests and meadows than to farming. Although the archaeological record is thin and incomplete, only moderately strengthened

EDWARD MORAN (1829–1901)
Henrik Hudson Entering New York Harbor, September 11, 1609, 1892
Oil on canvas, 36 x 53 in.
Berkshire Museum, Pittsfield, Massachusetts, Gift of Zena Crane

by period descriptions, indications are that these natives—the Mahicans of the upper to middle valley and the communities of Munsee speakers farther down, reaching to New York Bay—lived in hamlets consisting of no more than a few dwellings commonly referred to as wigwams. Their widely dispersed, impermanent distribution over the landscape reflected their seasonal movements in pursuit of food and necessary raw materials, a pattern different from that of their more sedentary Mohawk neighbors.[2]

Pressing questions with respect to the lands of the Hudson Valley, which the Dutch were anxious to and would acquire, revolve around how the original occupants—native people—viewed these holdings, and then, by extension, how their views may have changed over time. A quick survey of the literature suggests, with a consensus approaching conventional wisdom, that the first question has long been answered, not only for Hudson Valley peoples but also for those living elsewhere in the Northeast: namely, that Indians lacked entirely a concept of land ownership and did not conceive of anything approaching the jurisdiction and control assumed by European nation-states over their territories on the other side of the Atlantic. For all intents and purposes, the world

Landing of Hendrick Hudson, 1858
Printed after the original painting by ROBERT W. WEIR (1803–1889)
Martin, Johnson & Co., Publisher
In J. A. Spencer, *The History of the United States* (New York: Johns, Fry and Co., 1858).
Westchester County Historical Society

Inscription at bottom: "From the Original Picture by R. W. Weir in the possession of
Gulian C. Verplanck, Esq."

of these native people was absent metes and bounds. In their place, and in that
of other equally Western legal precepts, stood "usufruct," normally construed
as "use right," a claim laid and limited to lands on the basis of how they were
managed and to what ends. This was not a private or absolute right to the land;
instead, individuals or collectives might use or extract resources from a given
territory that they did not or could not hold in perpetuity, for an unspecified period of time. From these considerations the assumption of "communal
ownership" most likely evolved and, by extension, the existence of recognized
"rights" of community members—persons—to collect a range of resources
from the land for their own use. Such "rights" would have been an expression
of, and shifted with, an array of ecological uses as determined by native people
themselves.[3]

Unfortunately, there is little direct evidence in the seventeenth-century
record to shed light on how native people in the Hudson Valley regarded
"property" and "ownership" of any kind. One of the few hints is found in Adriaen van der Donck's mid-century *Description of New Netherland*, wherein he
observed:

Of all the rights, laws, and maxims observed anywhere in the world, none in particular is in force among these [Indian] people other than the law of nature or of nations. Accordingly, wind, stream, bush, field, sea, beach, and riverside are open and free to everyone of every nation with which the Indians are not embroiled in open conflict. All those are free to enjoy and move about such places as though they were born there.[4]

Van der Donck's somewhat alluring point of view must be examined in context. The "law of nature or of nations" may be less a comment on native perceptions of and behaviors toward land and its constituent elements than a recapitulation of certain legal theories as described by a fellow attorney and countryman, the influential Dutch jurist Hugo Grotius (1583–1645). Writing in 1604, Grotius had drawn a distinction between common or public property and private property, maintaining that the former, given that it was not

THEO VANDERWELDEN
Portrait of Adriaen Van Der Donck, n.d.
Ink on paper, 6 x 6 in.
Museum of the City of New York, gift of the artist, 32.243.1

JOHN OGILBY; ARNOLDUS MONTANUS
Novi Belgii, quod nunc Novi Jorck vocatur, Novaeque Anglia et partis Virginiae
(New Netherland, Which Is Now Called New York, and New England and
Part of Virginia), 1671
Hand-colored engraving, 14½ x 11 in.
Bert Twaalthoven Collection of Antiquarian Maps of New Amsterdam,
New York and New England, Fordham University Library, Bronx, New York
Map collection #13

JOHN OGILBY; ARNOLDUS MONTANUS
Cartouche detail depicting Indians engaged in hunting, preparing food, and other
details, Novi Belgii, quod nunc Novi Jorck vocatur, Novaeque Anglia et partis Virginiae
(New Netherland, Which Is Now Called New York, and New England and Part of
Virginia), 1671
Hand-colored engraving, 14½ x 11 in.
Bert Twaalthoven Collection of Antiquarian Maps of New Amsterdam,
New York and New England, Fordham University Library, Bronx, New York
Map collection #13

susceptible to occupancy or being occupied, was destined for the use of all
humankind. Private property, in contrast, is any thing subject to seizure and
possession by a person, something that is peculiarly one's own. "Common,"
maintained Grotius, was the simple antonym of "private."[5]

Whether Indians of the Hudson Valley had made use of such categories of
land tenure prior to or soon after the arrival of the Dutch is unknown. Com-
parative data, however, suggest that for the native people of the Northeast,
land, rather than being owned or subject to purchase, sale, or other forms of
formal conveyance, was seen as a geographical expression of social structure;
that is, land was allocated as an extension of kinship through "usufructuary
privilege," which was discharged primarily through families and corporate
groups such as lineages and clans.[6] An often overlooked detail is that access to
lands was acknowledged not only by members of these social units but also,
importantly, by adjacent, unaffiliated, and potentially uncongenial communities or groups. There is no reason to believe that the same acknowledgment did
not hold for Dutch colonial officials, whose position it was from the beginning
that native people were the true owners of the land and that possession could
be obtained only through regulated purchase. As Grotius explained it: "discov-

EDWIN WILLARD DEMING (1862–1942)
Peter Minuit Buying Manhattan Island from the Indians
Oil on board, 41 x 60 in.
Museum of the City of New York, Gift of Rita and Murray Hartstein, 96.13.1

ery imparts no legal right save in the case of those things which were owner-less [*res nullius*] prior to the act of discovery." Thus, he reasoned, native people "enjoyed public and private ownership of their own property and possessions, an attribute which would not be taken from them without just cause." But this idea of ownership, which included the ownership of land, did not originate with Grotius; it was, he wrote, "expounded by the Spaniard [Francisco de] Victoria with irrefutable logic and in agreement with other authorities of the greatest renown."[7] Victoria's lectures in 1532 set out the proposition that native people "'possessed natural legal rights as free and rational people,'" leading to the "Doctrine of Discovery" and the methods by which their lands could be acquired.[8] The Dutch, however, could not rely comfortably or solely on claims of first discovery and thus on unfettered access to the lands alleged to constitute New Netherland in the face of aggressive counterclaims by England. It remained, however, that under such a legal theory, land could be acquired only by purchase from native possessors.[9]

Discerning, creating, or depicting the boundaries delimiting native lands in the precontact period is impossible. And unless there exists a significant and rigorously generated and tested archaeological record, along with strong demographic data, it does not get much easier for the early years and decades following contact. What is demonstrable, however, is that, for any number of reasons, native people resident in the Hudson Valley were mobile and often shifted their settlements' location, a practice that would have given rise to shifting or fluid boundaries, however defined.[10] Among the most critical elements to affect intergroup boundaries would have been the exploitation of game animals, in particular the white-tailed deer, which provided meat and hides for clothing. Taking this a step farther, it has been suggested that competition over deer may have led to hostilities between native communities, predicated on the fact that deer populations and densities are known to expand and contract from season to season and year to year, and the extent of hunting territories would have changed accordingly.[11] After contact similar sorts of competition developed around the beaver and, to a lesser extent, other fur-bearing animals.[12] In addition, a significant but poorly understood factor affecting land use and occupation was the impact of European-introduced diseases, which began to strike native people in the Hudson Valley shortly after contact.[13] The high levels of mortality that resulted had an unknown although assuredly devastating effect on, for example, political and social organization, with the loss of leaders and other influential community members. As a consequence, tasks associated with subsistence, the maintenance of settlements, and the oversight of lands doubtlessly were reconfigured and modified, adapted to rapidly changing events and their aftermath.[14] But again, the relevant archaeological and documentary data for the seventeenth-century native residents of the Hudson Valley are either nonexistent or weak, making any assessment of boundaries problematical.

The acquisition of Indian lands by the Dutch began, as most everyone knows, with the purchase of Manhattan in 1626. Soon afterward lands were acquired in New Jersey, western Long Island, and Westchester County. The huge tract forming the patroonship of Rensselaerswijck at the northern extreme of the Hudson River was obtained in late summer 1630. Patents to land in the middle valley were secured in the 1640s and 1650s. And so it went.[15] Of note is that these transactions were conducted under the law as specified in the *Freedoms and Exemptions* of 1629.[16] Most informative, however, are the 1625 instructions to Willem Verhulst, the Dutch West India Company's first director in New Netherland, which detailed views on Indian lands and how they could be best and most appropriately acquired. In the search for a suitable place to build a settlement on Manhattan, company officials indicated that any land so chosen would first have to be "abandoned by the Indians or unoccupied." If no such lands could be found, then it would be necessary to deal directly with

Purchase of White Plains 1683, c. 1920s–30s
Reproduction image of diorama, Westchester County Historical Society, O-256

At the time of Dutch settlement in Manhattan, the part of current Westchester County around the city of White Plains was inhabited by the Weckquaesgeek tribe, who called the area Quarropas, meaning white marshes or white plains, for the fogs that hung over the swampland. Although non-native settlement occurred in 1683, land disputes went on until 1721.

the Indian proprietors and "for trading-goods or by means of some amicable agreement, induce them to give up ownership and possession to us, without however forcing them thereto in the least or taking possession by craft or fraud, lest we call down the wrath of God upon our unrighteous beginnings, the Company intending in no wise to make war or hostile attacks upon any one."[17] These instructions reflect, to a considerable degree, important elements of the Doctrine of Discovery and how, in accordance with it, Indian lands might be obtained: through a just war, evidently not an option for the Dutch, or if said lands were either unoccupied or abandoned. The third option, which the Dutch consistently chose, was through purchase.

How Indian lands were acquired by the Dutch and under what circumstances presents a complex and often confounding history. The first and most reasoned work to address these issues, by anthropologist Robert Grumet, began by asking what on its face was a straightforward question: Why did Munsee speakers sell their lands in present-day northern New Jersey to the Dutch in the first place?[18] The answers that Grumet proposed or discovered in the literature, however, appear to be post facto exculpations for what allegedly transpired. The foremost of these, invariably reiterated in subsequent historical studies, is "that the Native parties to the conveyances did not fully understand the meaning of the documents they affixed their marks to." Others include the "misunderstanding hypothesis," wherein the conveyances of land meant something different to native people than to the European purchasers; that Indians were "naturally guileless"; or that they disposed of land, or "sold it cheaply, as a gesture of friendship, high regard, or at worst, pity." Grumet also points to the explanation that accidental or deliberate mistranslations of deeds and related documents may have interfered with the Indians' understanding of land conveyances. The counterargument he offers is that the widespread use of a trade jargon, which purportedly "conveyed full understanding to the parties to the deeds," Indian or Dutch, was an important mitigating factor.[19] However, the language of the deeds in nearly all cases adheres to a form or style, a legal protocol, that is remarkably consistent and thus, on its face, transparent. What remains little understood is to what extent the Indian "proprietors" were read or otherwise told of the precise wording in a deed. A more strident view, in the context of what he derisively coined "the deed game," is that of historian Francis Jennings, who saw little more than trickery, fraud, and cheating in land transfers that took place in colonial New England.[20]

Whatever the case, many of the questions raised first by Grumet and then by historians who followed have not been satisfactorily answered; others have yet to be asked. For example: Who were the Indians who signed the deeds? Did they have the right to do so, and how would we know? More to the point, would it have made a difference to either party? Did Indians know what they were doing when they signed the deeds, and if they did, why did they sign them? What was it that the Indians believed they were, in fact, "selling"? What were the motives of the natives who were involved? And once the land was sold, did its location have anything at all to do with a native group's territory or boundaries? Finally, no matter how one might define ownership, was the land that the Indians—individually or collectively—sold to the Dutch actually theirs to sell? In light of the weakness of the documentary record and the inability to be certain of or understand at any level what was in the minds of the American Indian people, or even the Dutch for that matter, virtually none of these questions can be answered with confidence. What perhaps can be considered, however, are alternative explanations or possibilities.

New Netherland was founded and thrived on the trade in furs, most notably beaver. Within a relatively short period of time after the Dutch arrived and established a trading house at Fort Orange (1624) at the north end of the Hudson River, the economic interests of native people in the region and also from deep in the interior turned from traditional pursuits to accommodate a different way of life.[21] Goods that Dutch traders of all stripes made available to native people in exchange for their furs soon became necessities, forever transforming a people and their communities. However, in the lower reaches of the Hudson, in greater New York and surrounding areas, in coastal southern New England, and on Long Island, environments where the beaver had never been found in large numbers, they soon were eradicated. Thus, by about 1625, the fur trade was no longer a viable means by which the natives there could obtain the items that they desired and to which they had become accustomed.[22] But there were alternative commodities that the Indians could substitute so as to remain in the game, economically and politically, the first being wampum (*sewant*). These cylindrical beads, made from marine shells taken from the waters of Long Island Sound, were manufactured by the resident Algonquians. It is perhaps no coincidence, then, that by 1626 wampum had become the most valuable trade item at Fort Orange and elsewhere in the colony, used as a medium of exchange—a currency—with which supplies, trade goods, furs, and, of critical importance to the Dutch, land could be purchased.[23]

The business of land and its transfer, for Indians and the Dutch alike, was a somewhat more complex matter. For coastal natives and those whose communities were scattered throughout the lower Hudson Valley, selling land became a means by which to obtain trade goods, given that there were no longer furs to use in exchange. Virtually every surviving deed or other form of conveyance includes a listing of goods provided to the Indians in return for land; for example, purchases of Mahican lands were made with lengths of duffel or other cloth, axes, knives, guns and powder, kettles, adzes, swords, hatchets, smoking pipes and tobacco, beer, brandy, beaver pelts, and frequently, wampum. Identical items or simple mentions of "merchandise" accompanied sales of Munsee lands farther down the Hudson.[24] Whether these or other goods went to just the "sellers" of land or were redistributed by them among kin or other community members is unknown. Clearly, however, selling land to the Dutch was an important way these Indians were able to acquire the much-needed goods for which others traded furs.

The initial successes of the fur trade prompted the Dutch to begin building a colony whose citizens would furnish the support needed to maintain and expand the enterprise. Most of the population growth took place over the last fifteen years of the colony, from about 1650 to 1664, when, in the face of an economic downturn in the home country, out-migration for many became an option. The immigrants who arrived in the colony reflected a range of job skills and affiliations. There were soldiers, sailors, and ranking officials of the West India Company; independent merchants and those employed by trading houses; artisans; contract laborers; and the all-important farmers.[25] And they all required land on which to build homes, warehouses, barracks, breweries, brick factories, and other places to practice their occupations, and also for their farmsteads, pastures, and fields. That land, in accordance with various regulations and policies promulgated by the colony's governing bodies, could only be acquired from the Indians.

The process by which land was alienated by the Indians and purchased by the Dutch in New Netherland appears to have been straightforward. It must be assumed that Dutch officials sought out potential "sellers" or, less likely, native "proprietors" approached them with offers; surviving documents do not allow for an easy determination of who initiated what or anything at all about how arrangements to transfer land might have been made. The resulting deeds or other forms of conveyance contain information sufficient to fulfill the legal requirements of the colony: the names and frequently the offices or titles of the parties involved, Indian and Dutch; a description of the metes and bounds of the land conveyed; occasionally something of the quality and character of the land; and what was given or received in payment. Assertions made in the language of the deeds that the native "proprietors" were representatives authorized to transfer land on behalf of their communities or other social units; were leaders, headmen, of their communities; or indeed "owned" the land cannot be confirmed. Grumet, for example, in his research on Munsee and Mahican deeds, has conceded that it cannot be known for certain whether such alleged influential persons actually possessed authority, although he points the finger at European ignorance of Indian political systems rather than considering the possibility of native resourcefulness or self-promotion.[26]

What might be suggested is that native people were quick to discern that the Dutch were intent on purchasing the land on which they subsisted and that, in turn, they would receive valuable and needed goods in exchange. And among the possibilities is that, in their desire to adhere to stated policy, what mattered most to the Dutch was that deeds were drawn up, signed, and secured to fulfill the requirements of that policy, and if challenged, could be brought into one of their own courts for adjudication. There was no known equivalent forum in native communities, nor should one be expected. In the end, the Dutch may have been unconcerned about from whom the land was actually purchased. It was the deed—a legal agreement, an instrument—that counted, one not easily countermanded unless malfeasance could be established. The Indians fully understood that the Dutch wanted to buy land and, taking the position that there were economic and perhaps social advantages to be gained, sold whatever parcels the Dutch wanted. Did the Indians "own" or manage this land? Were they authorized to sell it? These questions are not answerable. It is pos-

JOOST HARTGERS
t' Fort nieuw Amsterdam op de Manhatans
(The Hartgers View of Manhattan as it appeared c. 1626)
Published in *Beschryvinghe van Virginia, Niew Nederlandt, Niew England . . .* ,
Amsterdam, the Netherlands, 1651.
Engraving, 3¼ x 4¾ in.
Museum of the City of New York, The J. Clarence Davies Collection, 29.100.792

sible that, however land tenure was practiced before the arrival of the Dutch, that process may have rapidly been transformed to address and accommodate changing circumstances. Native people, perhaps leaders in their communities or those who may have ingratiated themselves with the Dutch, or who saw opportunities in the making, likely were the initiators of these changes. The familiar view that Indians were simply and always the victims of the colonial land-taking juggernaut need not prevail. There is no reason to believe that native land tenure systems, and native people themselves, were incapable of the kinds of change and expedient adaptation suggested here. Indeed, there is sufficient evidence in the literature that a bias has been operating, a consequence of which has been a long-standing but wrong-headed assumption that Indians in fact could not adjust to the maelstrom of change around them. They did.

The trouble, and assuredly this is the appropriate word to use, began with the increase in Dutch population and the expansion of their settlements on the

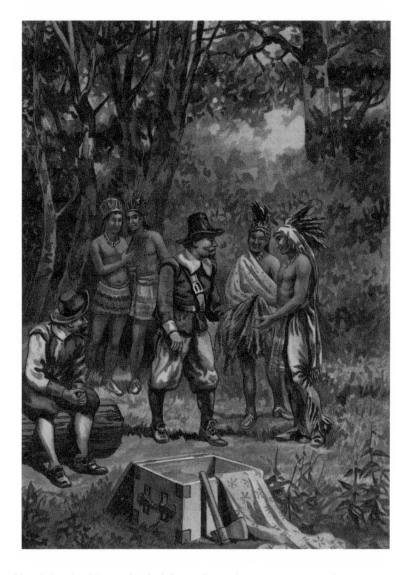

"Dutch Traders in New Netherlands," from *The American Continent and its Inhabitants Before Columbus*, by Annie Cole Cady (Philadelphia: Gebbie & Co., 1893). Hudson River Museum

tracts of land that had been deeded from the Indians. Beginning about 1640, almost immediately after the purchase of native lands on western Long Island, but also with disturbances on Manhattan and Staten Island, were the tensions leading to Willem Kieft's war (1640–1645). Historians have generally argued that the immediate source of the difficulties was Governor Kieft's administrative arrogance and recklessness, along with his imposition of an involuntary levy on Indians in the region to offset expenses linked to the presence of a substantial Dutch force and the building of fortifications.[27] Kieft and his council had argued that both of these military initiatives served to protect the Indians from their enemies, real or potential; accordingly, an ordinance was drawn up that required the Indians to contribute to their maintenance. "The excuse given that the Dutch had hitherto protected these tribes against their enemies," historian Allen Trelease has written, "was completely specious since that service was neither asked for nor rendered."[28] But there had been other sources of friction between natives and the Dutch, including disputes over livestock wandering into Indian cornfields, the damage done to poultry on Dutch farms by the Indians' dogs, theft, and the occasional murder, all of which were ultimately tied to the plain fact of continued Dutch intrusions on Indian lands, purchased or not.[29]

A second period of hostilities between natives and the Dutch took place in the lower Hudson Valley and the environs of Manhattan, Staten Island, New Jersey, and western Long Island from the mid-1650s to the early 1660s—the so-called Peach War and the first and second Esopus Wars. Although devastating to both sides, relentless Dutch military actions once and for all ended the dominance of native people in the region, who were forced to cede nearly all of their remaining ancestral lands.[30] As had been the case with Kieft's war, the essential, underlying causes could be traced to the Dutch presence on Indian land and the numerous and varied contentious encounters that took place as a result. Disputes arose over the heavy-handedness of Dutch administrative practices; a shortage of food and, for many Indians, places to grow their crops; the exchange of prisoners taken in this or that conflict; the lucrative but risky trade in contraband; the business of selling alcohol to the Indians and its long-recognized and destructive effects; and the continued taking of Indian lands.

After the arrival of the Dutch, the native people of a good part of the Hudson Valley found themselves without the furs required to be full partners in the trade. Soon, however, Algonquians residing on Long Island Sound began exchanging a locally made commodity—wampum—for the goods that they both desired and found increasingly necessary. Natives in the lower valley did not have direct access to wampum but were able to use another commodity—land—in order to obtain trade goods. This was not difficult at all as the Dutch, early on, had made it clear that they wished to purchase lands upon which to build their colony. For a short period there could not have been a more mutually advantageous relationship, as what had been lands settled by native people found their way into the hands of the Dutch of New Netherland. But land was a scarce and valuable resource for both the Dutch and the Indians, and contests over it spawned the violence and brutality of wars. In the end the native people of the Hudson Valley could not hold the land or their place on it.

NOTES
1. On the importance of the Mohawks in seventeenth-century diplomacy and trade, and early Dutch perspectives on these natives, see Daniel K. Richter, *The Ordeal of the Long-house: The Peoples of the Iroquois League in the Era of European Colonization* (Chapel Hill: University of North Carolina Press, 1992), 75-104; Francis Jennings, *The Ambiguous Iroquois*

Empire: The Covenant Chain Confederation of Indian Tribes with English Colonies from its beginnings to the Lancaster Treaty of 1744 (New York: Norton, 1984), Chapter 4, "An Iron Dutch Chain," and Chapter 6, "The Iroquoian 'Beaver Wars'"; José António Brandão, *"Your fyre shall burn no more": Iroquois Policy Toward New France and Its Native Allies to 1701* (Lincoln: University of Nebraska Press, 1997); Charles T. Gehring and William A. Starna, trans. and eds., *A Journey Into Mohawk and Oneida Country, 1634-1635: The Journal of Harmen Meyndertsz van den Bogaert* (Syracuse, N.Y.: Syracuse University Press, 1988); J. Franklin Jameson, ed., *Narratives of New Netherland: 1609-1664* (New York: Charles Scribner's Sons, 1909), 168-180. The archaeology of the Mohawks is best described in Dean R. Snow, *Mohawk Valley Archaeology: The Sites* (Albany: State University of New York, Institute for Archaeological Studies, 1995). See also James W. Bradley, *Before Albany: An Archaeology of Native-Dutch Relations in the Capital Region, 1600-1664*, New York State Museum Bulletin 509 (Albany, N.Y., 2007).

2. The best synthesis of seventeenth-century Hudson Valley archaeology and the native–Dutch experience there is Bradley, *Before Albany.*

3. See William Cronon, *Changes in the Land: Indians, Colonists, and the Ecology of New England* (New York: Hill & Wang, 1983), 58-65.

4. Charles T. Gehring and William A. Starna, eds., *A Description of New Netherland by Adriaen van der Donck,* trans. Diederik Willem Goedhuys (Lincoln: University of Nebraska Press, 2008), 74.

5. Hugo Grotius, *De Iure Praedae Commentarius—Commentary on the Law of Prize and Booty,* trans. Gwladys L. Williams, collab. Walter H. Zeydel (reprint, New York: Oceana, 1964), 221-231; Hugo Grotius, *The Freedom of the Seas or the Right Which Belongs to the Dutch to Take Part in the East Indian Trade* (New York: Oxford University Press, 1916), 20-25.

6. See Marshall Sahlins, *Stone Age Economics* (Chicago: Aldine-Atherton, 1972), 93; Marshall Sahlins, *Tribesmen* (Englewood Cliffs, N.J.: Prentice-Hall, 1968), 76.

7. Grotius, *De Iure Praedae Commentarius,* 221. For a thorough, erudite discussion on the Doctrine of Discovery and its legacies, see Robert A. Williams Jr., *The American Indian in Western Legal Thought: The Discourses of Conquest* (New York: Oxford University Press, 1990).

8. See Robert J. Miller, "The Doctrine of Discovery in American Indian Law," *Idaho Law Review* 42, no. 1 (2005): 15-16.

9. Ibid., 20-21. The land tenure system of the Dutch West India Company and the concomitant recognition of Indian land rights is discussed in Clarence White Rife, "Land Tenure in New Netherland," in *Essays in Colonial History Presented to Charles McLean Andrews by His Students* (1931; reprint, Freeport, N.Y.: Books for Libraries Press, 1966), 41-73.

10. Insofar as Iroquoian relocations or removals are concerned, see William A. Starna, George R. Hamell, and William L. Butts, "Northern Iroquoian Horticulture and Insect Infestation: A Cause for Village Removal," *Ethnohistory* 31, no. 3 (1987): 197-207; William A. Starna, "Aboriginal Title and Traditional Iroquois Land Use: An Anthropological Perspective," in *Iroquois Land Claims,* ed. Christopher Vecsey and William A. Starna (Syracuse, N.Y.: Syracuse University Press, 1988), 31-48.

11. See Michael R. Gramly, "Deerskins and Hunting Territories: Competition for a Scarce Resource of the Northeastern Woodlands," *American Antiquity* 42, no. 4 (1977): 601-605; William A. Starna and John H. Relethford, "Deer Densities and Population Dynamics: A Cautionary Note," *American Antiquity* 50, no. 4 (1985): 825-832. For a discussion of the range of factors leading to shifting settlements, see William Engelbrecht, *Iroquoia: The Development of a Native World* (Syracuse, N.Y.: Syracuse University Press, 2003), 101-104.

12. See Brandão, *Iroquois Policy*.

13. The earliest firsthand account of disease mortality, suggestive of an epidemic among the Munsees of the lower Hudson Valley, is from Isaack de Rasière, writing about 1628. Jameson, ed., *Narratives of New Netherland, 1609-1664*, 105. See also Dean R. Snow and Kim M. Lanphear, "European Contact and Indian Depopulation in the Northeast: The Timing of the First Epidemics," *Ethnohistory* 35, no. 1 (1988): 15-33.

14. William A. Starna, "The Biological Encounter: Disease and the Ideological Domain," *American Indian Quarterly* 16, no. 4 (1992): 513-514.

15. Charles T. Gehring, "Peter Minuit's Purchase of Manhattan Island—New Evidence," *de Halve Maen* 55, no. 1 (1980): 6-7, 17; E. B. O'Callaghan, ed., *Documents Relative to the Colonial History of New York; Procured in Holland, England, and France by John R. Brodhead*, 15 vols. (Albany, N.Y., 1853-87), 13:1-3, 5, 20; *Kingston Papers*, trans. Dingman Versteg, ed. Peter R. Christoph, Kenneth Scott, and Kenn Stryker-Rodda, 2 vols. (Baltimore, Md.: Genealogical Publishing, 1976), 1:ix.

16. A. J. F. van Laer, trans. and ed., *Van Rensselaer Bowier Manuscripts: Being the Letters of Kiliaen van Rensselaer, 1630-1643, and Other Documents Relating to the Colony of Rensselaerswyck* (Albany: University of the State of New York, 1908), 149.

17. A. J. F. van Laer, trans. and ed., *Documents Relating to New Netherland 1624-1626 in the Henry E. Huntington Library* (San Marino, Calif.: Henry E. Huntington Library and Art Gallery Press, 1924), 105-106.

18. Robert S. Grumet, "'We Are Not So Great Fools': Changes in Upper Delawaran Socio-Political Life, 1630-1758" (Ph.D. diss., Rutgers, The State University of New Jersey, 1979), 256.

19. Ibid., 256-262. See also Emerson W. Baker, "'A Scratch with a Bear's Paw': Anglo-Indian Land Deeds in Early Maine," *Ethnohistory* 36, no. 3 (1989): 237-239; David J. Silverman, "'Natural Inhabitants, Time Out of Mind': Sachem Rights and the Contest for Wampanoag Land in Colonial New England," *Northeast Anthropology* 70 (2005): 1-10. The argument made by several historians that deeds and other forms of land conveyances are useful devices for providing insight into Native sociopolitical organization or territorial boundaries receives a much-needed critical examination in Blair A. Rudes, "Indian Land Deeds as Evidence for Indian History in Western Connecticut," *Northeast Anthropology* 70 (2005): 19-48. Appropriate to the topic of this essay, there has been an attempt to delineate Mahican territorial boundaries employing period maps, deeds, and other land conveyances; oral testimony, primarily from the late eighteenth and early nineteenth centuries; and secondary sources. See Shirley W. Dunn, *The Mohicans and Their Land, 1609-1730* (Fleischmanns, N.Y.: Purple Mountain Press, 1994). The unsatisfactory result, however, is characterized by a spurious and inexpert methodology and historiography, in addition to an absence of ethnological insight.

20. Francis Jennings, *The Invasion of America: Indians, Colonialisms, and the Cant of Conquest* (Chapel Hill: University of North Carolina Press, 1975), 128-145.

21. A decade after the founding of Fort Orange (and New Amsterdam), the Dutch built a short-lived trading house on the Connecticut River.

22. For the 1625 date see Kevin A. McBride, "Fort Island: Conflict and Trade in Long Island Sound," in *Native Forts of the Long Island Sound Area*, ed. Gaynell Stone, Readings in Archaeology and Ethnohistory, vol. 3 (Stony Brook, N.Y.: Suffolk County Archaeological Association, 2007), 256; Cronon, *Changes*, 99.

23. See Bradley, *Beyond Albany*, 76-77; Lynn Ceci, "The First Fiscal Crisis in New York," *Economic Development and Cultural Change* 28, no. 4 (1980): 839-847. On the history and use of wampum see William N. Fenton, *The Great Law and the Longhouse: A Political His-*

tory of the Iroquois Confederacy (Norman: University of Oklahoma Press, 1998), 224-239.

24. Dunn, *Mohicans*, 279-287; Charles T. Gehring, trans. and ed., *Land Papers,* New York Historical Manuscripts: Dutch, vols. GG, HH, II (Baltimore, Md.: Genealogical Publishing, 1980), 1-10, 16, 62-63; O'Callaghan, ed., *Documents Relative,* 13: *passim.*

25. Jaap Jacobs, *New Netherland: A Dutch Colony in Seventeenth-Century America* (Leiden and Boston: Brill, 2005), 46-51.

26. Robert S. Grumet, "The Selling of Lenapehoking," in *Proceedings of the 1992 People to People Conference: Selected Papers*, ed. Charles F. Hayes III, Research Records No. 23 (Rochester, N.Y.: Rochester Museum and Science Center, 1994), 20.

27. Evan Haefeli, "Kieft's War and the Cultures of Violence in Colonial America," in Michael A. Bellesiles, ed., *Lethal Imagination: Violence and Brutality in American History* (New York: New York University Press, 1999), 18, asserts that "Economics was the proximate cause of this conflict."

28. Allen W. Trelease, *Indian Affairs in Colonial New York: The Seventeenth Century* (Ithaca, N.Y.: Cornell University Press, 1960), 62-65. See also Jacobs, *New Netherland*, 133-134.

29. See James Homer Williams, "Great Doggs and Mischievous Cattle: Domesticated Animals and Indian-European Relations in New Netherland and New York," *New York History* 76 (1995): 245-264.

30. Trelease, *Indian Affairs*, 138-168; Oliver A. Rink, *Holland on the Hudson: An Economic and Social History of Dutch New York* (Ithaca, N.Y.: Cornell University Press, 1986), 258-260.

PART TWO 1709 – The Persistence of Dutch Influence

Van-Cortlandt Manor-House
From Helen Wilkinson Reynolds, *Dutch Houses in the Hudson Valley Before 1776*
(New York: Payson and Clarke, Ltd., Prepared under the auspices of The Holland
Society of New York, 1929).
Hudson River Museum

4

Constructing the Tradition of Dutch American Architecture, 1609–2009

SEAN E. SAWYER

*The architecture, the decorations, the furniture of our early settlers
have a very definite relationship to the arts of today. It is true that our
modern life calls for conveniences unthought of in seventeenth century
New Amsterdam; but the charm of line, the judgment of location and the
spirit of simplicity of the homes of our ancestors are all a good influence
on a civilization which to some of us seems to be reverting to the more
humble and honest ideals.*[1]

In his 1936 introduction to Rosalie Fellow Bailey's seminal survey of the Dutch houses of southern New York and New Jersey, then President Franklin Delano Roosevelt drew an inspirational lesson for middle-class Americans in the depths of the Great Depression from the relative humbleness of the colonial-era homes of the people from whom he himself descended. His words suggested that domestic happiness, stability, and future success did not depend on privilege and affluence but on good judgment and endurance, values that he came to embody for the nation. The enthusiasm for the eighteenth-century Dutch colonial house as a model for American living through the first half of the twentieth century is one chapter in the larger history of the Dutch architectural presence in America. With the exception of the Dutch colonial revival, this is a regional story confined to what can be termed the Dutch American hearth area that includes the valleys of the Hudson River and its tributaries, the five boroughs of New York City, and northern and central New Jersey.

Given the diversity and relative briefness of the Dutch colonial experiment in North America, it is necessary to define what constitutes Dutch American architecture and the various labels used to categorize it over 400 years. The label "Dutch colonial" refers to the architectural forms employed in the colony of New Netherland itself, from 1624 through to its final surrender to the British in 1674, and their continuation into the eighteenth century. "Dutch American" refers both specifically to the distinct farmhouse typology that evolved in the mid-eighteenth century and broadly to the importation and reinterpretation of Dutch architecture in America. Finally, the phrases "Dutch Renaissance re-

Old Dutch Church, Sleepy Hollow,
after alterations in 1837.
From Helen Wilkinson Reynolds, *Dutch
Houses in the Hudson Valley Before 1776*,
(New York: Payson and Clarke, Ltd.,
Prepared under the auspices of The
Holland Society of New York, 1929).
Hudson River Museum

In 1837 the earlier church building
was renovated: the south entrance was
removed to the west and gothic arches
were added to the windows.

vival" and "Dutch colonial revival" describe the two principal revival movements of the late nineteenth and early twentieth centuries that reconstituted
sixteenth- and seventeenth-century Dutch urban architecture, on the one
hand, and the eighteenth-century Dutch American farmhouse, on the other,
for the modern, industrialized American context.

This analysis focuses on the architecture of the Dutch American farm, with
only tangential references to civic, ecclesiastical, or commercial typologies. The
New World Dutch barn is discussed as a prime constituent of Dutch American
architecture. Not only are the farmhouse and barn the only authentic architectural survivors of the Dutch colonial era, but also the Dutch American farmhouse and its offspring, the Dutch colonial suburban house, have been sites of
significant architectural evolution and innovation and are the most enduring
Dutch contributions to the American landscape.

1609: ARCHITECTURE IN NEW NETHERLAND

Evidence of the earliest forms of shelter erected by the inhabitants of New
Netherland during the first years of the Dutch West India Company's enterprise is extremely scant. It is largely archival, comprising a handful of references in contemporary journals and documents to provisional "dugout" shelters
constructed by excavating cellars, lining them with wood, and covering them
with bark-sheathed roofs.[2] Such expedient and communal shelters would have
served for several years while labor and materials for permanent residences
were marshaled. Similarly fragmentary archival and archaeological evidence
exists for this first generation of permanent habitations, but it suggests that
Dutch-sponsored settlers transplanted both architectural forms and settlement patterns from the Netherlands and that these were distinct within urban
and agrarian contexts.

The Castello Plan, c. 1665, copy redrawn and printed by
John Wolcott Adams (1874–1925) for publication by I. N. Phelps Stokes, 1916.
Museum of the City of New York, The J. Clarence Davies Collection, 29.100.709

This version was enlivened with much architectural, horticultural, and nautical detail.

The company's establishments at New Amsterdam on the southern tip of
Manhattan Island and at Beverwijck 150 miles up the North (Hudson) River
were fundamentally urban in conception from their foundation, in 1626 and
1624, respectively, and the colonial origins of what would become the cities of
New York and Albany under English rule. Fort Amsterdam and Fort Orange
anchored and defended mercantile depots around which civilian settlements
developed. The most complete and accurate representation of the development of New Amsterdam under the Dutch is the so-called "Castello Plan,"
which represents the state of the settlement in 1660.[3] This extraordinary aerial
axonometric survey plan delineates the loosely planned character of the settlement with its irregular and unequally sized blocks and lots. It also suggests
some attempt at replicating a radially planned, fortified urban enclave on the
model of seventeenth-century Amsterdam or other northern European cities, albeit fragmentally and on a minuscule scale. All principal streets lead to
and from the fort, most notably the wide expanse of the north-south Brede
Wegh (Broadway), which connected the fort with the main entrance gate into

the settlement. All essential structures, including church, windmill, and the Governor's House, are housed within the fort or in close proximity to its walls. Moreover, the survey that produced the "Castello Plan" itself demonstrated the desire for greater control over planning and construction on the part of Director-General Stuyvesant and his council, who were concerned that land speculation was inhibiting further settlement.[4] Having viewed the survey, the directors of the Dutch West India Company agreed, commenting on the "excessively large lots and gardens."[5] This is a clear expression of their intention that New Amsterdam be a densely built urban settlement. Thus, Manhattan was urban in character from the earliest years of European habitation, and real estate speculation was a primary factor in its development from its origins.

From the details of the "Castello Plan," it is clear that New Amsterdam's development followed the pattern of northern European commercial towns with narrow, rectilinear lots fronted by houses, whose entrance gables faced the street. The half dozen or so extant views and plans of seventeenth-century New Amsterdam, along with firsthand accounts, depict the growth of the settlement from a cluster of small wooden structures along the waterfront south and east of the fort to a burgeoning town of nearly 350 structures, most solidly constructed of brick or stone.[6] Based on the surviving evidence, it appears that these second and third generations of residential and commercial structures closely replicated established Dutch late medieval urban prototypes in construction, plan, and exterior and interior details and fittings. Since none of these townhouses survives in either New York or Albany, this is at best a generalization based on secondhand evidence. Nevertheless, by the time the English took control of New Amsterdam in 1664 it strongly resembled a small provincial Dutch city with a skyline anchored by church and town hall, an active commercial waterfront, and rows of closely built brick, stepped, or spout-gabled townhouses and warehouses.[7] These structures were characterized by: roofs covered with terra cotta pantiles; brick street façades anchored to internal timber-frame skeletons with iron tie rods; leaded-glass casement windows; and wooden stoops fronting the principal entry.

This same pattern of urban development played out on a smaller scale in Beverwijck, as seen in the single extant view of the settlement prior to the revolution.[8] The unplanned settlement spread north along the riverbank from the fort, attracting both those eager to engage in the lucrative fur trade with native tribes to the north and west and those reluctant to submit to the strictures of life on the Van Rensselaer family's surrounding patroonship. The civilian population had grown to such an extent by Stuyvesant's time that in 1652 he officially recognized the settlement as Beverwijck and made it a judicial seat for the surrounding territory, much to the chagrin of the Van Rensselaers.[9]

Twenty years later, the English built a new fort above the town, to the west at the top of what is now State Street, the principal east-west thoroughfare, and aligned with the Dutch church, which stood at the intersection of State and Market streets until 1806. As seen in eighteenth-century images, the frontier town behind its palisade was clearly Dutch in character. Indeed, Albany preserved its Dutch character up to the time of the revolution, and its entrenched Dutch families retained control of civic and social life for a generation or more after that, while New York City had become firmly Anglicized both socially and architecturally.

Nevertheless, the ultimately longer-lived and more dynamic chapter in the history of Dutch architecture in America is to be found in the agrarian precincts of New Netherland. The colonial Dutch agrarian presence was littoral, originating in the 1620s and 1630s in the extremely fertile plains and tidals flats of southwestern Long Island (now Brooklyn) as well as the vast, million-acre Van Rensselaer patroonship that flanked both sides of the Hudson north and south of Beverwijck.[10] From these bases the Dutch and their northern European associates expanded through the seventeenth and eighteenth centuries: south along both sides of the Hudson and inland along waterways and valleys, such as the Wallkill and Rondout valleys leading south and westward, respectively, from the settlement at Wiltwyck (now Kingston); north and west from New Amsterdam to encompass Manhattan Island and the region that is now northern New Jersey and Rockland County, New York; and south and west from Long Island across Staten Island and along the fertile reaches of the Raritan River valley and central New Jersey. Despite the explosion of urban and suburban development over the last century, Dutch agrarian material culture remains more or less discernible in all of these areas, either at historic sites and museums or in the significant number of farmhouses and barns in private ownership.[11]

The diverse agrarian settlers of New Netherland established themselves in the American wilderness using familiar northern European landholding patterns. David Cohen posits three distinct types: the isolated farm, the tenanted manor, and the agricultural village, the last of which only came into use in the 1640s.[12] Similarly, the farmers of New Netherland adopted familiar northern European, primarily Dutch and Flemish, architectural types. In Cohen's words, "there was a selection of certain architectural traditions from the various culture areas that crosscut the Netherlands and an adaptation of these traditions to a new environment in America."[13] There is some evidence that until about 1650 the combination house-barn form so characteristic of lowlands agrarian architecture was replicated throughout New Netherland along with smaller, stand-alone farmhouses, possibly derived from models in

North Holland.[14] This first generation of agrarian structures were as extemporized and impermanent as their urban counterparts, mostly built of wood with thatched roofs and often with no chimneys and unglazed window openings.[15] From mid-century they were replaced by the separate farmhouse with adjacent barn and outbuildings that became the prototypical Dutch agrarian complex in New Netherland.

Four distinct and widely recognized regional subtypes of New Netherland farmhouse developed over the period 1650 to 1750: the brick-sheathed farmhouse of the upper Hudson Valley; the stone farmhouse of the mid-Hudson region; the sandstone farmhouses of northern New Jersey and Rockland County, New York; and the wooden-clad farmhouses of western Long Island and central New Jersey. Clearly, the local availability of differing construction materials was the principal factor in this development. Other factors were the varying degrees of exposure to English influence and the relative isolation of a region. For instance, as Cohen demonstrates, brick-sheathed timber-frame houses were once found throughout New Netherland but gave way in the areas around New York City to newer forms while persisting through the early nineteenth century in the upper Hudson Valley.[16] This suggests that focusing on dominant regional subtypes in the analysis of the Dutch farmhouse can elide the substantial variety of house types across New Netherland.[17]

Despite the variety of exterior expression from the upper Hudson to central New Jersey, all Dutch farmhouses utilized the northern European H-bent, or anchor-bent, system of timber framing in some form, as did their urban counterparts. This fundamental commonality of construction technology identifies them as Dutch structures distinct from coeval English houses in New England and the South or German houses in Pennsylvania.[18] The H-bent system derives from northern European medieval building tradition and consists of a series of structural bents standing on sills and joined to each other at their tops by horizontal plates from which pairs of roof rafters rise, strengthened by collar beams, to form the roof structure. The individual structural H-bents consist of two uprights spanned by a large anchor beam attached with mortise and tenon joints several feet below their upper ends.

Of the four regional subtypes of Dutch farmhouse, the brick-sheathed houses of the upper Hudson Valley and the wooden-clad houses of western Long Island and central New Jersey utilized the H-bent system in its fullest form, with their brick or wooden exterior walls forming a sheathing for the timber frame. In brick houses, such as the Leendert Bronck house in Greene County, the sheathing was tied to the structural timbers by iron tie rods, as it was in brick townhouses, although it seems that urban houses frequently employed brick sheathing only on the publicly visible street-facing gables.[19] In wooden-clad houses, such as the Wyckoff house in Brooklyn, the sheathing took the form of either wide clapboards or shingles, and the walls were completed internally with infill materials ranging from primitive wattle-and-daub combinations in the seventeenth and early eighteenth centuries to brick later on.[20] The other two regional subtypes utilized locally available stone to create load-bearing masonry walls; however, the attic floor joists were generally set into the walls several feet below the top of the masonry, mimicking the form of the H-bent, albeit with the masonry walls substituting for the uprights.[21]

The purest expression of H-bent timber-framing technology appears in the so-called New World Dutch barn, built across the New Netherland region.[22] This is because the structure and form of the barn are completely congruous. The H-bents with their immense anchor beams form a wide central bay commonly used for grain threshing with a platform of saplings thrown across the anchor beams to form a loft for drying and storing grain crops. Flanking aisles accommodate a range of livestock and equipment. Interior partitions can be put up and moved as usage evolves, and the whole structure is sheathed with a single layer of weatherboards and a shingle roof. Here is a constructional system of great purity and directness, akin to the steel-frame skeleton as envisioned by the theoreticians of modernism.

There is a powerful logic and clarity to defining Dutch architecture in America by reference to the application of the H-bent system alone. Not only does this definition include both the New World Dutch barn and Dutch urban and rural house types, but it also circumvents the complexity and contradictions involved in analyzing the other potential determining characteristics for the Dutch house, in particular their floor plans. This is impossible in any case for the urban townhouse, since only fragmentary documentary evidence remains. For the farmhouse the principal complication is the frequent renovations made to most houses through centuries of use. Architectural historian John Stevens has made a life's work of teasing out these complex construction chronologies based on in-depth study and analysis of individual structures and presents over four dozen case studies in his recent publication, *Dutch Vernacular Architecture in North America, 1640–1830*.[23] The work of Stevens and others before him demonstrates that Dutch farmhouses generally began as one- or at the most two-room structures and were expanded and often substantially rebuilt from generation to generation.[24] As floor plans evolved they could take a variety of forms, but the most common was a linear arrangement of roughly square rooms, each with its own gable-end hearth and, often, with its own exterior entry door, as seen at both the Leendert Bronck house and the Johannes Decker house. The arrangement of multiple entry doors on the same façade has sometimes been identified as distinctly Dutch, yet there is

Exterior view of the Pieter and Leendert Bronck Houses, Coxsackie, Greene County, New York. From *Dutch Houses of the Hudson Valley*, 1929. Hudson River Museum

Exterior view of the Johannes Decker House; Wallkill, Ulster County, New York. From *Dutch Houses of the Hudson Valley*, 1929. Hudson River Museum

This complex represents the first and second generations of Dutch farmhouse in the upper Hudson Valley. Pieter Bronck built his one-room fieldstone farmhouse in 1663. His grandson built the two-room brick house in 1738.

Built by two generations of the Decker family over fifty years from the 1720s, this house represents the stone farmhouse of the mid-Hudson Valley.

Old Dutch Colonial Homestead

For Sale—This attractive nine room stone cottage on fine half acre corner in a beautiful, accessible and restricted residence suburb. Bearing fruit trees and vines. Shady lawn. Seven minutes' walk from station, 33 trains daily. A moderate expenditure would make this home a "show place" worth twice its present price.

RUFFIN A. SMITH, 47 West 34th St., New York

Exterior view of Campbell-Christie House; built in New Milford, New Jersey; moved in 1977 to New Bridge Landing State Park, River Edge. Bergen County Historical Society, New Jersey. Image courtesy of Sean Sawyer

Campbell-Christie House, New Milford, New Jersey, depicted in 1909 newspaper. Original source unknown. Bergen County Historical Society, River Edge, New Jersey

Built by Jacob Campbell, about the time of his marriage to Altche Westervelt in 1774, and represents the North Jersey sandstone farmhouse type. John Cristea (Christie) purchased the house in 1795 and operated a blacksmith shop and tavern at the busy crossroads. Threatened with destruction, the house was moved in its entirety in 1977 from New Milford to River Edge, onto land owned by Bergen County, and is part of the site operated by the Bergen County Historical Society.

no such tradition in the Netherlands.[25] However, it generally seems to indicate an earlier rather than later date of construction and remains one of the enduring puzzles in the field.[26] Contemporaneous with such reiterative floor plans, central chimney plans with central entries were being built, as seen in the Christopher Billop house on Staten Island of c. 1680 or the Jan Martense Schenck house, now restored within the Brooklyn Museum.[27] Cohen's analysis of 200 sites isolates four basic floor plans in use through 1750, all traceable to the Netherlands.[28] Regardless of arrangement, these plans contained similar rooms serving similar, multiple functions of cooking, eating, and sleeping in common, largely undifferentiated spaces.[29]

Another complex and contentious issue in attempts to understand the original appearance of Dutch farmhouses across New Netherland is the debate over roof forms. The analysis of existing roofs and the telltale evidence of their predecessors in houses across the region suggests that the earliest roof forms were steeply sloped straight gables, generally sheathed with wooden shingles but often with imported terra cotta pantiles. These conformed to the parapet gables of the upper Hudson Valley brick-sheathed house type, wherein the sloped edge of the roof surface was protected from weather by the brick gables rising above them.[30] In other regions the superstructure of the house was generally constructed of wood and there was greater choice in the roof form. A determining factor was the desire for the chimneys to emerge at the peak of the roof, for both practical and aesthetic reasons, and where there was a rear range of spaces behind the primary rooms this resulted in a saltbox-type roof, sometimes with the lower pitched rear roof reaching almost to the ground. Another factor was the use of loft spaces. Until the mid-eighteenth century they were typically storage for crops or auxiliary domestic work spaces for which lower roof profiles were adequate.[31] The most significant transformation of roof forms on Dutch urban and rural houses came from 1750 onward when the English gambrel form was widely adopted and adapted by Dutch Americans, as is examined below.

The interiors of Dutch farmhouses built during the period 1650 to 1750 were very similar in character and details to what is known of those in Dutch townhouses in New York and Albany. The distinctive Netherlandish jambless hearth was much remarked on by English visitors, as were the wooden floors and revealed H-bents, both often scrubbed to a brilliant whiteness.[32] Nevertheless, early Dutch colonial interiors in both urban and rural houses were, like their English counterparts, quite dim since window glass was a relatively rarified commodity, and windows were in the form of narrow casements, sometimes without glass and therefore shuttered during inclement weather.[33] A very few of these distinctive Dutch casement windows survive, mainly by omis-

Ogsbury Barn
Built at Guilderland Center, Albany County, New York, eighteenth century;
moved to Sleepy Hollow/Historic Hudson Valley, Tarrytown, New York in 1982.
Image by Michael Lord, Courtesy Historic Hudson Valley, Tarrytown, New York

Ogsbury Barn represents the prototypical New World Dutch barn with its central
threshing floor and quartering for livestock in the side aisles.

All-purpose room, Jan Martense Schenck House (or Schenck-Crooke House), Flatlands, Brooklyn, c. 1675–1676, given to the Brooklyn Museum, 1950.
Brooklyn Museum, 50.192mn, Gift of Atlantic and Pacific Company

This view shows the Brooklyn Museum's 2008 reinstallation with the central chimney and its jambless hearth, dining table, and bed box.

sion from renovation schemes, as at the Coeymans House near Albany, where a *kruiskozijn* or four-part casement was rediscovered within a closet.[34] They generally consisted of a combination of glazed, fixed openings and unglazed openings made weather-fast with shutters, thus both lighting and ventilating the house.

1709: CONTINUITY AND CHANGE IN EIGHTEENTH-CENTURY DUTCH AMERICAN ARCHITECTURE

Through the first seventy-five years of English rule in the provinces of New York and New Jersey, Dutch architectural forms and traditions continued to a remarkable extent, especially in areas and settlements distant from Manhattan, which was the nexus of English power and influence in the region. Even western Long Island and other areas just one river crossing removed remained rural and isolated enough to retain their essentially Dutch character.[35] In addition to geography, socioeconomic status was a prime indicator of exposure and aspiration to English culture: the greater an individual's status and wealth, the greater likelihood that they would choose to abandon medievalizing Netherlandish forms and build in a modern, classically inspired style characteristic

JOHN JOSEPH HOLLAND (C. 1776–1820)
[A View of Broad Street, Wall Street and the City Hall, New York, New York], 1797.
I. N. Phelps Stokes Collection, Miriam and Ira D. Wallach Division of Art, Prints and
Photographs, The New York Public Library, Astor, Lenox and Tilden Foundations, 54271

The stepped-gabled house dated 1698 in the right foreground was one of the last Dutch-
style structures to remaining standing in Manhattan.

of the fashionable elites of continental Europe and England. Moreover, in the
colonial context this stylistic choice spoke most strongly of aspirations to status and power to be gained by association.[36] Predictably, therefore, the seats
of civic and landed power were among the first structures to assume strongly
anglicized forms. In 1700 a new classicizing structure with Doric portico and
hip roof supplanted the stepped-gabled bulk of the Stadt Huys as New York's
city hall.[37] It is seen at the head of Broad Street in this view made in 1797, along
with the fashionable Georgian-style residences that gradually replaced the
Dutch gable-fronted townhouses of the city's Anglo-Dutch elite and merchant
classes through the eighteenth century. The devastating fires of 1776, 1835, and
1845 destroyed what fashion had left untouched.[38] The last of lower Manhattan's Dutch gables succumbed to the wreckers at least a decade before the Civil
War and, it seems, much to the pleasure of a city that embraced progress.[39] A
similar pattern unfolded in Albany, although almost fifty years later. English-

JAMES EIGHTS (1798–1882)
North Pearl Street—West Side from Maiden Lane North as it was in 1814, c. 1850
Watercolor on paper, 9½ x 12¾ in.
Albany Institute of History & Art, Bequest of Ledyard Cogswell, Jr., 1954.59.67

This is one of several detailed views of Albany that Eights made from sketches done decades before and shows the mix of Dutch- and English-style architecture that characterized the city through the nineteenth century.

style gambrel-roofed townhouses began to appear in the 1760s, but Dutch-style townhouses continued to be built through the revolutionary era. This representation of North Pearl Street in 1814 captures the mix of English and Dutch architectural forms that characterized Albany's streetscapes into the late nineteenth century.[40]

Even outside the urban environment, in the first half of the eighteenth century the region's Anglo-Dutch elite, often drawn together through strategic intermarriage, adopted the fashionable Georgian style for their residences. A prime example is Van Cortlandt Mansion, constructed for Frederick Van Cortlandt on the family's estate in southern Westchester County, now the Bronx, in 1748. Descended from Dutch merchant stock, Frederick inherited the property from his father Jacobus in 1739 and built a country seat embodying the family's newly established landed status as well as its mercantile wealth derived from international contacts. Built solidly of local stone, the principal south façade is symmetrical, with five bays of large sash windows and a central entrance leading to a broad central stairwell. Capacious parlors flank the entry on the south façade and have large English-style fireplaces set within elegant wood-paneled walls. The broad stair curves past a large arched window and leads to the family's principal chambers on the second floor. The third floor was the precinct of the lower-status members of the household, with a nursery and adjacent work space and slave quarters. Similar in plan and style were the impressive homes of other elite families, such as the earlier Philipse Manor Hall in nearby Yonkers or the mid-eighteenth-century Albany mansions of the Schuylers and Van Rensselaers.

While the colonial elites indulged in the latest English fashions, Dutch-descended families further down the socioeconomic scale were much more conservative in their architectural tastes, certainly due in part to a relative lack of resources but also, it seems, to a preference for the ways of their grandparents.[41] Across the region, from what was now Kings County to the Van Rensselaer lands around Albany, those living in the countryside gradually absorbed and adapted English architectural traditions. This was much more a process of adaptation than of assimilation: elements of Dutch material culture that worked well were steadfastly maintained. For instance, although there were subtle alterations in forms and proportions over the century, Dutch Americans continued to build barns in the same manner as their great-grandfathers had through the first four decades of the nineteenth century.[42]

Across the farmyard, however, the Dutch farmhouse experienced a gradual but thoroughgoing transformation as English design elements were selectively introduced and adapted. Cohen sees this as a fundamental structural shift that created a distinct Dutch American regional culture of which the farmhouse was a prime constituent.[43] There is a broad consensus among scholars that this shift occurred as the hold of Netherlandish culture slackened under increasing English social and political dominance and that it created a new, distinct style of hybrid farmhouse incorporating English features and labeled variously as "Dutch American," "New Style," or "Georgian."[44]

No matter the prestige of English culture, the adaptation of English architectural features embodied in the Dutch American farmhouse, as it will be referred to here, accorded with changed patterns of domestic life. As transportation and communication networks developed and Dutch farm families gained access to a broader range of markets and goods, patterns of daily living shifted and resulted in an increased differentiation of spaces within the house.[45] Formerly common, multiple-use spaces were realigned and redesigned to create dedicated cooking, dining, socialization, and sleeping spaces. Such distinc-

Exterior of the Van Cortlandt House commissioned by Frederick Van Cortlandt in 1748;
native fieldstone and brick, Bronx, New York.
Photograph, 1880s
Hudson River Museum, 75.0.71

The symmetry and classical detailing of the mansion's principal façade embodies the
fashionable Georgian elegance so highly valued by colonial New York's Anglo-Dutch
elite.

South façade of the
Van Cortlandt House,
Bronx, New York, early
twentieth century.
Print process postcard
Hudson River
Museum, INV.2761

The house and
property remained
in the Van Cortlandt
family until 1889, when
it was sold to New York
City; in 1897, it was
opened to the public
under the auspices of
the National Society of
the Colonial Dames in
the State of New York.

tions and refinements did not transpire overnight, and earlier Dutch farmhouses often designated one room as the *groote kamer*, or best room, with fittings and furnishings reserved for entertainment.[46] However, in the Dutch American farmhouse such practice became standard and necessitated often substantial additions or renovations to existing houses as well as new planning approaches in new ones.

A principal constituent of the Dutch American farmhouse was the so-called Georgian central hall, a dedicated circulation zone that provided the chambers to either side with privacy and the ability to be adapted to new uses as formal parlors, dining rooms, or bedrooms. The central hall also provided a dedicated and more formalized zone for vertical circulation, reflecting the enhanced use of upper floors within these larger homes. Blackburn summarizes the revolution in domestic functions brought about by the introduction of the central hall:

> The central hall became the buffer between public and private rooms and between outside elements and inside comfort. Once the front and rear doors entered a hall there was no longer the necessity for the stairway to be enclosed. It now became an elegant and graceful feature of the central hall, a statement of the social importance of the house and its owner. Upstairs bedrooms accessed only from the hall meant real privacy for the first time. That was what the newer style life and house was about.[47]

The regular habitation of the second floor of farmhouses in many cases necessitated altering or rebuilding the roof. Frequently dormers were added to provide light and ventilation; however, often older, low roofs were replaced with new English-style gambrel roofs.[48] The two-tiered gambrel form accommodated a maximum volume and introduced a new, fashionable profile in the countryside. Yet even as farmers were welcoming its practical advantages, they began adapting it to their cultural norms. In the lower Hudson Valley, Long Island, and New Jersey, many earlier Dutch farmhouses had extended eaves along their long primary façades, which regulated light and temperatures in the harsh American climate, minimizing the penetration of the high, hot summer sun yet allowing in the last raking rays of autumn and winter sunlight. The adoption of the gambrel with its steeper lower slope required ingenuity in order to preserve this functional and, as some argue, culturally significant feature.[49] What developed was a distinctive "bell-cast" eave form that combined with the gambrel form to create an elegant reverse S-curve silhouette capping these new, larger farmhouses and constituting a highly visible demonstration of Dutchness despite the English origins of the roof form.[50] Another significant and even earlier alteration to the exterior of farmhouses across the four regional subtypes was the replacement of medieval casement windows with single- or double-hung sash windows and larger window openings with increased availability of glass in the colonies. No longer were Dutch housewives shuttered in dim interiors on inclement days, and even farm families of relatively modest means swapped their outmoded casements for sash windows by the 1750s.[51]

The evolution of the Dutch American farmhouse also involved significant adaptations to the interiors of homes. Bedsteads were removed to dedicated bedchambers, and the noisome jambless hearth gave way to the more efficient English-style fireplace, often set within elaborately paneled and ornamented walls.[52] The elimination of the worst effusions of smoke and soot encouraged the expansion of plastered surfaces, and the finely hewn timbers of the distinctive H-bent structure were increasingly hidden behind paneled or plastered walls and drop ceilings. Yet even as Dutch farmers chose to adopt the English fireplace, they adapted it to express their own sense of heritage and culture by surrounding it with Dutch tiles of varying quality and iconography.[53] Thus the English fireplace was fully integrated and the newly constituted Dutch American hearth became a quintessential emblem of Dutchness in America for future generations.[54]

Despite the thoroughgoing transformation of the farmhouse in the mid-eighteenth century, there were fundamental points of continuity with both Dutch construction and design traditions. A very visible one was the preservation of the split or Dutch door, whose enduring practicality was not forsaken on the farm no matter its abandonment in fashionable urban houses. The most important point of continuity, however, was the use of the H-bent timber-frame system itself throughout the eighteenth and well into the nineteenth century. This continued to define the farmhouses built across western Long Island, the Hudson Valley, and New Jersey as Dutch American.

1809: EFFLORESCENCE AND ECLIPSE

The nineteenth century would seem not to have dawned too brightly for Dutch American architecture. Dutch gabled townhouses were outmoded and increasingly under threat in both Manhattan and Albany. What fashion failed to consume in the former, fire would over the first half of the new century. Upriver, the relocation of the state government from Kingston in 1797 and the opening of the Erie Canal in 1825 were significant spurs to Albany's growth and, concomitantly, to the destruction of its aging Dutch architecture. In the postrevolutionary period Anglicization even overtook the architecture of the Dutch Reformed Church, a pillar of cultural continuity in other regards.[55] The first generation of Dutch colonial churches had followed the Dutch pro-

All-purpose room, John DeWint House, Tappan, Rockland County, New York.
Library of Congress, Prints & Photographs Division, HABS, Reproduction number
HABS NY,44-TAP,2-12 Survey number HABS-NY4123
http://hdl.loc.gov/loc.pnp/hhh.ny0684

Built in 1700 with a brick exterior by Daniel DeClark, a Dutch settler, and
purchased in 1746 by Johannes and Antje DeWint, a West Indies planter and his
wife, who were patriots. In 1932 the Grand Lodge of Free and Accepted Masons of
the State of New York purchased the house, and remains the owner.

When the room was renovated with an English-style fireplace around the time
of DeWint's purchase of the house in 1746, both the original mantle molding and
biblical tiles of the original jambless hearth were accommodated in the
new hearth.

totype of the octagonal reformed chapel. The American Church's separation
from the authority of the Classis of Amsterdam in 1771 was a major break,
and the later eighteenth century saw the replacement of old-style churches
with steeple-fronted neoclassical structures. For instance, at Flatbush, in the
heart of Kings County's conservative agrarian communities, a new church was
built in a stripped-down neoclassical mode with a multitiered steeple over the
entrance and large round-arched windows flooding the interior with light,
just as any church in New England or Virginia might have been. Opened in
1796, it still stands at the intersection of Flatbush and Church avenues. On the
Philipse manor in what is now Sleepy Hollow, New York, the simple stone hall

ROBERT W. WEIR (1803–1889), painter
James Smillie, engraver
Washington's Head-quarters, Newburgh, N.Y. (Habrouck House, 1750)
Painted and engraved for the *New York Mirror*, 1884
Hudson River Museum

The exterior of the traditional Dutch form is native sandstone.
George Washington stayed at the house periodically from 1780 to 1783.

church of the 1690s was renovated after a fire in 1837 with a central entrance
and larger, fashionable Gothic arched windows, but more significantly it lost
its function, becoming a graveyard chapel while a new Greek revival structure
hosted the congregation.[56]

Despite these clear signs of decline and eclipse at the centers of power, in
the countryside of the lower Hudson Valley a resurgence and reconstitution
of Dutch American architecture was under way. This was in part associated
with the cultivation of a distinctly American culture and folklore during the
first third of the nineteenth century by literary New Yorkers such as James
Fenimore Cooper (1789–1851), James Kirke Paulding (1778–1860), and, most
significantly, Washington Irving (1783–1859). Irving's sensational best-seller,
*A History of New York from the Beginning of the World to the End of the Dutch
Dynasty,* published in 1809, may have had the long-term effect of undermining
contemporary academic efforts to include the Dutch in "the master narrative

Exterior view of Washington Irving's home, Sunnyside,
Tarrytown, Westchester County, New York, early twentieth century.
Hudson River Museum

Constructed around a Dutch stone farmhouse, Washington Irving's 1835 picturesque
cottage constitutes an early and anomalous Dutch colonial revival residence.

of United States history," but it and Irving's subsequent "Knickerbocker" tales
also catapulted the region's Dutch origins into the national consciousness and
international literary prominence.[57] Moreover, Irving's promotion and invention of a folklore for his native lower Hudson Valley, such as the elaboration of
the Dutch veneration of Saint Nicholas or the gothic creation of "The Legend
of Sleepy Hollow," gave new life to the Dutch presence in the region and ultimately planted the Dutch legacy deep within the American cultural consciousness.

A principal model for Irving's folkloric and literary enterprises was the
work of Sir Walter Scott (1771–1832).[58] Thus is it not surprising that Irving
made connections both implicit and explicit to Scott's lowlands manor, Abbotsford, when he constructed his own country seat, Sunnyside, with the assistance of the British watercolorist George Harvey beginning in 1835.[59] Most
emphatically, Irving made the medieval stepped gable the principal motif of
the house, as the Scottish versions were at Abbotsford. Yet the semiotics of
Sunnyside's gables were multivalent, referring at once to his admiration for

Scott and his self-made laird's demesne and, more pronouncedly, to the vanished and vanishing Dutch gables of Manhattan and Albany and through them to the authentic Dutch core of the house itself, the two-room stone tenant farmhouse that he had purchased in 1835. Despite its novelty, he also pronounced his home's chronological Dutchness by emblazoning the most visible riverfront gable with wrought-iron numerals citing the original farmhouse's supposed date of construction, squarely within the reign of Stuyvesant, whom Irving had almost single-handedly made the icon of New York's Dutch colonial past. Twenty years after Sunnyside's construction Irving completed the circle between past and present and fact and fiction by penning a fanciful tale of the farmhouse's builder, Wolfert Acker, entitled "Wolfert's Roost." The irony of Irving's appreciation of Sunnyside's authentic Dutch antecedent is that he subsumed it within his new structure, yet he would have been preternaturally ahead of his time to have considered it of historic significance and worth preserving itself when thousands of such houses still dotted the countryside. Rather, just as so many of his literary works took a strand of authentic Dutch colonial history or folklore and spun new fabric of it, he elaborated and extrapolated the simple farmhouse into an architectural fantasy of Dutchness, transplanting the stepped gables and weathervanes so strongly associated with lower Manhattan's urban precincts or Albany's old Dutch families into the bucolic countryside and staking his claim to fame and a portion of the Hudson riverscape.[60]

Sunnyside was more than a landmark of Irving's literary and cultural accomplishments, however; it was one of the most celebrated of antebellum country villas, cited by Andrew Jackson Downing (1815-1852) himself as a model for emulation. While Downing praised the stepped gables and "quaint old weathercocks," it was the associational *mis-en-scène* created by the combination of the house's Dutch elements, Irving's fame, and the picturesque Hudson River landscape that made Sunnyside an icon of what has been termed "genteel Romanticism."[61] Sunnyside can also be interpreted as a link between early nineteenth-century Romanticism and the later colonial revival, and its Dutch colonial artifice presages that of the early twentieth-century Dutch colonial revival house.[62]

Sunnyside revived the forms of the nearly vanished Dutch colonial townhouse but not the still vital Dutch American farmhouse, which through the nineteenth century still dominated the rural landscapes of the Dutch American hearth area. In the first quarter of the century it experienced a final efflorescence in Kings County that speaks to the farmhouse as the prime indicator of the Dutch American experience. One of the first points of settlement, the fertile flats and valleys of Kings County remained stolidly Dutch through the first half of the nineteenth century, yet the farming villages of Bushwick, New Utrecht, Gravesend, Flatbush, and Flatlands faced constant pressure from the expanding City of Brooklyn, and the last of them was annexed into it by 1896. Thus the farms of Kings County formed a key front in the adaptation and articulation of Dutch American culture and identity in the face of mass immigration and urbanization.

The last generation of farmhouses constructed in Kings County during the 1820s and 1830s shifted away from the assimilation and adaptation of English architectural elements to reassert Dutch forms explicitly and self-consciously. This phenomenon can be seen in the major renovation of his farmhouse in Flatlands undertaken by Abraham Wyckoff around 1820 to accommodate an extended family, including his elderly parents, his four children by his first and second wives, and at least three enslaved African laborers. Prior to the renovation the house had consisted of three H-bent framed principal chambers, each built separately over the prior 180 years and each served by its own entrance and hearth, laid end to end.[63] The two later chambers dated from the mid-eighteenth century, were built over full cellars, and likely had small service spaces outside their rear northern walls, which were sheltered under the long, low profile of a saltbox-shaped roof. Abraham replaced these service spaces with a range of three rooms to serve primarily as sleeping spaces. This necessitated replacing the roof over this portion of the house, and rather than retain the saltbox form or adopt the gambrel, the Wyckoffs and their builders constructed a broad, straight gabled roof with dramatically deep and flaring spring eaves. This distinctive profile set the Wyckoff house apart from the gambrel-roofed farmhouses built by the prior generation in Kings County, such as the Pieter Lefferts house of 1783. It seems to have harkened back to earlier, and perhaps what was considered purer, Dutch roof forms, such as that of the late seventeenth-century Jan Martense Schenck house, then still standing on nearby Bergen Island and possessed of a well-known and charismatic, indeed sensational, pseudo-history.[64] In the context of remodeling an ancestral homestead within a locality where Dutch traditions were under increasing pressure and criticism, the assertively Dutch form of the Wyckoff house's roof can be understood as a defiantly epideictic architectural form, broadcasting the family's status as proud descendants of one of the first generation of Dutch settlers in America.[65]

Yet by the third decade of the nineteenth century the evolution of the Dutch American farmhouse and New World Dutch barn ceased. Now in their seventh generation, Dutch American agrarian families in New York and New Jersey were increasingly intermarrying with those from other ethnic groups and becoming integrated into a national consumer society that was spread-

The Manor House of the Philipsburg Upper Mills, with tulip bed.
Photograph of the historic site as it looked during the late 1940s and 1950s
when it was called Philipse Castle Restoration.
Historic Hudson Valley, Tarrytown, New York

ing beyond the eastern seaboard.[66] Many families in the region continued to cherish their ancestral homesteads, but they had the wealth and immediate access to consumer goods necessary to adopt the latest fashions and domestic technologies and to make needed renovations. For older farmhouses, this was the era when lofts were converted to bedrooms, generally including the insertion of dormers; deep-set eaves became full-fledged porches, often replete with classicizing columns or elaborate gingerbread ornamentation; and interiors were wallpapered and fireplaces closed and replaced with cast-iron stoves.[67] In short, the Dutch American farmhouse assumed the appearance of the American picturesque cottage as so potently promoted by Downing and his followers.

Functionally, however, they remained farmhouses. Through the nineteenth century Dutch American farms in the region prospered, benefiting from their proximity to the nation's largest urban market and adapting to new demands and technologies.[68] Indeed, after 200 years of transporting their produce to Manhattan via ferry, Kings County's Dutch American farmers finally succeeded in securing their own central market adjacent to the Navy Yard at Wallabout Bay in 1884. New immigrants, mainly Irish and German, also entered farming

*The Pieter Claesen Wyckoff House
(Wyckoff Farmhouse Museum)*: south façade
(original entry façade), Brooklyn, Kings County,
New York, built between 1652 and 1819.
Wyckoff Farmhouse Museum, Brooklyn,
New York
Image Courtesy of Historic House Trust of
New York City. Photo by Madeline Isom.

The Wyckoff House represents the wooden-
clad Long Island farmhouse type, which spread
to eastern and central New Jersey as Kings
County families migrated there in the later
seventeenth century.

within the metropolitan area, often purchasing land from Dutch Americans.[69]
Yet this willingness to sell land that had been held in their families for multiple
generations was perhaps the most ominous sign that the forces of urbanization would ultimately overtake the region's farmlands.

Just as Manhattan had been the epicenter for the forces of Anglicization,
so it was for urbanization. By 1900 Dutch American farms within commuting
distance of the city faced certain demolition and development. Ironically, it was
at just this moment that growing appreciation of the city and region's Dutch
colonial heritage was fostering a revival of Dutch-inspired architecture.

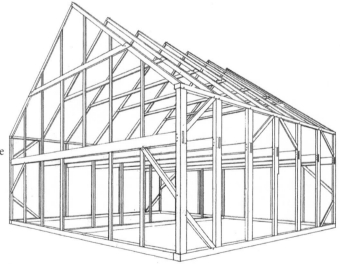

*Diagram of Dutch-American
anchor-bent framing*: seven anchor
bents 4 feet on center, with one
front room and two rear rooms.
Hand House, Dutch Neck, Mercer
County, New Jersey, c. 1740,
demolished 1978.
Drawn by Clifford W. Zink, image
courtesy of Clifford W. Zink.

Diagram of the H-bent timber-frame
system that defines both urban
and rural Dutch houses in colonial
America.

The first phase of this revival was explicitly urban in inspirations and focus. The 1880s saw the development of an urban, brick architecture in New York City and its environs that replicated and reconstituted forms from Dutch and Flemish Renaissance architecture.[70] Once again, the signature form was the stepped gable, but a variety of other, more ornamental gable forms were used as well, and other common features included tiled roofs, leaded casement windows, banded and colored brickwork, and elaborate terra cotta, stucco, and ironwork ornamentation. Moreover, the choice of brick as the primary building material was itself was symbolic of lowlands urban architecture.

Perhaps the most emblematic project of this brick-built Dutch Renaissance revival style was the Wallabout Market complex itself, which was completed in 1884 according to designs by William B. Tubby (1859–1944). A respected professional whose *oeuvre* was to include a number of other prominent civic commissions, Tubby worked in a variety of academic, historicizing styles.[71] The market complex's flamboyantly gabled and pinnacled forms clearly referred to Dutch or Flemish market squares, such as those in Delft or Antwerp.[72] The Wallabout Market's extravagantly ethnocentric architecture associated the marketing of produce in Brooklyn with the lowlands origins of Kings County's *boers* just as their 250-year-long hold over agricultural production was coming to an end.

In a somewhat peculiar and not unnoticed congruence of architectural sources, Robert W. Gibson's (1855–1927) West End Collegiate Church and School of 1891 also referred to lowlands market structures, in this case the early sixteenth-century Vleeshal in Haarlem.[73] A writer in *Harper's Weekly,* soon after the church's completion, expressed mild shock at its secular inspiration and condemned its compositional and ornamental exuberance: "It is a very attractive building by force of picturesqueness and quaintness, but the rollicking gayety of its expression is especially incompatible with churchliness."[74] It seems likely that this was exactly the affect the Reformed Church fathers desired as they, along with other denominations across the city, sought to both attract new members and lure existing congregants uptown to the newly developing and fashionable Upper West Side.

Indeed, Gibson's extravagantly detailed Dutch Renaissance-style complex formed the linchpin of a veritable Knickerbocker beachhead on West End Avenue between Seventy-second and Eighty-sixth streets. At the northwest corner of West Eighty-third Street McKim, Mead, and White built a group of five houses with Dutch gables in 1885, and one street north a whole blockfront of gable-fronted and tiled-roofed townhouses was completed in the early 1890s

Wallabout Market, 1905
From *Singer Souvenirs: Postcard Views,* Singer
Manufacturing Company, n.d.
Photographic print, 4¼ x 7 in.
The New York Public Library, Digital ID no. 800642

The market, built in 1884 and destroyed in 1941
for the Brooklyn Navy Yard expansion during
World War II, featured permanent, two-story brick
structures in fanciful Flemish-Dutch style, centered
on a tall clock tower. Gabriel Furman, in his *Notes
Geograpical and Historical, relating to the Town of
Brooklyn, in Kings County on Long-Island* (1824),
traces the name Wallabout from the Dutch "Waal
bocht," or "bay of the Walloons," referring to the
French-speaking passengers on *New Netherland*
who originally settled there in 1624. Wallabout Bay
is located along the northwest shore of Brooklyn
(*Bruykleen*) between the Williamsburg and
Manhattan bridges.

Brooklyn: B St.–E. Ave. (Wallabout Market Tower), 1925
Photographic print, Eugene L. Arabruster Collection
The New York Public Library, Mid-Manhattan Picture
Collection, Digital ID no. 707239F

to designs by Philadelphia architect Frank Miles Day (1861–1918).[75] Many other
stepped and scroll gables graced the side streets leading to Riverside Drive. The
same *Harper's Weekly* writer who criticized West End Collegiate's lack of decorum praised Day's block and the historical appropriateness of revived Dutch
domestic architecture in Manhattan coming after much stylistic experimenta-
tion:

> The more singular it has been, considering this pursuit of novelties and
> oddities for a decade, that the one style that has a particular historical claim
> upon New York, being at the same time a style eminently suitable to do-
> mestic uses, both practically and in its expression, should have been left
> untouched until within a very short time. We mean, of course, the Dutch
> Renaissance of the sixteenth and seventeenth centuries, of the time when

West End Collegiate Church and Collegiate School complex,
New York, New York, completed 1893.
In "Recent Brickwork in American Cities–New York," *The Brickbuilder* 3, no. 6
(June 1894): 106.

This view shows Robert W. Gibson's Dutch Renaissance Revival complex shortly
after its completion. The church faces south onto West 77th Street at the corner of
West End Avenue and is connected to offices and school buildings to the east.

the Dutch colonization of Manhattan Island took place, and New Amsterdam was made to reproduce, as nearly as the poverty of the settlers and the
unskilfulness of their mechanics could reproduce it, the aspect of ancestral
Amsterdam.[76]

Such enthusiasm for a revived Dutch architecture in New York City was
far removed from the glee expressed at the demolition of lower Manhattan's
Dutch colonial structures just forty years before. Public sentiment clearly embraced the revival of Dutch associations, and a range of Dutch Renaissance
revival residences, office buildings, schools, and firehouses were built through
the first decade of the twentieth century as public enthusiasm mounted to the
tricentennial of Hudson's voyage of discovery in 1909.[77] Similar structures were
built in urban areas and town centers around the region through the 1930s.

The best of them represented the development of a regional expression within the larger academic eclectic movement, while others were ersatz evocations of Dutchness.[78]

New York City's Dutch Renaissance revival may also be understood as related to both the broader colonial revival movement and the contemporary, nationwide enthusiasm for all things Dutch in the visual arts and popular culture, which Annette Stott has termed "Holland Mania." Stott's analysis connects "Holland Mania" of the period from 1880 to 1920 with both a renewed appreciation of the historic ties between the Netherlands and America and a xenophobic and prejudicial attitude that embraced Dutch culture as representative of a nonthreatening white, Protestant culture in the face of mass Catholic and Jewish immigration.[79] Within the metropolitan New York and Hudson Valley regions, "Holland Mania" and Dutch Renaissance revival architecture took on an added association with the assertion of Knickerbocker precedence and birthright as well as a genuine pride in having a personal connection to the historical narrative of colonial America. It was at this time that the principal Dutch American historical and genealogical organizations were founded: the all-male Holland Society was established in 1885 and The Society of Daughters of Holland Dames in 1895. Family associations evolved a generation later in the 1920s and 1930s; for instance, the Blauvelts organized in 1926, the Van Voorhees in 1932, and the Wyckoffs in 1937.

In 1910 The Holland Society gained a new member and Dutch American architecture a potent advocate in Franklin Delano Roosevelt (1882–1945), the rising son of one of New York's early Dutch families, who possessed a keen interest in genealogy and local history.[80] This interest deepened during the early 1920s as his recuperation from a severe paralytic illness forced a hiatus from politics, and in 1923 he joined the Board of The Holland Society. Over the course of a decade in which Roosevelt became Governor of New York and then President of the United States, he chaired a special committee of the society that supported and published the pioneering work of two architectural historians, Helen Wilkinson Reynolds (1876–1943) and Rosalie Fellows Bailey (1908–1991), on the houses of the Hudson Valley and those of northern New Jersey and southern New York, respectively.[81] Naturally, Reynolds and Bailey's work was structured by their sponsor's interests: they defined a Dutch house to be one built or occupied by a Dutch-descended family, and the great bulk of their four- to five-hundred-page volumes was given over to documenting each house with a summary of its builder's and owners' genealogies and an exterior photograph. However, their short prefatory essays presented keenly drawn historical and architectural analyses that were grounded in the direct observation of hundreds of structures and have largely been borne out by subsequent scholarship.[82] Principal goals that sponsor and authors clearly shared were to document the greatest possible number of structures and to inspire their preservation. Reynolds and Bailey were keenly aware of the threat posed to the houses they visited by both neglect and development. This was particularly the case with Bailey's work in New York City and its immediate environs, where a large percentage of the homes she documented were no longer standing by the time her book was finally published in 1936.[83] While it could clearly not delay or divert the socioeconomic forces reshaping the region, Reynolds and Bailey's work with its comprehensive catalogue of authentic models certainly fostered and sustained the Dutch colonial revival in American architecture, which had begun in the 1910s.

Through the first half of the twentieth century the Dutch American farmhouses of western Long Island and New Jersey served as models for the development of the so-called Dutch colonial house in almost every region of the country. Hundreds of thousands of these houses, ranging from substantial, rambling homes for affluent families in leafy suburbs to modest attached houses for the working classes in densely built urban areas, survive today. What marks the vast majority of them as Dutch colonial is the presence of the gambrel roof. Sometimes it is their only distinguishing feature, and in many instances it may be no more than a thin perimeter around a high, boxy dormer used to create the distinctive two-tiered gambrel profile. In the more sophisticated examples, such as the Jerome C. Bull house in Tuckahoe, New York, the geometrical flexibility of the gambrel's angles are exploited to accommodate a full-height second story, while the lower slope curves outward to provide for deep, sheltering eaves.

The Bull house was designed by Aymar Embury II (1880–1966), a New York City-born and Princeton-educated architect, who was a principal advocate of the twentieth-century Dutch colonial home.[84] In his best-known publication, *The Dutch Colonial House* of 1913, Embury's focus was squarely on demonstrating the applicability of the "old Dutch farmhouses" of western Long Island and New Jersey to contemporary design.[85] He explicitly disavowed any need to duplicate authentic plans, instead advocating their reworking to meet the uses and technologies of the modern household.[86] He celebrated the free interpretation of precedent as being "Dutch in spirit, and the sort of thing which the Dutch architects might have done had they happened to think of it" and acknowledged that many of the contemporary houses bore little resemblance to their erstwhile models.[87] He affirmed that the use of the gambrel roof was the principal common ground between old and new, and in its sheltering form he found the quintessence of the Dutch colonial style as a whole, its domestic picturesqueness:

Jerome C. Bull House, Tuckahoe, Westchester County, New York
From *The Dutch Colonial House* by Aymar Embury (New York: McBridge, Nast, & Company, 1913).

This substantial suburban house was designed by Aymar Embury II, a principal advocate of the Dutch Colonial Revival in residential design.

The style never was, and never can be, perfectly adjusted to houses of great size or formal character; it was essentially informal and picturesque. The genius of the Dutch race did not lend itself to the pomp of public life; . . . the Dutch simply do not know how to be stately. But if a country house is wanted which shall be homelike, quaint and lovely, the style is admirably adjusted to its use, especially since in a small house the lower the roof comes, the more intimately the building will fit its landscape, and houses of the Dutch type are essentially low in appearance.[88]

As Embury implies and is now widely recognized, it is historically inaccurate to label the twentieth-century gambrel-roofed house as Dutch colonial. As has been seen, the gambrel was an English form adapted by the Dutch well after the end of the Dutch colonial period, and such eighteenth-century houses are more accurately termed Dutch American. Yet they also represented the most substantial and refined of Dutch American domestic architecture that remained as models for early twentieth-century architects and builders, and

within the associational context of the broader colonial revival the Dutch colonial label was intended less as a historically accurate label than an evocative
descriptor for realtors' ad copy. The irony deepens in considering the preva-
lence of the style on the streets of the very residential developments that swal-
lowed up vast tracts of old-line Dutch American farmland and their authentic
structures during the first half of the twentieth century. There is a morbid-
ness to the omnipresence of ersatz Dutch colonial style houses in areas where
250 years of Dutch American architecture was demolished wholesale, such as
Kings County.

Perhaps the height of the backward compliment inherent in the Dutch colonial revival was the replication of specific historic houses. Stayton reproduces
a 1941 advertisement touting "A Series of Notable Colonial Architectural Museum Pieces" at the New Salem development in Port Washington, New York,
including a modernized version of the Jan Martense Schenck house.[89] In 1937
New York architect Randolph Evans (1901–1974) published a design for "an

View of Dutch colonial style house,
Cranford, Union County, New Jersey,
c. 1937.
Image courtesy of Sean Sawyer

Apparently based on a design published
by the Office of Randolph Evans in 1937
for a replica of the Dyckman farmhouse
in upper Manhattan to be built in
Scarsdale, New York.

exact duplicate" of northern Manhattan's Dyckman farmhouse with a caption suggesting that it was to be constructed in Scarsdale, New York.[90] Whether that house was built is not known, but another version does exist in Cranford, New Jersey, where the Dyckman farmhouse's picturesque combination of brick, stone, and clapboard are intact, but the rear of its kitchen wing has been distended for use as a garage. Ultimately, one senses that replication was not the sincerest form of flattery for the Dutch American farmhouse and that Embury's advocacy of free interpretation was more rational and respectful. The enduring popularity of the Dutch colonial style testifies to the success of the eighteenth-century Dutch American farmhouse as a design prototype. It also stands as a challenge for historians and museum professionals to produce a more integrated understanding of the relationship between the prototypes and the products.

2009: DUTCH AMERICAN ARCHITECTURE
IN THE TWENTY-FIRST CENTURY

After 400 years of decay, demolition, and development, the only remnants of original Dutch and Dutch American architecture in America are the farmhouses and barns that still dot the landscape from New York's Mohawk River Valley south to Monmouth County, New Jersey. In now urban or suburban areas such as Kings County, these survivors can be hard to find, as they have often been turned to conform to modern block patterns or disfigured by insensitive renovations. The majority of surviving structures remain in private hands, and many are not protected by any type of preservation designation or covenant and have been little studied and documented, if at all.[91]

Moreover, the process of demolition and development continues. While its focus has shifted to the farmlands of central New Jersey, even Brooklyn's few remaining Dutch American farmhouses face ongoing threats. In 2003 the 1791 Van Pelt-Woolsey house was demolished to make way for condominiums, and the Landmarks Preservation Commission required a decade of study before designating the restored Hubbard house in Gravesend as a New York City Landmark in January 2009.[92] The New World Dutch barn has seen a marked increase in interest and appreciation since the publication of John Fitchen's seminal study in 1968. Yet with the decline of agriculture throughout the region, they continue to succumb to disuse and decay, although today they are more likely to disappear as their prized timber-frames are bought for adaptation and reuse as residences or artists' studios.

While preservation continues to be a pressing concern, in assessing the state of Dutch American architecture at the beginning of the twenty-first century, historic interpretation presents the possibilities for the greatest advances in public understanding and appreciation. The popular success of Russell Shorto's recent retelling of the story of New Netherland, *The Island at the Center of the World*, should leave no doubt that there is significant public interest in well-researched history that is presented in a literate and engaging style.[93] Yet too many historic sites, no matter their character or content, have been content with stasis.

There are significant signs of development, however, as Dutch colonial and Dutch American sites across the lower Hudson Valley engage in dynamic interpretive work that seeks to significantly enhance and broaden the public's understanding of the Dutch presence in America. Historic Hudson Valley's reinterpretation of the Philipsburg Manor site in Sleepy Hollow, New York has led the way over the past decade in revolutionizing the understanding of the roles played by people of African descent in the development of agriculture and trade in the colonial period and in the development of Afro-Dutch culture through the seventeenth and eighteenth centuries. With support from the National Endowment for the Humanities, HHV has drawn upon the expanding body of scholarship in colonial and African American history to develop a range of public and educational programs that not only address issues of enslavement and servitude but also demonstrate the major contributions of Africans to agriculture, commerce, and culture in the region. Perhaps most visible is their revival of Pinkster, the Dutch colonial celebration of Pentecost,

Philipsburg Manor's Pinkster Festival.
Historic Hudson Valley, Tarrytown, New York
Image by Bryan Haeffele

The Wyckoff Durling Barn Education Center at the Wyckoff Farmhouse Museum, Brooklyn, Kings County, New York. This rendering shows the siting of the reconstructed barn within the public park adjacent to the Wyckoff farmhouse.
James Dart Architects, New York

a crucial period in the agrarian calendar when enslaved laborers were granted limited freedom of movement and expression as part of the delicate negotiation of the relationship between master and slave. Inspired in part by this work and with NEH support, the Wyckoff Farmhouse Museum in Brooklyn embarked on research to document and interpret the African presence on Kings County's Dutch American farms in 2004. In 2007 the Historic House Trust of New York City expanded upon this project to include a dozen or more of its sites across the city.

The Wyckoff Farmhouse Museum and the Historic House Trust, in partnership with the City of New York Department of Parks and Recreation, has also initiated an ambitious project to reconstruct an early eighteenth-century New World Dutch barn, originally from the Hoagland-Durling farm in Somerset County, New Jersey, at the museum site in Brooklyn.[94] The barn will serve as an educational center and will be the only Dutch barn within the city, thereby restoring one of the most historically significant varieties of Dutch American architecture to the landscape of Kings County, where it was among most distinctive features of the landscape for the first 300 years of European settlement. Equally ambitious is the New Amsterdam History Center project, proposed by Collegiate Church and the New Netherland Institute, which seeks to create a hub for Dutch-related historic, cultural, and business enterprises at the Corbin Building in lower Manhattan on land continually owned by the church since 1724.[95] On a smaller scale but with more immediate hopes for realization is the Metropolitan Museum's installation of the principal chamber of the Daniel Winne house of 1751 from Bethlehem, New York as part of its current renovation of the American Wing, which is anticipated to be completed in 2009.[96] Winne was a tenant farmer on the Rensselaerswyck manor, and the house had been hidden under later additions until 2002. This project will place a definitively Dutch colonial interior with prominent H-bents and jambless hearth at the heart of the Metropolitan's interpretation of colonial American architecture and decorative arts. The museum is also planning interpretive programs exploring the Winne room's relationship to both the Van Rensselaer hall and adjacent box-framed New England spaces.[97] Although this forging of connections across the department's collections is important, one could imagine the opening of the Winne room as an opportunity for the museum to encourage its hundreds of thousands of in-person visitors and millions of online visitors to visit related Dutch colonial and Dutch American sites around the region. No matter how professionally planned and executed, period rooms cannot substitute for the more visceral experience of visiting a complete structure, however imperfect, at the place where its inhabitants lived and died. From larger urban museums to small rural historic sites, the challenge for historians and museum professionals is to move past preservation to interpret Dutch American architecture in historically acute yet dynamic ways that will engage the public in a dialogue about the meanings of the Dutch presence in America.

NOTES

This essay derives from extensive study of secondary sources and six years of direct, hands-on experience in the interpretation of a Dutch American farmhouse as Director of the Wyckoff Farmhouse Museum from 2001 to 2007. Sources are specifically cited throughout, but four have particularly informed my understanding of the Dutch architectural presence in America: David Steven Cohen, *The Dutch-American Farm* (New York and London: New York University Press, 1992); Marc Linder and Lawrence S. Zacharias, *Of Cabbages and Kings County: Agriculture and the Formation of Modern Brooklyn* (Iowa City: University of Iowa Press, 1999); Kevin L. Stayton, *Dutch by Design: Tradition and Change in Two Historic Brooklyn Houses* (New York: The Brooklyn Museum in association with Phaidon Universe, 1990); and John R. Stevens, *Dutch Vernacular Architecture in North America, 1640-1830* (West Hurley, N.Y.: The Society for the Preservation of Hudson Valley Vernacular Architecture, 2005). I benefited greatly from the expertise of my colleagues at the Wyckoff Farmhouse Museum and the Historic House Trust of New York City, and conversations and firsthand exploration of Dutch American sites across the region with the following colleagues and friends have greatly informed this essay: Lucie Chin, Wyckoff Farmhouse Museum Docent; Laura Chmielewski, former Director of the Dyckman Farmhouse Museum and Assistant Professor of History, SUNY Purchase; Laura Carpenter, Director of the Van Cortlandt House Museum; Susan De Vries, Director of the Dyckman Farmhouse Museum; Joseph Ditta, Librarian, New-York Historical Society; Alyssa Loorya and Christopher Ricciardi, archaeologists; Felicia Mayro, Director of the St. Mark's Historic Landmark Fund; Kenneth F. Snodgrass, Executive Director of Locust Grove, and Michael V. Susi, my partner in life and in architectural exploration.

1. Franklin Delano Roosevelt, "Introduction," Rosalie Fellows Bailey, *Pre-Revolutionary Dutch Houses and Families in Northern New Jersey and Southern New York* (1936; reprint, New York: Dover, 1968).

2. David Steven Cohen, *The Dutch-American Farm* (New York and London: New York

University Press, 1992), 41; Paul R. Huey, "Archeological Evidence of Dutch Wooden Cellars and Perishable Wooden Structures at Seventeenth- and Eighteenth-Century Sites in the Upper Hudson Valley," in Roderic H. Blackburn and Nancy A. Kelley, eds., *New World Dutch Studies: Dutch Arts and Culture in Colonial America, 1609-1776* (Albany, N.Y.: Albany Institute of History and Art, 1987), 13-36.

3. Named for the Florentine villa where it was uncovered early in the twentieth century, the "Castello Plan" is a contemporary copy of Jacques Cortelyou's lost original survey plan of 1660 and documents 342 structures within the settlement's walls. Cortelyou was the official surveyor general of New Netherland under Pieter Stuyvesant. Paul E. Cohen and Robert T. Augustyn, *Manhattan in Maps, 1527-1995* (New York: Rizzoli International, 1997), 38-41.

4. Shortly after Stuyvesant's arrival in 1647 he appointed three surveyors to address irregularities in the layout of lots and intrusions into public thoroughfares. Cohen and Augustyn, *Manhattan in Maps,* 39-40.

5. As quoted in Cohen and Augustyn, *Manhattan in Maps,* 40.

6. The most comprehensive compilation of this graphic and documentary evidence is assembled in Roderic H. Blackburn and Ruth Piwonka, *In Remembrance of Patria* (New York: The Publishing Center for Cultural Resources for the Albany Institute of History and Art, 1988), 90-116.

7. The most closely observed representation of late seventeenth-century Manhattan is that drawn by Jasper Danckaerts around 1680, now in the collection of the Brooklyn Historical Society. See Blackburn and Piwonka, *In Remembrance of Patria,* 96-97. The town hall or *stadt huys* was a large, two-story brick tavern built under Director-General Kieft, which was co-opted for civic use with the granting of limited self-government in 1653. It served this function until 1699. In 1979-81 its site was the focus of the first large-scale archaeological excavation undertaken in Manhattan; see Anne-Marie Cantwell and Diana diZerega Wall, *Unearthing Gotham: The Archaeology of New York City* (New Haven and London: Yale University Press, 2001), 6-30.

8. Blackburn and Piwonka, *In Remembrance of Patria,* 93.

9. Janny Venema, *Beverwijck: A Dutch Village on the American Frontier, 1652-1664* (Albany: State University of New York Press, 2003), 50-56.

10. The company's earliest settlement directives mandated locations with water access. Cohen, *The Dutch-American Farm,* 67.

11. For a recent, well-illustrated overview of extant Dutch farmhouses and barns across these regions, including many open to the public, see Roderic H. Blackburn, *Dutch Colonial Homes in America,* photography by Geoffrey Gross and Susan Piatt, introduction by Harrison Frederick Meeske (New York: Rizzoli, 2002).

12. Cohen analyzes the Netherlands as containing five distinct culture areas that cut across northern Europe and posits that New Netherland's diverse settlers brought three distinct "farmhouse arrangements" with them, which were constructed in established settlement patterns also imported from the Netherlands. He traces the isolated farm pattern to the *kampen* of the reclaimed wastelands in what is now the province of Overijssel. He argues that patroonship landholding patterns originated in the *opstrekkende landerijen* or "elongated holdings," also used in reclaimed lands, particularly along the west coast of the Netherlands. His model for Dutch village landholding patterns, as at Flatbush, is the *brinkdorpen* of the Drenthe plateau. Cohen, *The Dutch-American Farm,* 28-29, 44, 68-73.

13. Cohen, *The Dutch-American Farm,* 40.

14. Cohen cites evidence for the combination house-barn form having been built around

THEO VANDERWELDEN

Portrait of Adriaen Van Der Donck

Ink on paper, 6 x 6 in.

Museum of the City of New York, Gift of the artist, 32.243.1

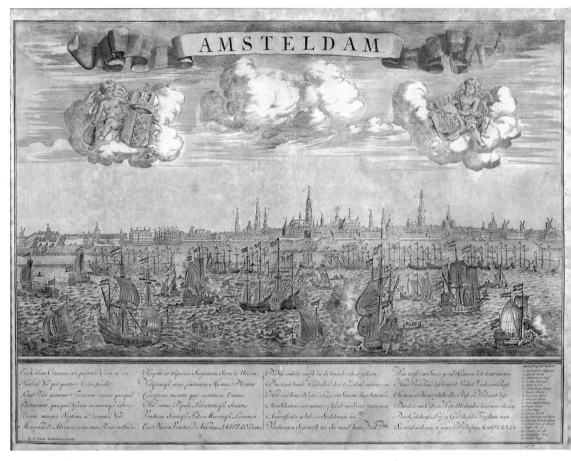

JACOB LOOTS

View of Amsterdam, c. 1660

Ink on paper with hand coloring, 20 x 28 in.

Van Cortlandt House Museum/The National Society
of Colonial Dames in the State of New York

ALBERT BIERSTADT, American, 1830–1902

Discovery of the Hudson River, 1874

Oil on canvas, 72 x 122 in.

U.S. House of Representatives, Washington, D.C.

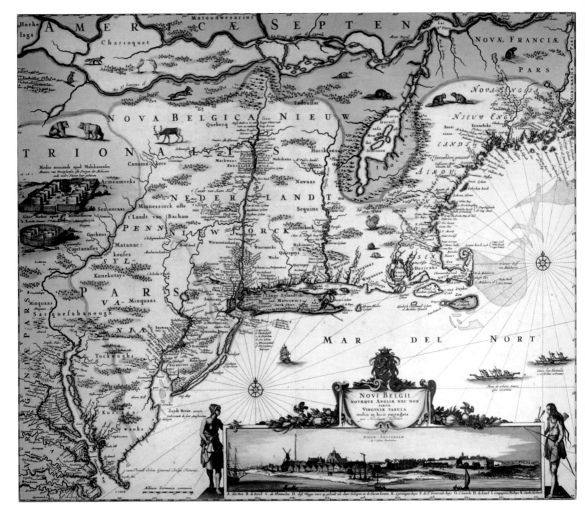

JUSTUS DANCKERTS

Novi Belgii Novaeque Angliae (New Netherland and New England),
mid-1650s

Hand colored engraving, 21¾ x 18¼ in.

Bert Twaalthoven Collection of Antiquarian Maps of New Amsterdam,
New York and New England, Fordham University Library, Bronx, New York

LAMBERT DOOMER (baptized 1624, died 1700)

Couple with a Globe, 1658

Oil on panel, 28½ x 21½ in.

Robert Hull Fleming Museum, University of Vermont, Gift of Prentis Cobb Hale Jr., 1957.21.1

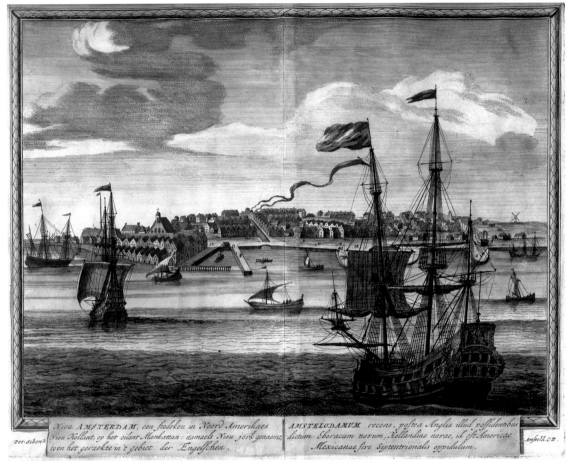

Nieu AMSTERDAM, een stedeken in Noord Amerikaes
Nieu Hollant, op het eilant Mankattan: namaels Nieu Jork genaemt,
toen het geraekte in 't gebiet der Engelschen.

AMSTELODAMUM recens, postea Anglis illud possidentibus
dictum Eboracum novum, Hollandiae novae, id est Americae
Mexicanae sive Septentrionalis oppidulum.

Pet: schenk

Amsteld. C:P.

PETER SCHENK

Nieu Amsterdam, een stedeken in Noord Amerikaes Nieu Hollant,
op het eilant Mankattan: Namaels Nieu Jork genaemt, toen het geraekte
in't gebiet der Engelschen, 1702

Hand-colored engraving, 10¼ x 7¾ in.

Bert Twaalthoven Collection of Antiquarian Maps of New Amsterdam,

New York and New England, Fordham University Library, Bronx, New York

UNIDENTIFIED ARTIST

Proposed Coat-of-Arms for New Amsterdam, New Netherlands, c. 1630

Watercolor, gouache and red chalk on paper with mat, 14 x 18 in.

The New-York Historical Society, Gift of Carson Brevoort, 1885.5

EDWARD MORAN (1829–1901)

Henrik Hudson Entering New York Harbor, September 11, 1609, 1892

Oil on canvas, 36 x 53 in.

Berkshire Museum, Pittsfield, Massachusetts, Gift of Zena Crane

JOHN OGILBY; ARNOLDUS MONTANUS

Novi Belgii, quod nunc Novi Jorck vocatur,

Novaeque Anglia et partis Virginiae, 1671

Hand-colored engraving, 14½ x 11 in.

Bert Twaalthoven Collection of Antiquarian Maps of New Amsterdam,

New York and New England, Fordham University Library, Bronx, New York

E. ROSCOE SHRADER, *"Henry Hudson got many furs from the Indians and made them all his friends,"* in *The Men Who Found America,* by Frederick Winthrop Hutchinson

(New York: Barse & Hopkins, Publishers, © E. Stern & Co., Inc., 1909), opp. p. 120. Hudson River Museum

The title of this romanticized scene is indicative of the narrow historical perspective of many late nineteenth- and early twentieth-century artists and writers.

All-purpose room, Jan Martense Schenck House (or Schenck-Crooke House),
Flatlands, Brooklyn, c. 1675–1676, given to the Brooklyn Museum, 1950.
Brooklyn Museum, 50.192mn, Gift of Atlantic and Pacific Company

JAMES EIGHTS (1798–1882)
North Pearl Street—West Side from Maiden Lane North
as it was in 1814, c. 1850
Watercolor on paper, 9½ x 12¾ in.
Albany Institute of History & Art, Bequest of Ledyard Cogswell, Jr., 1954.59.67

Within the map detail:

GOIAME.

R. Umbra

Zaire
Lacus.

Agag.

190.

o Noava

NIGRITARVM
REGIO.

45   50   55

JOAN BLAEU (1596–1673)

Congo, cartouche detail from page: *West and West Africa,* in [Atlas maior]
*Geographia, quae est Cosmographia Blaviana . . . Amstelaedami, Labore et
sumptibus Ioannis Blaev,* 1662–1665 [v. 1, 1665].

Hand-colored engraving, image: 15½ x 22¾ in; sheet: 22 x 25½ in.

Tracy W. McGregor Library of American History, Special Collections, University of
Virginia Library (A1662 .B53)

WILLIAM RICKARBY MILLER (1818–1893)
Old Dutch Church at Sleepy Hollow, 1861

Oil on canvas, 15½ x 22⅛ in.

Historic Hudson Valley, Tarrytown, New York, SS79.3 a-b

Attributed to JOHN HEATEN, active 1730–1745

Van Bergen Overmantel, c. 1733

Oil on wood, 15¼ x 74¾ in.

Fenimore Art Museum, Cooperstown, New York, Museum Purchase

JOHN WOLLASTON (active 1736–1775)
Mary Philipse, c. 1750
Oil on canvas, 36⅞ x 32¾ in.
Historic Hudson Valley, Tarrytown, New York,
Gift of Mrs. John D. Rockefeller, Jr., PM.80.2 a-b

JOHN WOLLASTON (active 1736–1775)
Margaret Philipse, c. 1750
Oil on canvas, 36 x 31⅜ in.
Historic Hudson Valley, Tarrytown, New York,
Gift of Mrs. John D. Rockefeller, Jr., PM.80.1 a-b

MATHYS NAIVEU (1647–1721)
Dominie Johannes Weeckstein (1638–1687,
minister of Old Dutch Reformed Church, Kingston), 1674

Oil on canvas, 27¼ x 22¾ in.

The New-York Historical Society, 1950.6

Kast, American, c. 1700

Pine, tulipwood, paint, 67¼ x 61⅜ x 19⅛ in.

Van Cortlandt House Museum/The National Society of Colonial Dames

in the State of New York, Gift of Miss Acrygg

Lidded Jars, Dutch, c. 1770
Tin-glazed earthenware, brass
H approximately 14 in.
Van Cortlandt House Museum/The National Society of
Colonial Dames in the State of New York

Wall clock with nautical scenes, Dutch, late eighteenth century
Wood, glass, metal, w 14¼ in.
Van Cortlandt House Museum/ The National Society of Colonial Dames in the State of New York, Gift of Mrs. Elihu Chauncey

QUIRINGH GERRITSZ. VAN BREKELENKAM
(born after 1622–died 1669 or after)
Old Man Scaling Fish, early 1660s
Oil on panel, 16½ x 21½ in.
Van Cortlandt House Museum/The National Society
of Colonial Dames in the State of New York

Bowl decorated with a dragon, Chinese
(excavated at Philipsburg Manor), 1620-1680
Porcelain, approx. 3 x 5 in.
Historic Hudson Valley, Tarrytown, New York

Chocolate cups
and saucers (two),
Chinese, c. 1750
Porcelain, Cup: 2⅝ x 3¼ in.,
Saucer: 1 x 5¼ in.
Historic Hudson Valley,
Tarrytown, New York,
PM.2003.4, .5, .8, .9

HOWARD PYLE (1853–1911)   TIFFANY STUDIOS (1902–1938)

Anthony Van Corlear, The Trumpeter of New Amsterdam, c. 1896

Leaded glass, mounted on wood light box, 64½ x 39½ in.

Delaware Art Museum, F. V. du Pont Acquisition Fund, 1984 DAM 1984-28

Albany and at Achter Col in New Jersey and for the latter type at both Rensselaerswyck and southwestern Long Island. Cohen, *The Dutch-American Farm,* 41-43.

15. Cohen, *The Dutch-American Farm,* 44-45.

16. Cohen, *The Dutch-American Farm,* 47. Zink sees the persistence of brick-sheathed farmhouses in the upper Hudson as also representing the influence Albany's urban Dutch townhouses in the surrounding countryside. Clifford W. Zink, "Dutch Framed Houses in New York and New Jersey," *Winterthur Portfolio* 22, no. 4 (Winter 1987): 266.

17. For instance, the lower Hudson region, including the Bronx, Manhattan, and Staten Island, constituted a transitional zone where stone-walled and wooden-clad types mixed.

18. Zink, "Dutch Framed Houses in New York and New Jersey," 265, 269; Kevin L. Stayton, *Dutch by Design: Tradition and Change in Two Historic Brooklyn Houses* (New York: The Brooklyn Museum in association with Phaidon Universe, 1990), 16; Cohen, *The Dutch-American Farm,* 6, 38-39.

19. Blackburn and Piwonka, *In Remembrance of Patria,* 108-114.

20. This evolution of wall infill materials is visible at the Wyckoff house, where sections of the wall structure are revealed in the seventeenth- and early nineteenth-century portions of the house.

21. Cohen, *The Dutch-American Farm,* 48.

22. The authoritative source for the history and analysis of the New World Dutch barn remains John Fitchen's seminal study, *The New World Dutch Barn: The Evolution, Forms, and Structure of a Disappearing Icon,* 2nd ed., edited and with new material by Gregory D. Huber (Syracuse, N.Y.: Syracuse University Press, 2001). Piet Van Wijk traces the New World Dutch barn to the *hallehuis* farmhouse type built in many areas of the Netherlands through the seventeenth century. Piet Van Wijk, "Form and Function in the Netherlands' Agricultural Architecture," in Blackburn and Kelley, *New World Dutch Studies,* 161-170.

23. John R. Stevens, *Dutch Vernacular Architecture in North America, 1640-1830* (West Hurley, N.Y.: The Society for the Preservation of Hudson Valley Vernacular Architecture, 2005).

24. Indeed, Helen Wilkinson Reynolds commented on the evidence of frequent alterations and additions based on her field survey of upper and mid-Hudson Valley houses conducted in 1925. Helen Wilkinson Reynolds, *Dutch Houses in the Hudson Valley Before 1776* (1929; reprint, New York: Dover, 1965), 7.

25. Cohen refers to Firth Fabend's assertion of the twin-door house as responding to Dutch practices of multiple-generation cohabitation and to its postrevolutionary resurgence in northern New Jersey and Rockland County as a self-consciously nostalgic gesture. He suggests, rather, that it may be a German tradition related to a desire to preserve the traditional central chimney floor plan while adhering to the dictates of symmetry imposed by eighteenth-century neoclassicism. Cohen, *The Dutch-American Farm,* 54-55.

26. As noted above, Cohen proposes a German association for this practice. In their recent publications, Stevens and Blackburn both refer to proposed Huguenot origins for it. However, Stevens debunks this and suggests that it was an indigenous development, and Blackburn sees the functional needs as determinate, including the better regulation of heat. Stevens, *Dutch Vernacular Architecture in North America, 1640-1830,* 20 and Roderic H. Blackburn, "Evolution of the Dutch House" in Blackburn and Kelley, *New World Dutch Studies,* 50.

27. The latter is perhaps the most visible of these early central chimney plans but represents a curatorial decision—made when the house was first relocated to the museum in 1964—to forsake the existing gable-end placement of the two fireplaces for a central chim-

ney with back-to-back jambless hearths based on evidence in the H-bents and framing of the roof. Stayton, *Dutch by Design*, 17-19. Cohen disagrees with the interpretation of this evidence. Cohen, *The Dutch-American Farm*, 52.

28. Cohen, *The Dutch-American Farm*, 38.

29. The presence of built-in Dutch style bed boxes would suggest some differentiation of use. However, the most prominent example of this is again the restored Jan Martense Schenck house, where Stayton himself notes that this was done "almost entirely on the basis of speculation alone, for there is no undisputed physical evidence of the use of such beds in American houses." Stayton, *Dutch by Design*, 34. Stevens's review of this evidence is inconclusive. Stevens, *Dutch Vernacular Architecture in North America, 1640-1830*, 97-98.

30. These houses generally did not have extended eaves, occasioning the provision of gutters or the later additions of porches in many cases, such as at the Leendert Bronck house.

31. There is also evidence that lofts served as slave quarters on the Dutch American farm. In particular, compelling evidence of African habitation of one of the loft spaces at the Hendrick I. Lott house in Brooklyn was found during archaeological investigation of the site in the 1990s. Personal communication with archaeologists Alyssa Loorya and Christopher Ricciardi.

32. See Stayton, *Dutch by Design*, 29-33 and Joseph Manca, "Erasing the Dutch: The Critical Reception of Hudson Valley Dutch Architecture, 1670-1840," in *Going Dutch: The Dutch Presence in America, 1609-2009*, ed. Joyce D. Goodfriend, Benjamin Schmidt, and Annette Stott (Leiden & Boston: Brill, 2008), 64-65.

33. On contemporary commentary on the darkness of Dutch houses see Manca, "Erasing the Dutch," 71.

34. For a discussion of Dutch casement types transplanted to New Netherland, see Stevens, *Dutch Vernacular Architecture in North America, 1640-1830*, 69-74 and 314-315 and Blackburn, *Dutch Colonial Homes in America*, 84-85.

35. As Cohen asserts: "After the English conquest, the Dutch urban merchants in America were quick to acculturate to English ways. It was in the agricultural traditions in the countryside that a distinct Dutch-American regional culture developed and survived through the end of the nineteenth century." Cohen, *The Dutch-American Farm*, 4-5.

36. Manca, "Erasing the Dutch," 75.

37. Serving as the national capital from 1789 to 1790, this new structure became Federal Hall, and was itself demolished in 1812 when the current City Hall was completed.

38. The fire of September 20-21, 1776 consumed approximately 500 structures in the southwestern portion of the old Dutch city. David McCullough, *1776* (New York: Simon & Schuster, 2005), 221-222. The fires of 1835 and 1845 burned over the remaining portions of what had been New Amsterdam. Eric Homberger, *The Historical Atlas of New York City* (New York: Henry Holt, 2005), 78-79. If an account of 1828 is to be believed, however, only five Dutch buildings remained by that date. John F. Watson, "Olden Time Researches and Reminiscences of New York City," as cited in Annette Stott, "Inventing Memory: Picturing New Netherland in the Nineteenth Century," in Joyce D. Goodfriend, ed., *Revisiting New Netherland: Perspectives on Early Dutch America* (Leiden: Brill, 2005), 13.

39. For the attack of words that accompanied the assault of fashion and fire on Manhattan's Dutch architectural heritage see Manca, "Erasing the Dutch," 66-71. In 1853 a writer in *Putnam's Magazine* recalled the demolition of the stepped-gabled house dated 1698 visible on the east side of Broad Street in George Holland's drawing (Figure 10) with glee: "We never waste a tear over the death of an old Fogy, especially a Dutch one, which … must be admitted to surpass in desolation all the other varieties of conservatism extant." As quoted

in John A. Kouwenhoven, *Columbia Historical Portrait of New York* (New York: Doubleday, 1953), 138.

40. Blackburn and Piwonka, *In Remembrance of Patria,* 108-114.

41. Blackburn sees the persistence of traditional architectural forms as integral to a medievally derived belief system: "The colonial Dutch knew of a more modern life style and elegant homes being advanced by the leading English and Anglo/Dutch citizens of their colony beginning in the late seventeenth century, but that did not ease their conscience into accepting these new ways. Change meant much more than changing houses and dress, it meant giving up a way of life long sanctioned by their God-fearing belief in their ancestral ways." Blackburn, "Evolution of the Dutch House," 31.

42. Fitchen, *The New World Dutch Barn,* xxxii; Cohen, *The Dutch-American Farm,* 89.

43. "I call this regional culture Dutch-American rather than Anglo-Dutch, because it was structurally different from either Dutch culture or English culture. It was a regional subculture of American culture." Cohen, *The Dutch-American Farm,* 5. Stayton agrees: "this style was not really Dutch, but neither was it fully English … it represented a peculiar Dutch-American form." Stayton, *Dutch by Design,* 61. Stayton notes the importance of cross-cultural ties, both forced and voluntary, during the Revolutionary War in these processes of assimilation and adaptation, particularly in the immediate vicinity of New York City, which was under British occupation for the duration of the war. Stayton, *Dutch by Design,* 68.

44. Stayton, *Dutch by Design,* 60-62. Blackburn refers to this as the "New Style" farmhouse. Blackburn, "Evolution of the Dutch House," 49-51. Stevens refers to all the houses within what he terms the Dutch vernacular tradition as Dutch American. Stevens, *Dutch Vernacular Architecture in North America, 1640-1830,* 15-25.

45. Blackburn sees the New Style house as representing the acceptance of broader English socioeconomic values: "Like houses, farmers and traders were evolving, finally accepting the English style of living, including its emphasis on wealth tied to class consciousness." Blackburn, "Evolution of the Dutch House," 51. An integral part of this adaptation of English attitudes was the institutionalization of African enslavement across the Dutch-American agrarian region. Although the Dutch West India Company imported African slave laborers starting in 1626, recent studies assert that the region transitioned from a society with slaves to a slave society under English colonial rule. See: Leslie M. Harris, *In the Shadow of Slavery: African Americans in New York City, 1626-1863* (Chicago & London: University of Chicago Press, 2003), pp. 26-30; Craig Steven Wilder, *Covenant with Color: Race and Social Power in Brooklyn* (New York: Columbia University Press, 2001), Chapters 1 and 2; and Ira Berlin and Leslie M. Harris, eds., "Uncovering, Discovering, and Recovering: Digging in New York's Slave Past Beyond the African Burial Ground," in *Slavery in New York* (New York & London: The New Press for the New-York Historical Society, 2005), pp. 10-11. The marked increase in slave labor on Dutch American farms, such as that of Abraham Wyckoff in Flatlands, New York, was a significant factor in the improving standard of living for farm families. See Sean Sawyer, "Slavery and Servitude at the Pieter Claesen Wyckoff House," in Berlin and Harris, eds., pp. 54-55.

46. Blackburn, "Evolution of the Dutch House," 49.

47. Blackburn, "Evolution of the Dutch House," 51.

48. On the English origins of the gambrel, see Blackburn, "Evolution of the Dutch House," 32-33; Cohen, *The Dutch-American Farm,* 33; and Stayton, *Dutch by Design,* 61. Stevens's investigations indicate early eighteenth-century use of the gambrel in Dutch cultural contexts but also in cases where other forms of Anglicization were present. Stevens, *Dutch Vernacular Architecture in North America, 1640-1830,* 56-57.

49. See Blackburn, "Evolution of the Dutch House," 46 and Cohen, *The Dutch-American Farm*, 35-36. It seems that in some instances the extended eaves on earlier houses were given a slight upward curve, creating a "kick" or "spring" eave, as in the Daniel De Klerck house of 1700 in Tappan, Rockland County, New York or the Voorlezer house of the 1690s on Staten Island. However, in the latter case, as well as several other well-known examples—for instance, the Minne Schenck house of c. 1730 at Old Bethpage Village—the spring eaves are restored features.

50. Zink notes that that this combination of gambrel and sprung eave "became the twentieth-century symbol for Dutch-colonial houses." Zink, "Dutch Framed Houses in New York and New Jersey," 291.

51. Stevens, *Dutch Vernacular Architecture in North America, 1640-1830*, 73.

52. Stevens, *Dutch Vernacular Architecture in North America, 1640-1830*, 92-95.

53. Tiles imported in the eighteenth century were manufactured in either the Netherlands or England, although in the Dutch style. Charlotte Wilcoxen, "Ceramics of the Albany Dutch, 1650-1750," in Blackburn and Piwonka, *In Remembrance of Patria*, 151-152.

54. See W. Barksdale Maynard, "'Best, Lowliest Style!' The Early-Nineteenth-Century Rediscovery of American Colonial Architecture," *The Journal of the Society of Architectural Historians* 59, no. 3 (Sept. 2000): 349.

55. Stayton, *Dutch by Design*, 62-65. The Dutch Reformed Church did more than any other element of society to preserve the Dutch language in America. The first English-language service was preached in New York City only in 1763, and in rural areas Dutch-language services continued well into the nineteenth century. Stayton, *Dutch by Design*, 65.

56. See Manca, "Erasing the Dutch," 72-75.

57. The former point is briefly argued by Goodfriend, Schmidt, and Stott in their introduction to the recent volume of essays on the Dutch presence in America. Joyce D. Goodfriend, Benjamin Schmidt, and Annette Stott, "Holland in America," in *Going Dutch: The Dutch Presence in America, 1609-2009* (Leiden and Boston: Brill, 2008), 1-26. Regarding the latter point, see Elisabeth Paling Funk, "Netherlands' Popular Culture in the Knickerbocker Works of Washington Irving," in Blackburn and Kelley, *New World Dutch Studies*, 83-93; and Stott, "Inventing Memory," 15-23.

58. Scott began his literary life by collecting and publishing folk ballads of the borders region and later played an important role in the creation of the image and mythology of the Scottish highlander. See Hugh Trevor-Roper, "The Invention of Tradition: The Highland Tradition of Scotland," in *The Invention of Tradition*, ed. Eric Hobsbawm and Terence Ranger (Cambridge and New York: Cambridge University Press, 1989), 15-42; for Irving's account of his seminal visit with Scott at Abbotsford in 1817 see Washington Irving, "Abbotsford," in *Works*, new edition, 1859, Vol. IX: *The Crayon Miscellany* reprinted in Michael Charlesworth, ed., *The Gothic Revival, 1720-1870: Literary Sources and Documents*, Vol. II, "Living the Gothic Revival" (The Banks, Mountfield, East Suxssex, UK: Helm Information, 2002), 353-390.

59. On the architectural and social history of Sunnyside see Kathleen Eagen Johnson, *Washington Irving's Sunnyside* (Historic Hudson Valley Press, 1995). For the broader context of Irving's accomplishment at Sunnyside, see Roger Panetta, "Westchester, the American Suburb: A New Narrative," in *Westchester: The American Suburb*, ed. Roger Panetta (New York: Fordham University Press, 2006), 13-15.

60. Irving claimed one of the Sunnyside weathervanes had come from the Stadt Huys, although it had been demolished over a century earlier, while the other did indeed come from one of Albany's grander homes, that of Johannes Beekman on North Pearl Street, where it can be seen in James Eights's view. See Blackburn and Piwonka, *In Remembrance*

of Patria, 108, fig. 64. With the addition of the Spanish-inspired tower to the house in 1847, Irving expanded the site's references from the literary to the autobiographical, considering that he had served as the U.S. Minister to Spain from 1842 to 1846.

61. For a discussion of Downing's praise for the associational qualities of Sunnyside in *A Treatise on the Theory and Practice of Landscape Gardening* (1841) and for the relationship between Downing, Paulding, and Irving's literary and architectural efforts, see Adam Sweeting, *Reading Houses and Building Books: Andrew Jackson Downing and the Architecture of Popular Antebellum Literature, 1835-1855* (Hanover, N.H.: University of New England Press, 1996), 88-89 and 133-139.

62. See Manca, "Erasing the Dutch," 84 and Maynard, "'Best, Lowliest Style!'" 352.

63. Stevens presents a diagrammatic chronology of the house's evolution in plan and elevation. Stevens, *Dutch Vernacular Architecture in North America, 1640-1830,* 195. Zink's article includes Henk Zantkuyl's diagram of an early seventeenth-century nave and single-aisle house type that strongly resembles the hypothetical appearance of the earliest form of the Wyckoff house. Zink, "Dutch Framed Houses in New York and New Jersey," 277, fig. 14.

64. In the later nineteenth century the Schenck house was popularly known as "Pirate Captain Schenck's Homestead," and Stayton cites an 1891 newspaper article claiming that Captain Schenck had been a Satanic pirate-sorcerer. Stayton, *Dutch by Design,* 22.

65. Other surviving contemporary examples of this roof form can be found on the Stoothoff-Baxter-Kouwenhoven house at 1640 East 48th Street, built in 1811, and the Hubbard house at 2138 McDonald Avenue, built in the 1830s.

66. Dutch-sponsored early settlement families had migrated westward from their first or second generation, first to New Jersey, Pennsylvania, and western New York and then northwest and beyond. Further research is merited on the effect of this extensive migration on vernacular architecture in these regions.

67. Stayton details and illustrates such mid- to late nineteenth-century modifications in the two Schenck houses. Stayton, *Dutch by Design,* 20-25, 28, 44, 85-89, 99, 106-107, 114. For older farmhouses, the end of slavery in New York in 1827 and in New Jersey in 1846 gave added incentive to convert loft space for family use. The Alice Austen house in Staten Island is a prime example of a Dutch farmhouse that was converted into a Victorian-era cottage, complete with gingerbread ornamentation. John Austen, a Manhattan businessman, purchased the late seventeenth-century farmhouse in 1844 as a summer retreat. *Historic Houses in New York City Parks* (New York: Historic House Trust of New York City, 2003), 54-55.

68. See Marc Linder and Lawrence S. Zacharias, *Of Cabbages and Kings County: Agriculture and the Formation of Modern Brooklyn* (Iowa City: University of Iowa Press, 1999), Chapter 3.

69. Linder and Zacharias, *Of Cabbages and Kings County,* 91, 208-209.

70. Annette Stott notes that American architects made little distinction between the ethnic and national architectures of the lowlands, in her words, "labeling all of it Dutch or Flemish with equal ease." When distinctions were made it was often to associate Dutch architecture with vernacular and rural forms and Flemish with urban high style structures. Annette Stott, *Holland Mania: The Unknown Dutch Period in American Art and Culture* (Woodstock, N.Y.: The Overlook Press, 1998), 152-153.

71. Born into a Quaker family in Des Moines, Iowa, Tubby attended Brooklyn Friends School and the Polytechnic Institute of Brooklyn, graduating in 1875. His works included an addition to the Pratt Institute, five Carnegie libraries that are now part of the Brooklyn Public Library network, the 83rd Precinct House in Bushwick, the Nassau County Courthouse, and a library and hospital in Greenwich, Connecticut, where he lived most of his life. "W. B. Tubby, Architect Here for 61 Years," *The New York Times,* May 10, 1944, 19.

72. The Wallabout Market was demolished to make way for the wartime expansion of the Navy Yard in 1941.

73. Gibson was English-born and educated and had a wide practice in the city, including the Century and New York Yacht clubhouses. "Robert W. Gibson, Architect, Dies," *The New York Times*, August 19, 1927, 17.

74. "New New Amsterdam," *Harper's Weekly* 38, no. 1948 (April 21, 1894): 370.

75. Robert A. M. Stern, Thomas Mellins, and David Fishman, *New York 1880: Architecture and Urbanism in the Gilded Age* (New York: The Monacelli Press, 1999), 766; "Recent Brickwork in American Cities—New York," *The Brickbuilder* 3, no. 6 (June 1894): 106-108; "New New Amsterdam," *Harper's Weekly* 38, no. 1948 (April 21, 1894): 370. All of these structures were replaced by larger apartment buildings within thirty years.

76. "New New Amsterdam," *Harper's Weekly* 38, no. 1948 (April 21, 1894): 370.

77. Not least among these was Henry Janeway Hardenbergh's (1847-1918) John Wolfe Building on Maiden Lane and William Street of 1895, which resurrected Dutch gables fifteen stories over lower Manhattan. Robert A.M. Stern, Gregory Gilmartin, and John Massengale, *New York 1900: Metropolitan Architecture and Urbanism 1890-1915* (New York: Rizzoli, 1983), 159.

78. For instance, a commercial structure inspired by Haarlem's Vleeshal graces the west end of Nassau Street in Princeton, New Jersey and a complex of stepped-gabled commercial and residential structures bridges Flatbush Avenue just south of King's Highway in Brooklyn. Myron Teller, an academically trained architect based in Kingston, New York, designed a variety of Dutch revival structures there. William B. Rhoads, *Kingston, New York: The Architectural Guide* (Hensonville, N.Y.: Black Dome Press, 2003), 181-184.

79. Stott, *Holland Mania,* 94-95.

80. The Roosevelt family descended from Claes Martenszen Van Rosenvelt, who arrived in New Netherland around 1650. For a detailed study of FDR's interest in and advocacy of Dutch American architecture, including his forays into the design of Dutch colonial–inspired structures on his Hyde Park estate and in Dutchess County more broadly, see William B. Rhoads, "Franklin Delano Roosevelt and Dutch Colonial Architecture," *New York History* (October 1978), 430-464.

81. Reynolds, *Dutch Houses in the Hudson Valley Before 1776,* and Bailey, *Pre-Revolutionary Dutch Houses and Families.*

82. Among the observations made by Reynolds and Bailey that have been sustained by subsequent scholarship are: the diverse origins of New Netherland's settlers and their development of distinct architectural prototypes; the modest character of the majority of Dutch colonial households; the complexity of individual building chronologies due to frequent renovations and additions; the importance of landholding patterns on house evolution; and the adoption and adaptation of English features from c. 1750.

83. There appear to be no studies analyzing the percentage of houses documented by Reynolds and Bailey still extant, but in subregion studies, such as Dilliard's on Kings County, it is possible to say that less than a third remain. Maud Esther Dilliard, *Old Dutch Houses of Brooklyn* (New York: R. R. Smith, 1945).

84. Prior to World War I Embury developed a reputation as a country house designer; however, he is most well known for his numerous public works across New York City as a consulting architect under Robert Moses. Hilary Ballon and Kenneth T. Jackson, *Robert Moses and the Modern City: The Transformation of New York* (New York and London: Norton, 2007), passim. For a brief summary of the significance of Embury and another promoter of the Dutch colonial, Isaac Henry Green (1858-1937), see Peter Kaufman, "The Dutch Colonial Architectural Revival on Long Island," in *Long Island Studies: Evoking a Sense of Place*, ed. Joann P. Krieg (Interlaken, N.Y.: Heart of the Lakes Publishing, 1988), 54-60.

85. Aymar Embury, *The Dutch Colonial House; Its Origin, Design, Modern Plan, and Construction; Illustrated with Photographs of Old Examples and American Adaptations of the Style, by Aymar Embury* (New York: McBride, Nast, 1913), ii.

86. Embury, *The Dutch Colonial House*, 61. He did advocate chaste, Dutch-influenced interiors, particularly dining rooms. Annette Stott has analyzed the development of an American taste for Dutch-inspired dining rooms as referencing broader cultural stereotypes of the morally pure and clean Dutch that infused American ideas of Dutchness during the period 1880-1910. Annette Stott, "The Dutch Dining Room in Turn-of-the-Century America," *Winterthur Portfolio* 37, no. 4 (Winter 2002): 229-231.

87. Embury, *The Dutch Colonial House*, 20.

88. Embury, *The Dutch Colonial House*, 11.

89. The ad copy reads in part: "Of particular interest are the fireplace log-bin, accessible from porch and living room; the conversion of the stone root cellar to a garage; the zone-control interior lighting; and the magnificently complete 'futura' kitchen." Stayton, *Dutch by Design*, 23.

90. The caption also notes that "the plan, of course, was made to conform with the needs of today" and "two of the three chimneys lost their function but not their form in the process of metamorphosis." *Pencil Points* (April 1937):202.

91. Since Reynolds's and Bailey's publications, no comprehensive survey of surviving Dutch and Dutch American structures has been completed.

92. Three of the surviving thirteen houses are not designated landmarks.

93. Russell Shorto, *The Island at the Center of the World* (New York: Random House, 2005). Shorto's book was a *New York Times* extended list best-seller and a featured selection of the Book of the Month Club, the History Book Club, and the Quality Paperback Book Club. It also was a winner of the New York City Book Award and the Washington Irving Prize for contribution to New York history. It was a *New York Times* Notable Book for 2004 and was chosen by the New York Public Library as one of its twenty-five outstanding books for the year.

94. Wyckoffs married into the Durling family in the mid-nineteenth century, and thus there is also a significant Wyckoff family connection between the barn and the Wyckoff farmhouse.

95. In March 2006 the building and its site were taken by eminent domain for the Metropolitan Transportation Authority as part of the new Fulton Street Transit Center; however, it will be preserved and available for use. Lisa Chamberlain, "Pressing a Claim for Dutch History," *The New York Times*, March 29, 2006.

96. Peter M. Kenny, "A New York Dutch Interior for the American Wing," *The Magazine Antiques* 169, no. 1 (January 2006).

97. Kenny, "A New York Dutch Interior," 185.

5

The Reformed Dutch Church and the Persistence of Dutchness in New York and New Jersey

FIRTH HARING FABEND

In 1833, the author and diplomat Washington Irving and his friend Martin Van Buren, the future President of the United States, traveled together down the Hudson Valley from Albany to Jersey City. In his journal Irving referred to this excursion as his "Esopus Dutch Tour," Esopus being the old name for Kingston, New York, when New York and New Jersey comprised the main part of the Dutch colony of New Netherland. As they made their way south, the two men marveled at the Dutchness of the towns and villages and their inhabitants. The farmers lived in what Irving described as "very neat Dutch stone houses," and in today's Piermont, New York, Irving noticed the "number of Dutch waggons returning from the [Hudson River] Landing." The "people talk Dutch," he wrote, and the women wore Dutch sunbonnets, the men quaint calico pantaloons. Later, Irving spoke of the "curious old Dutch places and Dutch families" he had visited, including, in Jersey City, the home of the Van Hornes, a "primitive [Dutch] family living in patriarchal style in the largest and best house of the place."[1]

This was more than two hundred years after the first Dutch settlers had arrived on Manhattan Island in the 1620s, yet in the area where they and their descendants had made their homes, Dutchness had persisted for seven or eight generations. Irving well noticed this, of course, but he did not ask why it was so. Although he was a close observer of his Dutch American neighbors in Westchester County, of whom he was fond, in all his writings about them he almost never mentions the cultural institution that defined and centered them: the Reformed Dutch Church. (Since 1867, this denomination has been known as the Reformed Church in America and still flourishes.)

This essay will explore the persistence of Dutchness in the Hudson and other river valleys of New York and New Jersey and attribute it to two factors: the devotion of the Dutch settlers and their descendants to the Reformed Dutch Church, and the intellectual link they made between the Dutch church and the Dutch language. It will end by discussing the social forces that resulted in the eventual Americanization of this ethnic group and its church.

The Brinkerhoff-Christie-Paulison Homestead,
Ridgefield Park, New Jersey, built c. 1685, as it appeared c. 1930
Photograph
Library of Congress, Prints & Photographs Division, HABS, Washington, D.C.,
Reproduction number HABS NJ, 2-RIDGP, 1-, Survey number HABS NJ-160

Dutch Reformed Church, Albany, New York
Exterior View, 1650s (destroyed 1806)
Engraving after a drawing by Philip Hooker, 1806,
14½ x 15⅞ in.

Interior of Dutch Reformed Church, Albany,
New York. In Joel Munsell, *Collections of the History
of Albany,* vol. 2. http://www.archive.org

The pulpit is located in the center, as typical in
early Dutch Reformed churches along the Hudson.

Reformed Protestant Dutch Church, view from
the northwest, Kingston, Ulster County, New York
(organized 1659), as it appeared 1680–1752.
Stone exterior with colored glass windows bearing
Dutch coats of arms.
Services were in Dutch until 1809.
Image published in Mary Isabella Forsyth, "The
Burning of Kingston, New York," *The Journal of
American History*, Fall, 1913, as reproduced at:
www.newrivernotes.com/ny/kingston4

Reformed Protestant Dutch Church,
view from west, Main Street, Kingston,
Ulster County, New York, organized 1659.
Photograph of third rebuilding, designed by
Minard Lafever, completed 1852.
Photograph, 1934
Library of Congress, Prints & Photographs
Division, HABS, Washington, D.C.,
Reproduction number HABS NY, 56-KING, 25-1.
Survey number NY5573

BACKGROUND

At the beginning of settlement, in 1624, the Dutch West India Company, which
almost literally owned the colony, instructed that the first settlers be provided
with a *ziekentrooster* or "comforter of the sick," whose duties, besides consol-
ing the ill, dying, and bereaved, included conducting Sunday worship services
by reading from the Bible, reading set prayers and sermons from a book by
a Reformed theologian, and leading the singing. Even though he was not
ordained, this official was also given permission to baptize and to perform
marriages, and it was he who catechized the children of the community. In
1628, an ordained minister arrived, and the denomination marks this as the
year of its official establishment in the New World. Worship services were conducted in a loft over a horse millnear the fort at the tip of Manhattan Island
until 1633, when a barnlike structure and parsonage were erected. In 1642,
inside the fort, a proper church replaced the "barn."[2]

Despite a shortage of ministers willing to endure frontier living conditions and poor pay, the history of the Reformed Church in New Netherland for the fifty years from 1624 until the second and final English takeover of the colony in 1674 was one of slow but steady growth, partly because, though "freedom of the conscience" was ensured for all, only the Reformed religion could be practiced in public. Even Lutherans, whose doctrine differed from Reformed doctrine in important ways, had to seek out the Reformed Church for the baptism of their children and other religious offices.

After 1664, the English permitted the Dutch under the terms of the Articles of Capitulation to continue practicing their religion unmolested. But they also decreed that other religions be ensured public worship. This meant that, for the first time in America, the Reformed Church had to endure competition for the churchgoing populace, which now had numerous religious choices to sample. Still, many continued to choose the Dutch church. It was during the 1690s and early 1700s, for instance, that the Reverend Guiliam Bertholf helped eleven different Reformed Dutch congregations to organize, four in New York (in Harlem Village, Port Richmond, Tappan, and Sleepy Hollow) and seven in New Jersey (in today's Passaic, Dumont, Tenafly, Belleville, Oakland, Pompton Plains, and Somerville).

Called the "itinerating apostle" of New Jersey, Bertholf served these churches on a supply basis, his home church being in Hackensack. His ministry attests to the desire of the people for religion and to his desire to serve them, not an easy task. To get to Sleepy Hollow, where in 1697 he was engaged to conduct the worship and perform the sacraments of baptism and Holy Communion four times a year, "the very learned and pious" Bertholf, accompanied by Tappan resident Teunis Van Houten, first had to travel by horseback to Tappan on a Friday and spend the night. Then, when the tide and the wind were right, Van Houten, who was paid by the Sleepy Hollow Church for his services, ferried the minister across the three-mile-wide Hudson River, where the two men procured fresh horses and proceeded to their destination, spending Saturday night and possibly Sunday night as well. Van Houten then conveyed Bertholf by the same method back to Hackensack.[3]

A chronic shortage of ministers and problems with their salaries continued into the last decades of the seventeenth century and the early eighteenth century, as did various political quandaries, especially the Glorious Revolution in England in 1688 and its repercussions in New York, Leisler's Rebellion, which divided both clergy and congregations into two vitriolic camps, those supporting Jacob Leisler and those opposed to him.

The Reformed Church's main difficulties were the desire of progressives for an assembly of their own, independent of the supervision of the Amsterdam

The Reformed Church of Tappan, New York, first church building, 1716. Pen and ink reconstruction based on Archibald Robertson's watercolor of 1778 and a view of the church drawn from an old seal, from David Cole, *History of Rockland County* (New York: 1884). In Richard J. Koke, *Accomplice in Treason: Joshua Hett Smith and the Arnold Conspiracy* (The New-York Historical Society, 1973).

Old Dutch Church, Tarrytown, Hudson River, late nineteenth century. Stereograph, 3^{7}/$_{16}$ x 6^{15}/$_{16}$ in. Hudson River Museum, Gift of Dr. Edward Friedman, 89.1.1116

Original church built in 1685 by Frederick Philipse on the Manor of Philipsburgh. Inscription on bell: If God Be For Us Who Can Be Against Us?

MATHYS NAIVEU (1647–1721)
Dominie Johannes Weeckstein (1638–1687, minister of
Old Dutch Reformed Church, Kingston), 1674
Oil on canvas, 27¼ x 22¾ in.
The New-York Historical Society, 1950.6

Old Queen's, designed by John McComb, 1809
Queens College (Rutgers University), New Brunswick, New Jersey.
In 1825 Queen's was renamed Rutgers College in honor of Colonel Henry Rutgers,
a Dutch American philanthropist, legislator, and hero of the American Revolution.
www.libraries.rutgers.edu

Classis; for a seminary to educate ministers on American soil; and for the ability to ordain ministers in America. Conservatives resisted these changes toward "independency," preferring to maintain the American churches' subordination to the Classis. The forces supporting change, called the *Coetus*, and those resisting it, called the *Conferentie,* contended in hostile and bitter fashion for decades. Not until after the American Revolution, during which, predictably, the *Coetus* members were patriots and the *Conferentie* members took the Tory side, did the two factions resolved their differences. Queen's College, the long-desired seminary, received its charter in 1766, but did not really get under way until after the war. (Queen's formed the nucleus of today's Rutgers University.)

THE LANGUAGE QUESTION

A fourth difficulty, the language question, is particularly pertinent to the persistence of Dutch culture in the river valleys of New York and New Jersey. By the first quarter of the eighteenth century, the younger generations of Dutch Americans were speaking English, at least in public, and they wanted English-speaking preachers. But the opposition to dispensing with Dutch preaching was intense; in New York City, this goal was not finally achieved until 1764, a hundred years after the original English takeover of New Netherland, when the Reverend Archibald Laidlie was called to the pulpit of the New Dutch Church on Nassau Street. Five years later, a second minister, the Reverend John Henry Livingston, also brought English preaching to the Dutch church in New York, and the use of Dutch was gradually phased out. In rural parishes in some Dutch-settled enclaves in the Hudson and Hackensack valleys, however, it continued into the nineteenth century.

As the author of one history of Westchester County put it, "the old Dutch settlers were very tenacious of the Dutch language. If there was anything in the world that was sacred, it was that. They talked and wrote and read and sang in Dutch. The minister preached in Dutch, and the church records down at least to April 28, 1777, were all kept in Dutch." The writer goes on to relate how, in 1785, a minister of the Old Dutch Church at Sleepy Hollow baptized a child in English, which "raised a small tempest in the congregation. The people were deeply offended, and they hardly considered the child baptized at all."[4]

The fierce resistance to giving up Dutch preaching had to do with a famous conference, the so-called Synod of Dort, held in the Dutch city of Dordrecht in the years 1618-1619. Attended by representatives of the European branches of the Reformed Church that had emerged from the Calvinistic wing of the Reformation, the synod was convened to settle a bitter controversy within the Dutch church concerning five points of disputed doctrine. The views set forth at Dordrecht have been called ever since the Canons of Dort.[5]

After a marathon 154 sessions in which the delegates resolved the disputed doctrines (not to the satisfaction of all), the Dutch delegates remained for another 25 sessions to agree upon, in what are called the Post-Acta, the translation first into Latin and then into Dutch of the canons and the various creeds, and to agree upon the polity, standards, and church order of the Reformed Dutch Church for all time, they hoped. In the Post-Acta, they also settled such matters as church ordinances, church visitation, the call to ministerial office, adult baptism, festival days, hymns, discipline, Sabbath observance, standards of schoolmasters, visitation of the sick, ministers' salaries, and more. But perhaps the decision with the most far-reaching effect was to translate the Bible for the first time into the Dutch language. This undertaking was published in 1637 and is known as the *Staten-Bijbel* in Dutch, or the States (i.e., official) Bible.

FRANÇOIS or FRANS SCHILLEMANS (born c. 1575, active c. 1620)
The Opening of the National Synod at Dordrecht, the Netherlands, November 13, 1618
Engraving
Rijksmuseum, Amsterdam, the Netherlands, inv.nr. RP-P-OB-77.278
http://www.rijksmuseum.nl.assetimage.jsp?id=RP-P-OB-77.278

This engraving shows the great hall of the Arquebusiers Targets with synod
participants and spectators. The print is accompanied by a verse by Jacob Cats from
1619, entitled "Ghedicht, The Gedenck weather sensible National Synod held in
Dordrecht, Anno 1618."

The influence of the States Bible on the history of the Reformed Church cannot be underestimated. Like the five Canons of Dort, the Dutch translation of the Bible quickly took on a sacred quality: the language of both was considered hallowed, godly, and inviolable, and this attitude remained firm for two hundred years. This explains why in 1837 Reformed churchgoers of a conservative bent still believed it was a profanation to hear prayers, preaching, holy scripture, creeds, confessions, and/or the Heidelberg Catechism (the church's main teaching tool) in any language other than the "good old Dutch of their Fatherland." The final word on God's Word had been received at Dort and translated into Dutch, and for the orthodox two centuries later, it was in Dutch that the Word must go on being received.[6]

However, this tenacious tradition of linguistic inviolability continued to emphasize the denomination's "foreign" image, clearly unsuited to the times. Since the 1820s, the progressives within the church's leadership had acknowledged that in the competition for members the Dutch church was in danger of falling by the wayside because the public perceived it as somehow "from abroad."

To compensate, the leaders devised a three-pronged strategy to alter the church's image. In the field of education, the Reformed Dutch Church now embraced the new concept of the Sunday school to educate children in the faith. It embarked upon its first venture into cooperative efforts with other denominations in the ecumenical American Sunday School Union. And it raised an endowment to ensure the stability of Queen's College in New Brunswick, New Jersey, soon to become Rutgers College, and a separate but linked institution, the New Brunswick Theological Seminary.

In a second direction, also in the 1820s, the Reformed Church began to urge its clergy and laity to take part in the moral reform and benevolence movements that were attempting to address the problems of immigration, ignorance, poverty, and crime. An unstated motive behind this was that it would expose the denomination to the wider society's modernizing influences and developments.

Third, as other denominations were doing, the Reformed Dutch Church began in the 1820s to publish a weekly newspaper, the *Christian Intelligencer*, whose stated purposes were to advance the missionary cause abroad and at home, to shape the minds and morals of church members, to defend the canons and decrees of the Synod of Dort, and to acquaint the rising generation with the glories of the Netherlands in its Golden Age and the Dutch people's heroic struggles against Catholic Spain.

Title page from Charlotte Elizabeth,
The Bible The Best Book (New York:
American Tract Society, n.d.).
Michigan State University Libraries,
http://digital.lib.msu.edu/projects/ssb/
display.cfm?TitleID=534&Format=jpg

This last effort, ironically, had an unintended effect, for in introducing readers to forgotten or never-known chapters in Dutch political, cultural, and religious history, the paper actually rekindled Dutchness in New York and New Jersey. Still, the *Intelligencer* also functioned as an important agent of cultural transmission, modernization, and eventually Americanization, by reprinting substantial amounts of political and diplomatic world news as well as news of the riveting religious revivals of the nineteenth century. As it dispersed this information into even very isolated rural hamlets in the Dutch culture areas, it enfolded them in a larger community and acquainted them with the evangelical activity that was convulsing America—and the urgent question of the day: What must I do to be saved?

THE SECOND GREAT AWAKENING

The Second Great Awakening in America, usually dated as beginning in the 1790s, got its second wind in 1824 with the appearance on the religious stage of the Reverend Charles Grandison Finney (1792-1875). With his flamboyant "New Measures" to achieve spiritual salvation, Finney, an ordained Presbyterian minister, ushered in what has been called the evangelical age or the age of revivals, a time of unified effort in the transcendent cause of saving Americans and America for Christ.

These New Measures included "protracted meetings," lasting from dawn to dusk for days, or every evening for weeks on end, in which the conversion of sinners was the main objective. Finney's adherents went from door to door personally inviting the unconverted to these meetings, which were

Bradbury's *Golden Shower of S.S. Melodies: A New Collection of Hymns and Tunes for the Sabbath School* Michigan State University Libraries, http://digital.lib.msu.edu/projects/ssb/display.cfm?TitleID=605&Format=jpg

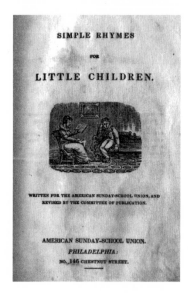

Title page of *Simple Rhymes for Little Children* (Philadelphia: American Sunday-School Union, 1835). Michigan State University Libraries, http://digital.lib.msu.edu/projects/ssb/display.fm?TitleID=558&Format=jpg

characterized by group prayer, wrenching personal testimonies of sin and salvation, and the anxious bench, where the worried unconverted were invited to hear prayers on their behalf. Other innovations were the inquiry room, where the anxious sinner could go to ask his or her faith questions; the card of intention, in which the sinner proclaimed a desire to be saved; lay participation in worship; extemporaneous prayer; public prayer meetings; and women speaking and even praying in public. Combined with Finney's exciting preaching, these methods brought the gathered to peaks of emotion, with converted and unconverted alike sobbing, fainting, and rolling on the floor.

An anonymous Reformed layman, "A. B.," in a letter to the *Intelligencer* titled "Colored Camp Meeting at Tarrytown," described in shocked tones the goings-on at an encampment at Beekman Woods, a square-mile grove of oaks, maples, and hickories forming a canopy over 60 or 70 "snowy white" tents, a preacher's platform, and seats for as many as 3,000. Here, among their cooking fires, groups of men and women gathered in close and animated conversation or worship. A chorus of a hundred voices sang, the infirm and aged looked on from their tent doors, youth strolled around or wandered off into the woods. In front of the platform was the "ring," where the leaders sang hymns and began to pray. Before long, the writer was startled to hear the "shrieks and shouts of some forty or fifty shrill and penetrating voices . . . [all] speaking at once . . . [shouting] 'Amen,' 'glory,' 'Hosannah,' 'bless God,' 'Jesus,' . . . mingled in one loud yell. . . . There was leaping, and dancing, and clapping of hands, and frightful contortions of body and limbs."[7]

In the center of this "wild and frenzied multitude," A. B. witnessed females, prostrate, rolling upon the ground in religious ferment. The excitement went on for hours, increasing as the time approached for the preaching to begin. When it did, through the preacher's whole discourse "he was cheered with the loud shouts of those within the ring [whom] . . . he raised to such a fury of excitement that they all sprung onto their feet, and danced, and jumped, and whirled, and screamed, and clapped, as if pandemonium itself had been on earth." The stunned observer left the meeting asking himself what such exhibitions had to do with the holy name of religion.

He was not alone. The Reformed Dutch leadership disapproved mightily of Finney's revival methods, for two reasons. They violated the denomination's venerable tradition, established at Dort, that all things be "done decently and in good order," and they introduced sensitive theological issues concerning the efficacy of human agency in the salvation of one's soul. Reformed theology held that one could and should work to achieve spiritual growth through faithful worship, the sacraments, prayer, meditation, Bible study, and good works. But it also held that in the end, the human will, by circuslike shouting and emoting, could not influence the workings of the divine will. Only God's grace could save one's soul.

Yet the New Measures presented a dilemma for the Reformed Church, because it was clear that people liked religious revivals and wanted them. If the denomination was to grow and flourish, the progressives among its leadership understood that they must resolve this, and they did so by distinguishing between the genuine revival and the spurious revival. The former, which was acceptable, originated in the hearts of the congregation, rather than being brought to them by outside forces. The genuine revival involved no exciting hoopla. The "Holy Spirit is in charge, and a deep solemnity pervades," as one minister put it, and most important, the changes wrought were lasting. In contrast, human agents scheduled the spurious revival and managed, advertised, and promoted it. Marked by "excitement, disorder, confusion, and wild, misguided zeal," its effects were short lived.[8]

Although conservatives were not wholly happy with this semantic solution, it was evidently successful, for the denomination grew. In 1850 the number of Reformed churches in New York and New Jersey had increased from 181 in 1826 to 281, the number of pastors from 104 to 185, and the number of congregants from 47,491 to 110,275. In 1870, there were 382 churches, 425 pastors, and 168,826 congregants. English preaching was now very widely accepted, except for special services when Dutch was used for nostalgic reasons.[9]

AMERICANIZATION PROCEEDS; DUTCHNESS PERSISTS

In its determination to join the American mainstream, the leadership of the Reformed Church increasingly embraced the era's popular moral-reform efforts and the "benevolent empire," the movements within Protestantism that became a mighty force for social change in the nineteenth century. Participation in these activities led to close association of huge numbers of Reformed clergy and laity with Americans from all other Protestant denominations, and Reformed Church leaders, both clerical and lay, sat on the boards of all the leading organizations of the day, including missionary societies, the ASSU, the American Tract Society, and the American Bible Society. They constituted a potent force in the modernizing process that was afoot.

For fifty years in the nineteenth century, the annual Anniversary Week in May was an integral and beloved part of religious culture. A kind of evangelical convention circuit, the meetings of this Protestant Holy Week, as it was called, were attended by thousands of churchgoers of all denominations who poured from every direction into the famous Broadway Tabernacle in Manhattan to hear the annual reports of the era's do-gooding organizations. For many within the Reformed Church, which continued to feel its outsider status, participation in Anniversary Week was unifying and integrating, allowing them to join in harmonious fellow feeling with their counterparts in other denominations—a de-ethnicizing experience that rendered labels and sectarian distinctions superfluous, at least for the time being.

Change happened slowly. The Reformed Dutch Church grew and prospered in the nineteenth century and modernized along with the larger culture, but it still retained its foreign aura, as did the particular Dutch American culture that had evolved out of it. A professor from the University of Utrecht visiting New York and New Jersey in 1850 commented that it was a pleasure to find the old Dutch ancestral customs maintained. In fact, so Dutchlike were manners and material culture in New York and New Jersey that more than one traveler to the Netherlands seemed to think the cultural influence flowed eastward: "Customs take deep root in Holland," one wrote, "and one sees many usages which are known [in New Jersey]. Amsterdam and Rotterdam are all over like

Chatham Street [in Manhattan] and South Street [in Philadelphia] combined." In 1855, an American in Amsterdam was reminded of the step-gabled Albany of his childhood and of the "old Dutch ladies, in high caps." He reminisced about having gone to school in one of those Dutch houses, and of the "Dutch dame" who taught him to read.[10]

This phenomenon of cultural retention was the result of factors central to the Dutch culture areas in New York and New Jersey. As we have seen, the Dutch language was one, although it was diminishing with each passing decade. The devotion to the Calvinism of the Synod of Dort was another. A third was the active promotion by Rutgers College and the New Brunswick Theological Seminary of an image of themselves as imbued with Dutch roots and a specific Dutch orientation. These two linked institutions encouraged members of the Reformed Church to view them with a "home feeling," where a sense of a distinctive history, a special peoplehood, and a reliable grounding in Reformed doctrine reigned, and no one questioned it. Send your sons to us, they suggested, and you can be sure they will hear, see, and learn nothing detrimental to traditional Reformed ideals.

Yet another factor was the marrying patterns of the Reformed clergy, which indeed formed a "band of brethren," as one clergyman termed it, with hundreds of Reformed ministers in the nineteenth century, along with hundreds of their female relatives, related by ties of blood and marriage. In 1840, there were 164 active clergymen in the Reformed Church in New York and New Jersey; in 1850, 285; and in 1860, 381, and almost all had a close relative or in-law in the profession. The Reverend John Scudder of the famous Scudder family fathered nine children who lived to maturity. Of his seven sons, all seven were ordained; ten grandsons were ordained, and five granddaughters went into the mission field. The laity followed their example, with countless numbers "marrying Dutch," i.e., marrying within the denomination.[11]

SOCIAL LIFE

Finally, one other important factor contributed to the endurance of Dutch ways and customs in the Hudson and other river valleys of New York and New Jersey: the settlement patterns of the seventeenth and eighteenth centuries, when New Netherland families united by ties of blood, marriage, friendship, religion, and even political leanings established neighborhoods of family farms that served as home to generations of their offspring. In such communities, by the third generation members of the same and related families—all lived near one another along adjacent roads, and all interacted year in and year out at home, at work, at church, at school, and in a constant face-to-face social life.

Inspired by an ideal of family coherence and based on a tradition long associated with the Netherlands—equal treatment of heirs—this settlement pattern provided family members with economic as well as affective and moral advantages. In other words, kinship networks were a dependable source of economic support and also of emotional and moral support, as well as cooperation, loyalty, advice and counsel, and sharing in times of need and joy. Such a settlement model also dictated a pool of marriage partners and patterns of social interaction that were inseparable from church life. From Albany to the Hackensack Valley to the Raritan Valley, in Manhattan, in Brooklyn—in every geographical area where the Reformed Church flourished—its members' intensely active social lives centered around church-related activities, often as many as six or eight a week, and a diverse range of purely secular activities, such as parties. In 1842, one young lady in the Raritan Valley recorded attending 196 parties, or nearly four per week, and she distinguished these from the more informal "visits," also very numerous, that did not require a written invitation.[12]

The most valid observation one can make about social life in the Dutch culture areas of New York and New Jersey in the nineteenth century is that Reformed people mingled almost exclusively with others reared in the same religious culture as themselves. The result, of course, was that shared values, beliefs, mores, expectations, and customs were constantly buttressed in the multitudinous and intertwining activities of church year and secular year. Daily contacts with the same people allowed Dutchness to reinvigorate itself.

Besides engaging in Sunday worship, Bible study, and prayer groups, nineteenth-century evangelicals participated in a range of religious activities that are now obsolete: not only the annual anniversary in May but also monthly concerts of prayer, refreshings and seasons of grace, donation days, fast days, days of humiliation and prayer, as well as weddings, funerals, clerical installations and ordinations, and new church dedications. The term "social religion" includes a host of other events with quasi-religious significance: church fairs, strawberry festivals, and Sunday school picnics. For Dutch Americans, commencement at Rutgers and the seminary were important occasions for socializing and renewing bonds of friendship and comity under the rubric of social religion, which covered everything from prayer meetings in private homes followed by refreshments and gossip to Fourth of July ceremonies where stirring sermons were succeeded by elaborate al fresco feasts and what one Reformed minister called a "noisy carnival of rum and gunpowder."[13]

THE BECKONING WORLD

Although the persistence of Dutchness in New York and New Jersey was intimately entwined with the ethnicizing influence of the Reformed Dutch Church, powerful de-ethnicizing, modernizing forces finally conveyed the Dutch and their church into the mainstream of American life. This was brought home at mid-century when a group of strict Dutch Calvinists who had seceded from the national Reformed Church in the Netherlands over theological differences arrived in New York, to a welcoming committee of distinguished American Reformed Dutch clergymen. It did not take the newcomers long to notice that their American brethren were very different from themselves. They worshiped in English, they no longer read the ancient writers in the seventeenth-century Dutch Pietist tradition, they sang hymns rather than solely Psalms, and worse, most of the hymns had been composed by non-Reformed persons. These were departures from Dort, as was the waning attention to the Heidelberg Catechism, all parts of which Reformed ministers were supposed to visit weekly on an annual cycle. Elders did not practice family visitation as strictly as they should, and elders and deacons sat with their families in church, no longer in official pews at the front of the congregation. Funerals and weddings were strangely elaborate and expensive. Christmas was not only celebrated; it was consumerized out of all recognition. And the Sunday school picnic resembled more a raucous harvest festival than a sedate gathering of the pious.

Even Jesus had changed. The Redeemer worshiped by Reformed people in America was now a new and modern "feeling" savior. One Reformed minister assured his listeners, "He is the great nerve-centre to which thrill all sensations which touch us who are his members." His temperament is "finely strung," like ours, and he is as sympathetic with our rheumatism, neuralgia, dyspepsia, inflamed muscles, and pangs of indigestion as a dearest friend. He never laughs at our whims and notions. Because "by his own hand he fashioned our every bone, strung every nerve, grew every eyelash, set every tooth in its sockets," he responds to every physical disorder with sympathy. He is touched by the imperfections of our prayers and kindly overlooks our lack of concentration while praying. Yet "he will pick out the one earnest petition from the rubbish and answer it." He even understands our imperfections of temper, and overlooks our "explosive temperament" and all our bunglings, as long as our intentions are good.[14]

In America, it was clear, the "good old way" was increasingly being replaced by a new way and new customs: the fashions of the religious culture of evangelical America. In embracing revivals, Sunday schools, fund-raising ladies' fairs and bird concerts, choirs and professional singers, the flamboyant anniversaries, the ecumenical benevolent associations, and the custom of closing the church in the summer, Reformed churchgoers, interacting with and relating to the world around them, had seamlessly merged into the mainstream of American Protestantism and become almost unrecognizable as fellow Reformed to

LYMAN COBB JR.
Residence of E.S.F. Arnold M.D.—Reformed Church—
Residence of Benjamin Mason, Esq., 1868
Print, mounted, 4½ x 7 in.
Hudson River Museum, 76.0.224

the strict and stern seceders from the Netherlands. The ethnicizing forces of Dort and doctrine, national history and national pride, seminary and college, and daily face-to-face socializing had proved less potent in the long run than the de-ethnicizing, modernizing forces of the larger culture.

Still, the good old way died hard. As Washington Irving and Martin Van Buren had been surprised by the Dutchness of the Hudson Valley on their way to Jersey City in 1833, so forty years later, in 1873, two travelers touring northern New Jersey had a similar reaction. They described a Reformed Dutch Church they came across in an "outpost of the Dutch country" as a "quaint old stone edifice in a moldy graveyard" and noted that some of the descendants of the early settlers they met spoke "a hideous jargon called Jersey Dutch." In parts of New Jersey and New York, Dutch was used in the Sunday afternoon church services into the 1860s and 1870s. In 1878, a visitor to what he called the "decayed village of Tappan" reported hearing it, and another wrote in 1899 that "hundreds who speak the tongue still live within a five-mile radius" of the Schraalenburgh Reformed Church in today's Dumont, New Jersey.[15]

But even in such Dutch strongholds as Bergen and Rockland counties, change was inevitable. During the Civil War, the Nyack branch of the U.S. Sanitary Commission held a fund-raising fair, one of whose features was an old Dutch kitchen. "Once again, and perhaps for the last time was seen the Dutch oven, the open fire-place, the crane, pot-hooks and trammels; once again did descendants of the Dutch settlers don short gown and petticoat, and busy themselves in cooking an old-fashioned Dutch dinner. When the feast was ready, the company sat around a table, then over two centuries old, loaded with savory viands, talked in the County Dutch patois and sang songs, long forgotten, in the same language." In other words, by the time of the Civil War, Dutchness in the Hudson Valley had become for many only a quaint memory.[16]

In 1854, progressives within the Reformed Dutch Church had proposed that the denomination drop the word "Dutch" from its name and become simply the Reformed Church in America. But this effort was stymied by conservatives who wished to retain the traditional name, believing that the reputation of the Dutch church in this country had "been earned by two centuries of undeviating adherence to the principles of the Reformation" and to "the doctrines and actions of the Synod of Dort." Oblivious to the fact that the church had been evolving slowly for two hundred years right under their noses, this faction had its way for the time being. But at last in 1867 the General Synod voted for the name change. As one young man had put it just the year before, "The Americanization idea should govern in the Church as well as in the State. We are an original people, no more like our Dutch progenitors than a steam-engine is like a windmill."[17]

THE MOTHER OF AMERICA

A naturalized Dutchman, Edward Bok, longtime editor of the *Ladies Home Journal,* was one of those who recognized America's political and cultural debt to the land of the windmill and the centuries-long persistence of Dutchness in the United States. In 1903, he wrote a two-part article for his magazine titled "The Mother of America," in which he listed everything from the invention of movable type to international law, from the office of the attorney general to the public school system, from the Declaration of Independence to the U.S. Constitution as having come to America from the Netherlands—everything, that is, except for the Reformed Dutch Church, whose long-lasting influence over the Dutchness of the culture of New York and New Jersey he seems to have overlooked, as had Washington Irving many years before.

Weather vane or weathercock,
from The Reformed Church of
Tappan, New York, installed by 1788
Iron, 16½ x 21 x ⅛ in.
James Smith Haring IV Collection,
Historical Society of Rockland County,
New City, New York

Probably fashioned in one of Rockland County or Bergen County's eighteenth- and
nineteenth-century iron foundries, the rooster-form weather vane indicated the direction
of the wind for Hudson River sailors, and reminded Tappan's colonists of Peter's denial
of Jesus. Later, from 1835 to 1856, the weather vane symbolized the simpler, vanishing
Dutch Hudson Valley rural life for Washington Irving, who collected and displayed
Dutch American weather vanes at his home, Sunnyside, in Tarrytown.

NOTES

1. Washington Irving Papers (1805-1866), Series III, Journals, New York Public Library,
Room 328, *ZL-310. See also Isabelle K. Savell, "Martin Van Buren and Washington Irving
in Rockland County," *South of the Mountains* (New City, N.Y.: Historical Society of Rockland County) (Oct.-Dec. 1983):3-8; (Jan.-Mar. 1984):12-17.

2. Gerald F. DeJong, *The Dutch Reformed Church in the American Colonies* (Grand Rapids, Mich.: Wm. B. Eeerdmans, 1978), is the best source for the denomination in the eighteenth century.

3. J. Thomas Scharf, *History of Westchester County, New York,* 2 vols. (Philadelphia,
1886), II:291.

4. Ibid., 289, 290.

5. Firth Haring Fabend, "The Synod of Dort and the Persistence of Dutchness in Nineteenth-Century New York and New Jersey," *New York History* 77, no. 3 (July 1996): 273-300.

6. Firth Haring Fabend, *Zion on the Hudson: Dutch New York and New Jersey in the Age
of Revivals* (New Brunswick and London: Rutgers University Press, 2000), 213. Hereafter
Zion. This and the following pages are based on this work, passim.

7. *The Christian Intelligencer*, September 25, 1845. Hereafter *CI.* Quoted in Fabend, *Zion,*
56.

8. Fabend, *Zion,* 49-56.

9. Fabend, *Zion,* Table 5.1, "The Reformed Laity: A Statistical Portrait, 1826-1870," 86.

10. D. Buddingh, *De Kerk, School en Wetenschap in de Vereenigde Staten van Noord-
Amerika,* 2 vols. (Utrecht, 1852), 2:xi; "Blyth in Holland," *CI,* December 20, 1855. Both
quoted in Fabend, *Zion,* 68, 213-214.

Reformed Dutch Church, Fishkill, New York, first building 1725, enlarged 1785–1795;
remains unchanged with its gilded weathercock atop the steeple.
Photograph, 1935
Library of Congress, Prints & Photographs Division, HABS, Washington, D.C.,
Reproduction number HABS NY, 14-FISH, 2-2- Survey number HABS NY-4-202

11. Figures computed from Edward T. Corwin, "The Ministry," *A Manual of the Reformed Church in America, 1628-1902,* 4th ed. (New York, 1902), 235-606. For more, see Fabend, "Pulpit and Pew, A Portrait," in *Zion,* 73-101.

12. Margaret Schenck, Diary, uncatalogued Nevius-Schenck Papers, Special Collections, Alexander Library, Rutgers University.

13. Rev. T. L. Cuyler, *CI,* July 19, 1855.

14. Rev. T. De Witt Talmage, *Around the Tea-table* (Philadelphia, 1875), 414-418.

15. Guy La Turette, *A North Jersey Jaunt* (n.p., 1873), 84-85. Quoted in Fabend, *Zion,* 214.

16. Frank B. Greene, *The History of Rockland County* (New York, 1886), 308.

17. Fabend, *Zion,* 224-225, 228. Quote from Henry S. Gansevoort, Diaries of Catherine Gansevoort, Box 255, Gansevoort-Lansing Collection, New York Public Library.

6

"I could not guess what she intended to do with it."

COLONIAL AMERICAN–DUTCH MATERIAL CULTURE

RUTH PIWONKA

When the Scots-born, university-educated Maryland physician Alexander Hamilton visited New York colony in June 1744, he indulged an instinctive impulse, using material culture to assess what he saw. Between New York City and Albany, contrary winds halted their sloop's progress up the Hudson, and Hamilton and his fellow traveler, Reverend John Milne, English minister at Albany,[2] disembarked on the western shore, below the Highlands opposite the northern end of Westchester County. They stopped at a small log house occupied by the Dutch Stanespring family, a couple in their thirties with seven children who Hamilton deemed quite "wild and rustic." When the children went out to gather blackberries for the travelers, Hamilton pronounced it "the greatest present they could make us." In return the men gave them a handful of copper halfpence. Hamilton fully reported Milne's analysis of the family's material culture, including

> several superfluous things which showed an inclination to finery in these
> poor people; such as a looking-glass with a painted frame, half a dozen
> pewter spoons, and as many plates, old and wore out, but bright and clean,
> a set of stone tea dishes and a teapot. These Mr. M-----ls said were superflu-
> ous, and too splendid for such a cottage, and therefore they ought to be sold
> to buy wool to make yarn; that a little water in a wooden pail might serve
> for a looking-glass, and wooden plates and spoons would be as good for
> use, and when clean would be almost as ornamental. As for the tea equipage
> it was quite unnecessary, but the man's musket, he observed, was a useful a
> piece of furniture as any in the cottage.[3]

This judgmental analysis is to modern readers at once informative and startling. It is perhaps not surprising that a highly educated young Scot would favor wit over considered observation when he wrote an account of his journey for the entertainment of a friend. But the commentary of Reverend Milne, who had been rector at the English church in Albany, is puzzling. He knew and lived within the Dutch culture area. For reasons we can now only guess,

QUIRINGH GERRITSZ. VAN BREKELENKAM (b. after 1622–d. 1669 or after)
Old Man Scaling Fish, early 1660s
Oil on panel, 16½ x 21½ in.
Van Cortlandt House Museum/The National Society of Colonial Dames in the
State of New York

Quiringh Gerritsz. van Brekelenkam is noted for paintings depicting country people
performing various domestic tasks. The room settings he shows often contain valuable
depictions of domestic utensils and tools—earthenware, barrels, and pails. Additionally
they show how people worked—often they are seen sitting down or even squatting on
the floor to prepare vegetables or meats. Like other painters of the period, he shows
kitchen utensils stashed on the floor.

Hamilton obscured Milne's identity by writing his name as "M----ls" or similarly throughout his account. Milne's wife, whom Hamilton met in Albany and
described as "a jolly fat Dutch woman," was Maria van Cortlandt (1680–circa
1750), a daughter of Stephanus van Cortlandt and the widow of Kiliaen van
Rensselaer, a deceased owner of the manor of Rensselaerswyck. If Milne had
pointed out Van Cortlandt properties in Westchester County, Hamilton did
not mention them. His English background surely played into his view of the
rural Dutch household, but knowing that tea and mirrors were broadly common and popular among the Dutch, it would be reasonable to expect Milne to
have a different perspective in this situation. His rigorous judgment of Dutch

material culture is in line with that taken by many who were not part of that cohort. In the broader context of colonial American material culture, the possessions of New York's colonial Dutch population today arouse interest because of their distinctive character.

Colonial Dutch material culture is most clearly expressed in its surviving domestic architecture and artifacts used by people of Dutch origins and heritage in their homes and communities.[4] Steep-roofed houses, large cupboards, and Dutch Bibles come quickly to mind. But these do not constitute a lifestyle. Estate inventories, which listed all possessions of deceased persons as part of the paper documentation related to an estate, can enlarge our knowledge of a household and its contents. Inventories included all "immoveable property" (such as a house or land), "moveable property" (including household furnishings, clothing, livestock, precious metals, and money), and debts owed the deceased as well as debts that needed to be paid. They held particular importance when there were minor and/or orphaned children, for the property might be sold in order to maintain the children or it might be sold and the sale revenue reserved for when they came of age.

Although some differences in law and custom with respect to overall estate administration among different nationalities existed, taking such inventories was customary among Europeans. Thus for colonial New Netherland and New York, inventories from a relatively early date through the revolutionary era have been preserved in some public records and archives and libraries[5] and represent the mix that made up New York's colonial population—Dutch, British, French, and Palatine German households. Later in the colonial era, the inventories reveal a changing and proliferating material culture. However, the surviving archived inventories—probably more than 600—are diverse and inconsistent: some have appraisals, others do not; some give descriptive information regarding furniture or textiles and many more do not. Some inventories leave an impression of diminished circumstances, but in reality may reflect the fact that heirs and relatives received goods from the estate before the inventory was made. Still other inventories leave an impression of genuine poverty. Such variations make systematic analysis difficult, if not impossible.

DUTCH HOUSEHOLDS IN NEW NETHERLAND

Despite inconsistencies and variations, estate inventories still express most fully distinctive lifestyle patterns and reveal people and their economic circumstances in most intimate settings, suggesting how material culture was used.

A good place to begin is with Jonas Bronck, who had settled in lands that would become part of early Westchester, almost immediately after his arrival in June 1639. Bronck, a native of Sweden, had apparently prospered as a seaman-

Seal ring, probably
Dutch, seventeenth
or eighteenth century
Silver, L 1⁷⁄₁₆ in.
Historic Hudson Valley,
Tarrytown, New York,
Gift of Mabel Brady
Garvan, SS.64.2

The flat engraved surface
topping of the ring
suggests that it would
have been used to impress
the family crest on wax,
perhaps next to a family
member's signature.
This example bears the
DePeyster family coat of
arms.

merchant involved in the Baltic trade. He came to sojourn or live in the Netherlands and in 1638 married a Dutch woman, Teuntje Jurriaens. Then Bronck financed a substantial share of the ship *Fire of Troy* in order to bring some laborers, livestock, and goods to New Netherland. Rather than settle on Manhattan, Bronck lived opposite the island in the area that has become the Bronx, a part of Westchester County until 1895.

After Bronck died at his farm, "Emmaus," in April 1643, his widow and a kinsman, Pieter Bronck, listed property belonging to Jonas. The document is among the colony's earliest surviving estate inventories and reveals varied and unexpected cultural richness in a near-wilderness. It also indicates that his five-year-old settlement had been successful.

Bronck's masonry house with a tile roof was included in the inventory.[6] His wardrobe was substantial, with four suits, a doublet, two mantles (one of them old), gloves, and seven shirts. On occasion, he could enhance it with a silver-mounted rapier and his gold signet ring. The furnishings given as his are impressive and appear to surpass those of many householders in New Netherland—thirty-seven pewter plates of several sizes, seven substantial pieces of silver, two mirrors (one framed with ebony and the other with gilt), an extension table, a chest containing porcelain pieces, six little alabaster saucers, eleven pictures large and small, and three beds with six pairs of sheets, four pillows, and four tablecloths with sixteen or seventeen napkins. Three iron pots, three brass kettles, a brass skimmer, and "a lot of old iron" supplied the kitchen. Other specific kitchen and hearth utensils, as well as chairs or stools, are lacking; but such essential household furnishings might have been property belonging to his widow.

Though the livestock and produce of the farm are not strictly material culture, they were counted as important property among Dutch settlers, and Bronck's inventory indicates a relatively large operation—two five-year-old mares, a six-year-old stallion, a two-year-old stallion, five milk cows, and one two-year-old milk cow; additionally, there were an unknown number of hogs running in the woods. His efforts in animal husbandry were paying off, as the operation also boasted a successful breeding program that had yielded two year-old mares, a yearling stallion, three yearling heifers, and four bull calves born in 1643. Oxen are unusual to find on a Dutch farm, where horsepower was preferred; though it is possible Bronck secured them from a New England settlement, it seems more likely that he drew on his own Scandinavian agricultural tradition in supplying his farm with these powerful animals. Crops apparently nearly ready for harvest included six schepels of wheat, sixty-six of rye, three of winter barley, and seven of peas and attest to agricultural development.

The livestock and crops lend substance to the farm buildings and utensils. The ox plow was likely a swing plow and may have been of Scandinavian origin. It was evidently not the typical Dutch plow, which had a colter and wheels and was drawn by horses. The foot plow was likely a two- or three-pronged forked hand tool, leveraged with a human foot—not unlike today's garden fork; however, the mention of "appurtenances" suggests that it had moving parts, and was larger and perhaps manipulated by more than one person. It was possibly more focused than the ox plow in the removal of roots. The harrow had many teeth set in a frame and was dragged through the soil after plowing to further break clods and refine the soil for planting. The hoes, hand tools for breaking soil around the plants and removing weeds, refined cultivation. The scythes and sickles raise further questions: they were evidently not the Flemish scythe or sith used with a mattock typically employed by the Dutch.

Compared with the farm utensils provided by Johannes de la Montagne for his farmer Bout Fransen at the Vredendael farm, across the East River from Jonas Bronck's Emmaus farm, Bronck's stash seems to consist of things he brought with him. Although the inventory may have been imperfectly taken, equipment for separating grain from chaff is absent. That such utensils could have belonged to his wife is possible but seems less likely. Nonetheless his old grain tubs, small brew kettle, large liquid measures, and malt vats attest to grain harvest and beer production.

A churn and three milk tubs relate to dairy production. The five milk cows were a number typical of a household, suggesting that they provided mostly

Dutch, Circle of DAVID TENIERS II (1610–1690)
Men Smoking, c. mid-1600s
Van Cortlandt House Museum/The National Society
of Colonial Dames in the State of New York

Although New Netherland is most noted as a source of beaver and other furs, tobacco
was also much desired by the Dutch in Europe. The Dutch in New Netherland devoted
some effort to cultivating tobacco, but its quality, compared with Virginia tobacco, was
inferior and this commodity never became a major product.

for Bronck's domestic needs; some additional dairy products (milk, butter, and
cream) would likely have been sold or bartered for other goods.

It appears that Bronck had cleared land, harvesting the wood needed to
frame his house or its roof, his barn, and the barracks and tobacco house. The
blockwagen (translated "dray," a heavy, low, usually sideless wagon) is usually
understood to be a sturdy carriage for hauling logs. Of the twenty-three new
axes and four old ones, some must have seen some serious use (on occasion
perhaps even as an aid to removing roots from ground being prepared for
cultivation). The carpenters' axes, adzes, and other tools would have finished
timber to the degree adequate for house carpentry, though boards and smaller
pieces would have been milled at the saw mill on lower Manhattan. The numerous new axes may also have been intended for trade with Indians.

With so much livestock, a good barn and two barracks to hold hay for their
fodder were important. Raising tobacco was another important early endeavor
in New Netherland, for in the Netherlands there was an enormous demand for
this New World product. So the tobacco barn and the hogshead (a standard

tobacco shipping container) round out this farm's products as expressed in material culture.

Bronck's remarkable assortment of household, agricultural, and craftsman's utensils and related property express a high degree of self-sufficiency. The most striking feature of his inventory are the twenty-one books, listed by name. Apart from Bibles, book titles are infrequently given in New Netherland and New York inventories; "a parcel of books" is the usual term. So Bronck's books are quite noticeable, and the inventory takers must have thought so too, for they placed the list at the beginning of the inventory. The books were in diverse languages (Latin, Dutch, German, and Danish); fourteen were Protestant religious works and included both Reformed Calvinist thought and Lutheran. Four Danish works included a history, a child's book, a calendar (probably a type of almanac), and a law book, which would have upended Dutch legal practices. Three books pertaining to navigation were major works: Apianus's astronomical work; Blaeu's famous sea atlas, *Zeespiegel* (1623); and a copy of the relatively new sea atlas and navigational work by J. H. J. van der Ley, who included instruction on a new way of finding exact longitude and latitude. These demonstrate the era's rapid dissemination of geographical knowledge and evoke its impact on sea voyaging. The detailed list in Bronck's inventory is particularly illuminating.[7]

Other inventories and lists of sales and auctions of domestic goods surviving from the New Netherland period are relatively few in number—about forty. These include some "partial inventories" made for special circumstances—such as a claim for a portion of an estate, a list of goods deposited with an associate for safekeeping, or detailed inventories of farming utensils included in farm leases. Most from the 1630s and 1640s seem to pertain primarily to agricultural circumstances in the lower Hudson Valley; those from the 1650s and 1660s mostly relate to people living in and around Beverwyck (modern Albany). So the view of early colonial material culture they offer is limited, but useful. Often the earlier inventories do not include real estate (which would be expected in Dutch inventories), suggesting the deceased lived in rented property or were perhaps employees of the Dutch West India Company who owned little in addition to the their clothing and perhaps some hand tools.[8] Although the extant inventories probably do not fully represent the variety of household goods that many living in the Dutch colony possessed, collectively they express patterns of lifestyle that often include evidence of comfort and even touches of luxury.

After livestock and tools, the most prominent articles found in the inventories are clothing, bedding, and cooking and eating utensils. Textiles hold such a leading place and deserve attention for several reasons. By the seventeenth

Wall clock with nautical scenes, Dutch, late eighteenth century Wood, glass, metal, w 14¼ in. Van Cortlandt House Museum/ The National Society of Colonial Dames in the State of New York, Gift of Mrs. Elihu Chauncey

Maritime scenes in paintings and on decorative arts reflect the strong connection between the Dutch and the sea.

century, the Dutch had gained stature and wealth in both the trade and the manufacture of textiles. These items held a mystique of sorts: they were, so to speak, newly beautiful, and a rich variety was available for the first time to a developing middle class. They were used for clothing that protected the body and brought comfort to sleeping arrangements and further ornamentation to households. Textiles were a significant part—fine felted beaver hats—of the larger reasons that had brought the Dutch to North America. The material wealth that they expressed, evident in many Dutch paintings of the seventeenth century, was not confined to the Netherlands.

Jacob Vernu, an Englishman married to a New Netherland woman and who had died by October 1640, had a high percentage of textiles among his possessions, thirty of forty-three items: twentythree articles of clothing, five pieces of bedding, six napkins, and a pair of curtains. The remaining thirteen items were mostly for the hearth and kitchen (eight items), some livestock (sows and a hog), a box, two pine chests, and a fishing rod.[9]

The 1641 estate of the insolvent Willem Quick list only twenty-seven items, fourteen of which were textiles. Of note in this inventory are several pewter articles—two platters, a cup, two small saucers, and a chamber pot. One wooden bowl is listed, and it is of some note that plates, dishes, and other food service ware was invariably of pewter and not wood. This is a distinct contrast to New England inventories, where wooden food service pieces are widely found. Quick's wife, Anne Medford, described as a "sorrowful widow in a foreign land," was English and may have liked having a wooden bowl at hand. Another exceptional inventory is the 1658 Beverwyck sale of Bastiaen de Winter's property, where eighteen wooden plates changed hands.[10]

Some other lists or partial inventories of goods were made for varying circumstances. In 1642, Jan Willemsen Schut claimed some articles from his brother's estate, which was in Harlem, The Netherlands—a black cloth mantle, a purple coat, a velvet bag, and one bed and pillow.[11] And in 1646, Jan Jansen Wansaer, a ship captain, left valuable goods in New Netherland with Jacob Wolphertson. They included textiles and gold and silver pieces—a large silver chalice, a silver bowl weighing one and a half pounds, a plated coconut with a foot (that is, a mount), a hat band with gold tassels, a gold ring, forty-seven ells of fine and coarse linen in diverse pieces, a bedsheet, a broadcloth sheet, a handkerchief with lace border, a pair of linen drawers, a black hat, a chimney valance, a Spanish cotton petticoat, a small tortoiseshell box, and eleven ells of light canvas. Wolphertsen in effect signed a receipt before witnesses and promised to keep them in good care until Wanaser returned.[12]

Two longer inventories present a fuller impression of the goods and lifestyles of people involved in agriculture and evidently trade and urban affairs.

Not quite three years before Jan Jansen Damen's death in 1651, he had contracted with Jeuriaen Hendricksz to build in Manhattan (in today's Wall Street area) a new house, "60 feet long and on each side a passageway throughout, the frame 24 feet wide." Thus Damen's front room was to be 24 by 24 feet (minus the side aisles) with the attic floor to be "tongue and groove ... and to wainscot the front room all around; two bedsteads, one in the front room and one in the chamber, and a winding stair so that one can go from the cellar to the attic. . . . In the front room a window casing with transom and mullion and also a mantel piece."[13] The remaining 36 feet was a barn for livestock and storage of harvested grains. Combining the dwelling and barn in one structure was typical in New Netherland. Damen and his wife, Ariaentje Cuvilje Vigne, one of the colony's earliest settlers, lived at this site for a short time; their heirs sold it to Oloff Stevense van Cortlandt and Dirck Dey.

Remarkably, Damen's inventory is somewhat room-by-room and begins with the heading "In the large front room," with seven framed pictures on paper, a looking glass, and evidently ornamental brass wreaths. The house seems to have been sparsely furnished, with only two tables and three chairs mentioned, though the seven green chair cushions may imply that other chairs were there as well. Or the encased bedstead may have made up for that deficit with ample bedding—an old single bed and bolster, a double bed and bolster, four pillows, two green blankets, one white woolen blanket, two white linen sheets, and one bolster.

There were in this room also four chests—evidently all locked—that contained an array of clothing, additional bedding, and textiles to be sewn into future garments, in all about sixty different items. Tablecloths and napkins, towels, neckwear, and various stockings, including a pair of Faroe stockings, are some examples. While most of these textiles were linen or plainer woolens, the six men's "printed callico" night caps indicate a remarkable use of an early printed cotton, a new sensation imported to Europe from India. The white bombazine was a durable but rather fine fabric woven from silk and woolen thread. The blankets were wool. Also in the chests were several books, fourteen different kinds of currency, and a cellaret with twelve empty bottles. In a blue chest, fourteen good and bad white linen sheets, sixteen mostly old pillow slips, and a piece of bed ticking three quarters ell long. Also in the front room were carpenter's tools, a wooden inkstand, and various pewter pieces, including a chamber pot.

The entrance hall, so-called in the inventory, contained all evidence of being a well-stocked kitchen alongside a pantry. Although there were five wooden plates, fifteen pewter plates, nine porringers, and nine dishes supplied food service along with twenty-two spoons. Other pewter cups and jugs provided

Spoon rack, New York, 1700–1790
Tulip, poplar, 22 x 8⅞ x 2⅛ in.
Historic Hudson Valley, Tarrytown,
New York, PM.65.588

Spoon racks are a traditional form that
first emerged in New York documents of
the late seventeenth century. They were
carved with rustic, geometric patterns in
high contrast to the rich carving found on
some cradles and other domestic pieces.

Cradle, Dutch, late seventeenth century
Oak, 31¼ x 37¼ x 19 in.
Van Cortlandt House Museum/The National Society of Colonial Dames in the
State of New York, Gift of Mrs. Adam Gordon Norrie

The post and boldly carved-panel construction, and the low hood is a characteristic
of Dutch cradles.

for beverages. For butter there was a churn and also a wooden mold for a decorative shape. Candles, meat, beer, and butter tubs were stored in the cellar.

The attached barn and its loft harvested grain, all manner of tools to keep the agricultural operation in good repair, and further utensils for agriculture including scythes; rope and lines for plows, cows, and horses; and a hay wagon. Evidently in the yard were livestock—horses, cattle, and pigs—along with an old wagon, plows, and harrows, and in the front yard of the house was well with an ironbound bucket. A brewery on the premises was possibly a building separate from the great house and barn. It was well equipped with a brew kettle, vats, tubs, malt storage, and a new vat for draft. In the barn itself were stored two half sacks of hops that had just arrived from the Netherlands.

Damen's inventory lists about 354 items—73 (20 percent) were textiles; the remaining 281 included 15 types of livestock (counted by species and by age), 20 pieces of pewter, 34 items used in food storage and preparation, and 112 items associated with agriculture and farm operation.[14]

Fort Orange and Beverwyck (modern Albany) records contain diverse articles. Various linen pieces surrounding childbirth and apparently infants reveal more about textiles. The 1657 inventory of Kit Davidts's estate included goods of his deceased wife Cornelia Vos; among mostly women's textiles in a great chest were seven swathing cloths, five bibs, five tuckers, five women's handkerchiefs, and two packages of "child's bed linen," at least one of which was wrapped in a square linen cloth. Quite similar goods recur in other women's estate inventories, suggesting that they were saved to be used in the next generation.[15] By the end of the seventeenth century, the "swathing cloths" (sometimes understood as "swaddling clothes") were typically specified as red, a color that would not show the staining typical of infant diapers. The packages of childbed linens seem to refer to linen sheets and perhaps towels that were kept exclusively for a woman during and after childbirth. In the seventeenth century, childbed linen was also separately preserved by English New Yorkers, such as William Richardson, a Quaker who purchased two acres of land on the Bronx River.[16] Richardson's 1692 will bequeaths to Mary Cock "all his last wife's"[17] wearing apparel with childbed linen.[18] That these and infant cloths were preserved, rather than used as regular bedding or household cleaning towels, make clear that special significance was attached to these things.

Besides textiles holding special meaning in family rituals, the Dutch prized cleanliness. English novelist Charlotte Lennox, who was in Albany circa 1738-1740, recorded some of the care and ritual cleaning attending childbirth. The custom was evidently not at all agreeable to the English; the account dramatically highlights strong cultural antipathies. In her novel *Euphemia*, Lennox describes in first-person narrative the experiences of the wife of a British officer garrisoned at Albany circa 1740. This character describes Mr. Neville, who

seizing my arm with dreadful gripe, exclaimed—"Oh! Madam, come in, see what these Dutch devils have done, —they have killed my wife!"

While Mr. Neville continued cursing and raving at the nurse, who being entitled by her age and her wealth to wear a forehead cloth, a distinction which the matrons here are extremely fond of, considered herself as highly affronted by this behavior. I enquired of Fanny, who stood by in great agitation, the meaning of the strange appearances I beheld.

She told me the nurse, as soon as I was retired, had called up the housemaid, and ordered the room to be scoured. "I remonstrated against it in vain," pursed Fanny, weeping, "and said it would kill my lady—that it was not the custom in our country. But finding that I could not prevail, I called my master, who was so shocked at their having wetted the room, which he said would kill his wife with cold, that he kicked down the pail a rage, and set it all afloat as you see."

Lidded Jars, Dutch, c. 1770
Tin-glazed earthenware, brass
H approximately 14 in.
Van Cortlandt House Museum/The National Society of Colonial Dames in the State of New York

Delftware was and has remained a treasured product of Dutch manufacture. By the late eighteenth century, both the form and decorative styles had evolved along with other styles, while the clays used to manufacture them and their blue decoration remained. Pieces like these jars were sometimes collected by Dutch descendants in the late nineteenth and early twentieth centuries.

I ordered a large fire in the room; and collecting all the carpets in the house, laid them one upon another on the floor. Mrs. Neville was anxious only for her child. I opposed very bad arguments to her reasonable fears, but it was absolutely necessary to quiet her mind; as for Mr. Neville, he continued to rail and swear.

"Did you ever hear of such a savage custom?"; said he, "what! Scour the chamber of a lying-in woman?"

"The greatest mischief," I replied, "is likely to happen from the pail of water that was thrown down."

"Aye," said he, "that was unfortunate, to be sure; but it was very natural for me to be in a passion you know, when my wife's life was endangered by that old Dutch woman's absurdity." . . .

Mrs. Neville and the child are perfectly well. She makes an admirable nurse and loses none of her delicacy by doing the duty of a mother. This little stranger has been received with great joy by the father. . . .[19]

Few contemporary accounts of birth or cleanliness are so passionate or so revealing. A few inventories list brushes used for cleaning, and the 1693 New York inventory of Elizabeth Bancker superlatively details a range of brushes and brooms. They are infrequently mentioned in estate inventories, but judging from the reports of cleanliness by contemporary observers and travelers, they had had an important place in colonial Dutch households. Their appearance was illustrated by Jan Luykens.

Between late 1663 and June 1665, Jan Gerritsz van Marcken seemed mired in a tangle of debts he owed and debts due to him. He had been appointed Farmer of the Excise at Beverwyck and Rensselaerswyck in the 1650s. Inventories of his goods were made in December 1663 and a second time in March 1664, after Jan had broken the seal and opened the press and taken some goods from it. The press was taken to the house of Jochem Wesselse for safekeeping. The March 1664 inventory is more detailed and appears to contain many more items than those listed in December 1663. Jan lived for about two decades or more after this inventory was made and was the highest municipal official invited to the funeral of Jeremias van Rensselaer in 1674, so it seems that his financial issues of the early 1660s were straightened out.

While neither room-by-room nor particularly agricultural in nature, van Marcken's inventory is rich in diverse goods—20 pieces of earthenware, some of which would have been the slightly coarse utility red wares while other pieces are clearly delft plates, platters, salt cellars, mugs, or cups. Six paintings and a "great looking glass" decorated his walls, along with a *lepelbort* or spoon rack and an almanac mounted to hang up. Also fixed to a wall was a *kapstock*, "a place to hang cloaks," an article found in some Dutch houses as recently as the late twentieth century. He had *een kolff*, "a golf" or golf club. An ordinance passed at Beverwyck in 1659 prohibiting golf playing in the streets because of damage to windows and risk of personal injury[20] did not quell enthusiasm for this sometimes popular game. He also had a *tric-trac* table—that is, a backgammon board fixed on a table. This game was a forerunner to backgammon as it has come to be known, but then it was popular in taverns and was the cause of an argument that went to court in Kingston. Balancing his sporting life was a *kerck stooff* or "church stove," more commonly called today a "foot stove," a small box of wood or brass pierced to keep airflow fanning the coals in a small earthenware pot inside. These were intended for women to slip under their petticoats when they sat for long services in unheated churches. Few chairs are mentioned, but five chair cushions were counted, and one lone round table (and three tablecloths). Out of 185 items, 69 (37 percent) were textiles—41 of linen (including red and green infant swathing cloths); 28 of wool; 2 specifically silk, and 5 others likely a blend of silk and wool.

Armchair, New York, c. 1790
Maple, rush, 47¼ x 18¼ x 20¼ in.
Van Cortlandt House Museum/The National Society
of Colonial Dames in the State of New York

This chair emulates a style seen in Dutch prints in the
earlier and middle seventeenth century.

Platter with armorial decoration representing the province of Overysel,
Chinese, c. 1720
Porcelain, 2¼ x 15 in.
Historic Hudson Valley, Tarrytown, New York, PM.64.7

This platter is an excellent example of the cross-pollination of different decorative styles,
as European nations developed trade with China. It is possible this piece was created for
a member of the prominent Beekman family, which originally came from Overysel, the
Netherlands. This platter was purchased by Philipse Castle Restoration in 1943 for early
interpretation in Philipsburg Manor period rooms.

DUTCH HOUSEHOLDS UNDER THE ENGLISH

There is a gap in time between the earlier New Netherland inventories of more
prosperous and prominent settlers like Bronck and Damen and those of the
residents who remained after New Netherland became an English colony. Surviving New Netherland inventories do not include such notable persons as
Adriaen van der Donck (whose house was burned), Petrus Stuyvesant (who
died in 1672, well into the English period), or Arent van Curler (died 1667).
And inventories for them do not survive in later colonial New York records.

After the English takeover, the English policy resulted in an unusual balance
of cultures. In Europe, Dutch furniture design, manufacture, and use, derived
from French examples, was a growing influence in the last half of the seven-

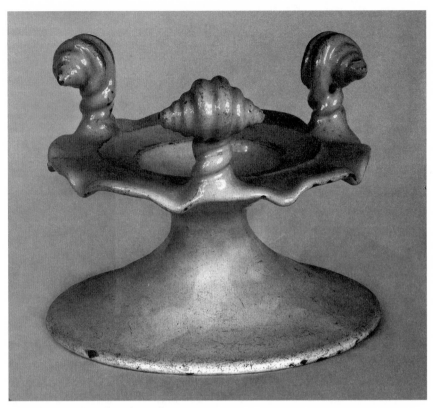

Salt cellar, Dutch, early eighteenth century
Tin-glazed earthenware, 8 x 10 in.
Van Cortlandt House Museum/The National Society
of Colonial Dames in the State of New York

This highly ornamental ceramic form may have inspired
works by New York silversmiths, of which there is at least one
known surviving example.

teenth century; in turn, it had begun to influence English furniture. In New
York these cultural developments coincided and made an easy blend for the
Dutch, who were now in a position that required them to follow new trends and
to respond to opportunity. Further, the economy was more prosperous in New
York City and environs in the late seventeenth century and enabled people—
Dutch or English—to enrich their households. The course of prosperity in the
Hudson Valley and old Albany County followed a slightly different course.
Inventories for Nicholas van Rensselaer (1634–1678) of Albany and Cornelis
Steenwyck (died 1685/86), a New York City mayor and prosperous merchant,
point to significant change, some of it cultural and some economic.

To the discouragement of his family, van Rensselaer sought a religious life
rather than a mercantile one. When he arrived in Albany, he expected to be

the minister at the Albany church. Although this had been approved by the English King Charles II, it did not please his family, the Dutch domine Schaets, or the community at large. In 1675 he married Alida Schuyler, nineteen years his junior, and the couple established a small household in Albany. His inventory, taken by Robert Livingston, probably reflects his religious penchant, for he had an enormous quantity of books, about 200 (all unnamed), and also a celestial globe, understood at the time to be a symbol of philosophers and perhaps more a reflection of his mysticism than of any fashion of the day. This item was written as "1 globe of the world vizt celestiall"—indicating that Livingston made a correction in his description.

Even though van Rensselaer had spent some time in England before coming to New York, the contents of his house are otherwise almost entirely Dutch in attitude. He and his young wife had not accumulated many of the expected textiles, but they had bed hangings and bedding, tablecloths and napkins. There were two mirrors, three small pictures, and a full array of pewter, fine and coarser earthenwares, and even a porcelain tea service. There were a number of pieces of silver—a beaker, two salt cellars, mustard pots, and a dozen spoons (broken and whole). Here is a note of change, for these dozen silver spoons were nearly enough to use with the nineteen fine earthenware plates. Further, he had several pieces of impressive-sounding furniture: a "brown chest of nutwood" and five nutwood chairs (possibly stools, because the Dutch word *stoelen* indicated either stools or chairs), an oak table, and a chest of drawers. An ideal comparison with previous tables and chairs cannot be made because all the household goods were appraised using currency in beavers and because kinds of wood were not given, but it is noticeable that the five nutwood chairs and table are together in the inventory, and the oak table suggests something more massy that the "small tables" described in previous inventories. Above all, the chest of drawers marks a new trend, as do the numerous silver spoons and earthenware plates.[21]

Cornelis Steenwyck's 1686 inventory shows even more "advances" in quantities and style. Steenwyck was a rich New Yorker involved with international trade who entertained colonial governors; his household goods reflect that fact. His goods were appraised in English pounds, so comparison and evaluation of van Rensselaer's nutwood furniture with Steenwyck's "French nutwood" cupboard (perhaps a *kas*) is not possible. It is easy to see, however, that some of the goods in his house reflected other changes, new fashions, and political and economic pressure.

For Steenwyck this amounted to having many more tables and chairs, and some pieces made of special materials. His five tables were round, oval, square; a wood table; and a table with a wooden frame and marble top. Distributed

Sconce, Dutch, early eighteenth century
Brass, 18⅜ x 9¹³⁄₁₆ x 6⅛ in.
Van Cortlandt House Museum/The National Society
of Colonial Dames in the State of New York

Hammered repoussé sconces similar to this one are found
throughout New York. Kept brightly polished, they would enhance
the light given by one candle.

BARTHOLOMEW SCHAATS (New York, New York, 1670–1758)
Two-handled cup, c. 1750
Silver, 2 x 5½ in.
Hudson River Museum, 71.0.91

through his house were thirty-three chairs—ten Russia leather chairs and two others, seven Russia leather chairs, two chairs, five Russia leather chairs, three matted chairs, and four "other chairs." The chairs in particular represent a change in how people would move in and use space in a house. Nonetheless, distinctive Dutch elements remained: two *capstocken*, wooden racks or shelving for dishes, chimney cloths, thirty-three pictures, two mirrors (one large and the other more utilitarian), and a large store of linen and earthen wares. The kitchen was well supplied with standard hearth equipment, kettles, and pans, as well as some specialized cookware. He also had a *tric-trac* board, thirty-one cleaning brushes, and twenty-four pounds of Spanish soap. His inventory, by comparison with others of this period, is exceptional; it would be misleading to suggest that his household represented thelifestyle of very many Dutch in New York.[22]

The 1749 inventory of Adolphe Philipse points in a direction well established by that time. Though his city house was opulent, the household he kept at Philipsburg was, in principal, typical of rural lifestyles throughout the Hudson Valley. In New York, the mid-eighteenth century was a crucial period when the trend distinguishing differences between and among various social groups

Chocolate cups and saucers (two),
Chinese, c. 1750
Porcelain, Cup: 2⅝ x 3¼ in., Saucer: 1 x 5¼ in.
Historic Hudson Valley, Tarrytown, New York,
PM.2003.4, .5, .8, .9

Chocolate was imported in New York in the
second quarter of the eighteenth century
and became an exceedingly popular drink
accompanied with its own service and as much
formal ritual as tea drinking had. This example
was recovered from the *Geldermalsen*, a Dutch
East India ship that sank in the South China Sea,
1752.

Bowl decorated with a dragon,
Chinese (excavated at Philipsburg Manor),
1620–1680
Porcelain, approx. 3 x 5 in.
Historic Hudson Valley, Tarrytown, New York

Some porcelains imported from China by the
Dutch made their way to their North American
colony, New Netherland. While it is not unusual
to find fragments in archaeological investigations
at Manhattan and Albany, a whole piece is rare
and treasured.

became entrenched. Apart from observable features of colonial life, differences
between Dutch and English, this was a period of great social change in Europe
and America. Manners, etiquette, and fashion began to influence lifestyle in
ways not generally experienced before. Rather than measuring the number of
chairs and tables or comparing the total value of estates delineated in inventories, analysis of cultural differences is better based on an understanding of
dining and social customs.

Classifying inventories accordingly produces new social categories that
permit a better view of eighteenth-century New York material culture. The
classification system was devised by Barbara Carson for her study of Federal
period Washington, D.C.[23] In the absence of an estate inventory for George
Mason, staff at the Gunston Hall restoration used the classifications to develop
a furnishing plan for his house and have compiled an inventory database of
regional households surrounding Mason's Neck, Virginia, for the 1740–1780
time period.[24] The classifications are:

Elite—Inventories of the wealthiest decedents which exceed in quantity and quality all the criteria of the "aspiring" classification. These persons would have been able to serve a seated dinner to approximately twenty or more guests.

Aspiring—Fairly extensive households which have spoons, knives, and forks, as well as enough equipage to seat a dinner for ten persons.

Decent—Inventories which include spoons, knives, and forks, but do not have enough equipage to seat a dinner for ten persons. Hospitality appears to have been extended over tea rather than dinner.

Old-Fashioned—Inventories which do not contain forks fall into this classification. Some of these might otherwise have been considered Aspiring or Elite.

Identifying manners and customs as expressed in the presence or absence of table forks works especially well for understanding class status in the later colonial era. Both the Gunston Hall study and Carson's original study reveal

Pair of candlesticks, Dutch, seventeenth century
Brass, 8⅜ x 6⅛ in.
Historic Hudson Valley, Tarrytown, New York, PM.65.262-263

Brass was a preferred material for candlesticks. Its weight cast into a form with a heavy base and fixed with a drip-pan made them somewhat safer, and polished brass created a brightness suited for more formal settings. Iron candlesticks were also widely used.

that forks were less common earlier in the eighteenth century. The use of forks was coming into fashion and their adoption in daily use was not widespread in New York. There is some evidence that personal knife and fork sets were owned by less than a handful of seventeenth- and eighteenth-century Dutch before 1750. Peter Kalm, boarding in a Dutch household at Albany in 1749, remarks how food was presented in a main serving dish, and shared by dipping bread. Beyond this, spoons were most important hand-manipulated food service article across the Dutch colonial era.

All of this puts into perspective the six silver forks and twelve silver spoons (six new and six old—but no table knives) found in Adolphe Philipse's rural Philipsburg house. He had become so accustomed to new English and Dutch styles and must have felt so much at ease with them that they were necessary for his personal lifestyle. Furthermore, there were fourteen knives and twelve forks in the "upper kitchen." They were not silver, but were among numerous pewter pieces—eleven dishes, thirty-three plates, bassons, a tankard, a colander, and a mustard pot—so were likely of pewter as well. Such examples are little known today, though pewter spoons have had a better rate of survival. Yet Philipse appears to have maintained what would otherwise be a household more typical, albeit quite prosperous, of any Dutch countryman. The ubiquitous pewter service, the somewhat fluid use of rooms suggested by random assortments of furnishings and other goods spread throughout the house are consistent with Dutch ways. The inventory was taken by Joseph Reade, an English kinsman, who noted first the backgammon table kept in "Mr. Philipse's roome" and a copper chafing dish (commonly found in eighteenth-century inventories), a brass candlestick and tin candle snuffer, and a Dutch Bible and an English one, along with a parcel of unnamed books. By the mid-eighteenth century, backgammon had gained popularity in England and made its way to New York. Nonetheless, the table certainly echoes the distinctly old-fashioned Dutch game of *tric-trac*, a detail which Joseph Reade might not have recognized.[25]

Over time, one of the main characteristics of Dutch material culture is its conservatism, increasingly evident in the mid- and later eighteenth century and in some locales, even in the nineteenth century. William Smith, describing New York colony's people and their manners as they had become established by 1762, pointed this out:

> English the most prevailing language amongst us, but not a little corrupted by the Dutch dialect, which is still much used in some counties . . . .
> The manners of the people differ as well as their language. In Suffolk and Queen's county, the first settlers of which were either natives of England, or

the immediate descendants of such as begun the plantations in the eastern colonies, their customs are similar to those prevailing in the English counties from which they originally sprang. In the city of New-York, through our intercourse with the Europeans, we follow the London fashions; though, by the time we adopt them, they become disused in England. Our affluence, during the late war, introduced a degree of luxury in tables, dress, and furniture, with which we were before unacquainted. But still we are not so gay a people as our neighbours in Boston, and several of the southern colonies. The Dutch counties, in some measure, follow the example of New-York, but still retain many modes peculiar to the Hollanders.

The city of New-York consists principally of merchants, shopkeepers, and tradesmen . . . .

With respect to riches, there is not so great an inequality amongst us as is common in Boston and some other places. Every man of industry and integrity has it in his power to live well, and many are the instances of persons who came here distressed by their poverty, who now enjoy easy and plentiful fortunes.[26]

While such conservatism was not limited to the Dutch settlement areas in New York and New Jersey—it was also found among Virginia and New England households, typically in more rural places—in the Hudson Valley it seems to have added character because the Dutch simply retained a more old-fashioned lifestyle and did not adopt changing trends in furniture, table service, dress, and agricultural methods.

In some ways, later Dutch householders seem to have reinforced their identity by adapting to changing fashion in two ways: through continual use, traditional Dutch forms reinforced a cultural identity; and elements of a new style were borrowed and imposed upon Dutch style. The principal examples of this are the kas or kast and the so-called Hudson Valley Queen Anne chair, also known in New England as "York chairs."

New Netherland and especially New York inventories mention the *kas* among household goods. This word, in the seventeenth and eighteenth centuries without a t at the end, referred to cupboards, cases and chests of various sizes, and in the early inventories cannot be ascribed to mean a *kas* or *kasten* (the *-en* suffix denotes plural) as we have come to understand it today. Used in various ways and in combination with other words, it was applied to a watch case, a letter case, and large forms such as the "great dutch Cas" listed in Margreta van Varick's 1696 inventory. In the early period few, if any, specifically great or large *kassen* are apparent, though various *kas* and *kassen* are found in households. The word *kist* referred to a box or chest, and combined with other

Kast, American, c. 1700
Pine, tulipwood, paint, 67¼ x 61⅜ x 19⅛ in.
Van Cortlandt House Museum/The National Society
of Colonial Dames in the State of New York,
Gift of Miss Acrygg

Grisaille-painted *kasten* appeared in America around the turn of the eighteenth century. The painted ornament emulated the carved patterns found on elaborately carved Netherlands-made *kasten*.

words to mean a coffin (*doed kist*), a clothes chest (*kleer kist*), a strong box (*geld kist*). But seemingly in the early eighteenth century, the word *kas* came to refer to the large cupboard recognized today as "the *kas,*" or as spelled in modern Dutch, "*kast*."[27]

Large *kassen*, often heavily ornamented with paneled doors and deeply molded cornices, from Europe were not common in America. Here in the eighteenth century, however, a simpler style seems to have derived from that one, and with local variants it became an important furnishing for many Dutch families. An even more simplified form with respect to paneling and cornices was ornamented with grisaille painted motifs, such as fruit. These large (and sometimes relatively smaller) cupboards held as much Dutch identity as they held household linens and became important family icons in the nineteenth century. In rural areas, a few early nineteenth-century inventories still referred to large old cupboards.

The Queen Anne Hudson Valley chair eloquently demonstrates the process of adaptation of new stylistic elements into household furnishings. It began as a turned chair and was given carved, shaped parts at its "top rail" that appeared as a yoke, and in place of the usual horizontal splats, it was given a vase-shaped vertical splat that echoed Queen Anne design. Its slipper feet and trumpet-shaped leg replaced the sausage-turned legs of older Dutch chairs. This style of chair, made from about 1750 to 1810, seems to have originated in the Daniel Coutant workshop in New York City, and with an enormous following in the Hudson Valley, they were advertised by James McChesney, Albany chair maker, as late as 1810. The design was followed by other chair makers in rural places, who added their own flourish (or lack thereof). Apart from their somewhat massy character, there is nothing demonstrably Dutch about them. Yet—perhaps because they were (and are) a relatively numerous old chair form found in Dutch families—they came to be equated with the Dutch and the Hudson Valley in the twentieth century. To the extent that they were coeval with Windsor chairs, the association is a fair one. This seems to belie the idea that the Dutch and their material culture were entirely conservative, but it points to their desire to use material culture to retain their identity with a distinctive artifact.

Compared with people in other colonies, more people of Dutch heritage probably had and enjoyed a material culture that reflected distinctive stylistic preferences in furnishings, and more particularly in paintings and pictures, diverse and sometimes rich textiles, a great range of agricultural tools and utensils, and kitchen wares. However, by the time food service and associated etiquette was introduced, they were not ready to make that cultural change so rapidly. Notwithstanding the examples of the New York elite, for most Dutch in America it must have seemed an English invention to be eschewed. Forsaking English manners and trying to retain a cultural identity, they used and embellished their own material culture to express and reinforce that identity.

NOTES

1. Confronted by a Dutch landlady bringing a warming pan to the supper table, Dr. Hamilton had his first taste of fried clams. Alexander Hamilton, *Hamilton's Itinerarium being a Narrative of a Journey . . . through New York, New Jersey, . . . from May to September 1744* (1907; reprint, New York: Arno Press & The New York Times, 1971), 46.

2. Reverend John Milne was rector of Albany's Anglican church between 1727 and 1736. Arriving in Albany about 1726, he married, in the Dutch church, Maria van Cortlandt (1680-circa 1750), widow of Kiliaen van Rensselaer (1663-1719), proprietor of Rensselaerswyck.

3. Hamilton, *Itinerarium,*64-65.

4. Material culture refers to man-made objects. The historic time period and/or people and the place where the objects are used identifies a particular material culture. For the North American colonial era, further distinctions can be made based on different time periods within its one and three-quarter century span, climate and geography, and food supply; and since several cultures from different European countries were transplanted to America, consideration of European origin. Documented material culture exists in estate inventories, some account books, records of sales, and travelers' accounts. Most commonly, physical remains are found in museum and private collections, as well as in possession of descendants. Archaeologists find some articles in the ground. In the instance of the Dutch, it is also evident in the subject matter of seventeenth-century Dutch paintings and prints, where it provides significant guideposts.

5. Inventories dating from before 1664 are found in various New Netherland records such as the Register of the Provincical Secretary and Fort Orange Records. The largest collection of estate inventories for the English period is now in the New York State Archives, Albany, New York, and is part of the Court of Appeals records (these inventories were part of estates that had been contested and were subsequently used in settling the estates). Other county surrogate offices may hold additional examples, though archival issues appear to have affected their survival in most counties.

6. There is an ambiguity as to whether Bronck's house was stone or brick. In the ms. inventory (New York State Archives) it is termed *een steenen huys*, which strictly translates as "stone house." However, modern scholars note that in the Netherlands proper, this term was widely used to mean "brick house," an abbreviation of the term for brick, *baksteen* or "baked stone."

7. *New York Historical Manuscripts: Dutch. Register of the Provincial Secretary, 1642-1647,* trans. A. J. F. van Laer, ed. Kenneth Scott and Kenn Stryker-Rodda (Baltimore: Genealogical Publishing Co., 1974), II:121-123.

8. Tenancy—leasing living quarters or a whole farmstead from the Dutch West India Company or a patroonship—did not have the negative connotation it would acquire by the nineteenth century. It was perceived as a fair means to encourage settlement and give aid to newly arrived individuals. Farm leases often included the livestock tools necessary to work the land and harvest: in such instances, farm tools and some livestock would have been excluded from an inventory. Typically, in most leases, which were five or seven years in length, the issue of livestock was divided equally between the landlord and the tenant.

9. *New York Historical Manuscripts,* 1, 320-322.

10. *New York Historical Manuscripts,* 4, 114-15 for Quick's inventory. For Bastian de Winter's sale, September 23, 1658, see *Early Records of the City and County Albany,* trans. Jonathan Pearson, rev. and ed. A. J. F. van Laer (Albany: The University of the State of New York, 1869), 4, 78-80.

11. *New York Historical Manuscripts,* 2. Reg of Prov Sec., 77.

12. *New York Historical Manuscripts,* 2. Reg of Prov Sec., 339-340.

13. *New York Historical Manuscripts,* 3 Reg Prov Sec III: 63-64. See also Shirley Dunn, "Influences of New York's Early Dutch Architecture," *Dutch Barn Preservation Society Newsletter* 16, no. 2 (Fall 2003) for a discussion of early farmhouses with attached barn in New Netherland.

14. *New York Historical Manuscripts,* Dutch. 3 Reg of Prov Sec., 267-276. 6 July 1651.

15. Charles T. Gehring, *Fort Orange Records 1656-1678* (Syracuse, N.Y.: Syracuse University Press, 2000), 21.

16. Excerpt from "Genealogy of some of the Vail Family descended from Thomas Vail, at Salem, Massachusetts 1640, Together with Collateral Lines by William Penn Vail, MD, 1937," prepared by Gray & Thompson Advertising, Chapel Hill, North Carolina.

17. This was Amey Borden (1653-1683), born at Newport, Rhode Island, died "on shipboard at New York," and buried at Gravesend, Long Island. William Richardson married her as his second wife in March 1678 (V. Needham, The Needham Family, 2007, http://jrm.phys.ksu.edu/Genealogy/Needham/d0005/I3342.html). Mary Cock (1655-?) married John Bowne in June 1693. Their only surviving child, Amey Bowne, was evidently named for Amey Borden Richardson. George William Cocks, *History and Genealogy of the Cock-Cocks-Cox Family descended from James and Sarah Cock* (New York, 1914), 14.

18. William Pelletreau, *Early Wills of Westchester County, New York from 1664 to 1784* (New York: Francis Harper, 1898), will abstract No. 19. Dated the "20th day of 10th month 1692; proved April 20, 1693; and recorded in Liber 3. P. 428.

19. Charlotte Lennox, *Euphemia* (London: T. Cadell and J. Evans, 1790), III:121-124.

20. Charles T. Gehring, *Fort Orange Court Minutes 1652-1660* (Syracuse, N.Y.: Syracuse University Press, 1990), pp. 473-472.

21. Jeremias van Rensselaer's inventory, January 16, 1679, LDS Church Microfilm Roll Q-3, Surrogate's Office Inventories 1730-1780.

22. Steenwyck's inventory is given full treatment in Esther Singleton and Russell Sturgis, *The Furniture of Our Forefathers* (New York: Doubleday, Page, 1901), 245-247. This work and Singleton's *Dutch New York* and *Social New York Under the Georges* give accounts drawn from many New York inventories and stress the Dutch character and lifestyle of the colony. The books are informatively illustrated, but the dating assigned to many examples is often off by a generation or more.

23. Barbara Carson, *Ambitious Appetites: Dining, Behavior, and Patterns of Consumption in Federal Washington* (Washington, D.C.: American Institute of Architects Press, 1990).

24. "Probate Inventory Database—Virginia and Maryland Inventories 1740-1810," http://www.gunstonhall.org/probate/index.html.

25. The Philipsburg portion of Adolph Philipse's inventory was taken on January 24, 1749, and is found in Philipse family papers at the New York Public Library; a transcription is at Historic Hudson Valley Library, Sleepy Hollow, New York.

26. William Smith, *The History of the Province of New-York, from its Discovery to the Appointment of Governor Colden in 1762,* 2 vols. (New York: The New-York Historical Society, 1829), 1:277.

27. Peter M. Kenney, Frances Gruber Stafford, and Gilbert T. Vincent, *American* Kasten*: The Dutch-Style Cupboards of New York and New Jersey 1650-1800* (New York: The Metropolitan Museum of Art, 1991), vii, discusses this word and offers a study of various large New York and New Jersey cupboards. The *kas* was also the subject of Joyce Volk and Roderic H. Blackburn's "The Dutch Cupboard and Dutch Decorative Painting" in Roderic H. Blackburn and Ruth Piwonka, *Remembrance of Patria Dutch Arts and Culture in Colonial America 1609-1776* (Albany: Albany Institute of History and Art, 1988), 253-273.

PART THREE 1809 – Romanticizing the Dutch

UNKNOWN ARTIST
Portrait of Washington Irving, late nineteenth century
Photo-mechanical print process, 9½ x 7½ in.
Hudson River Museum

The Days of the Patriarchs

7

WASHINGTON IRVING'S

A HISTORY OF NEW YORK

PHILLIP LOPATE

Washington Irving was America's first professional man of letters. Other fine writers—clergymen, lawyers, housewives—preceded him, but Irving was the first to make a living by his pen. This distinction inspires both our gratitude and suspicion, insofar as he not only paved the way for all future American masters, but for all our glib periodicalists and hacks as well. In fact, Irving belonged to both camps: at different times master and hack writer.

He was also the first American writer to gain a European audience; and, having spent considerable time on the Continent, became a living bridge between the two cultures. Irving's shrewd essay, "English Writers on America," demonstrates his worldliness and tact, arguing as it does that 1) British writers have distorted American life, out of chauvinistic malice toward the New World; and 2) Americans ought not to take excessive offense at this condescension, but should continue to try to learn what they can from English culture.

Irving was, finally, America's first important belle-lettrist, which may help to explain why he is so little read today. Had he been a novelist or poet, he might have fit better into the canon, as precursor to the curricular giants of American literature. Instead, he was primarily an essayist and travel writer—a practitioner of "creative nonfiction"—a scribbler, whose most famous book was aptly titled *The Sketch Book of Geoffrey Crayon, Gent.* In his day, Irving operated stylishly in the bacheloric-spectatorial-nostalgic vein initiated by Addison and Steele. The *Sketch Book* and its successors, *Bracebridge Hall* and *Tales of a Traveler,* contain many genial, diverting pages, but they also seem to the modem reader—even to me, his defender—overly tame, decorous, and syrupy, especially compared to the far riskier essays of his great essayist contemporaries, William Hazlitt and Charles Lamb.

It was Hazlitt who wrote a sharp critique of Washington Irving, accusing him of having "skimmed the cream" of the best-known, older English writers:

> He gives us very good American copies of our British Essayists and Novelists, which may be very well on the other side of the water, or as proofs of the capabilities of the national genius, but which might be dispensed with

FELIX OCTAVIUS CARR DARLEY (1822–1888)
Scene from *Knickerbocker's History of New York* by
Washington Irving [pseud. Diedrich Knickerbocker]
Engraved by Child

here, where we have to boast of the originals. Not only Mr. Irving's language is with great taste and felicity modelled on that of Addison, Goldsmith, Sterne, or Mackenzie: but the thoughts and sentiments are drawn at the rebound, and, as they are brought forward at the present period, want both freshness and probability.

There is more than a touch of patriotic pique in this put-down of the American *arriviste*, and anger at Irving for being more popular at the time than his friend Lamb. But Hazlitt rightly nails Irving as a tourist, who went looking for

FELIX OCTAVIUS CARR DARLEY (1822–1888)
Scene from *Knickerbocker's History of New York* by
Washington Irving [pseud. Diedrich Knickerbocker]
Engraved by John William Orr (1815–1887)

In 1949
Washington
Irving's iconic
vision of the
Headless
Horseman was
given the Disney
treatment in
*The Adventures
of Ichabod and
Mr. Toad*, a
double feature
of Irving's story
and *The Wind in
the Willows*.
Image courtesy
Photofest, New
York

the quaint English types of his reading ("He has Parson Adams or Sir Roger
de Coverley in his mind's eye"), and failed to note enough the social tensions
and complexities of the current English scene. (Ironically, this reliance on pre-
conceptions over observation is just what Irving faulted the English writers
for doing when they reported on America). It is Irving's English writings that
Hazlitt objects to—as much as to say, "Stay off my turf." He adds cautiously,
"Of the merit of his *Knickerbocker* and New York stories we cannot pretend to
judge." Presumably Hazlitt says this because he hadn't read the author's earlier
volume, Irving's comic chronicle of mock-learning and literary parody, *A History of New York*, though it was much admired by Scott, Byron, Coleridge and,
later, Dickens, who wore out his copy.

Today's readers generally know Irving, if at all, only through his two *Sketch
Book* stories, "Rip Van Winkle" and "The Legend of Sleepy Hollow." "Rip" is a
first-rate tale, while "Sleepy Hollow" strikes me as a little too coy. About both
it might be said that Irving's secular rationalist side dilutes the uncanniness
one finds in Poe or Hoffmann with an excessively joshing tone, as though the
author were somewhat embarrassed to be proffering the supernatural. In any
case, these chestnuts prevented me too long from experiencing *A History of*

Tim Burton took on Irving's legend with *Sleepy Hollow* (1999), starring Johnny Depp as Ichabod Crane and Christina Ricci as Katrina Van Tassel. Image courtesy Photofest, New York

Redfield Brothers Inc. *Float, Legend of 'Sleepy Hollow'* Color process photo postcard; 3½ x 5½ in. Hudson River Museum, INV.9702

New York, which now seems Irving's strongest, boldest, funniest, and most idiosyncratically original work.

The book's full title, as it first appeared in 1809, was *A History of New York from the Beginnings of the World to the End of the Dutch Dynasty*. The author was listed as Diedrich Knickerbocker, and Irving went so far with the hoax as to place notices in newspapers, pretending to be searching for the where-abouts of the old gentleman author, who was missing from his lodgings. (The book's "frame," that beloved 19th-century device, consisted of Knickerbocker's landlord claiming he had found these historical papers, left behind by his im-pecunious tenant in lieu of back-rent, and was publishing them in an effort to recoup his losses.)

Walter Huston leads the kick line as a peg-legged Peter Stuyvesant in the 1938 Broadway musical *Knickerbocker Holiday.* The show featured a book and lyrics by Maxwell Anderson and music by Kurt Weill.
Image courtesy Photofest, New York

Why the need for Diedrich Knickerbocker? A familiar essayist rather than a personal one, Irving shied away from direct autobiographical disclosure, especially of a painful nature. He required masks, aliases: his two most notable being Geoffrey Crayon and Diedrich Knickerbocker. These two personae were very different. The first seems more or less a stand-in for the author, sharing with him the same age, bloodline (English), education, marital status (single) and connoisseurial, affable temperament: Washington Irving minus the celebrity and accomplishment. In fact, I would say Geoffrey Crayon is not a successful masquerade, precisely because Irving never bothered to differentiate himself sufficiently from his surrogate to make him into an individual character. Nor did he disclose his own personal self sufficiently, like Montaigne, to render such fictionalizing unnecessary.

In Diedrich Knickerbocker, on the other hand, he created a character markedly distinct from himself. Irving was twenty-six at the time his *History of*

The 1943 film version of *Knickerbocker Holiday* starred
Nelson Eddy, Charles Coburn, and Constance Dowling.
Image courtesy Photofest, New York

New York first appeared; Knickerbocker was supposedly a cranky old codger
close to being "chilled forever." Knickerbocker's cheeky authorial vanity, testi-
ness and perverse contrariety were essential in supplying the work a comic
edge.[1] Irving was comfortably middle-class by background and aristocratic in
values; Knickerbocker was penniless, déclassé. Most important, Irving was of
Scottish-English stock, a representative of the victorious Yankee caste; he im-
personated Knickerbocker, a proudly Dutch New Yorker whose ancestors had
been defeated by the English. If history is said to be written by the winners,
Irving chose for his own reasons the tarter viewpoint of the vanquished.

Diedrich announces, on the first page, his melancholy motive for writing a
municipal history:

With great solicitude had I long beheld the early history of this venerable
and ancient city, gradually slipping from our grasp, trembling on the lips of

HENRY A. OGDEN
Dutch Citizens in a Crowd, costume
sketch for the play, *Peter Stuyvesant*, 1899
Pencil on paper, 11 x 6½ in.
Museum of the City of New York,
Gift of Herbert Brook, 82.105.4

narrative old age, and day by day dropping piece meal into the tomb. In a little while, thought I, and those venerable dutch burghers, who serve as the tottering monuments of good old times, will be gathered to their fathers; their children engrossed by the empty pleasures or insignificant transactions of the present age, will neglect to treasure up the recollections of the past, and posterity shall search in vain, for memorials of the days of the Patriarchs.

It is curious, this agenda to solemnize the patriarchy, considering that the author's own relations with his stern, deacon father were distant and fearful. Washington Irving, the youngest of eight surviving children, doted on by his mother and older siblings, seemed ever-willing in life to play the Son's role, if

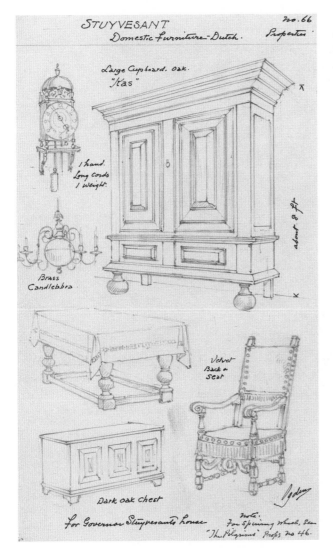

HENRY A. OGDEN
Dutch Domestic Furniture,
Prop sketch for the play,
Peter Stuyvesant, 1899
Pencil on paper, 11 x 6½ in.
Museum of the City of New York,
Gift of Herbert Brook, 82.105.61

not without conflicted feelings toward the Father. The "History's" filial form of ancestor worship meets its oedipal come-uppance, as it were, in the narrator's ensuing portrait of "the Patriarchs" as something less than heroic. (One might say the same about the Biblical Patriarchs.) Indeed, Irving has fun showing these New Amsterdam colonialists as a race of gluttonous, smoking-addicted, timorous burghers.

Yet, underneath the tongue-in-cheek, Yankee satire of the Dutch, Irving seems truly to have identified with his narrator's sense of inner exile. Here is Knickerbocker on a tear, venting his rancor:

Luckless Diedrich! born in a degenerate age—abandoned to the buffetings of fortune—a stranger and a weary pilgrim in thy native land; blest with

The 1958 episode of Shirley Temple's *Storybook* featured "The Legend of Sleepy Hollow,"
with Temple as Katrina, Jules Munshin as Ichabod Crane, John Ericson as Brom Bones,
and Boris Karloff as the Irving stand-in Storyteller.
Image courtesy Photofest, New York

no weeping wife, nor family of helpless children—but doomed to wander
neglected through those crowded streets, and elbowed by foreign upstarts
from those fair abodes, where once thine ancestors held sovereign empire.
Alas! alas! is then the dutch spirit forever extinct? The days of the patriarchs, have they fled forever?

I would hazard a guess that Knickerbocker's tribal alienation from the con-
quering Yankee ethos mirrored Irving's own feelings of estrangement—as a
Romantic intellectual, lover of ruins and Old World culture—from the brash,
crass, money-grubbing optimism of the young Republic. Irving's was the first
of many fastidious literary detachments from the feast of American progress:
Hawthorne, Thoreau, Henry Adams. Hawthorne's fence-sitting, witty Miles
Coverdale, in *The Blithedale Romance*, bears more than a little resemblance to
Irving's prior bachelor-narrators. (Hawthorne actually sent Irving a tenderly
respectful note along with the book, acknowledging his debt.)

Irving also was first to sound the expatriate note in American letters. He
spent seventeen consecutive years abroad: always an outsider, split in alle-

giances and homesickness, eventually serving as a foreign diplomat. Just as he tried to bridge the two transatlantic cultures, so he attempted to explain the New York Dutch to the Yankees—and vice versa. That a social distance persisted between the two groups may be seen by Knickerbocker's wry comment: "so inveterately did they [the Dutch-Americans] retain their abhorrence of the British nation, that in a private meeting of the leading citizens, it was unanimously determined never to ask any of their conquerors to dinner." (Ichabod Crane, the gawky schoolmaster of "The Legend of Sleepy Hollow," can be seen as the embodiment of this failed social bridge: a Yankee parvenu who vainly aspires to marry the daughter of a wealthy Dutch burgher.)

Irving seems to have been attracted to New York's Dutch past partly for geographical reasons. He spent much time as a young man (and later made his home) in the Hudson River Valley, where many of the old Dutch families and byways remained intact. Irving was an amateur folklorist, who loved legends

FELIX OCTAVIUS CARR DARLEY (1822–1888)
From set of drawings for "Rip Van Winkle," New York City, c. 1848
Ink and watercolor on paper, 8⅞ x 10⅞ in.
Historic Hudson Valley, Tarrytown, New York, SS.64.557

FELIX OCTAVIUS CARR DARLEY (1822–1888)
From set of drawings for "Rip Van Winkle"
New York City, c. 1848
Ink and watercolor on paper, 8⅞ x 10⅞ in.
Historic Hudson Valley, Tarrytown, New York, SS.64.559

and storytelling, and the old Dutch New York society appealed to him as an aural, largely preliterate culture. He developed a yearning to preserve that past, along with a frustration about being able to do so.

Irving's central theme, I believe, is American amnesia; his work is a reproach to it. In "Rip Van Winkle," you will recall, the eponymous hero falls asleep for twenty years and returns to find no one remembers the old Dutch town he knew. They are all gung-ho for politics and speechmaking in the brand-new independent Republic. I would like to point out that during the Revolutionary War, a fire destroyed almost all of the Dutch remnants in New York City; the city rebuilt as if nothing had happened. The fire was as amnesiac in its effect as the veil of Rip's slumber.

Has a writer ever been more obsessed with sleep than Irving? Even before "Rip Van Winkle" and "The Legend of Sleepy Hollow," *A History of New York* teems with Dutch city fathers dozing during council meetings. The colony itself is compared to a sleeping giant: "the guileless government of the New Netherlands . . . like a worthy unsuspicious old burgher, quietly settled itself down into the city of New Amsterdam, as into a snug elbow chair—and fell into a comfortable nap—while in the mean time its cunning neighbors stepp'd in and picked its pockets." Sleep is associated with honesty, virtue—and un-protectedness. The fathers sleep; the sons mourn. Sleep is the sin of the Patri-archs. Aside from its obvious, wan humor as a comic device, sleep must have had some deeper psychological meaning to Irving, springing, perhaps, from his desire to stop the march of time and its attendant losses. We know that he lost his father, sister and betrothed around this period; we also know that he was often overtaken by phases of lethargy and inability to work.

Sleep and resistance to change—here he explains his reason for choosing Sleepy Hollow:

> It is in such little retired Dutch valleys, found here and there embosomed in the great State of New York, that population, manners, and customs remain fixed; while the great torrent of migration and improvement, which is mak-ing such incessant changes in other parts of this restless country, sweeps by them unobserved.

FELIX OCTAVIUS CARR DARLEY (1822–1888)
From set of drawings for "Rip Van Winkle"
New York City, c. 1848
Ink and watercolor on paper, 8⅞ x 10⅞ in. each
Historic Hudson Valley, Tarrytown, New York, SS.64.558

FELIX OCTAVIUS CARR DARLEY (1822–1888)
From set of drawings for *Rip Van Winkle,* New York City, c. 1848
Ink and watercolor on paper, 8⅞ x 10⅞ in.
Historic Hudson Valley, Tarrytown, New York, SS.64.560

A History of New York also invokes an ordered, bucolic past to reproach the bustling, dangerous, heterogeneous present:

> In that delightful period, a sweet and holy calm reigned over the whole province. The Burgomaster smoked his pipe in peace—the substantial solace of his domestic house, his well petticoated *yffrouw,* after her daily cares were done, sat soberly at her door, with arms crossed over her apron of snowy white, without being insulted by ribald street walkers or vagabond boys—those unlucky urchins, who do so infest our streets. . . .

The paradox is that Irving on the one hand champions historical remembrance, and on the other, portrays the Dutch colonial past as a prelapsarian Eden dozing in ahistorical stasis.

N.C. WYETH (1882–1945)
Cover illustration for *Rip Van Winkle* by Washington Irving
(Philadelphia: David McKay Company, 1921).
Hudson River Museum, INV.9811

Thrice happy, and never to be forgotten age! when everything was better than it had ever been since, or ever will be again—when Buttermilk
channel was quite dry at low water—when the shad in the Hudson were all
salmon. . . .

Of course, young Irving is partly parodying the sound of the old complainer
Knickerbocker here. But part of him seems to buy the fantasy of old New York
in a state of grace:

No sooner was the colony once planted, than like a luxuriant vine, it took
root and throve amazingly; for it would seem, that this thrice favoured island is like a munificent dung hill, where everything finds kindly nourish-
ment, and soon shoots up and expands to greatness. The thriving state of
settlement . . . gradually awakened the leaders from a profound lethargy,
into which they had fallen, after having built their mud fort.

By these alternations of lethargy and activity, Irving is elongating the experience of time and giving the history of Dutch New York a mythological dimension, like Garcia Marquez's Macondo. Lending it more weight, perhaps, than the actual record warrants. It is worth recalling that the Dutch occupied New York for only half a century: Henry Hudson explored it in 1609, the Dutch West India Company began sending colonists over two years later, and by 1664 they had surrendered it to the British. One reason they gave it up without a fight was that it was not turning enough of a profit. The Dutch empire was indeed impressive at the time, stretching as it did worldwide; but the men in control of it, according to historian Michael Kammen,[2]

were far more intrigued by prospects in Guinea on the African coast, in Guiana on the South American coast, and in the Caribbean than by New Netherland. They could not grow exotic spices in North America, nor exploit an indigenous labor force, nor find fantastic mines. Sandwiched between Jamestown's settlement southward and the Pilgrims in New England, New Netherland's location did not even provide much of a chance to tweak the Spanish snout. The expanse of land stretching from the Delaware to the Connecticut rivers offered only furs, timber, and perhaps agricultural support for settlements more favorably situated. None of these commodities were contemptible; but neither were they high priorities. Accordingly, from the outset New Netherland was relegated to a supporting role in the West India Company's scheme of things. Its position was slow to change, vulnerable to chance, and when the crisis of 1664 came, expendable by choice.

This is not the picture Knickerbocker paints: he would have us believe that New Amsterdam was the plum of plums. If Irving concurs, it may be to justify stretching out the brief tale of Dutch rule in New York to 450-plus pages. Earlier, he had published only short pieces in the collection entitled *Salmagundi*. But he took as his models for *A History of New York* the fat comic tomes of Cervantes, Rabelais, Sterne and Fielding; and he splashed around in the garrulous plenitude of a young writer, discovering his full powers for the first time.

Indeed, much of the book's comedy extends from its resistance to straight narration—its delays, digressions, reader addresses, and preposterously long preambles. The book's subtitle (*From the Beginning of the World*) gives the game away. The first chapters are actually taken up with mock-scholarly enumerations of creation myths, such as:

The Mohawk Philosophers tell us that a pregnant woman fell down from heaven, and that a tortoise took her upon its back, because every place was covered with water; and that the woman sitting upon the tortoise paddled with her hands in the water, and raked up the earth, whence it finally happened that the earth became higher than the water.

Having reviewed the testimony, historian Knickerbocker declares:

It appears, I say, and I make the assertion deliberately, without fear of contradiction, that the globe really was created, and that it is composed of land and water. It further appears that it is curiously divided and parcelled out into continents and islands, among which I boldly declare the renowned ISLAND OF NEW YORK, will be found, by anyone who seeks for it in its proper place.

Irving is a master at this accordion-like inflation and deflation of rhetorical rodomontade. His comedy feasts on the resources of language—syntax itself. For instance, the following passage depends for its joke on the placement of one interpolated clause:

To give this menace the greater effect, he drew forth his trusty sword, and shook it at them with such a fierce and vigorous motion, that doubtless, if it had not been exceeding rusty, it would have lightened terror into the eyes and hearts of the enemy.

At times Knickerbocker is in on the joke; at times the author is having it at the narrator's expense. Irving employs a whole panoply of ironies. He mocks the phony effusions of other historians about the fall of empires ("You who have noses, prepare to blow them now!"). He pretends he has no idea what's coming next:

I generally make it a rule, not to examine the annals of the times whereof I treat, further than exactly a page in advance of my own work; hence I am equally interested in the progress of my history, with him who reads it, and equally unconscious, what occurrence is next to happen.

He startles us with contrarian epigrams:

To a profound philosopher, like myself, who am apt to see clear through a subject, where the penetration of ordinary people extends but half way, there is no fact more simple and manifest, than that the death of a great man, is a matter of very little importance.

These epigrams, usually at the start of a chapter, get worked up into ingenious little essays:

The world, to tell the private truth, cares but little for their loss, and if left to itself would soon forget to grieve; and though a nation has often figuratively drowned in tears on the death of a great man, yet it is ten chances to one if an individual tear has been shed on the melancholy occasion, excepting from the forlorn pen of some hungry author. It is the historian, the biographer, and the poet, who have the whole burden of grief to sustain; who—unhappy varlets!—like the undertakers in England, act the part of chief mourners—who inflate a nation with sighs it never heaved, and deluge it with tears, it never dreamed of shedding.

One is reminded of Richard Nixon's passing. Irving has made the point, and made it well. But, with that cornucopic excess of elaboration which is so much a part of the comic spirit (Rabelais, Cervantes, etc.), he takes it one step further, addressing the specific death of the Dutch governor, William Kieft:

His exit occasioned no convulsion in the city of New Amsterdam, or its vicinity; the earth trembled not, neither did any stars shoot from their spheres—the heavens were not shrouded in black, as poets would fain persuade us they have been, on the unfortunate death of a hero—the rocks (hard hearted vagabonds) melted not in tears; nor did the trees hang their heads in silent sorrow; and as to the sun, he laid abed the next night, just as long. . . .

There is also an absurd anachronistic humor, as when Irving lists all the military defenses Peter Stuyvesant chose not to avail himself of, adding:

My readers will perhaps be surprised, that out of so many systems, governor Stuyvesant should find none to suit him; this may be tolerably accounted for, by the simple fact, that many of them were unfortunately invented long since his time. . . . .

Irving's relationship to his readers is playfully mischievous, right up to the edge of impudence. He interrupts a point of historical high drama with:

Having therefore got him in my clutches—what hinders me from indulging in a little recreation, and varying the dull task of narrative by stultifying my readers with a drove of sober reflections about this, that and the other thing—by pushing forward a few of my own darling opinions; or talking a little about myself—

Later, after apologizing to readers for being "a little cold and reserved at first," he says:

Besides, why should I have been sociable to the host of how-d'ye-do acquaintances, who flocked around me at my first appearance? They were merely attracted by a new face; many of them only stared me full in the title page, and then walked off without saying a word; while others lingered yawningly through the preface, and having gratified their short-lived curiosity, soon dropped off one by one.

He explains that he was testing them, as King Arthur did potential knights, with "two or three knotty chapters, where they were most woefully belabored and buffetted, by a host of pagan philosophers and infidel writers."

Irving is partly expressing, through the testy Knickerbocker, the very real uncertainty that a new writer has about his audience. Until he has acquired a stable readership and knowledge of its tastes, he is apt to feel both cringing and hostile towards the public. At this early juncture in his career, Irving was given to showing his claws more, and the aggressiveness was salutary to his prose; the latter Irving turned more dulcet and sentimental, and played his readers like a lute, with lulling physical descriptions that now seem padded. As Perry Miller puts it:

> But between 1809 and 1819 he discovered, and for the rest of his life was to remain happy with the finding, that a lush yet refined cultivation of the gentle tear, interspersed with bonhommie and a pleasant affectation of useless erudition, was readily marketable in the early nineteenth century.

The Irving who wrote *A History of New York* (1809) was intent on establishing a more demanding conversation with his readers, and tweaking them into alert response. Irving saves some of his best ironies for serious subjects, like the mistreatment of the Indians. He has Knickerbocker pose the question: "What right had the first discoverers of America to land, and take possession of a country, without asking the consent of its inhabitants, or yielding them an adequate compensation for their territory?" Boasting that "My readers will now see with astonishment, how easily I vanquish this gigantic doubt," he offers some logical double-talk of devastating, Swiftian irony:

> Now it is notorious, that the savages knew nothing of agriculture, when first discovered by the Europeans, but lived a most vagabond, disorderly, unrighteous life,—rambling from place to place, and prodigally rioting upon the spontaneous luxuries of nature, without tasking her generosity to yield them any thing more; whereas it has been most unquestionably shown, that heaven intended the earth should be ploughed and sown, and manured, and laid out into cities and towns and farms, and country seats, and pleasure grounds, and public gardens, all which the Indians knew nothing about—therefore they did not improve the talents providence had

bestowed on them—therefore they were careless stewards—therefore they had no right to the soil—therefore they deserved to be exterminated.

It is true the savages might plead that they drew all the benefits from the land which their simple wants required—they found plenty of game to hunt, which together with the roots and uncultivated fruits of the earth, furnished a sufficient variety for their frugal table; —and that as heaven merely designed the earth to form the abode, and satisfy the wants of man; so long as those purposes were answered, the will of heaven was accomplished. —But this only proves how undeserving they were of the blessing around them—they were so much the more savages, for not having more wants; for knowledge is to some degree an increase of desires, that distinguishes the man from the beast. Therefore the Indians, in not having more wants, were very unreasonable animals; and it was but just that they would make way for the Europeans, who had a thousand wants to their one, and therefore would turn the earth to more account, and by cultivating it, more truly fulfill the will of heaven.

Here, placed in Knickerbocker's mouth, is the bland doctrine of progress whose nightmarish underpinnings so alienated Irving from the early Republic. The passage, in its controlled indignation, is a strong anti-colonialist indictment. Elsewhere, Irving ridicules fanatical certainty in general, mocking the New England Puritans "for indulging the preposterous idea of convincing the mind by toasting the carcass. . . ." He is also quite witty on the Salem witch trials. Knickerbocker marvels that these "ignorant, decrepit" old women, most of whom "were totally unversed in the occult mysteries of the alphabet," should have mastered

this terrible art, which so long has baffled the painful researches, and abstruse studies of philosophers, astrologers, alchymists, theurgists, and other

WILLIAM HEATH (1795–1840)
Peter Stuyvesant's Army Entering New Amsterdam, c. 1850
Sarony & Major, New York lithographers

The Strobridge Litho Co, Cincinnati
and New York
*Wm. H. Crane as Peter Stuyvesant,
Governor of New Amsterdam*, 1899
Color lithographic poster, 28 x 18¾ in.
Library of Congress, Prints and
Photographs Division, Washington, D.C.

William H. Crane played the title role
in this play, written by Brander Matthews
and Bronson Howard and performed in
Wallack's Theatre at Broadway and 30th
Street, New York.
The play opened on October 2, 1899
and lasted for 28 performances.

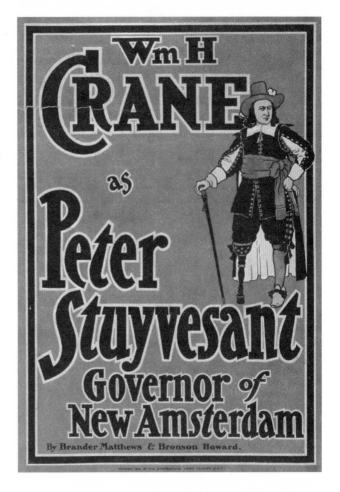

sages. . . . Though exhorted in the most solemn persuasive and affectionate manner, to confess themselves guilty, and be burnt for the good of religion, and the entertainment of the public; yet did they most pertinaciously persist in asserting their innocence. Such incredible obstinacy was in itself deserving of immediate punishment, and was sufficient proof, if proof were necessary, that they were in league with the devil, who is perverseness itself.

Irving notes slyly that the good people of New England, having purged themselves of witches, "turned their attention to the more profitable hocus pocus of trade, and soon became expert in the legerdemain art of turning a penny."

In such passages, Irving comes across as both predecessor and prototype of the New York literati: liberal, secular, ironic, skeptical, competitive toward New England. He shows progressive sympathy for the poor, as when he characterizes the Dutch courts as winking "at the offences of the rich," while hounding those who come before the bench in the "disgraceful rags of poverty." Liberal in his defense of minorities, outsiders and the marginalized, he was not, how-

HOWARD PYLE (1853–1911)
TIFFANY STUDIOS (1902–1938)
Anthony Van Corlear, The Trumpeter of New Amsterdam, c.1896
Leaded glass, mounted on wood light box, 64½ x 39½ in.
Delaware Art Museum, F. V. du Pont Acquisition Fund, 1984
DAM 1984-28

ever, a great fan of democracy. There is that gentleman's distrust (shared by Poe, among others) of "the greasy multitude," and that approval of an authoritarian leader like Peter Stuyvesant, who "possessed a sovereign contempt for the sovereign people."

Much of the book's second half, in fact, favorably contrasts the rule of Stuyvesant with that of his predecessor, William Kieft. Stuyvesant is shown as a courageous, headstrong character who takes his own counsel; Kieft is portrayed as a crackbrained inventor, inconsistent, over-trusting of proclamations instead of armies, and prey to impractical democratic notions. Many commentators believe that Irving's portrait of Kieft is a satire on Thomas Jefferson, then President. Certainly, when he refers to Kieft as "this learned, philosophic, but unfortunate little man," one suspects he has another target in mind.

To what degree Irving was using the pretext of history-writing for political satire, or was actually attempting to write a serious history, is difficult to

JOHN ROGERS (1829–1904)
Rip Van Winkle Returned,
patented 1871
Painted plaster, 21½ in. high
Hudson River Museum, Gift of
Samuel L. Rosenfeld in memory
of his wife, June S. Rosenfeld,
1993.17.6

say. The book has long had the distorted reputation of being what we would now call "wild history": a completely comic burlesque of the facts. There are, true, occasional tall tales inserted into the text, like one about the derivation of the place name "Anthony's Nose" (a trumpeter named Anthony had a huge nose, and the sun's rays, reflecting off it, killed a mighty sturgeon). And there are charming local legends, like the one about the layout of Manhattan streets (pre-grid): the council, unable to make up its mind,

> the cows, in a laudable fit of patriotism, took it under their particular charge, and, as they went to and from pasture, established paths through the bushes, on each side of which the good folks built their houses; which is one cause of the rambling and picturesque turns and labyrinths, which distinguish certain streets of New York, at this very day.

Yet what is surprising is how closely Irving follows historical events, and how accurate his record actually is, given the paucity of annals, chronicles and documents he had to work with. "More and more it appears that *A History of New York* is a curious mixture of genuine and spurious erudition," conclude

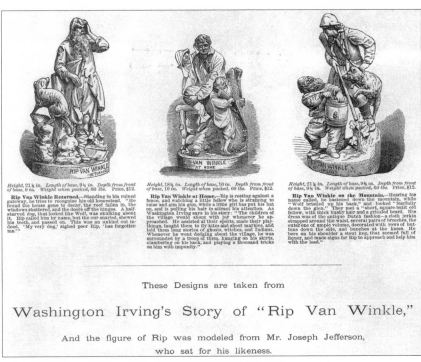

Washington Irving's Story of "Rip Van Winkle," in *Groups of Statuary by John Rogers*, New-York, promotional sales brochure, 1886, p. 3
Hudson River Museum

Stanley Williams and Tremaine Mcdowell. Irving spent considerable time researching the subject in the fledgling New-York Historical Society, to which he dedicates the book, and obviously saw himself as something of an historian. (Later, he wrote biographies of Columbus and Washington.) For better or for worse, Irving's was, in fact, the first published history of New York. "That I have not written a better history of the days of the patriarchs is not my fault— had any other person written one, as good, I should not have attempted it at all." Thus spake Diedrich Knickerbocker—and maybe Washington Irving.

We do have Irving's Author's Apology, some three decades later, in the prologue for a revised edition (1848). Describing his struggles to limit the subject, he writes:

> I accordingly resolved to confine it to the period of the Dutch domination, which, in its rise, progress, and decline, presented that unity of subject required by classic rule. It was a period, also, at that time almost a terra incognita in history. In fact, I was surprised to find how few of my fellow-citizens were aware that New York had ever been called New Amsterdam, or had heard of the names of its early Dutch governors, or cared a straw about their ancient Dutch progenitors. This, then, broke upon me as the poetic age of

Pach Bros.
"Rip Van Winkle" as played by
Joseph Jefferson, 1895
Photogravure from the limited-
edition book, 10¼ x 7⅛ in.
Hudson River Museum, Gift of
Samuel Rosenfeld in memory of
his wife, June S. Rosenfeld, 94.5.2

Joseph Jefferson was a
celebrated actor who made a
long career of playing Rip Van
Winkle. His success was so great
that he became the stereotypical
embodiment of the character.

our city; poetic from its very obscurity; and open; like the early and obscure days of ancient Rome, to all the embellishments of heroic fiction.

Having expressed regret for hurting the feelings of certain Dutch families (who reacted touchily after the book appeared), he says, with some justice, that at least the liberties he took encouraged other historians to rummage the forgotten archives. Then he adds:

> The main object of my work, in fact, had a bearing wide from the sober aim of history. . . . It was to embody the traditions of our city in an amusing form; to illustrate its local humors, customs, and peculiarities; to clothe home scenes and places and familiar names with those imaginative and whimsical associations so seldom met with in our new country, but which live like charms and spells about the cities of the old world, binding the heart of the native inhabitant to his home.

New York's problem from its start has been the tension between an energizing but centrifugal pluralism and the task of building cohesive community. Irving now states that his aim all along was to "link our whole community together in good humor and good fellowship." Then, with a certain pathetic boastfulness, like the doddering Diedrich Knickerbocker he has finally grown into, he notes that

Pach Bros.
"Rip Van Winkle" as played by Joseph Jefferson, 1895
Photogravure from the limited edition, 10¼ x 7⅛ in.
Hudson River Museum, Gift of Samuel Rosenfeld in memory of his wife, June S. Rosenfeld, 94.5.2

I have reason to believe that I have in some measure succeeded . . . and when I find, after a lapse of nearly forty years, this hap-hazard production of my youth still cherished among them; when I find its very name become a "household word," and used to give the home stamp to everything recommended for popular acceptation, such as Knickerbocker societies; Knickerbocker insurance companies; Knickerbocker steamboats; Knickerbocker omnibuses; Knickerbocker bread; and Knickerbocker ice; and when I find New Yorkers of Dutch descent priding themselves upon being "genuine Knickerbockers," I please myself with the persuasion that I have struck the right chord . . . that I have opened a vein of pleasant associations and quaint characteristics peculiar to my native place. . . .

This Chamber of Commerce tone shows how thoroughly he has forgotten the sharp-edged, provocative young man he was—or how much more his book once had on its mind than "pleasant associations and quaint characteristics." You might say that the elderly Irving has suffered amnesia. Not only

GEORGE BENSELL (1834–1879)
Rip Van Winkle, n.d.
Oil on canvas, 50 x 39½ in.
Westmoreland Museum of American Art, Greensburg, Pennsylvania, 1977.129

has he forgotten the book's mischief, but its dangerous sadness as well. That persistent, surprising undertow of gravity and melancholy, in a work intended to be comic, is not the least of its attractions for the reader of today. It is, after all, a long tale of loss, decline, nostalgia without solace, premature aging, and bitterness at the present's disrespect for the past.

Why such melancholy? Legend and scholarship together assert that Irving had hoped to marry the beautiful Mathilda Hoffman, who died in the course of his writing the book. Whether this entirely explains his compositional state

ALBURTUS DEL ORIENT BROWERE (1814–1887)
Rip in the Mountains, 1880
One of four paintings from the *Rip Van Winkle* Series
Oil on canvas, 30 x 44¼ in.
Shelburne Museum, Shelburne, Vermont, 27.1.7-17

of mind, or whether this "lost love" is the usual romance cooked up by literary biographers faced with the blank of an author's lifelong bachelorhood, we have no way of knowing. Irving, with his customary reticence, took us only partway into his confidence, in a memoir fragment written years later:

> I had begun a satirical & humorous work (The History of New York) in company with one of my brothers; but he had gone to Europe shortly after commencing it, and my feelings had run into so different a vein, that I could not go on with it. . . . When I became calm & collected I applied myself, by way of occupation, to the finishing of my work. I brought it to a close, as well as I could, and published it but the time & circumstances in which it was produced rendered me always unable to look upon it with satisfaction.

This poignantly laconic statement does account, at least, for the work's shifting tones and emotional richness. It is not as smoothly even-handed as *The Sketch Book* or *The Alhambra*—and profits accordingly. *A History of New York* is one of those books that seems to take you directly into the bumpy inner life

Bencke & Scott
"Dis von don't count." Mr. Joseph Jefferson, in his celebrated character of Rip Van Winkle, c. 1895
Color lithograph
Library of Congress Prints and Photographs Division, Washington, D.C., (PGA - Bencke & Scott—Dis von don't count . . . (B size) [P&P])

This popular print was based on the photograph shown on the opposite page. The image of Joseph Jefferson became so associated with Rip Van Winkle, that when called to illustrate him, artists conjured the image of the actor.

of its author. I am convinced it offers the key to the elusive Irving; after reading it, the rest of his work seems much clearer, sadder and more appealing.

Years later he was to go back and revise extensively this youthful production, smoothing over, tightening and bowdlerizing what he now saw, from the literary standards of the European drawing room, as vulgarities. Fortunately, modern scholarship has chosen to reprint the original, racier, if baggier, *History of New York*.

In the ensuing debate about whether America should generate its own indigenous, buckskin literature, or imitate European models, Irving came to stand for the latter, more conservative position. Most of *The Sketch Book* was given over to English themes; and he cemented his cosmopolitanism by penning books about Spain and Mohammed. Though he was later to return to America and write about the West, his viewpoint was more that of a continental tourist; it was, as his biographer Stanley T. Williams noted, "the contrast in these to those of Europe which fascinated him." But his initial popularity, especially in Europe, has derived from the public's perception that he was offering something new, fresh, directly American—in his *History of New York* and the

Pach Bros.
"Rip Van Winkle" as played by
Joseph Jefferson, 1895
Photogravure from the limited-
edition book, 10¼ x 7⅛ in.
Hudson River Museum, Gift of
Samuel Rosenfeld in memory of his
wife, June S. Rosenfeld, 94.5.2

two famous Hudson Valley tales. As London's *Atheneum Magazine* phrased it
in 1829, from the perspective of twenty years after first publication: "'Knickerbocker's History of New York' was an honest and manly attempt to found
an American literature. Those who read it must have exclaimed involuntarily
'Yes, this is the work which was wanted. The umbilical cord is now severed.
America is indeed independent.'"

Washington Irving lived to seventy-eight, long enough to hear himself
called (ironic word) "the patriarch of American literature"—and long enough
to see his style of literature elbowed aside. The rap on him was that he was too
eager to please, and too "easily pleased." Irving's desperate attempts in middle
and old age to repeat his early success belies this happy-go-lucky characterization. A letter he wrote late in life has a poignant ring:

> In the early part of my literary career I used to think I would take warn-
> ing by the fate of writers who kept on writing until they "wrote themselves

down," and that I would retire while still in the freshness of my powers—but you see circumstances have obliged me to change my plan, and I am likely to write until the pen drops from my hand.

So Irving, our first in many ways, also seems to have initiated that unfortunate pattern in American literature, of the writer who is lionized for his youthful exuberance, and spends the rest of his life fruitlessly and mechanically trying to regain the touch. Let us then honor the inspiration of these early, pleasure-giving successes by continuing to read them, and the dignified sweat of his later exertions by refusing to read them.

NOTES

1. Interestingly, Irving's two most famous stories, "The Legend of Sleepy Hollow" and "Rip Van Winkle," both were ascribed to the late Diedrich Knickerbocker's narration, even though they appeared in Geoffrey Crayon's *Sketch Book*. Thus, Irving seemed to need the alter ego of Knickerbocker for all his best work.

2. His *Colonial New York* (Charles Scribner's Sons, 1975) is the best summary of pre-Revolutionary New York.

8

Imagining Dutch New York

JOHN QUIDOR AND THE ROMANTIC TRADITION

BARTHOLOMEW F. BLAND

In John Quidor's paintings, the Dutch live wildly and well. Stereotypes of windmills, taverns, pipe smokers, and a peg-legged Peter Stuyvesant all parade through his canvases, giving visual form to the enduring power of Washington Irving's legendary, if highly inaccurate portrayal of Dutch life in the Hudson Valley.[1] Quidor was one of the key artistic purveyors of a rugged but lush nineteenth-century American romanticism. He is best known for a series of approximately two dozen paintings, scenes from the stories of Irving's old Dutch New York. Although Quidor drew the imagery and inspiration for the majority of his canvases from Irving's tales, he also adapted Irving's work for his own purposes, subtly intensifying the drama inherent in the written word. Quidor's work is not simple illustration and, in fact, his paintings are not known to have been used as illustrations for any printed edition of Irving's writings. Nor were his paintings created in any recognizable sequence—instead, Quidor seems to have picked whatever dramatic scenes took his fancy and expanded upon them, imbuing them with his own nineteenth-century anxieties and his own perspective of Irving's Dutch characters.

A product of an anxious age and eventually a commercial one, unsuccessful as an artist and a farmer, Quidor produced paintings imbued with the unease caused by changes occurring in society from the 1820s through the 1850s. In this sense, the impulse that drove him to depict Irving's stories has double meaning: a backward glance at a time that was being viewed as a kind of coarse Arcadia, from a time filled with danger and dread. In embracing the work of Irving and his depiction of a deeply romanticized New Netherland, Quidor appears as an important harbinger of the many American artists who would later embrace "Holland Mania" at the end of the nineteenth century.

Quidor was neither the first nor the last artist to draw inspiration from Irving's colorful fables, but his images both capture and enhance the rustic charm and the grotesque qualities inherent in the writings, as well as provide windows into the way artists in the nineteenth century used Irving as a lens to view New York's history. Quidor was by no means the best known of Irving's interpreters: sculptors like John Rogers domesticated his tales, emphasizing the suitably soothing, cozy aspects, ensuring a demand by families in middle-class homes who desired charming tabletop depictions of Katrina Van Tassel and Ichabod Crane courting in the parlor. However, more than any other artist, Quidor engaged the exaggerated, vulgar, even grotesque aspects of Irving's work. It is these aspects, many cases outright distortions, of Irving's stories that give Quidor's work its independent power beyond illustration. Quidor's style was consistent in its caricature through most of his career, although his technique was not, moving from thickly painted brushstrokes to thinly painted, nearly monochromatic works that suggested illustrations from antique books. Irving's wry skepticism toward his own characters obviously appealed to Quidor. It is perhaps surprising that Quidor was never drawn to the short stories of Hawthorne or Poe, as some of the gothic aspects of their work might have appealed to him, but those authors lack Irving's ironic sense of humor.

Historical information about John Quidor is fairly limited.[2] He was born in 1801 in Tappen, New York, in the heart of the Hudson Valley, not far from Washington Irving's Sunnyside in Tarrytown. At the time, the artist's family had lived in the Hudson Valley for more than 150 years. During his youth, the family moved to the rapidly growing New York City, where Quidor, the son of a teacher, was apprenticed to the artist John Wesley Jarvis from 1818 to 1822, along with another pupil, the artist Henry Inman (1801–1846).[3] The apprenticeship was evidently not a success, and Quidor eventually sued Jarvis for failing to perform adequately as a teacher.[4] In the end, this suit may have been more damaging to Quidor's reputation than to Jarvis's, since his seeming public admission that he had not been well trained cast a permanent critical pall over his skill as an artist. This experience as an apprentice does not seem to have inspired him to become a model mentor to his own pupils later in life; he is remembered for being a particularly laissez-faire instructor. As his student Thomas Bangs Thorpe (1815–1878) recounted, "In all the time we were with Quidor, many months, I do not remember of his giving us anything but easel room and one or two very common engravings to copy. He would absent himself from his studio for days and weeks together. When present, if not painting on a banner or engine back, he would generally lie at full length on the long bench."[5] His comparatively lowly status in New York's artistic hierarchy may be gleaned from the fact that although he exhibited several times at the National Academy, for much of his early career he made his living doing decorative work, with considerable success, for New York's fire companies, which during the early nineteenth century consisted of extremely competitive firehouses akin to modern sports teams.[6]

Modestly successful in the art world of his own day, in retrospect Quidor was a significant figure of nineteenth-century romanticism, whom one critic has called one of the key eccentrics and visionaries in American painting, his artistic importance belied by his relatively obscure status. The little biographical information that survives suggests Quidor was as rowdy as one of his painted figures, eschewing the decorous demeanor thought suitable for an artist, which may explain his failure to be considered acceptable as a member of the National Academy.[7]

Quidor reached his artistic maturity during the 1830s, an especially turbulent decade in New York City; his studio, located at 46 Canal Street, may have been destroyed in a large fire on December 16, 1835. There were two major cholera outbreaks, which led to a great fear of contagion. This, combined with a financial crisis and a financial crash in the late 1830s, led to Quidor's abandoning New York for a farming life in Illinois around 1837, which reduced the amount of time he spent actively painting.[8]

Of his estimated thirty-five known canvases, the majority are drawn from Irving's tales of Dutch New York. Although Irving's several dozen volumes of writings were widely available in bound author's sets after 1848, when Quidor was still actively painting, the artist chose to base his Irving canvases exclusively on the Dutch-inspired tales, eschewing source material ranging from biographies of the life of Mahomet to the life of George Washington to picturesque descriptions of Spain. Like many in the American romantic tradition, Quidor was drawn to the dark, gnarled woods of the Hudson Valley.

Quidor's Irving paintings, now almost all in major museum collections, exemplify the growing nineteenth-century acceptance of the colorful roots of New York's past, in the period before Progressive Era ideology transformed the view of the Dutch into upstanding, upright paragons of what we would currently term the WASP elite. It is no coincidence that Quidor's reputation declined to nonexistence during the late nineteenth and early twentieth centuries. In pushing the characters in Irving's stories to grotesque extremes, Quidor's depictions of the Dutch are the polar antithesis of the traditional "Dutch" values that Progressive Era elites sought to instill as suitable in new American immigrant groups: Quidor's figures are slovenly, whereas revised depictions of Dutch virtues suggested cleanliness; drunken instead of sober; and lazy instead of hardworking.

Quidor presented a reckless and superstitious peasantry not at all becoming of a group that Progressive Era reformers sought to present as an acceptable alternative to an aristocratic British past. Any self-respecting "Knickerbocker" would take one look at Quidor's canvases and shudder before claiming kin with these oddly proportioned, dissolute creatures. Although his works were actively sought by several prominent collectors during his lifetime, these factors, combined with Quidor's limited commercial success and his relatively

JOHN QUIDOR (1801–1881)
Ichabod Crane Flying from the Headless Horseman, c. 1828
Oil on canvas, 22⅝ x 30¹/₁₆ in.
Yale University Art Gallery, Mabel Brady Garvan Collection, 1948.68

Tim Burton's 1999 version of *Sleepy Hollow*, showing
the dramatic appearance of the Headless Horseman.
Image courtesy of Photofest, New York.

small oeuvre, combined to kept his name obscure until the 1930s, when curator John I. H. Baur rediscovered his work, presenting the first major exhibition devoted to the artist at the Brooklyn Museum in 1942.[9]

As one critic has noted, Irving's stories provided Quidor "with subject matter, but it also left him free, as no living subject would, to develop the fancies of his own mind."[10] Two of Quidor's favorite sources, to which he returned on multiple occasions, are simultaneously two of Irving's most popular and most fantastic tales: "The Legend of Sleepy Hollow" and "Rip Van Winkle." Both first appeared in *The Sketch Book*, supposedly as posthumous writing fragments by Diedrich Knickerbocker, the popular (and fictional) historian of Dutch ancestry in one of Irving's most popular early books, ironically titled *A History of New York from the Beginning of the World to the End of the Dutch Dynasty*, first published in 1809, exactly two hundred years after Henry Hudson first sailed into New York Harbor.

The basic plot of "The Legend of Sleepy Hollow" is familiar to most people, if not through Irving's writings, then through the popular Disney or Tim Burton film adaptations. In particular, the iconic moment of Ichabod's encounter with the Headless Horseman inspired nineteenth-century American artists from George Washington Allston Jenkins (1816–1907) to William Wilgus (1865–1949), each of whom created a variation on this scene, though often with distinct similarities. Quidor made two distinct versions, and they provide a good example of his evolving style. The earlier canvas *Ichabod Crane Flying from the Headless Horseman*, c. 1828, now in the collection of the Yale University Art Museum, presents a bleaker, more claustrophobic, and more gothic vision of Dutch New York than is described in Irving's story, in which Ichabod is something of a buffoon and it is clear that his romantic rival, Brom Bones, is in fact the ghostly Headless Horseman. In this nearly monochromatic image, Ichabod appears less goofy, less a figure of fun or caricature than is often the case in depictions of the story. Contrary to Irving's description of Ichabod as a poor rider as he flees his doom, here he appears nearly at one with the horse. Quidor's horse is a remarkable creation, its eye literally popping from its head in terror. It is also at odds with the decrepit nag described by Irving:

> The animal he bestrode was a broken-down plough house, that had outlived almost everything by viciousness. He was gaunt and shagged, with a ewe neck and a head like a hammer. . . . One eye had lost its pupil, and was glaring and spectral, but the other had the gleam of a genuine devil in it. Still, he much had fire and mettle in his day, if we may judge from the name he bore of Gunpowder.[11]

Quidor's horse looks more like a light, limber Arabian, with delicate limbs compacted like a grayhound's, every inch capable of outrunning the terrors of the dark. In the painting Ichabod rides low and close, but the proportions are distorted so that if he were standing, he would be considerably taller than the horse. The overall effect is to create a sense of urgency, that the horse, though nimble, is not a large enough means of transportation and could collapse under his weight at any moment. The tree limbs are shimmering highlights, barely visible, and the roots in particular seem almost clawlike, able to reach out and snatch Ichabod back. The picture is lit from the left with dramatic, raking moonlight that serves as a beacon, drawing him closer to the safety of the bridge where he believes that the Headless Horseman will disappear. The dramatic use of light anticipates later American artists like Ralph Albert Blakelock (1847–1919) (who himself exhibited paintings with the subject of Rip Van Winkle)[12] and inspiration drawn from the earlier, lush romantic moonscapes of German artist Casper David Friedrich (1774–1840), although both Blakelock and Freidrich used their heavily silhouetted night scenes as a device to suggest calm, timeless reflection rather than the frenzied action displayed in Quidor's painting.

Perhaps the most notable feature about Quidor's first variation of this scene is the restraint, what it leaves out: the Old Dutch Church, the bridge, and the Headless Horseman himself are nowhere to be seen; the absence of these plot signifiers gives the painting a universal quality, suggesting imagery as diverse as Rembrandt's *Polish Rider* and Longfellow's "Paul Revere's Ride," and the terrifying account in Revelation 6:8 of Death on a pale horse.[13] This lack of a more obvious narrative led to the altering of the painting more than fifty years after its completion, with another artist adding the shadowy figure of the Headless Horseman, since removed.[14]

Thirty years later in his career, Quidor returned to the theme of Ichabod's wild ride with 1858's *The Headless Horseman Pursuing Ichabod Crane*, a work rediscovered in the 1990s and now in the collection of the Smithsonian Museum of American Art.[15] These two paintings drawn from the same dramatic moment provide a number of interesting contrasts. The 1858 painting has colors that are "softly elegiac" compared to the monochromatic tones of the earlier work; it is also more in keeping with what is expected of literary illustration.[16] The Smithsonian's later version is more clearly set in time and place, depicting the moment of confrontation of the Headless Horseman and the famous pumpkin about to be hurled at Ichabod's head. While the earlier painting has an otherworldly, universal quality, the Smithsonian's painting more fully follows Irving's description of the story's locale. In the distance, the viewer can just make out the Old Dutch Church and its graveyard, filled

JOHN QUIDOR
(1801–1881)
The Headless Horseman Pursuing Ichabod Crane, 1858
Oil on canvas, 26⅞ x 33⅞ in.
Smithsonian American Art Museum, Museum purchase made possible in part by the Catherine Walden Myer Endowment, the Julia D. Strong Endowment, and the Director's Discretionary Fund. 1994.120

WILLIAM RICKARBY MILLER (1818–1893)
The Mill Pond, Sleepy Hollow, Tarrytown, New York, 1853
Wood engraving, 6⁵⁄₁₆ x 9⅜ in.
Hudson River Museum

The bucolic landscape of Tarrytown depicted by Miller belies Ichabod Crane's terrifying nighttime encounter as imagined by Quidor. A print of this engraving was shown in the Hudson-Fulton Celebration exhibition held at the New York Public Library in 1909.

GEORGE WASHINGTON ALLSTON JENKINS (1816–1907)
Headless Horseman in Pursuit of Ichabod Crane, c. 1842–1865
Oil on canvas, 26 x 36⅛ in.
Historic Hudson Valley, Tarrytown, New York, Gift of
Benjamin G. Jenkins, SS.64.538a-b

with weeping willow trees. Quidor sacrifices the deep shadows of the night to
more fully illuminate his scene, which occurs here in the golden autumn light
of late afternoon. However, in this later variation of Ichabod's encounter with
the Headless Horseman, Quidor turns the biblical allusion to Death on a pale
horse on its head, placing Ichabod on the pale horse and Death (in the shape
of the Headless Horseman) on a black steed. Irving pointedly mentions that
Brom Bones rides a horse, "Daredevil, a creature, like himself full of mettle
and mischief, and which no one but himself could manage."[17] There is a running association of darkness and blackness with fear of foreignness, death, and
the devil in Quidor's paintings that exaggerates various descriptions by Irving
and says as much about Quidor's cultural anxieties over race relations in the
first half of the nineteenth century as it does about the colonial Dutch. Despite
Ichabod's white horse, he is certainly no knight in shining armor, and despite
Brom Bones' dark horse, he is not the unlikely newcomer. In this story Ichabod is not an attractive enough character for it to be entirely obvious which
suitor the reader should prefer.

JOHN QUIDOR (1801–1881)
Ichabod Crane at a Ball at Van Tassel's Mansion, 1855
Oil on canvas, 23½ x 34 in.
Historic Hudson Valley, Tarrytown, New York,
Gift of Mabel Brady Garvan, SS.64.556 a-b

By 1858, Quidor was entering the last fruitful years of a sporadically successful and declining career derailed in New York by a period of approximately
ten years' stay in Illinois.[18] A number of critics have charged that his work lost
dramatic impact and creativity as his energies ebbed. *The Headless Horseman
Pursuing Ichabod Crane* is one of Quidor's strongest late works, but it bears
a striking similarity to George Washington Allston Jenkins's painting *Headless Horseman of Sleepy Hollow*, dated between 1840 and 1865, and may have
been suggested by Jenkins's canvas. Jenkins exhibited at the National Academy
between 1842 and 1865, during the period that Quidor had returned to New
York and was in critical decline, and Quidor may have seen his work there and
been inspired to do his own variant on the composition.[19] The two paintings
undoubtedly bear some relationship. Ichabod's pose in each is nearly identical,
fingers spread and arm raised in horror, as is the position of the church, nestled in a glen in the background. For all the similarities, Quidor's, however, is
the version with greater intensity. In his painting, the saddle has slipped from
Gunpowder and trails along the ground, emphasizing the precariousness of

Ichabod's ride, while the Headless Horseman's black horse dramatically rears up in a pose identical to the horse Quidor's 1856 painting *Tom Walker's Flight*. In addition, in Jenkins's painting, it is fairly obvious that the Headless Horseman is, in fact, the disguised Brom Bones, his real head concealed by his coat, while in Quidor's version the truth is more ambiguous and the rider, swathed in billowing fabric, does in fact appear headless. In comparison, it is also interesting to note how closely Disney's animation hewed to the Jenkins/Quidor imagery for the climactic moment of the film final sequence: "Just then he saw the goblin rising in his stirrups and in the very act of hurling his head at him."[20]

Quidor drew imagery for a third extant painting from "The Legend of Sleepy Hollow." However, *Ichabod Crane at a Ball at Van Tassel's Mansion*, 1855, deals with a much less fraught moment in the story. The painting dates from Quidor's late period, the 1850s to early 1860, when he produced a burst of final canvases before a long retirement. It depicts Ichabod's pleasure in dancing with Katrina Van Tassel, daughter of the most prosperous farmer in Tarrytown. Irving describes the scene:

> Ichabod prided himself upon his dancing as much as upon his vocal powers. Not a limb, not a fibre about him was idle; and to have seen his loosely hung frame in full motion, and clattering about the room, you would have thought Saint Vitus himself, that blessed figure of the dance, was figuring before you in person.[21]

In *Ichabod Crane at a Ball at Van Tassel's Mansion*, Quidor uses a familiar theatrical framing device of swagged curtains pulled back on a scene, suggesting that "all the world's a stage," which the artists would have recognized from a number of sources, most notably Charles Wilson Peale's famous 1822 self-portrait *The Artist in His Museum*. Despite the refined elegance suggested by the *Ball* of the title, the picture depicts the ruddy Dutch yeomanry gathering for an evening of raucous rural pleasure. Quidor also chose to keep the focus on the central figures of Ichabod and Katrina and not to portray the rival Brom Bones, a romantic triangle that has been popular with many of Irving's illustrators.

Quidor has considerably varied the physiognomy in his depictions of Ichabod. In the earlier Yale picture, he is a resolute, even determined, figure, purposefully and grimly intent on escape from his unseen pursuer. In the later Smithsonian picture, his gesticulations are hysterical with fear, and he appears a younger man, with long, flowing locks. He also mimics the facial features of his horse, which adds to the comedic effect. In *Ichabod Crane at a Ball at Van Tassel's Mansion*, Ichabod appears as a middle-aged figure with a gray, reced-

ARTHUR
IGNATIUS
KELLER
(1866–1924)
*Ichabod Crane
Romancing*, n.d.
Watercolor on
paper,
22 x 16½ in.
New Britain
Museum of
American Art,
Gift of Mrs.
Edith Keller
Johnson,
1972.35LIC

·ing hairline in contrast with Katrina's petite, youthful buxomness. His figure is lankier and more in line with Irving's description. Quidor's Ichabod is skilled at dancing, but the grim determination of his set mouth and his great height make him less a figure of fun than a slightly malevolent, even predatory figure. His rustic black clothes (his only suit) almost make him appear like a kind of crow or bird of prey. Quidor has shown Ichabod's mercenary thoughts of marrying a wealthy heiress. Katrina, "the fat partridge," as Irving describes her, has a smiling, sweet, but vapid dumpling face. In these rather acidic character types, Quidor remains truer to Irving's sensibility of the Dutch than does the refined, almost ludicrously Gainsboroughesque elegance of late nineteenth-

EDGAR MAYHEW BACON (1855–1935)
Stone Farmhouse (Home of Katrina Van Tassel,
"Legend Of Sleepy Hollow"), c. 1896
Oil on wood door, image: 23½ x 24¾ in.;
door 73½ x 36 x 1¼ in.
The Historical Society, Serving Sleepy Hollow
and Tarrytown, Gift of Edgar Mayhew Bacon

century artists such as Arthur Ignatius Keller, who, in works like *Ichabod Crane Romancing*, reflected the growing Progressive desire to see the early Dutch colonists (even the fictional ones) as evidence of New York's refined heritage. This impetus to meld historical fact and literary fiction can be seen in such examples of early "artistic" historical preservation as Edgar Mayhew Bacon's *Stone Farmhouse (Home of Katrina Van Tassel)*, c. 1896, a painting created on an architectural fragment from the building that was reputedly the inspiration for Katrina Van Tassel's home.

Like *Ichabod Crane at a Ball*, Quidor's paintings *The Money Diggers* and *Wolfert's Will*, both 1856, reflect the idea of the Dutch as greedy and corrupt, which is indicated in several of Irving's tales and may reflect English bias against the Dutch that occurred when the colony was taken over by the English. These canvases illustrate the greed and sloth of one Wolfert Webber, a cabbage farmer who embodies the Dutch stereotype of greed and sloth. In *The*

JOHN QUIDOR (1801–1881)
The Money Diggers, 1856
Oil on canvas, 27 x 34 in.
Private Collection

Money Diggers, Webber abandons farming to take up treasure hunting, with disastrous results, and in *Wolfert's Will*, he makes a sudden deathbed recovery upon hearing that his farm is worth a fortune.

In *Ichabod Crane at a Ball*, Katrina's buxom figure is encased in a bodice of nineteenth-century design, her short skirts corresponding to Irving's descriptions of New Amsterdam's Dutch maidens as preferring petticoats of a shockingly short length to display their well-turned legs. This fashion so greatly disturbed Peter Stuyvesant that he issued an (ultimately unsuccessful) edict to the women of the colony, ordering them to wear longer petticoats covered in concealing ruffles of a more respectable length, although it is hard to imagine the lusty Stuyvesant depicted in Quidor's work giving such a chaste decree.

Quidor's paintings frequently incorporate strong, gesticulating hand movements. In *Ichabod Crane at a Ball* the figure directly in the center of the picture, behind Ichabod and Katrina, perfectly re-creates a pose that Quidor had used

JOHN QUIDOR (1801–1881)
Wolfert's Will, 1856
Oil on canvas, 26¾ x 33⅞ in.
Brooklyn Museum, Dick S. Ramsay Fund, 42.46

for a dancing figure of a black man sixteen years earlier in *Antony Van Corlear Brought into the Presence of Peter Stuyvesant*, 1839. In both paintings, Quidor amplifies and exaggerates images of racial difference and dangerous loss of control, which are comparatively innocuous in Irving's stories. On the extreme right side of the *Ichabod Crane at a Ball* canvas, an animated black man wildly plays the fiddle, a sinister presence with historical reference to the devil. Nearby, the huge, wide-open fireplace roars, a stand-in for the flames of hell, as the guests metaphorically dance on their graves. Despite the seeming cheerfulness of the subject, danger is a constantly lurking presence, and a foreshadowing of Ichabod's fateful ride home. However, as critics have noted, Quidor's wild black fiddler springs from his own imagination, since Irving's fiddler is "an old grey-headed negro. . . . His instrument was as old and battered as himself. The greater part of the time he scraped on two or three strings."[22]

JOHN QUIDOR (1801–1881)
Antony Van Corlear Brought into the Presence of Peter Stuyvesant, 1839
Oil on canvas, 27 x 34 in.
Munson-Williams-Proctor Arts Institute, Museum of Art, Utica, New York, 63.110

"Rip Van Winkle," Irving's other famous story from *The Sketch Book*, is an interesting fictional example of transitional of Dutch culture in upstate New York, despite the fantastical elements. Although the story takes place in the late eighteenth century, in the years leading up to and after the American Revolution, the characters, all with Dutch surnames, retain both their traditional culture and the sleepiness that characterized the century after the Dutch had lost actual political power. The concept of Dutch culture retaining its essential character through another transfer of political power, this time from the British to the United States, is inherent in the story. Although Rip is rightly disoriented when he wakes up after his twenty-year sleep to find his village changed and more animated, it is not so essentially transformed that he cannot quickly fall back into his established patterns of inactive leisure. Quidor painted *Rip Van Winkle and His Companions at the Inn Door of Nicholas Vedder*, 1839,

JOHN QUIDOR (1801–1881)
Rip Van Winkle and His Companions at the Inn Door of Nicholas Vedder, 1839
Oil on canvas, 27⅛ x 34⅛ in.
Museum of Fine Arts, Boston
Bequest of Martha C. Karolik for the M. and M. Karolik Collection of
American Paintings, 1815–1865, 48.469

Detail of Work Above

when he was at the peak of his artistic powers. The figures are bursting with life and the composition is bursting with swirling energy. The winding path leads the viewer's eye to the picturesque background: the vernacular architecture of a building with a traditional Dutch gable and a thatched cottage nestled in a valley of the Catskills. The sheep and tiny figures of shepherdesses in the scene give an idyllic Arcadian quality at odds with the dissolute figures in the foreground.

In Quidor's best work there is a crude power inherent in his style. This vigor can be seen in a comparison of Quidor's tavern scene with N. C. Wyeth's book illustration of the same scene outside Vedder's tavern, painted more than eighty years later. Wyeth's skill as an artist is still clearly story illustration, and in some ways he is more faithful to the tone of Irving's story. The figures in front of Wyeth's version of the inn appear lazy and sleepy. The Dutch door remains only cracked for viewers to guess at the activities within, and the whole scene has a tidier, quieter, more prosperous air than it does in Quidor's painting.

Quidor more successfully captures the louche, ruddy qualities of the Dutch as described by Irving, but not their laziness—there is too much coiled energy and animation in his figures, but it is these elements that give his paintings their power and make them independent works of art rather than book illustrations. Even the sleeping figures seem likely to spring into action at any time—in this sense they also display a greater degree of cunning then Irving may have indicated in his books. In such a way the artists reflect the changing view of the Dutch from the early nineteenth century to the early twentieth. This evolving image, from slatternly to upright citizens representing cleanliness and thrift, can best be seen in the upright posture of Wyeth's inn painting, in which the figures even in their leisure are straight with rectitude.

Quidor's depiction shows Rip on the far right side of the canvas in an unusual Mannerist pose, which suggests he is an isolated and alienated man, not at all the gregarious soul described by Irving. This unusual composition was analyzed by Christopher Wilson, who first theorized that Quidor designed *Rip Van Winkle and His Companions at the Inn Door of Nicholas Vedder* as a pendant to a lost earlier version of a painting in the National Gallery of Art, *The Return of Rip Van Winkle*, 1849. Although *The Return of Rip Van Winkle* is more thinly painted in Quidor's later looser style, a side-by-side comparison proves this thesis compelling: Rip Van Winkle under the tree in the earlier painting creates a mirror image of the father and son.

The same distinctive Dutch-gabled building in the background of the earlier painting can be seen up close in the second. Although critics have argued that viewers of Quidor's day would have recognized the rapid disappearance of Dutch culture and the destruction of many old Dutch buildings that Quidor

N. C. WYETH (1882–1945)
"Here they used to sit in the shade through a long lazy summer's day. . . ."
From *Rip Van Winkle* by Washington Irving, 1921
Hudson River Museum, INV.9811

was witnessing in New York in the 1820s and '30s, their presence in both the "before" and the "after" paintings also suggests the stable continuity of Dutch culture in a changing world.[23]

In the foreground of *The Return of Rip Van Winkle*, a scroll symbolically dropped on the ground and ignored by the crowd reads "Election, Rights of Citizens, Bunker Hill"—Washington has replaced George III on the Union Hotel, and a young boy inches up the rickety-looking flagstaff, suggesting that the advance of the new generation is somewhat precarious. Most telling of all is an old Dutch-style cap, which literally "caps" the flagstaff above the new American flag, suggesting the merging of Dutch culture into the new national identity. Despite all the surface changes, the characters seem to retain their essential nature. Horrified, Rip recognizes his younger self, but even the fact that

JOHN QUIDOR (1801–1881)
Tavern Scene, 1867
Oil on canvas, 26¾ x 34 in.
Neuberger Museum of Art, Purchase College,
State University of New York, Gift of Roy R. Neuberger
Image by Jim Frank

the son is so recognizable suggests that the patterns of life are being repeated unchanged.

Although many other illustrators have focused on Rip's bewilderment upon returning to his village, Quidor shows an accusing and confrontational Rip at odds with the community around him. Some scholars have suggested that this intense alienation may have had as a source the massive societal changes in New York at the time. It is notable that Quidor has depicted Rip's raging against the community, rather that the happier reconciliation and re-integration that Rip achieves fairly quickly. Unlike Quidor's dramatic scene, Irving's description in "Rip Van Winkle" suggests that pleasure and idleness are dangerous, but not fatally so.

Having noted the vigor of so much of Quidor's work, particularly in depicting the society of Irving's Dutch characters, one comes upon *Tavern Scene*, 1867, now in the collection of the Neuberger Museum of Art, which makes an striking contrast with the inn scene in *Rip Van Winkle and His Companions at the Inn Door of Nicholas Vedder*. *Tavern Scene* is one of Quidor's few paintings

JOHN QUIDOR (1801–1881)
A Battle Scene from Knickerbocker's History of New York, 1838
Oil on canvas, 27 x 34⅝ in.
Museum of Fine Arts, Boston
Bequest of Martha C. Karolik for the M. and M. Karolik Collection of
American Paintings, 1815–1865, 48.468

not to draw upon a known literary source. A generic scene of rural life in the
Hudson Valley, the painting depicts water in the distance. Thinly painted in the
golden tones of much of his later work, the figures have staid, quiet, demure
qualities that seem the very antitheses of Irving's literary descriptions. Critics
have been in nearly universal agreement that these last few canvases show a
marked decline in both Quidor's ambition and his technical skill, yet *Tavern
Scene* perhaps most successfully captures the quietly idyllic aspect of rural life.
The ramshackle tavern, shutters falling off, under the rule of an unspecified
Dutch or English monarch, gives piquancy to the painting; a sober reflecting
tone, it is not a grand summation of an artist who never fully achieved his ambition, but neither is it a whimper. It is as if at the very end of his artistic career,
Quidor had finally come to appreciate stillness.

Apart from *Rip Van Winkle* and the *Legend of Sleepy Hollow*, the bulk of
Quidor's scenes of Dutch life were drawn from Irving's *A History of New York*.
Although Ralph Waldo Emerson expressed distaste for the *History*'s 'deplor-
able Dutch humor," the book was phenomenally popular from the time of its

first printing in 1809 and was a natural source of subject matter for Quidor, who undoubtedly recognized the commercial appeal of images derived from the book.[24]

His earliest known major canvas from this book, *A Battle Scene from Knickerbocker's History of New York*, 1838, depicts a wickedly funny account of "Dutch Courage" in the New Amsterdam colonists' battle against the Swedes that is one of his most pointedly humorous translations of an Irving story to canvas and also one of his best. Quidor depicted Peter Stuyvesant leading the troops in their successful attempt to take Fort Christina at the Swedish stronghold led by General Jan Risingh, with swirling, almost hurricane-force movement. The painting was not well received at the National Academy in 1838, and it was described as "a sad medley of broken shins and bloody noses; a confused, ill-assorted mass of flesh and smoke, almost without form and without colour; and yet, here and there, about an inch square of real humour and positive merit."[25]

The scene looks more like a schoolyard brawl than an important battle over

ALBERTUS DEL ORIENT BROWERE (1814–1887)
Recruiting Peter Stuyvesant's Army for the Recapture of Fort Casimir, 1838
Oil on canvas, 24 in x 28¾ in.
Biggs Museum of American Art, Dover, Delaware
Image by Carson Zullinger

the fate of the New World. Quidor chooses to portray the exact moment when Stuyvesant fires a decisive "fatal" cork. The soldiers are comedic, shooting at geese, getting drunk, and lurching about, singing, and even chasing after a cow in the distance. They may remind the viewer of a burlesque of a battle of biblical proportions reconceived by a comedic Hieronymous Bosch. Although the Dutch look silly, the Swedes still manage to lose the battle—a metaphorically impudent leader charges forward with a broken sword. As lightning strikes in the background, one is led to wonder if the Dutch could only have won this battle through predestination. In the humorous patterns, there are echoes of the Lilliputian battle scenes from Jonathon Swift's *Gulliver's Travels*. A comparison of Quidor's 1838 *Battle Scene* with Albertus del Orient Browere's painting *Recruiting Peter Stuyvesant's Army for the Recapture of Fort Casimir,* painted the same year, is illuminating. While possessing a naïve charm, Browere's canvas is a much stiffer execution of similar military subject matter drawn from Irving, and the painting highlights Quidor's strength in conveying movement and action on a static surface. However, Quidor's style had softened as well.

JOHN QUIDOR (1801–1881)
The Vigilant Stuyvesant's Wall Street Gate, 1863
Oil on canvas, 27⅛ x 34⅜ in.
The Metropolitan Museum of Art, Gift of Roy R. Neuberger, 1961 (61.79)
Image © The Metropolitan Museum of Art

The Vigilant Stuyvesant's Wall Street Gate, 1863, depicting the victorious warriors, painted a quarter century after *A Battle Scene*, shows the artist in a mode less determinedly satirical and almost earnestly commemorative of Dutch life. At the top of the painting, a traditional Dutch weather vane stands as an alert sentinel against the approaching fall of New Amsterdam.

Peter Stuyvesant appears in several other Quidor paintings. Unlike the enraged and comic figure in *A Battle Scene*, in *Peter Stuyvesant Watching Festivities on the Battery*, 1860, he is benevolent and patriarchal in his golden years, watching the frolicking youth. In *Ichabod Crane at a Ball*, the subject of the scene is merry on the surface but has a slightly sinister subtext; similarly, *Peter Stuyvesant Watching Festivities*, created just before the outbreak of the Civil War, with its soft autumnal scene, has a melancholy subtext. The viewer senses that this the end of an era, a conflation of Irving's description of the waning years of Dutch rule with the close of the Antebellum period in the nineteenth century. More than ten feet wide, *Peter Stuyvesant Watching Festivities* is far larger than any other existing work by Quidor and was perhaps inspired by his awareness of the growing popularity of the grand landscape canvases of the Hudson River School painters. In any event, the painting was clearly important to Quidor and was shown at the National Academy in 1861.[26] Its golden tones beautifully capture Irving's description:

> Weekly assemblages were held, not in heated ballrooms at midnight hours, but on Saturday afternoons, by the golden light of the golden sun, on the green lawn of the Battery—with Antony the Trumpeter for master of ceremonies. Here would the good Peter take his seat under the spreading trees, among the old burghers and their wives, and watch the mazes of the dance. Here he would smoke his pipe, crack his joke, and forget the rugged toils of war in the sweet oblivious festivities of peace, giving a nod of approbation to those of the young men who shuffled and kicked most vigorously—and now and then a hearty smack, in all honesty and soul, to the buxom lass who held out longest, and tired down every competitor—infalliable proof of her being the best dancer.[27]

As in *Ichabod Crane at a Ball*, the skirts of the female dancers are surprisingly short. Unlike those in Quidor's earlier works, the individual characters and specific narrative are subverted to the overall atmosphere of the piece, a kind of twilight fairy world, reminiscent of *A Midsummer Night's Dream*. The vegetation that surrounds the scene creates a storybook oval, a compositional format unusual for Quidor. Peter Stuyvesant sits in a high-backed Dutch chair, his peg leg sticking straight out as though he would use it to gently keep time

JOHN QUIDOR (1801–1881)
Peter Stuyvesant Watching the Festivities on the Battery, c. 1860
Oil on canvas, 83½ x 129⅜ in.
Hunter Museum of American Art, Chattanooga Tennessee, Museum purchase in
honor of Cleve K. Scarbrough, Jr., Director of the Hunter Museum of American Art,
1976–2000, HMAA. 1996.12

with the music. A comparison of this concept of Stuyvesant with the character
Quidor painted twenty years earlier in *Antony Van Corlear Brought into the
Presence of Peter Stuyvesant*, 1839, is a study in contrasts. In the earlier painting Stuyvesant is a randy, bloated, blatantly sexual presence surrounded by
phallic imagery. Additional comparison reveals that this dissolute character is
in marked contrast to the much more respectable and commanding figure of
Stuyvesant in *Peter Stuyvesant and the Cobbler*, c. 1850, portrayed by a more
conventional artist, John Whetton Ehninger (1827–1889).

Peter Stuyvesant was obviously a compelling figure for Quidor, and yet another version of him can be seen in one of the last canvases, *Peter Stuyvesant's
Voyage Up the Hudson River*, 1866. This painting, in the collection of the Mead
Art Museum at Amherst, has been recently cleaned and reveals a technique
typical of Quidor's late style—using a series of thin glazes, composed of oil
paint and natural resins, to make the trademark "golden tone" reminiscent
of the old masters over an underdrawing of thin brown paint.[28] This method,

JOHN WHETTON EHNINGER (1827–1889)
Peter Stuyvesant and the Cobbler, c. 1850
Oil on canvas, 36 x 48⅛ in.
The New-York Historical Society, Gift of Mr. Hugh W. Long, 1950.335

which lent an antiquated quality to Quidor's late works, led one critic to fancifully describe him as "perhaps the first of American artists to work from his imagination outward, suggesting an underground survival in the town that had once been New Amsterdam of the great old painters of the school of Rembrandt."[29]

The scene of Stuyvesant's voyage depicts a particular moment when, as Irving describes, a beam of light bounces off the large nose of Stuyvesant's right-hand man, Antony the Trumpeter, and kills a sturgeon in the water, which is feasted on by the crew. This happy event, Irving claims, leads to the naming of the nearby bluff Antony's Nose.[30] However, as in *Peter Stuyvesant Watching Festivities on the Battery*, the character of Stuyvesant, his peg leg seen resting on the deck of the ship, is subverted into the swirling landscape. *Peter Stuyvesant's Voyage Up the Hudson River* is compositionally related to a pair of Quidor's slightly earlier paintings entitled *Embarkation from Comminipaw*

JOHN QUIDOR (1801–1881)
Peter Stuyvesant's Voyage Up the Hudson River, 1866
Oil on canvas, 26⅞ x 33⅞ in.
Mead Art Museum, Amherst College, Amherst, Massachusetts,
Gift of Herbert W. Plimpton: The Hollis W. Plimpton (Class of 1915)
Memorial Collection, AC 1980.88

and *Voyage to Hellgate*, both 1861, both showing episodes drawn from Irving, depicting the Dutch attempt to relocate from their initial colony along the present Jersey shore to a community along the Long Island Sound in order to remove themselves from the threat of English colonists.

One critic has described *Embarkation from Communipaw*'s lively sea voyage as part of an overall design that suggests adventure: "not only the participants but also the trees and branches and clouds are engaged together in a kind of quivering all-encompassing dance, a cosmic dance as it were."[31] All three of these paintings depicting water voyages have the same golden tones, storybook quality, and makeshift seventeenth-century boats. Looking at them as a group of marine paintings, it is notable that, as far as is known, Quidor resisted the temptation to create an illustration based on Henry Hudson's initial dramatic sea voyage to New Amsterdam, a subject that has proven irresistible to many other artists, despite an overt call by Irving in *A History of New York*:

JOHN QUIDOR (1801–1881)
Voyage to Hell Gate From Cummunipaw, 1861
Oil on canvas, 27 x 34 in.
The Roland P. Murdock Collection, Wichita Art Museum,
Wichita, Kansas

Such was Hendrick Hudson, of whom we have heard so much, and know so little; and I have been thus particular in his description for the benefit of modern painters and statuaries, that they may represent him as he was, —and not, according to their common custom with modern heroes, make him look like Caesar, or Marcus Aurelius, or the Apollo of Belvedere.[32]

Although Quidor depicted Peter Stuyvesant, the last and most famous governor of New Amsterdam, in multiple canvases, only a single Quidor image survives of the colony's second governor, William Keift, known as "William the Testy." In *The Edict of William the Testy Against Tobacco,* c. 1865, the governor appears at the doors of his "castle" to rail against the colonists who continue puffing away in open defiance of his smoking ban.[33] In the distance can be seen the two great symbols of New Amsterdam architecture: the Dutch gabled house and the windmill.

The continuing survival of Dutch culture in the sparsely populated Hudson
Valley was largely due to the region's unpopularity with settlers from England
and other European nations, because of land was controlled by a few wealthy
owners. Most new settlers preferred to go to other regions and become land-
owners rather than be tenants in the Hudson Valley. Almost all of the population growth in the late seventeenth and early eighteenth centuries was due to
Dutch fertility rather than to an increase in immigration. For this reason, as
late as 1749 the botanist Peter Kelm noted when traveling through the region
that although the Hudson Valley had been ruled by the British for more than
eighty years, and although styles of dress had become more English, the language, houses, and manners of the people were still decidedly Dutch.[34]

Two of Quidor's late canvases, *A Knickerbocker Kitchen,* 1865, and *A Knickerbocker Tea Party,* 1866, give detailed views of Irving's conception of Dutch

JOHN QUIDOR (1801–1881)
The Edict of William the Testy Against Tobacco, c. 1865
Oil on canvas, 27¼ x 34¼ in.
Shelburne Museum, Vermont 27.1.7-14

domestic habits. The paintings were probably originally designed as pendants, as they are linked by size, date, compositional format, and several of the same gluttonous family members who appear in both scenes. Most important, the subjects follow linked descriptions in Irving, first of a traditional Dutch kitchen and its huge hearth and then of a "primitive" Dutch tea party.[35] The paintings most likely feature members of the same family. Both are thinly painted in Quidor's late style and have a deceptive coziness that is belied by careful observation. In *A Knickerbocker Kitchen*, the patriarch of the family calmly observes a small child brutally muzzling a dog, while *Tea Party* satirizes the very healthy Dutch appetite.

Tea made a major cultural impact on manners and social customs in the Netherlands, Europe, and its American colony. As one historian has noted, "many humorous tales exist about the quantity consumed at popular late-

JOHN QUIDOR (1801–1881)
A Knickerbocker Tea Party, 1866
Watercolor on paper, 27 x 34 in.
New Britain Museum of American Art, Charles F. Smith Fund, 1953.06

seventeenth-century tea parties, where purportedly, between twenty and one hundred small cupfuls per person were drunk."[36] Quidor's figures at table with their competitive greed live up to this description, although they may also serve as allegories for Quidor's discomfort with the growing competitive capitalism in New York as the Civil War drew to a close.

Of all Quidor's beloved Irving characters, the artist's travels and sporadic career might align him most closely with Rip Van Winkle. The overtly romantic idea of a lost place and lost time clearly had special resonance for the artist, and seemingly also poetic parallels with his career that spurred Quidor's ongoing interest in a picturesque (at times grotesque) "lost" Dutch New York. Both Quidor and Rip were absent from New York for years and returned only to find themselves bewildered, missed by few, and undeservedly undervalued by their contemporaries. One of the messages of the story of "Rip Van Winkle,"

JOHN QUIDOR (1801–1881)
A Knickerbocker Kitchen, 1865
Oil on canvas, 27 x 34 in.
Museum purchase, Addison Gallery of American Art,
Phillips Academy, Andover, Massachusetts

that cultures may change and yet many things remain recognizably the same, resonates well with the historic moment for this publication, the quadricentennial of Henry Hudson's travels up the Hudson River. On first glance, it seems that much of New York's Dutch influence has quietly disappeared, perhaps unmissed, but it remains powerfully alive as a romantic legend in Quidor's art.

NOTES

1. I would like to thank A. J. Minogue and Penelope Fritzer for their invaluable suggestions in developing this essay.

2. The biographical material on Quidor is relatively scant, the last published exhibition catalogue of his work having been printed in 1973. Two Ph.D. dissertations (Christopher Wilson, "The Life and Work of John Quidor," Yale University, 1982 and David M. Sokol, "John Quidor: His Life and Work," New York University, 1971) remain the major sources of reference.

3. Christopher Wilson, "The Life and Work of John Quidor" (Ph.D. diss., Yale University, 1982), 20.

4. For the most compete account of this dispute, please see Wilson, "The Life and Work of John Quidor," 21-24.

5. John I.H. Baur, *John Quidor 1801-1881*(New York: Brooklyn Museum, 1942), 9.

6. David M. Sokol, "John Quidor: His Life and Work," (Ph.D. diss., New York University, 1971), 39.

7. Sarah Burns, *Painting the Dark Side: Art and the Gothic Imagination in Nineteenth-Century America* (Berkley: University of California Press, 2004), 103.

8. Wilson, "The Life and Work of John Quidor," 82.

9. There have been three major exhibitions devoted to John Quidor's work. The first exhibition was organized by John I.H. Baur and held at the Brooklyn Museum in 1942; Baur returned to Quidor's work in an exhibition organized by the Munson-Williams-Proctor Institute in 1965, which traveled to several venues, including the Whitney Museum of American Art. The third exhibition was organized by David M. Sokol at the Wichita Museum of Art in 1973, and was based on his dissertation research. The gathering of Quidor paintings in the exhibition *Dutch New York: The Roots of Hudson Valley Culture* is the largest since 1973.

10. Lillian Schlissel, "John Quidor in New York," *American Quarterly* 17, no. 4 (Winter 1965): 757.

11. Washington Irving, *The Sketch Book* (Philadelphia: J. P. Lippincott, 1872), 476.

12. David M. Sokol, "Washington Irving: Friend and Muse to American Artists," *Visions of Washington Irving: Selected Works from the Collections of Historic Hudson Valley* (Tarrytown: Historic Hudson Valley, 1991), 27.

13. I am grateful to Susan Callanan for her illuminating conversation with me regarding the universal aspect of Rembrandt's "Polish Rider."

14. Wilson, "The Life and Work of John Quidor," 45.

15. *The Headless Horseman Pursuing Ichabod Crane* was purchased by the Smithsonian Museum of American Art in 1994.

16. Abraham A. Davidson, *The Eccentrics and Other American Visionary Painters* (New York: Dutton, 1978), 69.

17. Irving, *The Sketch Book*, 480.

18. Wilson, "The Life and Work of John Quidor," 95.

19. Kathleen Eagan Johnson, "Headless Horseman of Sleepy Hollow" in *Visions of Washington Irving: Selected Works from the Collections of Historic Hudson Valley* (Tarrytown: Historic Hudson Valley, 1991), 98.

20. Irving, *The Sketch Book*, 494.

21. Irving, *The Sketch Book*, 482.

22. Irving, *The Sketch Book*, 481-482.

23. Wilson, "The Life and Work of John Quidor," 165.

24. Qtd. in Andrew B. Myers, *The Worlds of Washington Irving, 1783-1859* (Tarrytown: Sleepy Hollow Restorations, 1974), 4.

25. *New York Mirror*, June 9, 1838; qtd. in Wilson, "The Life and Work of John Quidor," 109.

26. Ellen Simak, *A Catalogue of the American Collection Volume 2—Hunter Museum of American Art* (Chattanooga: Hunter Museum of American Art, 2001), 16.

27. Washington Irving [Diedrich Knickerbocker, pseud.], *A History of New York* (Philadelphia: Lippincott, 1872), 455-456.

28. Matthew Cushman, e-mail message describing the treatment of the painting, to Stephen Fisher on behalf of the author, November 6, 2008.

29. Van Wyck Brooks, *The World of Washington Irving* (New York: Dutton, 1944), 323.

30. Wilson, "The Life and Work of John Quidor," 217.

31. Davidson, *The Eccentrics and Other American Visionary Painters*, 131.

32. Irving, *A History of New York*, 102.

33. Although the Shelburne Musuem continues to date *Edict of William the Testy* to c. 1865, based on style, Christopher Wilson dates the painting slightly earlier, to 1857.

34. Kenneth Meyers, "The Catskills and the Creation of Landscape Taste in America," in *The Catskills: Painters, Writers, and Tourists in the Mountains 1820-1895* (Yonkers: The Hudson River Museum, 1987), 24.

35. Wilson, "The Life and Work of John Quidor," 211.

36. Peter G. Rose, "Dutch Foodways: An American Connection," in *Matters of Taste: Food and Drink in Seventeenth-Century Dutch Art and Life* (Albany: Albany Institute of History and Art, 2002), 20.

Return in Glory

THE HOLLAND SOCIETY VISITS "THE FATHERLAND"

9

LAURA VOOKLES

When twenty-six members of the Holland Society of New York boarded the steamer *Rotterdam* with family and a few friends on July 29, 1888, they joined the ranks of many Americans whose fascination with the Dutch inspired transatlantic voyages.[1] Holland Society secretary George Van Siclen was central to the trip's initiation and realization; his eulogy in the Holland Society's 1904 *Year Book* pointed out that "the trip of the Society to Holland is still the subject of agreeable reminiscence among those who participated and excites the envy of those who were unable to adopt Mr. Van Siclen's suggestion and visit the Fatherland."[2] Van Siclen probably would have been pleased to have his contribution recalled more than fifteen years later, and it does reveal how significant the romance of the one-time trip was in the creation of the society's identity. Fifteen more years later, the memorial for Charles Lydecker, a younger member of the party, concluded, "He was one of those pilgrims who made the memorable trip to Holland in 1888." Yet the renown of the trip also suggests it was not repeated as a group activity, at least not as regularly. This unique event is an apt lens for looking at Dutch heritage societies and the allure of Holland in the late nineteenth century. Both the Holland Society's founding in 1885 and their trip to the Netherlands, proposed and planned only two years later, reflect two trends gathering momentum at the end of the nineteenth century: pedigree mania and what scholar Annette Stott has termed "Holland mania."[3] This essay is an interpretive look at that journey—its planning and purpose, the people who went, how their impressions of places and activities compared with other tourists' experiences, any prestige attached to the trip, and in regard to this, the role of the press in making the public aware of this private enterprise.

KNICKERBOCKERS ON THE WAVE[4]

Tours to the Netherlands were newly popular with Americans in the 1880s, and in many ways the society's trip was similar. Like other Americans, the travelers sought in Holland the evidence and roots of U.S. culture, but they also had greater and more intensive contact with contemporary Netherlanders

Postcard: Dutch costumes, Zeeland, early 20th century
Hudson River Museum, INV.10340

than ordinary tourists. Secretary Van Siclen had planned the tour on a recognizance trip the year before, and both visits took on aspects of diplomatic missions, with formal banquets, speeches, and tours guided by local politicians and businessmen.

A pilgrimage was unusual for a heritage society and made news headlines, garnering the group a *New York Herald* correspondent as a traveling companion. Journalist Lehman Israels was himself a Dutch immigrant and brother of a celebrated contemporary Dutch artist, Josef Israels. The society's own account of the voyage, written by members Sheldon Viele and Reverend J. Howard Suydam, is filled with examples of a complex dualism of past and present. Their trip launched a continuing relationship with the existing Netherlands government and institutions that enriched New Yorkers' popular and historical images of Holland and contributed to the initiation and planning for the Hudson-Fulton Celebration twenty years later.

Map of Central Europe, including The Netherlands
From *Frye's Complete Geography* by Alex Everett Frye (Boston & London: Ginn & Company, 1895). Hudson River Museum

Heritage associations like the Holland Society of New York have long played a role in the social culture of America. In 1835 Washington Irving had helped create the Saint Nicholas Society, limited to men of pre-Revolutionary War heritage and focused on the early history of New York City. The club was in part a response to the preexisting Saint George's Society of New York (1770), the Saint David's Society of the State of New York (1835), and The Friendly Sons of Saint Patrick of New York (1784), organized for the English, the Welsh, and the Irish, as well as the New England Society in the City of New York (1805). In the spirit of Irving's mythologized tales of old New Amsterdam and the Hudson Valley, he and his Saint Nicholas Society members revered their roots with congenial frivolity.[5]

ROBERT
WALTER WEIR
(1803–1889)
Saint Nicholas,
1838
Oil on wood
panel, 30 x 25 in.
The Butler
Institute of
American Art,
Youngstown,
Ohio

The Saint
Nicholas Society
took its name
from the Dutch
patron saint
of Christmas,
popularized
in the United
States by
Washington
Irving.

TOMPKINS H.
MATTESON
(1813–1884)
*Santa's
Workshop*, 1856
Oil on canvas,
25½ x 30½ in.
W. Graham
Arader III /
Arader Gallery

The New England Kitchen at the Centennial Exhibition, Philadelphia,
wood engraving by F. S. Church in *Harper's Weekly*, July 15, 1876
Hudson River Museum

After the Civil War, pride in the nation's upcoming centennial, as well as
ambivalence toward industrialization and immigration, spurred nostalgia and
a desire to celebrate the country's heritage.[6] This in turn inspired numerous
popular and scholarly inquiries into colonial history. Early nineteenth-century
scholars of U.S. history had downplayed the importance of Dutch contributions, but this was beginning to change.[7] There was no group with more incentive to promote the importance of early Dutch presence in New York State
than the elite founders and members of The Holland Society of New York, men
who traced their ancestry to pioneers arriving before 1674, the second time the
Netherlands ceded its North American holdings to Britain. The club can be

seen as a reflection of, as much as a contributor to, a general trend of embracing one's roots dating as far back as Irving, but they certainly embraced it with gusto. A large part of their mission was to revive interest in the Dutch roots of the Hudson River Valley and preserve that historical record.

AN ENTIRE FOREST OF GENEALOGICAL TREES[8]

Sentimental reflections on colonial ancestors contributed to the founding of unprecedented numbers of heritage societies toward the end of the late nineteenth century. Many scholars have also pointed to the connections between the escalation of immigration after the Civil War and the assertion of preferred lineage and other expressions of nativistic unease. By the 1870s, there were many types of societies devoted to heritage, military service, and national origin, but it was mainly heritage societies, like the New England Society in the City of New York and the Saint Nicholas Society, that emphasized pedigree. Not all were concerned with dates of arrival. The Irish and Scottish associations, in particular, were more focused on inclusive socializing and mutual benefit or charity. Of the exclusive variety, there were certainly fewer than five relevant before the Civil War, about five founded from 1876 to 1889, and nearly twenty founded in the 1890s alone. Starting in 1885, the Holland Society marked the beginning of this astonishing scramble for aristocratic trappings as the Gilded Age approached the millennium. Some of these associations are familiar, if often confused names, like the National Daughters of the American Revolution or the Colonial Dames of America and its rival the National Society of the Colonial Dames of America.[9] Others, like the Baronial Order of the Magna Charta, founded in 1898, might inspire both awe and a skeptical eyebrow lift.[10] Most of these groups, many of which were for women, focused on patriotic colonial contributions more than nationality or origin. Yet it was this very focus on the English colonial period that had galvanized men of New York's oldest Dutch families to take action.

THE MASTERFUL INFLUENCE OF THE DUTCH[11]

New York residents had been reminded of the city's vanished Dutch heritage in 1867, when the famous pear tree planted by Peter Stuyvesant and protected for over two hundred years was felled in a carriage collision. In the next two decades, two other prominent events were the centennial-year organization of the General Society Sons of the American Revolution in 1876, and, only two years before the Holland Society's founding, the Huguenot Society of America in 1883. Many Huguenots had fled to New Netherland during Dutch days to gain religious freedom, and several early Holland Society members, including Sheldon Viele, had Huguenot ancestry.[12]

The Old Pear-Tree Planted by Governor Stuyvesant, 1861
Lithograph by Sarony, Major & Knapp, published in *D.T. Valentine's Manual*
Museum of the City of New York, 93.1.1.6378
Anonymous

American
Cross-section of Stuyvesant Pear Tree, 1650–1750
Wood, 7 x 30 x 34 in.
The New-York Historical Society, Gift of Rutherfurd Stuyvesant, 1867.439

Considered a relic of New York's past, the tree was protected with an iron fence and sections were later preserved.

EDWARD PENFIELD (1866–1925)
Windmills, from *Holland Sketches*, by Edward Penfield,
published by C. Scribner's Sons, 1907
Hudson River Museum, Purchase 2008

The colonial revival's initial focus on the English had slighted not only many pedigreed old New York families but also New Yorkers and New York State in general. Responding expressions of Dutch heritage ranged from using windmills to advertise flour to more serious historical inquiry and reappraisals of New Netherland's contributions. In 1882, Yonkers celebrated the bicentennial of the Philipse Manor Hall, one of the oldest buildings in Westchester County with Dutch colonial connections. The ceremonial address was a detailed history of Yonkers written and delivered by Reverend David Cole of the local Dutch Reformed Church. Cole would become an early member of the Holland Society. Another event that no doubt attracted the attention of some later founders was the 1883 publication of translations of some of the early records of New Amsterdam.[13]

In 1877, the year after the centennial celebration, the death of John Motley was headline news. The *New York Times* published a memorial tribute to the celebrated American scholar of Dutch history, in addition to his obituary.[14] Motley's three-volume *Rise of the Dutch Republic*, first published in 1856, had been seminal in generating interest in Dutch history, particularly with his slant, now recognized as flawed, toward the Dutch era as predictive of the American Revolution. This renewed interest in Motley was refocused by the republication of his classic text in 1879.[15] Americans interested in colonial history often

The Centennial—An Old Fashioned Wind-Mill,
Agricultural Hall, from *Harper's Weekly,* June 10, 1876, p. 473.
Hudson River Museum, INV. 3599

referenced and quoted him, as does the anonymous author of an 1880 article in *The New York Times* about a tour of Holland. The writer gives Motley credit for making the locale seem much more romantic than does the guidebook: "My Baedeker's Guide . . . only gives me bare tantalizing facts, simply informs me that from this platform through a telescope I can see 'almost the whole of Holland.'" She goes on "to quote the first lines of the best historical work of this century, *The Rise of the Dutch Republic* by John Lothrop Motley."

> To be great and powerful a nation need not occupy a vast territory. Russia . . . is a dwarf in history compared with Holland, nearly all of whose land and water can be seen through a telescope from the cathedral tower of Utrecht. It is not to be wondered that England feels a tremor of anxious sympathy with the Dutch as often as there comes about a rumor of the desire of Germany to annex the land of the Hollanders, which is one of the links in the chain of human progress and liberty forged in the glorious revolutions which maintained the right in Holland, Zealand, England, and the United States of America during the sixteenth, seventeenth, and eighteenth centuries.[16]

New York.—Bi-Centennial of the Building of the Philipse Manor Hall at Yonkers, October 18—the Historic House and its Surroundings, from sketches by a staff artist in *Frank Leslie's Magazine,* Oct. 21, 1882. Hudson River Museum, INV.9845

Motley, who had conducted much of his research in primary sources in the Netherlands, was also well respected there. M. Brouwer, their host in Leiden, quoted him in his speech: "Has not your great historian, John Lothrop Motley, made the remark that the resistance to England's despotism found its example in our resistance to Spain?"[17]

THE LAND OF DYKES AND DUNES AND MILLS[18]

All of these historical details surely paved the way for the moment when several Knickerbocker lawyers, including Van Siclen, decided to form an association and soon after plan a trip abroad; but Holland mania included interest in not only colonial Dutch roots but also the Netherlands of the present day, a visit to which was seen as living time travel. It is interesting but largely speculative to make a list of events that may have focused New Yorkers' attention abroad to contemporary Holland in the decade prior to the founding of the Holland Society of New York. The Netherlands did not have its own building at the Philadelphia centennial exhibition, but their engineering displays were particularly admired.[19] In the early 1880s, Holland was frequently in *The New York Times* for a variety of reasons, including articles about Old Master and contemporary Dutch artists. Other events considered newsworthy during those years included a World's Fair in Amsterdam in 1883 with a theme of colonial empire building and the opening of the Rijksmuseum's new building the very year of the Holland Society's founding.[20]

Tile Picture of a Painting by Franz Hals, c. 1900
By Joost Thooft & Labouchere, Dutch
Glazed tiles in a wood frame
Hudson River Museum, Gift of
Mrs. Arthur W. Little, 35.113
Photograph by John Maggiotto

The ornate interiors of Dutch steamers included decorations such as this. Sheldon Viele noted, "The smoke-room was fully appreciated both for its comfort and its quaint panels illustrating Dutch life and character."

In any case, the modern nation was on the minds of Holland Society members from the start. At the first annual dinner, society president Van Vorst made a point of saying, "Holland and her people, with whom we in the past are closely connected, and to whom we are now linked by strong ties, is worthy of our continued interest and love."[21] Furthermore, one of the letters of regret in response to the dinner invitation read at the event, from G. Van Weckerlin, the minister Plenipotentiary and Envoy Extraordinaire of the Netherlands, thanked them for the "attention they have shown the Dutch government" and called it "a new mark of friendship."[22]

ACROSS THE BOUNDING DARK BLUE SEA
GOES FORTH OUR HOLLAND SOCIETY[23]

Interest in America's and New York's roots affected the growth of overseas tourism. During the Victorian age, innovations in the speed and economy of transportation and its growing base of leisured consumers spawned the modern travel industry. The increasing ease of communication and changes in the field of journalism, including organization of the Associated Press in 1848 and the

JOSEF ISRAELS (1824–1911)
A Ray of Sunshine, 1875, painting illustrated in "The Collection of
Mr. Alexander Young—IV. The Modern Dutch Pictures," by E. G. Halton,
The International Studio, Feb. 1907, p. 297.
Hudson River Museum

Nearly twenty years after the Holland society's trip, Halton called Josef Israels
"the leader of the modern Dutch school . . . . the great poet painter of the
humble life of his country." He also called this painting "the finest example
of Israels' later work in the collection."

With Roosevelt Through Holland, by M. J. Brusse, illustrated with pen and ink sketches by J. G. Veldheer, published by the Holland America Line, 1911.
Hudson River Museum, Purchase 2008

When Theodore Roosevelt, a charter member of the Holland Society, toured the Netherlands in 1910, the Holland America Line used his fame and heritage to promote tourism. The author seemed overwhelmed with awe and anticipation: "The visit of the great Roosevelt has, of course, been an event of exceptional interest for the small country of Holland. . . . For does not this ex-president of the United States . . . more or less belong to the family in Holland? . . . . our own distant cousin TEDDY OF DELFT . . ."

completion of the transatlantic cable in 1866, also encouraged and facilitated overseas contact. Although Europe was still a luxurious destination in terms of expense and time invested, England, France, Italy, and Germany became popular with more and more Americans. Holland only gradually became an object of interest, beginning in the 1870s and 1880s, when Holland mania was on the rise, and becoming something of a fad by 1900. Motives that sent Americans to the Netherlands in droves included a desire to find Dutch ancestors, witness sites trodden by the Pilgrims before their voyage to New England, and seek out stereotypical scenes of tulips, windmills, and wooden shoes. The increased interest of American artists and collectors in Dutch painting and scenery was another key element. Artists sought out old-fashioned scenes as well, contributing to Americans' imagining that the more traditional locales in Holland, including their residents, must look like New Amsterdam had.[24]

These quests were aided and encouraged by guidebooks and travelogues. By 1900 there was a flood of books of all types about the Netherlands, including a Holland America Line promotional booklet about a 1910 tour by Theodore

Roosevelt, himself a famous Holland Society member.[25] But there were few publications available in the years leading up to the Holland Society's visit. The major guides were still all foreign—the German Baedeker and the British Murray and Cook—but were beginning to cater more to American tourists.. All three companies made guides to several countries. Murray was one of the earliest, with the 1871 edition entitled simply *A Handbook for Travellers on the Continent*, and a subtitle specifying that this meant not only Holland but also Belgium, Prussia, northern Germany, and the Rhine. Baedeker's handbook was also not just about the Netherlands but also included Belgium; Cook's included a trip up the Rhine.[26]

An early work that was more literary than a mere travel guide was the Italian *Holland and Its People* by Edmondo de Amicis, which was translated into several languages. The English versions, including Putnam's first American edition in 1880 and a deluxe edition four years later, lavishly illustrated with etchings, were highly popular with Americans.[27]

That the Holland Society tourists were well aware of at least some of the standard guides and travelogues is apparent from Sheldon Viele's reference to De Amicis as their day-tour boat steamed away from Amsterdam en route to Marken: "As we left the harbor, the weeping tower, so beautifully described by de Amicis, was pointed out to us." He was referencing this passage:

> Among these towers there is one called the "Tower of the Corner of Lamentation," or "Tower of Tears," because there in ancient times Dutch sailors embarking for long voyages took leave of their families who came to see them off. Over the gate is a rusty bas-relief, bearing the date of 1569, and representing the port, with a ship about to sail, and a weeping woman. It was put up in memory of a sailor's wife who died of grief at the departure of her husband.
>
> It has been observed that almost all strangers who go to see that tower, after having given a glance at the bas-relief, and at the guide-book which explains it, turn towards the sea and look thoughtfully out, as if in search of the departing vessel. What are they thinking of? Perhaps what I myself was thinking of. They follow that vessel into the Arctic seas, to the whale fishery, and in search of a new road to the Indies.[28]

Other foreign travelogues that members of the Holland Society might have read or seen include books by Henry Havard, like *The Dead Cities of the Zuyder Zee: A Voyage to the Picturesque Side of Holland,* and Augustus John Cuthbert Hare's *The Heart of Holland.* Annette Stott points out that authors not under the sway of American Holland mania did not always view Holland scenery and the Dutch people through such rose-colored glasses.[29]

American books were also beginning to appear. Just two months before the Holland Society was founded, Harper & Brothers published *Sketching Rambles in Holland*, written and illustrated by painter George Henry Boughton, which received lengthy coverage in *The New York Times*. The reviewer compared the writing to De Amicis and found Boughton more "practical and humorous."[30] That Holland Society members were aware of such books is revealed by their asking artist F. Hopkins Smith, author and illustrator of *Well-Worn Roads of Spain, Holland and Italy* (1887), to speak at the 1888 dinner.[31]

I'M A VAN OF A VAN OF A VAN OF A VAN OF A VAN OF A WAY BACK LINE[32]

This was the milieu of interest in Holland and the Dutch roots of New York in the years just prior to the founding of the Holland Society in 1885. The story of its founding does not directly point to any of these factors, but it is not surprising that if a group of New York blue bloods were to decide to form a Dutch heritage association they might be motivated to do so around 1885. From the beginning, the association concerned itself almost equally with scholarly and social pursuits, often combining the two by featuring speakers on historical subjects at the dinners and by featuring scholarly and social topics in the actual reports.[33] There was also immediate interest in establishing relations with officials in modern Holland. As typical of Victorian Americans, they were in awe of Dutch royalty, and this fascination coexisted uncritically with their promotion of Dutch society as democratic.[34]

LAND OF OUR FATHERS WE THY SHORES ARE SEEKING[35]

The goal of connecting to present-day Holland seems to have been unique to the heritage associations that placed a great deal of emphasis on pedigree. Van Siclen and the other members no doubt had a number of motivations, ranging from the relative exoticism of Holland to the desire to collect historical information and strengthen New York's claim to a unique status, to the notion of quasi diplomacy and even investment potential. Already in the *Year Book* of 1886–87, there was a report that they had been in touch with Leiden's Third of October Association, a patriotic historical group, which they saw as analogous to themselves. They contributed funds toward the Dutch group's grand anniversary celebration of the Siege of Leiden. The *Year Book* included a long reply from the association president, N. Brouwer, and secretary, along with a photograph of a Holland Society banner their group had made and paraded, but stopped short of actually inviting them to visit.[36]

The expedition was a motion by Secretary Van Siclen during a regular meeting, but Holland was an obvious excursion that could have already been

George Van Siclen,
Secretary of the Holland Society
From *Year Book of the Holland Society
of New-York*, 1888–1889
Hudson River Museum, Gift of the
Dutchess County Historical Society,
2008

on the minds of others. Van Siclen certainly worked to make the tour happen
and did so with panache. The *Year Book* of 1887–88 reports that the members
authorized the trip, though all or part of it had been set by May 19 the previous
year—the date of that meeting. A tour of such size and complexity required extensive preparation, especially considering the formal reception of the members at nearly every stop. Van Siclen was noted to be going on a trip "for purpose of cultivating more close and friendly relations with our Fatherland and
its people."[37] The transatlantic cable had been in place for twenty years, but his
scheme required more diplomacy than those brief communiqués would allow.
Van Siclen traveled to the Netherlands in the summer of 1887 to make the
necessary plans. That he was a lawyer and also creator of an investment group,
the Holland Trust, seems to have caused misunderstanding among some of his
hosts, leading them to believe that the Holland Society members were seeking
investment opportunities in the Netherlands.[38]

All the society members were from old New York families, but Van Siclen
was the only tourist conversant in modern Dutch. His planning visit attracted
a flurry of attention, including from the Holland America Line (then called
Nederlands Amerikaanse Stoomvaart Maatschappij), for which the tour meant

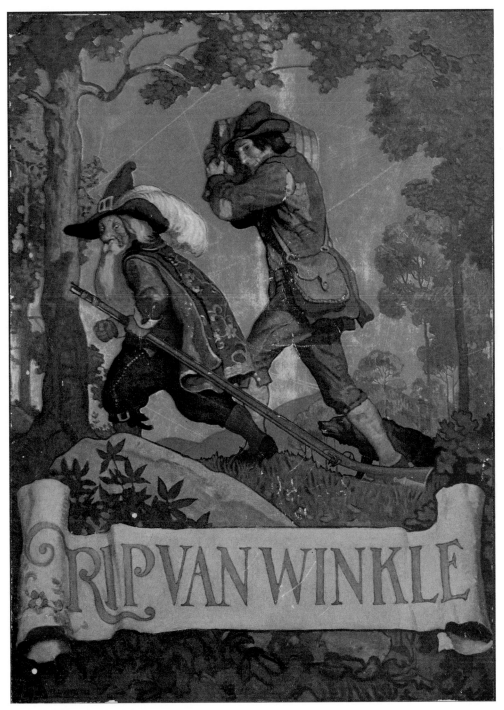

N. C. WYETH (1882–1945)

Cover illustration for *Rip Van Winkle* by Washington Irving

(Philadelphia: David McKay Company, 1921).

Hudson River Museum, INV.9811

ALBURTUS DEL ORIENT BROWERE (1814–1887)

Rip in the Mountains, 1880

One of four paintings from the *Rip Van Winkle* Series

Oil on canvas, 30 x 44¼ in.

Shelburne Museum, Shelburne, Vermont, 27.1.7-17

BENCKE & SCOTT

"Dis von don't count." Mr. Joseph Jefferson, in his celebrated
character of Rip Van Winkle, c. 1895

Color lithograph

Library of Congress Prints and Photographs Division, Washington, D.C.,

(PGA—Bencke & Scott—Dis von don't count . . . (B size) [P&PJ])

JOHN QUIDOR (1801–1881)
The Money Diggers, 1856
Oil on canvas, 27 x 34 in.
Private Collection

JOHN QUIDOR (1801–1881)

Ichabod Crane at a Ball at Van Tassel's Mansion, 1855

Oil on canvas, 23½ x 34 in.

Historic Hudson Valley, Tarrytown, New York, Gift of Mabel Brady Garvan, SS.64.556 a-b

JOHN QUIDOR (1801–1881)

The Headless Horseman Pursuing Ichabod Crane, 1858

Oil on canvas, 26⅞ x 33⅞ in.

Smithsonian American Art Museum, Museum purchase
made possible in part by the Catherine Walden Myer Endowment,
the Julia D. Strong Endowment, and the Director's Discretionary Fund. 1994.120

In 1949 Washington Irving's iconic vision of the Headless Horseman
was given the Disney treatment in *The Adventures of Ichabod and Mr. Toad*,
a double feature of Irving's story and *The Wind in the Willows*.
Image courtesy Photofest, New York

JOHN QUIDOR (1801–1881)

Rip Van Winkle and His Companions at the
Inn Door of Nicholas Vedder, 1839

Oil on canvas, 27⅛ x 34⅛ in.

Museum of Fine Arts, Boston

Bequest of Martha C. Karolik for the M. and M. Karolik Collection

of American Paintings, 1815-1865, 48.469

JOHN QUIDOR (1801–1881)

The Return of Rip Van Winkle, 1849

Oil on canvas, 39¾ x 49¹³⁄₁₆ in.

National Gallery of Art, Washington, D.C.,

Andrew W. Mellon Collection, 1942.8.10

Image courtesy of the Board of Trustees, National Gallery of Art, Washington, D.C.

JOHN QUIDOR (1801–1881)
A Knickerbocker Kitchen, 1865
Oil on canvas, 27 x 34 in.
Museum purchase, Addison Gallery of American Art,
Phillips Academy, Andover, Massachusetts

JOHN QUIDOR (1801–1881)

Peter Stuyvesant's Voyage Up the Hudson River, 1866

Oil on canvas, 26⅞ x 33⅞ in.

Mead Art Museum, Amherst College, Amherst, Massachusetts,

Gift of Herbert W. Plimpton: The Hollis W. Plimpton (Class of 1915)

Memorial Collection, AC 1980.88

JOHN QUIDOR (1801–1881)

Antony Van Corlear Brought into the Presence of Peter Stuyvesant, 1839

Oil on canvas, 27 x 34 in.

Munson-Williams-Proctor Arts Institute, Museum of Art, Utica, New York, 63.110

JOHN WHETTON EHNINGER (1827–1889)
Peter Stuyvesant and the Cobbler, c. 1850

Oil on canvas, 36 x 48⅛ in.

The New-York Historical Society, Gift of Mr. Hugh W. Long, 1950.335

Postcard: Dutch costumes, Zeeland,
early twentieth century
Hudson River Museum, INV.10340

Tile Picture of a Painting by Franz Hals, c. 1900

By JOOST THOOFT & LABOUCHERE, Dutch, Glazed tiles in a wood frame

Hudson River Museum, Gift of Mrs. Arthur W. Little, 35.113

Photograph by John Maggiotto

MARCIA OAKES WOODBURY (1865–1913)

Cinderella, 1892

Watercolor on paper, mounted on board, 27¼ x 20½ in.

Carl Van Dell

Photograph by John Maggiotto

J. C. LEYENDECKER
(1874–1951), *Young
Dutch Girl—Study*,
painted for the cover of
*The Saturday Evening
Post*, April 3, 1926.
Oil on unstretched canvas,
19½ x 10¾ in.
Curtis Publishing
Company
Image courtesy of Archives
of American Illustrators
Gallery, New York

EDWARD PENFIELD (1866–1925)
Marken Bedroom, from *Holland Sketches*,
by Edward Penfield, published by C. Scribner's Sons, 1907
Hudson River Museum, Purchase 2008

TOMPKINS H. MATTESON (1813–1884)

Santa's Workshop, 1856

Oil on canvas, 25½ x 30½ in.

W. Graham Arader III/Arader Gallery

OFFICIAL PROGRAM

HUDSON-FULTON CELEBRATION

PRICE TWENTY-FIVE CENTS

COPYRIGHT 1909 BY THE HUDSON-FULTON CELEBRATION COMMISSION

REDFIELD BROTHERS INC.
Official Program of the Hudson-Fulton Celebration, 1909
10 x 7 x ⅛ in.
Hudson River Museum, 75.0.433.1 (3)

Hudson-Fulton Poster Postcard, 1909

Printed postcard, 5½ x 3¼ in.

Hudson River Museum

NAVAL PARADE

HUDSON-FULTON
CELEBRATION 1909

Hudson-Fulton Celebration Postcard, 1909

Printed postcard, 3 x 5 in.

Hudson River Museum purchase

UNKNOWN ARTIST

Kingsbridge Road Near Dykemans [sic] Farm, c. 1866

Lithograph, 7¾ x 8¼ in.

Dyckman Farmhouse Museum, New York, New York

A Merry Christmas, postmarked 1909

Embossed color postcard, 3½ x 5½ in.

Hudson River Museum, INV. 5003

Dutch Cleanser
advertisement (detail)

From *Good Housekeeping*
magazine, February, 1944
Hudson River Museum
Purchase

Even today, popular
imagery and stereotypes
of the Dutch maintain a
strong hold on the public
imagination.

Cleans with Lightning Speed

By actual test, Old Dutch cleans 34 more bathtubs per can than any other leading cleanser! Cleans with lightning speed—without scratching beautiful porcelain and enamel finishes!

And here's why. Because grease is one of the worst problems of cleaning, Old Dutch is made with a fast grease dissolver that emulsifies grease quickly... loosens its hold on the dirt. Then Seismotite erases the loosened dirt—easily—quickly.

Prove the superiority of Old Dutch yourself! Compare cleansers in your own home... keep a *record. You* may get even *more* sensational results than those obtained by independent laboratories!

GET THE CLEANSER USED BY MORE WOMEN THAN ANY OTHER

COPYRIGHT 1943, CUDAHY PACKING COMPANY

Chases Dirt

OLD DUTCH
CLEANSER
MADE WITH SEISMOTITE

Guaranteed by
Good Housekeeping

144   February 1944 Good Housekeeping

good business. The company invited officers of the Holland Society to an on-board dinner to celebrate Van Siclen's trip. The text of the invitation noted that they "appreciate that he is traveling to Europe in an official capacity."[39]

Van Siclen reported on his recognizance trip in a speech at the 1887 dinner and noted that the secretary of the Third October Association of Leiden had boarded ship to greet him. He encouraged members to join that organization.[40] He described having visited typical Dutch houses in Leiden and presented what was becoming a widespread view of the Pilgrims as highly influenced by Dutch virtues. Van Siclen used the word "Puritan" interchangeably with "Pilgrims"—quite common at the time.[41] He went into some detail about the historical references of places on his visit, including a house dated 1492, and notes that in Dordrecht they were driven through "old streets where carriages are seldom seen." He concluded by saying that even if Holland were to be lost to the sea, the virtues she had imparted to the United States would remain "political liberty, freedom of conscience and free public instruction." He did not particularly mention a proposed trip or invitation, but considering the elaborate nature of the arrangements, the group tour must have been under consideration for some time already.

DESCENDANTS OF THE PATROONS IN THE LAND OF THEIR ANCESTORS[42]

A large party were going, more than 25 members, some traveling separately, as well as 9 women—wives, daughters, and friends—and several sons, probably future members. There were also several other nonmember guests. The Holland Society had grown rapidly in the first few years of its existence. At the time of the 1886 dinner there were 200 members; by May 1887, there were 440. In August 1888 there were at least 500, which meant about 5 percent went to Holland. This relatively small list of travelers revealed just how widespread the Holland Society was becoming (see chart).[43] The members represented 14 cities from the metropolitan area of New York City, Brooklyn, and Jersey City to the length of the Hudson Valley, represented by Irvington, Nyack, Poughkeepsie, and Albany. There was a significant upstate group, including Sheldon Viele of Rochester, the historian of the trip, and Dr. John Van Duyn of Syracuse, chosen during a meeting at sea to be the "pictoriographer," as well as members from Schenectady, Rochester, and Buffalo. Besides Jersey City, the spread of the Dutch to that state was further indicated by travelers from Freehold and New Brunswick. At the time, John H. Voorhees lived in Washington, D.C.

The well-heeled group included six lawyers, two ministers, an architect, a lumber merchant, and a doctor. The members were a who's who of current

Dr. John Van Duyn and
Charles Beseler Company
Mr. Israels
Herald Correspondent,
lantern slide (#59)
The Holland Society of
New York

and future society officers ranging in age from thirties to late sixties.[44] A few key members not traveling with them did come to some of the events and day trips, including Robert Roosevelt, newly appointed ambassador to the Netherlands; State Senator C. P. Vedder, serving Cattaraugus County near Buffalo; and Warner Van Norden, a private banker and later President of the Bank of North American and the Holland Society. The trip was not only a memorable event for them; it was, in comparison with the activities of similar groups, a journalistic sensation, appearing in the press twenty-two times from preparation to aftermath—in *The New York Times*, the *Brooklyn Eagle*, and primarily the *New York Herald*, which dispatched special correspondent Lehman Israels. At the time, the *Herald* was engaged in an intense competition for readership with Pulitzer's *New York World*, and losing ground.[45] This could have prompted the decision to exploit the Holland Society trip as a major story.

Sheldon Viele and Reverend J. Howard Suydam gave a list of the participants and a thorough chronology of the trip in their travelogue, published in the society's annual report in 1889. The tourists and their itinerary are summarized below. Documentation of the trip also included Dr. Van Duyn's photographs. Each members contributed $3 for "a collection of photographs for the archives."[46] Viele purchased professional shots similar to a group of tourist

Members	Residence
Blauvelt, James A & son	Nyack
Ditmars, Isaac E.	New York City
Elmendorf, Rev. J., D.D. & wife	New York City
Elsworth, Hon. Edw.(mayor) & daughter	Poughkeepsie
Elsworth, Eugene	Irvington
Fort, Peter V. & daughter & granddaughter	Albany
Hasbrouck, Frank	Poughkeepsie
Hubbard, H. B. & son	Brooklyn
Lydecker, Chas. E.	New York City
Suydam, Rev. J. Howard, D.D.	Jersey City
Swits, John L.	Schenectady
Van Allen, Hon. L. L. & sister	New York City
Vander Beek, Frank I. & son	Jersey City
Vander Bogart, G. Y.	Schenectady
Van Duyn, Dr. John & wife	Syracuse
Van Heusen, Theo V. & son	Albany
Van Siclen, Geo. W.	NYC
Veeder, Dr. Harmon W.	Schenectady
Van Voast, James A.	Schenectady
Van Voorhis, Menzo	Rochester
Viele, Sheldon T.	Buffalo
Vredenbergh, W. H.& son	Freehold, N.J.
Van Wyck, Robert A.	New York City
Voorhees, Dr. Chas. H. & wife	New Brunswick, N.J.
Voorhees, John H.	Washington, D.C.
Voorhees, Judah B. & wife & 2 other women guests	Brooklyn (Deputy Surrogate)

souvenirs now in the collection of the Hudson River Museum, but over 100 lantern slides in the Holland Society's library attest to the fact that Van Duyn was also an amateur photographer.

The language of narrative surrounding this event—the press, the accounts of the trip historians, and the supposedly verbatim speeches recorded therein— reflects the complex and conflicted feelings about Holland in the 1880s and 1890s. Many people's notions of colonial history were based largely on folk- lore and current perceptions, attitudes, and relationships.[47] This interplay of

DATES	ITINERARY OF THE HOLLAND SOCIETY, 1888
Sat., July 28– Thur., Aug. 9	aboard steamship *Amsterdam* sailing from Jersey City
Thur., Aug. 9– Tue., Aug. 14	arrive Rotterdam; train to Amsterdam
12	Rijksmuseum
13	Leyden
14	island of Marken; old city of Hoorn (day trip from Amsterdam)
15	Delft and The Hague
16	Rotterdam
	steamer day trip down the Maas to Brielle; onward to Dordrecht
	Rotterdam
17	Alkmaar
19	most tourists leave Rotterdam on board the *Amsterdam*
20	Leeuwarden in province of Friesland
21	Groningen (day trip)
22?*	Sneek Yacht Races; train back to Leeuwarden that night
	next morning—joined at station by the Van Nordens
23?	Arnhem; reception at the residence of Peter de Vries.
24?	Utrecht
25?	Middelburg, Flushing
29?	Antwerp, Belgium
30?	Brussels, Belgium—impromptu invitation by a member of the Dutch Club at Brussels
Sept. 1–13	Rotterdam; return travel of second group on the steamer *Rotterdam*

* no further dates until departure—these deduced from recorded activities

left: Dr. John Van Duyn and Charles Beseler Company,
Mr. Van de Beek, Mrs. Van Duyn, Mr. Van Zuyler, & Little Miss Delahanty, 1888
lantern slide (#49)
The Holland Society of New York

Anticipating the dawn of the snapshot age, Van Duyn took numerous candid
shots on ship, including this one with his wife stage center. "Little Miss Delahanty"
may have been the youngest tourist.

right: Dr. John Van Duyn and Charles Beseler Company,
Marken Street, 1888
lantern slide (#105)
The Holland Society of New York

Scholar Nancy Steiber quotes diarist Charles Lydecker as writing that the men
on the trip purchased tall top hats because they were standard attire for Dutch men
of their class (see note 82).

past and present, positive and negative, fact and fiction is exemplified in the
Holland Society and their trip. During the main part of the trip, Van Siclen
made several formal responses to their hosts in Dutch; and near the end of
their journey, at Middelburg, with the party down to four men, lawyer John
Voorhees gave a speech that laid out what he thought the tourists had actually
known and actually learned. With carefully organized eloquence, Voorhees
said that they had known much of the history of Holland via "our Motley" and
had also known of the Dutch struggles to protect and even create land from
the sea—a story of commitment and perseverance often repeated by Americans. And of course, they were also aware of the Old Master painters, whose
works were being so avidly collected by wealthy socialites in New York and
other major U.S. cities. He concluded with these effusive and flattering words
for their hosts: "But one thing we did not know; it is the charm of your home
life, the lessons of the hearth and the family altar . . . the secret of the influence of Dutch civilization and colonization. It is the education of the home,
the Bible in the house, the mother teaching the deference to age and parental
authority."[48]

Fine Arts Museum Amsterdam (Rijksmuseum), c. 1885–88
Photographer unknown
4¾ x 7⅛ in., Hudson River Museum, INV.2363

Today some of these speeches seem rather condescending, with their implications that the new home the Dutch colonists created was more impressive than the homeland they had left behind. For example, at Leiden, Reverend Suydam made an extended analogy with the Dutch explorers and settlers as Jason and the Argonauts and America as the Golden Fleece, which was not returned but put to good use.[49] If they sensed any tensions, the visitors nevertheless clearly enjoyed themselves and felt they were privy to a more intimate experience of Holland than the average tourist, with the personal attention, invitations, dinners, specially arranged historical exhibitions, and visits to the homes of prominent people. However, most of the sites they saw and the activities they did were entirely typical of ordinary tourists' experiences, highly influenced by the popular guidebooks. They visited the Rijksmuseum to see Rembrandt's *Night Watch*, marveled at the hundreds of windmills as they passed by Zaandam, and took a day trip on a small steamer to the island of Marken, which was steeped in the traditional culture of an old-time fishing village. Unlike most tourists, they also spent some of their time at the Rijksmuseum scanning labels for the names of their ancestors.[50]

Water Street-Zaandam, Holland, n.d.,
Stereograph by unknown maker, 3½ x 7 in.
Hudson River Museum, Gift of Dr. Edward Friedman, 89.1.502

CONFOUNDING HOLLAND OF THIS CENTURY WITH
HOLLAND OF TWO CENTURIES AGO[51]

The isolation of Marken, which the group visited on August 14, was an artificial construct by that point. [52] Not much more than a stone's throw from Amsterdam, it was visited daily by numerous tourists, who gaped at the residents. One example of this simulated atmosphere was the widow Marretje Thijssen Teerhuis, who let tourists and artists see the interior of her house, for a fee, thus simultaneously supporting herself and sparing her neighbors the indignity of strangers knocking at their doors. Due to this limitation, for three decades most photographs and artworks of Marken interiors depicted her room, always from one specific angle.[53]

In Marken and other areas preserved from modernization, some tourists even attempted to purchase items of traditional garb off the residents' bodies. John Voorhees, Menzo Van Voorhis, Frank Hasbrouck, and Reverend J. Howard Suydam, the four members of the Holland Society who continued to tour the countryside after the majority had dispersed, apparently tried to do this in Groningen, because Reverend Suydam, who was the historian for that portion of the trip, confessed that the ladies could not be induced to part with their traditional head coverings. They had to content themselves with a display at a nearby museum, reinforcing the melding of past and present in their experience of Holland. On some level the tourists must have been aware of the self-conscious preservation of the past: in describing their visit to the famous

Children of Marken-Holland, c. 1885–88
Photographer unknown, 4¾ x 6¾ in.
Hudson River Museum, INV.5266

Marken-Holland (Bedroom of Widow
Marretje Thijssen Teerhuis) c. 1885–88
Photographer unknown, 5 x 8 in.
Hudson River Museum, INV.2366

EDWARD PENFIELD (1866–1925)
Marken Bedroom, from *Holland Sketches*,
by Edward Penfield, published by C. Scribner's Sons, 1907
Hudson River Museum, Purchase 2008

Cheese Market at Alkmaar, Sheldon Viele made the revealing comment that the local men were dressed in traditional clothing, "in honor of our visit."

Although Marken was a must-see destination, most tourists stayed a mere hour or so and then, as recommended by the guidebooks, returned to the modern comforts of their Amsterdam hotels. The Holland Society visitors apparently saw no contradiction or irony in their appreciation of these comforts, though they "seemed astonished at the modernization of Amsterdam."[54] Viele described their approach to the city by train as like coming into New York City from the north.[55]

In Amsterdam, the travelers stayed at the Amstel Hotel, which was new and one of the most popular and lavish in the city. Its construction was

spearheaded by Samuel Sarphati (1813–1866), a Jewish doctor, public health crusader, and urban planner who influenced much of the modern development in mid-nineteenth-century Amsterdam.[56] His prominent position and the background of *Herald* correspondent Lehman Israels, an immigrant from Groningen and brother of the most famous Dutch painter of the day, serve as a reminder of the long-standing importance of the Jewish community in the Netherlands. Some of the earliest Dutch settlers in New Amsterdam had been Jews, though none of their descendants was among the founders and early members of the Holland Society.

Unlike its nineteenth-century cousins visiting from America, Dutch society in Europe and New Netherland had been quite diverse. The image of the Dutch as religiously tolerant comes up in speech after speech on the Holland Society

At Home-Marken-Holland, c. 1885–88
Photographer unknown
4¾ x 7⅛ in.
Hudson River Museum, INV.5275

trip and at the annual dinners, and was expressed as early as the first banquet, in 1886. Chauncey Depew, member and president of the New York Central & Hudson River Railroad, summed up one prevailing rationale for Holland mania bluntly with these words: "We hear much of the Puritan and Plymouth Rock. The true Puritan was a bigot. . . fighting to preserve his own religious liberty and to destroy that of everyone else. . . . Those Pilgrim Fathers that journeyed to New England by way of Holland never burned witches." Despite these fighting words, Depew, like many other members of elite heritage societies, held multiple memberships, including the New England Society, the Society of Colonial Wars, the Huguenot Society, and the Saint Nicholas Society.[57]

OUR SPECIAL CORRESPONDENT,
IN WHOM WE TOOK MUCH PRIDE[58]

Lehman Israels, who came to New York in 1851, was part of a new wave of Dutch immigrants to the United States.[59] He was from Groningen, which had a thriving Jewish community up to World War II. Israels served in the Civil War, then had a long career as a journalist. With his connections and his personal knowledge of the Dutch language, country, and art world, he made an ideal overseas correspondent; one source states he was foreign editor of the *World* for several years.[60] Based on census data on the occupations of Dutch

MARCIA OAKES WOODBURY (1865–1913)
Cinderella, 1892
Watercolor on paper, mounted on board, 27¼ x 20½ in.
Carl Van Dell

By the 1890s, Dutch imagery was so pervasive that it appeared
in contexts not necessarily connected to Holland or colonial New
Amsterdam.

Zeilvereeniging Sneek
From *Yearbook of the Holland Society of New-York*, 1888–1889
Photograph by Edward Bierstadt
Hudson River Museum, Gift of the Dutchess County Historical Society, 2008

After the main part of their trip, Reverend J. Howard Suydam and his three remaining Holland Society traveling companions were invited to and much enjoyed the annual Sneek yacht races. This was familiar territory, representing contemporary rather than historical co-interests. They later sent a trophy cup as a gift.

Jewish immigrants to the United States, his choice of career was unusual.[61] Unfortunately, at various times he was a subject of rumors, accusations, and bad recommendations.[62] It is tempting to wonder if some of this was related to his ethnicity. Surely these setbacks were at least partly why he later branched out into real estate press.

No records have been found of how Lehman Israels came to be employed on the Holland Society assignment, but he was certainly a natural choice. Sheldon Viele makes almost no mention of the reporter's presence in his account of the trip, other than to name him and state his purpose. Though Lehman Israels was surely at The Hague when the Holland Society members met and socialized with his brother Josef—whom Veile called "the celebrated painter Israels"—and his own sister-in-law, his presence is not noted.[63] The tourists returned in two groups, and Israels is not listed on either return trip, so he may have stayed longer to visit family.

Amsterdam, c. 1885–88
Photographer unknown, 4⅞ x 7⅛ in.
Hudson River Museum, INV.2361

Although Amsterdam was a modern city in many respects, tourists
preferred areas where many traditional buildings were standing.

Amsterdam, c. 1885–88
Photographer unknown
4⅞ x 7½ in.
Hudson River Museum, INV.2365

The only extended description of Israels' activities in the narrative are some condescending remarks about his interviews regarding their colonial ancestry. Viele poked fun at the fact that the reporter wanted details with maximum news impact.

> We were directed to . . . hand to Mr. Israels, the versatile special correspondent of the "Herald," who accompanied us, a succinct account of our Dutch descent; and we were particularly instructed to insert therein any romantic incidents or legends that occurred in our family traditions. "But," said Van, "suppose we haven't any?" "Then," said the autocrat, "invent some. . . ." Accordingly we all went to work, and at intervals "our special correspondent," in whom we took much pride, was presented with our effusions.[64]

Lehman Israels' coverage consists of eleven articles—long ones sent by steamer and very brief ones dispatched by cable.[65] Most are straightforward and informative, with sensational headlines like THE DUTCH TAKE HOLLAND and DUTCH RAIDERS. In contrast to Lehman's other reports, his last dispatch to New York began with a scathing criticism of what he thought had been an awkward, even insulting toast offered by Reverend Suydam to the Princess Wilhelmina at the farewell banquet in Rotterdam. Israels quoted the minister as toasting "the health and success of the young princess, who is ere long to succeed the aged monarch with the expiration of whom the House of Orange will cease to exist."[66] As a native Dutchman, Israels felt that the comments about Wilhelmina's succession representing the end of a royal line were tasteless and showed a typical American lack of understanding of Holland's past and present international role. Digressing from the recap of the dinner, Israels launched into an attack on out-of-touch royals and aristocrats, who feared the "intelligent masses." He started out by asserting that the Dutch were governed by the will of the people, despite the vestiges of monarchy, but ended up suggesting that the true democracy of the United States would set the example for the future.

In this more positive light, Lehman Israels concluded by quoting Emerson, saying that as years go by, the Holland Society tourists might realize their trip had a legacy, that they "builded better than they knew." This line was often summoned during the late nineteenth century, usually in reference to the prescience of the Founding Fathers and other creators of the American system of government.[67] To suggest that the Holland Society might ultimately wield influence in that regard is highly flattering. It would be enlightening to know what the society members thought of the article, which ran in the *Herald* before the first group to depart arrived home. Perhaps one indication is that

The Procession in Leiden
From *Yearbook of the Holland Society of New-York*, 1888–1889
Hudson River Museum, Gift of the Dutchess County Historical Society, 2008

Israels was a guest, along with forty-two other invited nonmembers, at their January 8, 1889 annual dinner.[68]

PRINCES OF THE BLOOD[69]

Although the trip to the Netherlands was overall a positive experience for the participants, there was some tension and controversy regarding the Holland Society's ongoing relations with the Third of October Society, which they had visited in Leiden.[70] This group had been formed even more recently than the Holland Society, from whom they sought memberships and contributions. The Americans were at first happy to oblige, at least from the point of view of George Van Siclen. However, Van Siclen was guilty of implying that the Holland Society was connected to an investment firm, called the Holland Trust, which he founded the year of the trip and for which he used similar stationery.[71] A major reason for the grand reception in Holland may have been less political diplomacy than the Dutch hosts wining and dining potential investors whom they thought could benefit themselves and their country. This impression would have been despite the fact that whenever asked, even by Dutch press, about the investment rumors or the society's purposes in general, Van Siclen strongly denied that the trip was anything but sentimental and recreational—"only as an act of piety."[72]

The Gorham Company, Designed by Frank J. Ready
Memorial to Henry Hudson: The Arrival of the Halve Moon, 1609, 1908
Stained glass, 149½ x 65½ in.
The New-York Historical Society Library, Installed by the Daughters of the
Holland Dames, 1908
Image courtesy of The New-York Historical Society, 79209d

Holland Society Chair of the Memorial Committee,
Tunis G. Bergen on board the Half-Moon, in *Year Book of the*
Holland Society of New York, 1910
Hudson River Museum, Purchase 2008

The actual details only emerged later. The Holland Trust was never very successful and became entangled in a scandalous money loss, which disgraced Van Siclen and alienated him from some Holland Society members. The trust declined in financial solvency until it finally disbanded in the 1890s.[73] But this was long after Sheldon Viele and Reverend Suydam had returned and prepared their glowing narrative of the trip.

THE THROBBING OF THE BLOOD IN OUR VEINS[74]

In a period of increasing American tourism to the Netherlands, the Holland Society trip was fairly early. Thus, it is tempting to imagine that the expedition, particularly in light of the amount of publicity surrounding it, may have encouraged the curiosity of other Americans, contributed to the cachet of Holland via the prestige of the old New York families involved, and helped the spread of Holland mania as much as reflected it.

The explosion of heritage mania in the next decade included the formation of the Daughters of Holland Dames. In fact, there were two rival groups. The still active Society of the Daughters of Holland Dames was founded in 1895; soon a contender appeared, run by the headstrong and bizarre Lavinia Dempsey.[75] Miss Dempsey had herself crowned Queen of the Holland Dames in the ballroom of the Waldorf-Astoria Hotel. Certainly intending irony, a *New York Times* reporter gave the article covering this event the subtitle "an occa-

N. C. WYETH (1882–1945)
Portrait of Ann Stuyvesant, 1926
Oil on canvas, 42 x 30 in.
Private collection
Image by Ashley Slade, Brandywine River Museum.

This detailed imaginary portrait was likely painted to complement
Wyeth's *Half Moon in the Hudson* for the Hendrick Hudson Dining Room
at New York City's Hotel Roosevelt.

sion for which there is no known precedent." Dempsey paraded through the
streets of New York as part of her coronation and later traveled to Holland
to witness the actual coronation of Queen Wilhelmina.[76] Ultimately, she was
discredited in a series of articles in *The New York Times*, which included severe
criticism by her own brother, who was "sick of the Holland Dames business."[77]

J. C. LEYENDECKER (1874–1951)
Young Dutch Girl—Study, painted for
the cover of *The Saturday Evening Post*,
April 3, 1926
Oil on unstretched canvas, 19½ x 10¾ in.
Curtis Publishing Company
Image courtesy of Archives of American
Illustrators Gallery, New York

Meanwhile, the original group flourished and later funded a stained-glass window for the New-York Historical Society Library, depicting Henry Hudson. This was installed on the eve of the Hudson-Fulton Celebration.[78]

So many associations with such ridiculously narrow and elite descriptions were founded in the 1890s that in 1900, Eliot Gregory, a well-known artist and writer, published a satirical essay about them, "The Genealogical Craze."[79] A particularly good paradigm of this trend is an event at the Metropolitan Opera House in 1897. The National Society of New England Women organized a series of historical tableaux from the Pilgrims to the Civil War, enacted by "many lineal descendants of the original characters portrayed." In addition to

the organizers and the Holland Society, the following other groups participated: the Society of Mayflower Descendants; the Sons of the American Revolution; the Founders and Patriots of America; the Daughters of the Revolution;
the Daughters of the Cincinnati; the Colonial Dames of America, New York,
and New Jersey; and three different chapters of the Daughters of the American
Revolution.[80] This roster alone seems to prove Gregory's sneering comment:
"Indeed, the vogue of these enterprises has been in reverse ration to their use-
fulness or raison d'être, people apparently being ready to join anything rather
than get left out in the cold." According to him, the "Circle of Holland Dames
of the New Netherlands" required royal descent. And he referred to a crowning, which must be Lavinia's. Recalling an exclusive club he and his friends
created when he was a boy, he made the analogy that it was childish to "band
together, blackball friends, crown queens and perform other senseless mum-
meries, such as having a weathercock of a departed meeting house brought in
during a banquet, and dressing restaurant waiters in knickerbockers for 'one
night only.'"

Gregory might be writing today, when it is all too easy to take this stance
and rail self-righteously against late nineteenth-century heritage groups with
their exclusive written and unwritten restrictions, thinly veiled anti-immigra-
tion fears and actions, and condescending superiority toward everything from
the nouveau riche to other countries. But these attitudes were unfortunately
the norm for a high percentage of the upper class of Gregory's day. The Holland Society also played a significant role in the recording and preservation of
the historic documentation of early New York and New Jersey history. They
reached out to contemporary Holland and established connections that enabled them to play a large role in the planning for the Hudson-Fulton Celebration. In particular, the society arranged for the building and display of the
replica of Henry Hudson's *Half Moon*. The glitter of America's colonial aristocracy dimmed with the rising political and social power of immigrant groups,
the disillusionment of two world wars, and the equalizing financial collapse of
the Great Depression. Still, an eminent intellectual like modernist poet Wallace Stevens could spend years of research on his own, and with hired experts,
unsuccessfully trying to prove that his Dutch roots went back as far as the
Holland Society required and in 1926, the 300th anniversary of the purchase
of Manhattan by Peter Minuit occasioned a small flurry of celebratory events
and artworks.[81] Through it all, the Holland Society of New York embodied and
exemplified the spirit of Holland mania, and their trip to the Netherlands crys-
tallized that devotion to heritage and fatherland into a moment that expressed
much of the complexity and contradiction that make the Gilded Age such a
fascinating study of human nature and culture. [82]

NOTES

1. The two main sources of primary material for this trip are Sheldon Viele and Reverend J. Howard Suydam, "The Narrative of the Visit of the Holland Society to the Netherlands," *Year Book of The Holland Society of New-York, 1888-1889*, ed. George Van Siclen (New York: The Holland Society of New-York, 1889) and eleven articles by Lehman Israels that appeared in the *New York Herald* between July 28 and September 2, 1888. The Viele and Suydam account had a broad circulation at the time that it was reviewed in the *Magazine of American History* XXV 1891, 346-347. I am grateful to David William Voorhees, *The Holland Society: A Centennial History, 1885-1985* (New York: The Holland Society of New York, 1985) and Annette Stott, *Holland Mania: The Unknown Dutch Period in American Art and Culture* (New York: Overlook Press, 1998), 138, which are the key secondary sources for the event.

2. Henry L. Bogert, ed., *Year Book of The Holland Society of New York* (New York: The Knickerbocker Press, 1904), 239.

3. Stott, *Holland Mania*. Stott seems to be the first to use the term "Holland mania," but the phrase "pedigree mania" dates back at least to the eighteenth century, one instance being Eliza Kirkham Mathews and Charles Mathews, *The Pharos* (London: T. Hookham, 1787), 28.

4. Lehman Israels, "Knickerbockers on the Wave/The Holland Society to Visit the Homes of Their Ancestors," *New York Herald*, July 28, 1888.

5. Francis J. Sypher Jr., ed., *The Saint Nicholas Society of the City of New York: A 150 Year Record* (New York: The Saint Nicholas Society of the City of New York, 1993), 3.

6. Michael Kammen, *Mystic Chords of Memory: The Transformation of Tradition in American Culture* (New York: Knopf, 1991).

7. Stott, *Holland Mania*, 78ff.

8. Eliot Gregory, "The Genealogical Craze," in *The Ways of Men, New York* (New York: C. Scribner's Sons, 1900), 155.

9. Societies listed in the *Hereditary Society Blue Book* (http://members.tripod.com/~Historic_Trust/society.htm). Wallace Evan Davies, *Patriotism on Parade: The Story of Veterans' and Hereditary Organizations in America, 1783-1900* (Cambridge, Mass.: Harvard University Press, 1955), 55, 69, 80; chapters 3, 4, and 5 (44-118) provide excellent context for the hereditary society movement.

10. Ridiculed by Gregory in "The Genealogical Craze," 158.

11. George Van Siclen, *Year Book of The Holland Society of New-York, 1887-8* (New York: The De Vinne Press, 1888), 87.

12. Lehman Israels, "Dutch Raiders/Descendants of the Patroons in the Land of Their Ancestors," *New York Herald*, August 21, 1888.

13. Rev. David Cole, D.D., "Yonkers," in J. Thomas Scharf, *History of Westchester County* (Philadelphia: L. E. Preston & Co., 1886), 1-172; "New-Netherland," review of *Documents Relating to the History of the Early Colonial Settlements*, by Berthold Fernow, *The New York Times*, November 25, 1883; "Books of the Month," review of same in *The Atlantic Monthly* LIII, no. CCCXV (1883): 150.

14. "Motley, the Historian" and "Obituary, John Lothrop Motley, Historian," both in *The New York Times*, May 31, 1877.

15. Stott, *Holland Mania*, 79-81, 130, 137.

16. "The Dutch and their Land/*Holland Through a Telescope*. In Utrecht's Cathedral Tower—the Whole Country at a Glance," *The New York Times*, May 9, 1880.

17. Robert Wheaton, "Motley and the Dutch Historians," *The New England Quarterly*, v. 35, n. 3 (Sep. 1962): 318-336; Viele and Suydam, *Year Book of The Holland Society of New-York, 1888-1889*, 76.

18. Charles E. Lydecker, "The Pilgrimage to Holland" (song) in Viele and Suydam, *Year Book of The Holland Society of New-York, 1888-1889*, 20.

19. United States Centennial Commission, *Reports and Awards* (Philadelphia: J. B. Lippincott, 1877), Item notes: Group 21-27, 548.

20. "The Holland Exhibition," *The New York Times*, Jan. 15, 1883.

21. *The First Annual Dinner of the Holland Society of New York . . . Hotel Brunswick, Jan. 8, 1886* (New York: Holland Society of New York, Published by De Vinne Press, 1886), 12.

22. Ibid., 14-15.

23. Lydecker, "The Pilgrimage to Holland," 19.

24. Stott, *Holland Mania*, 120-151, 43-77, chapters on "Tourism and Travel Literature" and "American Artists in Holland."

25. M. J. Brusse, *With Roosevelt Through Holland*, illus. by J. G. Veldheer, published by the Holland America Line, 1911.

26. Baedecker, *Belgium and Holland, Handbook for Travellers*, 1881; *Cook's Tourists Handbook, Holland, Belgium, and the Rhine*, 1880, published in London but title page also lists a New York office.

27. Edmondo de Amicis, *Holland and Its People* (New York: Putnam & Sons, 1880). Edmondo de Amicis, *Holland and Its People*, illustrated by Joseph Pennell, R. Swain Gifford and others (New York: Putnam & Sons, 1885).

28. Viele and Suydam, *Year Book of The Holland Society of New-York, 1888-1889*, 86. De Amicis, *Holland and Its People*, 254-255.

29. Like Henry Havard, *The Dead Cities of the Zuyder Zee: A Voyage to the Picturesque Side of Holland* (Published by McKay, 1884) or Augustus John Cuthbert Hare, *The Heart of Holland* (London: Richard Bentley, 1875). Stott, *Holland Mania*, 126-127.

30. George Henry Boughton, *Sketching Rambles in Holland*, illustrated by Boughton and Edwin A. Abbey (New York: Harper & Brothers, 1885). "Holland Sketches," review of *Sketching Rambles in Holland* by Boughton, *The New York Times*, January 15, 1885.

31. Viele and Suydam, *Year Book of The Holland Society of New-York, 1888-1889*, 199-201.

32. Viele, "The Son of a Van" (song), *Year Book of The Holland Society of New-York, 1888-1889*, 17.

33. Voorhees, *The Holland Society: A Centennial History*, 30-31, 42-43, 47, and also apparent in perusing of early editions of the *Year Book of The Holland Society of New-York*.

34. Stott, *Holland Mania*, 130 (general trend).

35. Rev. J. Elmendorf, "The Holland Society of New York to Old Holland" (song), Viele and Suydam, *Year Book of The Holland Society of New-York, 1888-1889*, 38.

36. George Van Siclen, *Year Book of The Holland Society of New-York, 1886-7* (New York: The De Vinne Press, 1887), 6-11. Arti Ponsen, "Vivent les Gueux!" August 1888: 'The Holland Society of New-York' meets the '3rd of October-Association' of Leiden, Holland," 2008, 2 (unpublished paper by amateur historian on staff of Leiden University, sent to Holland Society by Stedelijk Museum De Lakenhal, Leiden).

37. *The Holland Society of New-York*, Trustee Minutes, May 19, 1887, 96ff., Van Siclen, *Year Book of The Holland Society, 1887-8*, 7.

38. Arti Ponsen, "Vivent les Gueux!" 3-4.

39. Van Siclen, *Year Book of The Holland Society, 1887-8*, 12-14.

40. Van Siclen, *Year Book of The Holland Society, 1887-8*, 32-33.

41. Kammen, *Mystic Chords of Memory*, 207-208.

42. Israels, "Dutch Raiders."

43. Information on charts consolidated from Viele and Suydam, *Year Book of The Holland Society of New-York, 1888-1889*.

44. Biographical information from obituaries and officer lists in several editions of *Year Book of The Holland Society of New-York*, 1901-1920.

45. Elizabeth Lorang, "'Two more throws against oblivion': Walt Whitman and the *New York Herald* in 1888." *Walt Whitman Quarterly Review* 25, no. 4 (Spring 2008): 168–169.

46. Viele and Suydam, *Year Book of The Holland Society of New-York, 1888-1889*, 15.

47. Stott, *Holland Mania*, 78-100, and Kammen, *Mystic Chords of Memory*, 132-193.

48. Viele and Suydam, *Year Book of The Holland Society of New-York, 1888-1889*, 158-160.

49. Viele and Suydam, *Year Book of The Holland Society of New-York, 1888-1889*, 67-68.

50. Viele and Suydam, *Year Book of The Holland Society of New-York, 1888-1889*, 59.

51. *The New York Times*, November 22, 1880 (in a review of Putnam's de Amicis translation).

52. Viele and Suydam, *Year Book of The Holland Society of New-York, 1888-1889*, 86.

53. Stott, *Holland Mania*, 146.

54. Lehman Israels, "Holland Society/A Band of Visitors from New York to the Dams of Dutchland," *New York Herald*, August 10, 1888.

55. Viele and Suydam, *Year Book of The Holland Society of New-York, 1888-1889*, 44.

56. Web site of the Jewish Historical Museum of Amsterdam.

57. Yale Obituary Record, 1927-28, 4-8.

58. Viele and Suydam, *Year Book of The Holland Society of New-York, 1888-1889*, 13.

59. Elisabeth Israels Perry, *Belle Moskowitz: Feminine Politics and the Exercise of Power in the Age of Alfred E. Smith* (Boston: Northeastern University Press, 1992), 24; Robert P. Swierenga, *The Forerunners: Dutch Jewry in the North American Diaspora* (Detroit: Wayne State University Press, 1994), 65, 68-70, 328.

60. Thompson Cooper, *Men of the Time: A Dictionary of Contemporaries* (London: G. Routledge and Sons, 1872), 529; Victor Plarr, *Men and Women of the Time: A Dictionary of Contemporaries* (London: G. Routledge and Sons, 1895), 458 (at end of entries on Josef Israels).

61. Swierenga, *The Forerunners*, 106-110.

62. Perry, *Belle Moskowitz*, 24.

63. Viele and Suydam, *Year Book of The Holland Society of New-York, 1888-1889*, 93.

64. Viele and Suydam, *Year Book of The Holland Society of New-York, 1888-1889*, 13.

65. Lehman Israels, *New York Herald*, 1888: long articles July 28, August 10, 12, 21, 27, September 2; short dispatches August 13-17 (microfilm at New York Public Library).

66. Lehman Israels, "Holland's Silent Influence/Holding the Balance of Power Between Continental Extremes/Her Geographical Position a Menace/One Hand on the Sword, the Other on the Water/An American's Awkward Toast," *New York Herald*, September 2, 1888.

67. Ralph Waldo Emerson, "The Problem," *The Dial: A Magazine for Literature, Philosophy, and Religion*, By Margaret Fuller, Ralph Waldo Emerson, Published by J. Monroe, #1, 1841; annotations in *Ralph Waldo Emerson*, ed. Edward Waldo Emerson (Boston: Houghton Mifflin, 1904), 405.

68. Viele and Suydam, *Year Book of The Holland Society of New-York, 1888-1889*, 174.

69. Lehman Israels, "Victorious Again/The Holland Society of New York Takes Leyden by Storm/An Enthusiastic Reception/Hollanders Treat the Visiting Americans Like Princes of the Blood," *New York Herald*, August 27, 1888.

70. Viele and Suydam, *Year Book of The Holland Society of New-York, 1888-1889*, 63.

71. Arti Ponsen, "Vivent les Gueux!" 3.

72. Viele and Suydam, *Year Book of The Holland Society of New-York, 1888-1889*, 49.

73. "Mr. Vansiclen Resigns," *The New York Times*, October 22, 1891; "Fraud and Conspiracy Charged," *The New York Times*, August 10, 1894.

74. Van Siclen, Letter "To the editors of the leading newspapers of Holland, Amsterdam, Aug. 25, 1888," Viele and Suydam, *Year Book of The Holland Society of New-York, 1888-1889*, 171.

75. "New Society Founded by Women/Descendants of the Dutch Secure Incorporation Papers," *The New York Times*, December 11, 1895; "Two New Dutch Societies/Miss Dempsey Says She Was Kept Out of the One She Planned," *The New York Times*, January 16, 1897; "Society of Holland Dames/NYC Women Incorporate a New Organization" *The New York Times*, January 16, 1897.

76. "Miss Dempsey Crowned," *The New York Times*, February 10, 1898; "Queen of the Holland Dames Back," *The New York Times*, September 26, 1898.

77. "Queen Lavinia in Trouble," *The New York Times*, May 21, 1899; "Queen in a Prison Cell/Miss Dempsey of the Holland Dames Accused of Larceny," *The New York Times*, March 10, 1900.

78. "Historical Society Meets," *The New York Times*, January 6, 1909.

79. Gregory, "The Genealogical Craze," 161.

80. "A Series of Tableaux Given by the New York Society People in the Metropolitan Opera House—Patriotic Societies to Take Part in the Display," *Brookyn Eagle*, December 1, 1897.

81. Milton J. Bates, "To Realize the Past: Wallace Stevens' Genealogical Study," *American Literature* 52, no. 4 (January 1981): 607-627; "MANHATTAN BOUGHT AGAIN IN A PAGEANT; Tableau in Battery Park on 300th Anniversary Depicts Trade of Indians and Dutch; $24 CALLED EXTRAVAGANT, Price Was $2,000, Judged by Values Today, Says Speaker, and It Brought Chiefly Barren Land," *The New York Times*, May 26, 1926.

82. Another very recent study analyzing the trip is Nancy Steiber, "Amsterdam Eternal and Fleeting: The Individual and Representations of Urban Space," in *Biographies and Space: Placing the Subject in Art and Architecture*, ed. Dana Arnold and Joanna R. Sofaer (London: Routledge, 2008), 73-98. Steiber focuses on Sheldon Viele and documents some additional source materials new to this author, including Viele's souvenir photo album, a diary by Charles Lydecker and articles in the *New Amsterdam Gazette*, 95, n. 29.

PART FOUR 1909 – Searching for Dutch Heritage

left: Attributed to JOHN WATSON (1685–1768)
Mrs. Kilaen Van Rensselaer, ca. 1730
Oil on canvas, 50 x 41½ in.
The New-York Historical Society, Bequest of Waldron Phoenix Belnap, Jr., 1950.242

right: *Good Housekeeping* magazine advertisement, *"Mrs. Brookfield Van Rensselaer Smokes Camels"* (detail), October 1935, Hudson River Museum

10

The Hudson-Fulton Celebration of 1909

ROGER PANETTA

The Reverend J. H. Suydham from Rhinecliff, New York wrote to the *New York Tribune* on July 30, 1893, no doubt inspired by The World's Columbian Exposition, whose fairgrounds had opened to the public three months earlier on May 1, 1893, and proposed a celebration to commemorate the 300th anniversary of the 1609 discovery of the Hudson River. Dr. George Frederick Kunz, in an article in the *North American Review* in September, wrote, "There should be a World's Fair in 1909 on Manhattan Island in honor of the ter-centenary of Henry Hudson's arrival in the Half Moon." In linking Columbus with Hudson, Suydham and Kunz yoked not only the great explorers but also the import of their discoveries to American history. Suydham hoped such a celebration would reintroduce his fellow New Yorkers to their long-neglected Dutch ancestors and recognize their centrality to the history of the city and state.

Celebrations, pageants, and fairs like the one Suydham was suggesting have received increasing scrutiny from historians, who see in such events collective symbolic moments that express power relationships and cultural values, and create public memory.[1] They are often ways for elites to build a common identity and for the middle class and immigrants to imagine a secure place for themselves in the American landscape. These celebrations often use the language of consensus in their public rhetoric to cover class, ethnic, and racial divisions. Historian John Bodnar sees a fundamental battle between the forces of the official culture seeking to create a common identity and the vernacular that celebrates the particular, the personal, and the local.[2] At stake in a public moment is a fundamental difference in how we construct communal or national identity—the centrifugal approach, which pushes us outward toward a decentralized and diverse set of traditions, and the centripetal pull toward a unified core of values and behaviors.

The Hudson-Fulton Celebration of 1909, long neglected by scholars and largely unknown to the general public, was fully engaged with these questions and, I suggest, offered an alternative framework for cultural identity that for its own time was progressive and hopeful. The challenge for historians is to look past the official rhetoric of the organizers and the boosters to uncover their

Redfield Brothers Inc.
Official Program of the Hudson-Fulton Celebration, 1909
10 x 7 in.
Hudson River Museum, 75.0.433.1 (3)

inner tensions and cultural assumptions and the impact of the event on the various publics who were involved as active participants or spectators.

New York City's failure to host the World's Columbian Exposition (also called The Chicago World's Fair) held in Chicago in 1893 cast a long shadow over these early discussions. From October 8 to 13, 1892, New York staged its own Columbian Celebration, which was eclipsed in March 1893 with the public opening of "that little afFAIR" in Chicago, leaving the city humbled and aggrieved. Chicago was not the only precedent for New Yorkers to draw upon—the city had hosted two major celebrations still fresh in memory. The city had welcomed Admiral Dewey on September 28, 1898, in a carefully staged pageant that was the most sensational and emotional since Lafayette's visit in 1824. Its central iconic structure was the Dewey Arch, a plasterlike temporary beaux-arts colonnade modeled after the Arch of Titus in Rome.[3]

New York had a long ceremonial heritage that began in 1788 with the Federal Procession celebrating the ratification of the Constitution. This was followed by celebrations of Lafayette's visit and the openings of the Erie Canal, the Croton Aqueduct, the Brooklyn Bridge, and the Statue of Liberty, on through Dewey's victory, which along with Chicago's Columbian Exposition established the basic format—naval parades, fireworks, street marches, floats,

A Glimpse of the Court of Honor, 1893
From *Portfolio of Photographs of The World's Fair*, 1893–94
Published by the Werner Co., Chicago, Ill. 11 x 13½ in.
Hudson River Museum, INV.0485 B

and elaborate built structures—all of which heightened the public's expectations for subsequent pageants.[4]

New York City's commercial-minded Board of Trade and Transportation, which had a record of aggressively pursuing political conventions and international expositions, established the Fulton Centennial Celebration Committee at City Hall on July 13, 1905, to mark the anniversary of the first trip of

The Dewey Arch, 1899
Photograph, 6½ x 7½ in.
Hudson River Museum, Gift of Mr. and Mrs. Richard Kaeyer,
1986, INV.10391

the *North River/Clermont* on the Hudson River in 1807. Over the next twelve
months they recognized a shared interest with the Hudson Tri-Centennial
Commission and merged the two organizations. While they embraced a common river and city, they would come to represent two distinct directions. The
Hudson tricentennial looked back to the past and sought to use history as
a source of legitimation and affirmation of New York's colonial credentials,
while the Fulton centennial pointed to the future and the spirit and inventive-
ness of American technology.

The Hudson-Fulton Commission, strengthened by the addition of dozens
of subcommittees and a host of volunteers from the city's urban elite, accelerated its work plan in 1907. The roster of membership reads like a who's who of
New York City's political and cultural leadership, with a heavy concentration
of the descendants of Dutch families. While the commission espoused broad-
based participation, control of the celebration remained in the hands of this
tightly knit group of insiders—civic-minded upper- and middle-class professionals and artists working for nonpartisan reforms to soften the excesses of

Hudson-Fulton Poster Postcard, 1909
Printed postcard, 5½ x 3¼ in.
Hudson River Museum

This was the signature image for the Hudson-Fulton Celebration, showing a female allegorical figure dressed in the attributes of Mercury (God of Trade), as well as Henry Hudson and Robert Fulton with their respective boats.

capitalism, and of course secure their own standing in society. The influence of these individuals and their worldview in shaping the character and direction of the 1909 celebration was decisive.[5] Indeed, one of their first successful strategies, to center the celebration in the city, succeeded when Manhattan became the headquarters and the principal venue for the major events.

With the creation of Greater New York in 1898, a master stroke instigated by Andrew Green, a new metropolis brought together the diverse communities of the Bronx, Brooklyn, Queens, and Richmond, making New York the largest city in the United States and the world's premier international city.

Special efforts were made to include New York's newly consolidated boroughs, celebrate the city's new size, and draw its constituents closer together. This new metropolis also had historical and economic ties to the river valley extending from the suburbs of Westchester to the capital at Albany and embracing the numerous river towns along the Hudson, many of which now insisted on participating in the celebration.

The first proposed plan, which called for a New York World's Fair, was rejected because it "elicited no public enthusiasm." Rather, the commission argued that the City of New York was the metropolis of the country, second city of the world, and a self-contained vast exposition. Here we see New York as spectacle—its commerce, its people, and its streets and rivers would provide

the stage for the celebration. Commissioner Theodore Sutro favored a celebration that would "beautify the city and elevate the people, and not one devoted
to commercialism." He referred to "the primeval beauty of Manhattan Island
and the Hudson." Richard G. Hollaman added, "Let us glorify the occasion as
well as the discovery of New York; let us spread our wings and let the eagle
scream for New York."[6] The hope was that a direct experience of the city's life
would dispel negative stereotypes and establish its credentials as a world city.

Fundamental to this plan was the rejection of the commercial—no admission fees, no advertisements, and no business endorsements or underwriters.
This commitment was a prerequisite for a historical commemoration designed
to educate the public in their local and regional history and to inculcate a sense
of civic pride. The underlying fear was of a commercialized event deteriorating
into a cheap amusement, packed with rowdy and unruly crowds—the very ele-

COPYRIGHT 1909 BY J. KOEHLER. N. Y.

1609 · HUDSON - FULTON CELEBRATION · 1909 ·

Sept. 25 Commencement Day N. Y.
,, 26 Religious Observance Day N. Y.
,, 27 Reception Day N. Y
,, 28 Historical Parade N. Y.
,, 29 Commemoration Day N. Y,
,, 30 Military Parade Day N. Y.
Oct. 1 Naval Parade N. Y,
,, 2 Naval Carnival Parade N. Y.

Oct. 3 Religious Day Upper Hudson
,, 4 Dutchess Co. Day
,, 5 Ulster Co. Day
,, 6 Greene Co. Day
,, 7 Columbia Co. Day
,, 8 Albany Co. Day
,, 9 Rensselaer Co. Day

Hudson-Fulton Postcard with
Schedule of Events, 1909
Printed postcard, 5½ x 3⅜ in.
Hudson River Museum

This image is symbolic of the
unification of the Hudson and
Fulton Committees to create a
single celebration.

ments that had come to characterize far too many Fourth of July celebrations.
The planners were ever vigilant in the name of decorum and order, commend-
ing the well-behaved citizenry and noting the low incidence of crime during the celebration. The city fathers imagined themselves as guardians of the
commonwealth's reputation, which ought not be sullied by crass commercial
interests and cheap pleasures. This was a moment, if not an opportunity, to
build civic identity—a coming out party.

New York's power brokers, distressed at the rapid transformation of their
modern city's landscape through commercialization, industrialization, and
immigration, found solace in a fictive history described as "Old New York."
They hoped to use this constructed history to shape public memory and reaf-
firm their social and cultural standing. The heyday of "Old New York" was
1888 to 1920, and the concept was supported by a determined effort to provide

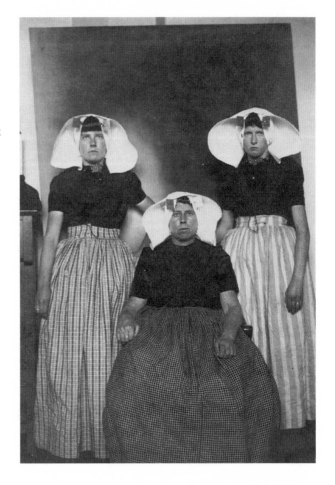

urbanites and especially the recently arrived southern and eastern European immigrants with a history primer. Pageants like the Hudson-Fulton Celebration that offered "a history lesson three miles long" could be effective in reaching the underclass and the undereducated, especially the children of immigrants.[7] The commissioners, inspired by "Holland Mania," a vogue of "Dutchness" from about 1880 to the end of World War I that influenced many aspects of American life, and supported by a series of revisionist histories, directed attention to American roots in the Netherlands, constructing a new theory of American history in which Holland played the central role. The 1909 celebration provided a special opportunity to connect New Yorkers with their Dutch past—the rightful source of fundamental American democratic values of liberty and tolerance.[8]

Jonkheer J. Loudon, Minister of the Netherlands, reiterated this argument:

I feel at home and in unison with the citizens of this great Empire City and Empire State, that once bore the name of New Amsterdam and New Neth-

erlands; a satisfaction because this Celebration comes at a moment when minute historical research has definitely established the fact that the early Dutch settlers, and especially the influence of the old Netherlands, have left indelible traces on the banks of the Hudson and far beyond in the New World.[9]

Interestingly, this thesis has been resuscitated by Russell Shorto, who in his 2004 book, *The Island at the Center of the World,* argued that New York City's commercial prowess and cosmopolitan sensibility were rooted in New Amsterdam; for Shorto "it helped to set the whole thing in motion."[10]

The Hudson-Fulton Celebration promised a civics lesson that by the nature of the instruction had to be experiential, participatory, and out-of-doors and be effectively imprinted on to the imaginations of the city's newcomers. Would New Yorkers come to associate the landscape with historic events and recognize their local neighborhoods as places encoded with the tracings of those who came before?

Hudson-Fulton Celebration Postcard, 1909
Printed Postcard, 3 x 5 in.
Hudson River Museum

This didactic use of history had two purposes. In addition to immigrants and the undereducated, the city fathers were hoping to reach a wider public and to upgrade New York's second-class reputation and poor standing in the national historic consciousness. They lamented the absence of first-rate city histories and sought to shake free from the interpretative choke hold Washington Irving had on New Amsterdam and the colonial history of the metropolis. They targeted a national audience and indeed an international community who needed to be convinced that New York deserved a place with the founding states of Massachusetts, Pennsylvania, and Virginia in the pantheon of American history.[11]

In addition to achieving the objectives of education and status reclamation, the commission hoped "to cement more firmly our friendly international relations and promote the cause of international peace." Here they made good use of Fulton as an agent of international commerce and as a catalyst for better international understanding through improved communication. The Fultonites argued that steam navigation made the world more intimate and safer. Both distance and potential international misunderstandings would diminish in a world drawn closer by the steamboat.[12]

Throughout much of 1907 and 1908 the commission was rapidly increasing its size, with new appointees from the boroughs of Greater New York, specialized interests, and mayors of river towns. They reviewed numerous proposals for inclusion in the celebration. The plan to create a permanent Hudson park at Verplanck's Point and a Manhattan memorial water gate to honor Robert Fulton slowly faded while the extension of the celebration upriver and other plans for memorials and parks expanded. By the winter of 1909, drawing heavily on the Chicago Columbian Exposition and the Quebec Tricentennial, a basic format began to emerge. A series of parades beginning with the cornerstone naval parade and its sister military parade were the bookends for the Historical and Carnival parades. A Children's Festival would be the centerpiece of the educational effort and include numerous exhibits, programs, and concerts in all the boroughs. Elaborate formal banquets would honor international guests, local and national political leaders, and naval officers while fireworks shows and electric light displays would entertain the general public. The celebration would extend up the Hudson from Manhattan to Albany and continue for fourteen days. The careful and intense planning reflected the scale of the celebration, the stake New York City and State had in a successful outcome, and the highly prized attributes of planning in the Progressive world of prewar America.

The celebration began on Saturday, September 25 with the Inaugural Naval Parade and the formal opening that evening at the Metropolitan Opera House.

FREDERICK COZZENS (1846–1928)
'Half Moon' and 'Clermont' in Hudson River, New York, 1909
Watercolor, graphite and gouache on board, 6 x 15 in.
The New-York Historical Society, Gift of Mrs. William Sulzer, 1943.483

The Half Moon Ramming the Clermont
Illustration from the *Hudson-Fulton Commission Report*, September 25, 1909
Fordham University Library, Bronx, New York

An international fleet of seventy-eight warships, the largest ever assembled, stretched eight miles up the Hudson. While some saw the gathering as a witness for peace, the signs of a naval arms race were unmistakable in the comments of the admirals gathered for the evening banquet and the presence of the white-hulled American vessels that had been part of the Great White Fleet, back from its circumnavigation of the globe from December 16, 1907 to February 22, 1909. Some saw that Pacific tour as an extension of the "triumphalist discourse of imperialist cosmopolitanism. The success of the naval parade depended on the use of spectacle to transform New Yorkers into tourists able to imagine the workings of globalization and the emerging American imperial space.[13]

The centerpiece of the first day was the entrance of the re-created *Half Moon* and the *Clermont* in the Kill van Kull. Original plans of both vessels had been lost, and their new incarnations were triumphs of Dutch generosity and sleuthing engineers. Their presence constituted a commitment to historical veracity and an essential element in this great public civics lesson. The diminutive scale of both vessels, especially against the backdrop of the world's cruisers and battleships, magnified the singular courage and achievement of both Hud-

HENRY ALEXANDER OGDEN
(1856–1936)
*The 'Half Moon' [with Hudson
River Day Line steamer Hendrick
Hudson]*, 1909
Black, gray, and white gouache,
black crayon, and graphite on
heavy board, 23¼ x 16⅝ in.
The New-York Historical Society,
Gift of the Estate of Harry A.
Ogden, X.281

son and Fulton. Historical legitimacy was enhanced by the costumed crews, stand-ins for Hudson and Fulton, and the presence of Livingston and Fulton family descendants on board the *Clermont*.

Hudson and Fulton were the subjects of many celebratory biographies, including Assistant Secretary Hall's *Hudson and Fulton*, published by the commission in 1909, and Alice Crary Sutcliffe's *Robert Fulton and the Clermont*, published in the same year. Both men were the subject of many exhibits that identified their work and courage with the modern era. In Sutcliffe's words, Fulton

anticipated the enlightenment of this century. He emphasized truths which prevail to-day and are termed modern: a hope for Universal Peace; a claim for Intellectual Freedom through a system of general, free education; a discernment that a Nation's wealth is the sum of the talents and handiworks of its citizens; and a sacrifice of any personal claim to leisure that through labor a world might be served; —these were the ruling motives of his life.[14]

In similar expression of indebtedness to Hudson, his voyages and courage are linked to the advances of the modern world and the history of the city.

On the evening of September 25 the fleet lying still in the lower Hudson came to light with a simultaneous electrical illumination of all the vessels, harmonizing with a city whose buildings and bridges were now outlined by thousands of lights. The Ryan Scintillator at 115th Street, with its bank of large searchlights diffused by columns of steam, drew thousands to Riverside Drive. Electric lighting had quickly become the mainstay of fairs; the Columbian Exposition and the Ferris Wheel "doubled the technology . . . by transforming a scene that was spectacular into a more powerful vision."[15] David Nye suggests this was an attempt to create a text without words, to seduce the public and legitimate the position of the social elite.

All of this constituted the city spectacular and established the preconditions for modernism.[16] Technology with growing influence and power in popular culture was employed to create a common experience, unchecked by race and class, freely and simultaneously visible to all New Yorkers, providing a powerful component in the construction of a historical memory.

Robert Fulton's *Clermont* represented the conjunction of the themes of republican values and technological progress that envisioned speed and efficient transportation as critical national imperatives and were reiterated throughout the celebration and embodied in the flight of Wilbur Wright. In the competitive world of public air shows and demonstrations and the battle for altitude and endurance records, Wright and Glen Curtiss would compete over the Hudson. Wright recognized the resonance between his work and Fulton's accomplishment. If he was to fly for 10 miles or one hour he would to capture a prize of $15,000. Wright took off on Wednesday, September 29 from an improvised air field on Governor's Island, with a canoe strapped to the bottom of his plane, and circled the Statue of Liberty. On Sunday, October 3 he left the island at 10 a.m. and flew north up the Hudson to Grant's Tomb in front of a million spectators. The thirty-three minute flight of "Bird Man" was judged the marvel of the celebration.[17]

Sunday, September 26 was reserved as a day of prayer and reflection, with the evening set aside for musical concerts throughout the city. Irish and German fraternal music and singing groups dominated these events throughout the first week, giving the celebration an ethnic coloration. These organizations along with other fraternal societies, of Irish and Italians participated as escorts for the Historical Parade and the Carnival, marching in traditional folk cos-

Float No. 11: Title Car, Dutch Period
In *Hudson-Fulton Commission Report*, 1909
Fordham University Library, Bronx, New York

tumes. The German societies were very active in the organizational and planning efforts, securing a place in public events and signaling a more inclusive attitude by the city's elite toward its immigrant and ethnic populations. The city was moving away from the centripetal approach of the melting pot toward an acceptance of multiplicity and diversity. Internationalizing the event and opening it to the city's ethnic groups, at least those who were organized, envisioned the city as a cosmopolis—the beginnings of a modern redefinition.[18]

The Historical Parade floats moved on Tuesday, September 28 from their workshop on 145th Street south to the assembly point on 110th to begin their procession down Central Park West to 59th Street and east along Fifth Avenue, past the Court of Honor at 42nd Street. The 54 moving vehicles were "beautifying graphic and instructive in themselves, they will stimulate study of the connecting moments in the great historical chain of which the events depicted form a part."[19] The history of New York was segmented into four thematic divisions—Indian, Dutch, English and Colonial, and The United States. Selected episodes in each of these histories were re-created in floats that combined papier-mâché figures and landscapes with costumed human figures.

Float No. 12: The Half Moon, In General View in Central Park West Historical Parade
In *Hudson-Fulton Commission Report*, 1909
Fordham University Library, Bronx, New York
Photo by Jessie T. Beals

The object was to unite in the procession the representatives of as many as possible of the nationalities composing the cosmopolitan population of the State, so as to make them feel that the heritage of the State's history belonged to them as well as to those more distinctively American.[20]

This animated public history text resonated with schoolchildren, who often excitedly called out the names of the various floats—having been prepared by their teachers, a state-sponsored curriculum, and specially designed reading and visual materials. Floats portraying such themes as "The Purchase of Manhattan," "Pulling Down the Statue of George III," "The Legend of Ichabod Crane," and "The Introduction of Croton Water" mixed traditional historical events with folklore and technological innovation.[21] The crowd, estimated at between two and two and a half million, increased subway ridership during the celebration, with spikes during events like the historical pageant.

The context for this event was a series of exhibitions in New York City's museums, historical societies, and cultural centers. The Dutch Masters, displaying the collecting prowess of New York's wealthy, and an American Crafts exhibit could be found at the Metropolitan Museum of Art, while Robert Fulton was the featured exhibit at the New-York Historical Society. The American Museum of Natural History profiled Native American history and culture while the Botanical Garden and the Zoological Society, in an action that speaks to an emerging environmental sensitivity, inventoried the surviving trees and animal species that had been here at the time of Hudson's arrival. Maps, historical monographs, and prints, along with a series of concerts, provided a broad range of program materials.

The Hudson-Fulton Commission encouraged these activities and kept close tabs on attendance at each of the venues. This was part of the effort not only to educate the public using vocabulary and images drawn from a continum of high and popular culture but also to demonstrate to the world New York's cultural maturation and sophistication—another reiteration of the cosmopolitan. Indeed, a close scrutiny of the iconography of various official insignia, medals, and banners supports the notion that Hudson-Fulton was attempting to link modern citizens to the long-standing cultural traditions of classical civilizations.

Sensitivity to the feelings of the newly consolidated boroughs compelled the organizers to encourage local planning and deepen the levels of participation. Colleges and universities, public and private schools were invited to sponsor programs and festivals, many in Iroquois and Dutch costume. Race was a sensitive issue for the celebration. Iroquis, "real Indians" from an upstate reservation, served as surrogates for all the displaced Native peoples and remnants of a dying civilization, marched in the Historical Parade, and participated in the dedication of several memorials. Three hundred African Americans participated in the Historical Parade but under the rubric of an immigrant group; black sailors were barred from the naval parade. Clearly the new cosmopolis found it easier to incorporate ethnic diversity than racial difference.[22]

A series of monuments and statutes memorialized Fort Amsterdam, Verrazano, Hudson, and Fulton and dozens of tablets marked the sites of revolutionary battles in Washington Heights, Fort Tryon, and Stony Point and throughout the Hudson River Valley. Collectively they would concretize historic memory and provide durable outdoor civics lessons for all citizens. At the dedication of the Fort Tryon memorial, George F. Kunz, President of the American Scenic and Historic Preservation Society and a key force in the workings of the commission, noted, "Tablets like this and everything that helps to stimulate civic virtue and encourage high ideals in our immense population are of inestimable value, and nothing is better calculated to accomplish this than memorials of the heroism and self-sacrifice of our ancestors."[23]

The preservation of historic memory and the natural beauty of the river landscape were elite responses to a growing concern over the pace of urban change, the loss of authority, and the perceived level of public indifference.[24]

In Manhattan at 1 p.m. on Thursday, September 30, 25,000 soldiers and sailors from the United States and other countries marched and were met with great enthusiasm—the loudest cheers of the celebration. One commentator noted that the excessive pride in the national guard was part of the "great interest . . . for all things military."[25] The mood of the military parade was captured best by Gustav Kobbe:

> The ooze changed to a flow, the flow became pervaded with a suggestion of set undulation, which in turn became charged with rhythmic rise and fall, not yet as separate atoms, but as of one huge mass being shoved steadily forward by an unseen force from the rear. At last—it was half past two—it took on the shape, color, throb of a marching army, its banners flung to the wind, its bayonets glistening in the sun.[26]

Isisdore Konti and crew installing his Hudson Fulton Monument, Yonkers, 1924
Photograph courtesy of Richard Kaeyer

While many believe peace has its own special kind of pageantry, this day's protean expressions of the martial spirit seemed to tip the balance toward the military. The streets were a part of the show, introducing American tourists and international visitors to New York's emerging skyline, the vertical city, and its new fashionable shopping district on Fifth Avenue.

On Saturday evening, October 2, the Carnival Parade followed the same route as the Historical Parade. The tradition of the carnival involved moving vehicles or floats to present allegorical, mythological, and historical scenes. The Hudson-Fulton version included floats depicting moments of northern Europe history and high culture including "Father Rhine," "Germania," and "Uncle Sam Welcoming the Nations" as well as "Lohengrin," "Aeolian Harp," and "The Crowning of Beethoven." The commission believed that the Carnival Parade should demonstrate that

Dutch Girls Parading, 1909
In *Hudson-Fulton Commission Report*, 1909
Fordham University Library, Bronx, New York

great body of Old World folklore which has inspired so much of the beautiful imagery of the poetry, song and drama of all civilized nations. Although the legends and allegories represented were not indigenous to America, yet they form a real part of our culture, inherited, like the cumulative facts which constitute our progressive civilization, from the past.[27]

While the program was dominated by the well-organized German social and fraternal societies, its important positioning in the celebration and the commission's stated objectives recall Randolph Bourne's "Trans National America." Unlike the centripetal pull of the melting pot, Bourne proposed a form of national incorporation in which particularity is honored as a means to maintain the richness and variety of New York's cultural mix.[28] Thus the Carnival Parade would legitimate the contributions of European immigrants and their parent cultures and encourage spectators to think anew about notions of national identity and the character of the modern city.

The educational commitment of the commission inevitably led to the primary schools. Approximately 300,000 children from private and public schools organized a variety of programs including historical plays, folk dances,

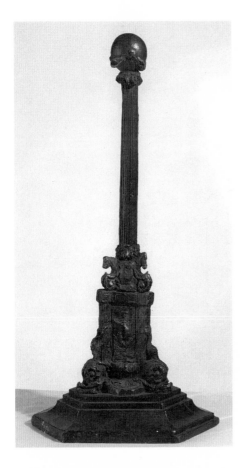

pageants, and festivals, performed in costume in 50 local parks. These programs were inspired by Progressive reform ideals stressing experiential learning and the value of parks and playgrounds as educational spaces. The Festival at Mulberry Bend involved thousands of children who began by pledging to the flag, thus explicitly linking the Children's Festival with the new emerging cosmopolis. In the words of the commission,

> many thousands of children, scarcely without exception, were of parents who have within comparatively recent years emigrated to this country from nearly every other country of the globe. From the schools of the lower East Side came children of many nationalities, Italian and Hebrew in the majority, with others from Syria, China, Japan, Turkey, Hungary, Spain, Greece, Portugal and so on through the nationalities of the earth.[29]

The spectacular city festivities and the anointing of New York as a world city can lead to the mistaken conclusion that the celebration was a city affair. To correct this misperception we need to look northward from a vantage point upriver, at the border of Manhattan.

Detroit Publishing Company
Hudson Memorial Monument, Riverside Drive, New York, 1910–1920
Glass plate negative of printed page, 8 x 10 in.
Inscribed on monument: "To commemorate the discovery of the Hudson River
by Henry Hudson in the year [16]09"
Library of Congress, Prints and Photographs Division, Washington, D.C.
(LC-D4-73034P&P)

On September 27, 1909 at 2 p.m., rain and mist enveloped a crowd of over five hundred dignitaries, members of numerous patriotic societies, and local residents sitting in an open grandstand. They had assembled on Spuyten Duyvil Hill in northern Manhattan to lay the cornerstone of the Henry Hudson Monument on a site of a Weckquaskeeks village, whose "native owners" witnessed Hudson's voyage in 1609 and who on October 1 engaged in a bloody conflict with the crew on the *Half Moon*'s return. Spuytin Duyvil Hill was also the location of three Revolutionary War fortifications, qualifying as a place rich in historical association.[30]

The planned monument, funded by private subscriptions, had a flutted Doric column standing upon a cubical plinth surmounted with a statue of Henry Hudson clad in seafaring garb. The total height was 300 feet, memorializing Hudson's 1609 arrival. The column was finished in 1912, but money ran out and not until the intervention of Robert Moses, with support from Mayor

Fiorella La Guardia, was the monument completed in 1938. The site was expanded into Henry Hudson Memorial Park between 1935 and 1937.

At the July 5, 1909 groundbreaking, four young women represented the Indians who welcomed Hudson, the Dutch who sponsored the trip, the English of his national home, and the Americans who erected the fortifications, creating a place whose history was marked by four cultures and offering a reprise of the thematic organization of the Historic Parade and New York City as the New Cosmopolis.

Cleveland H. Dodge in his welcome speech noted that while few New Yorkers knew of the location, that would change when Spuytin Duyvil Hill was connected to Inwood by the proposed Henry Hudson Memorial Bridge. He suggested that with the completion of the bridge the "greatest boulevard in the world" would pass by the Hudson monument[31]—referring to the proposed extension of Riverside Drive from northern Manhattan. The lower level of the bridge would provide a four-track extension of the rapid transit system.

This bridge proposal called for the erection of a reinforced concrete arch bridge "to form an imperishable memorial of the voyage of discovery made by Henry Hudson."[32] With its unprecedented size, it would stand among the greatest arched bridges, symbolizing "the combination of British pluck and Dutch enterprise of Henry Hudson."[33] This idea was an outgrowth of the popularity enjoyed by the temporary Dewey Arch at Madison Square from 1896. The picturesque and historic location also defined the boundary of Manhattan and reiterated its separateness as an island.

Critics complained that the excessive cost and ambitious design would forestall the construction for two decades. The proposal attempted to provide a scenic automobile link running parallel to the Hudson and connecting Manhattan with its northern borough and the more distant Westchester suburbs, a significant transportation innovation.[34] The Hudson River's north-south axis of exploration, transportation, settlement, and commercial development prefigured such a riverside highway. We can see here the emerging idea of metropolitanization and the creation of interlocking networks binding downriver New York City with the cities, towns, and villages upriver.[35] Proponents argued that this bridge embodied the adventuresome spirit of Hudson, in the words of Governor Hughes, "a man who knows no terror, who counts no difficulty too great," but it is in fact a more befitting memorial to Robert Fulton, whose steamboat established the commercial feasibility of river travel and linked the city and hinterland in profound and durable ways.

Spuyten Duyvil Hill provides a bird's-eye view of the Hudson from Manhattan to the Tappan Zee, a reminder of the river's centrality to the celebration

Parade in Getty Square at McKenzie Building during Hudson-Fulton Celebration, 1909
Albumen print photo, 16 x 20 in.
Hudson River Museum, Gift of Miss Lillian Roper, 44.61
Reproduction photograph by John Maggiotto

and the ways it served as the primary integrative element in 1909. This focus on the Hudson River was manifested in the publication of several memorial histories, including Clifton Johnson's *Picturesque Hudson*.[36]

In fighting for an extension of the eight-day city-based celebration, Mayor Henry Hudson of Hudson, New York proposed a second week to include the major upriver cities and towns. The idea was accepted when all his fellow mayors became members of the commission. One can sense in the minds of the early organizers a preoccupation with Manhattan and its Dutch founding, to the detriment of a more open view that recognized the symbiotic relationship between upriver and downriver—two antipodes yoked by the Hudson.[37]

Nothing better illustrates this connection than the dedication of the Palisades Interstate Park on September 27, 1909 in Alpine, New Jersey, just across the river from the Henry Hudson Monument. The park rescued the Palisades from the quarrymen whose continued removal of stone threatened to deface this geological wonder. New York Governor Theodore Roosevelt appointed George W. Perkins Chairman of the New York Commission in 1900. In the same year, with the help of J. P. Morgan, he stopped the quarrying. In his dedication speech Perkins outlined the frugal manner in which the property had been acquired and noted the increasing number of permits issued for campers and visitors since 1905, a vindication of the commitment to make the park accessible to all.[38] The principal speaker, present at most of the public ceremonies during the celebration, was Charles E. Hughes, Republican Governor of New York State from 1907 to 1910. His words provide a continuous progressive voice throughout the commemoration.

He began by encouraging the turn from historical association toward preservation and emphasizing the need to examine the natural conditions of the river and "conserve this priceless gift of nature." He warned the audience that for too long a time they had been content with the lavishness of nature and unmindful of "the reckless waste and speedy spoliation." He admonished them to keep the river free from pollution, preserve it as wholesome, and not permit it to become a "mere sewer." Hughes was aware of the exigencies of industry and its importance to local prosperity but insisted we must "keep our streams pure." He then exalted the power of nature not only as an economic force but also for the opportunity it provided to cultivate the beautiful, which he argued was the richest blessing of the Hudson River, "its most gracious ministry to the spirit of man . . . the free gift . . . which no wealth could ever create." The highest duty, he declared, was the preservation of the scenery of the Hudson, a responsibility "impose on those who are the trustees of its manifold benefits."[39]

Hughes was no idealist; he called attention to the river's capacity to renovate and inspire the toiling "masses." How fortunate for New York City with its growing population to have such an extensive area of natural beauty so close and so accessible. Later in his dedication speech he marveled that

> Within a short distance of the great metropolis, within easy reach of its teeming population, lies this extensive area of natural beauty, making with its fascinating story a special appeal to the patriotic American heart. Easily

Historic Philipse Manor Hall decorated for the Hudson-Fulton Celebration in Yonkers, 1909 Postcard, 3½ x 5½ in. Hudson River Museum, 76.0.18

The *'Half Moon' at Yonkers*, 1909
Photographic postcard
Hudson River Museum, 75.0.180

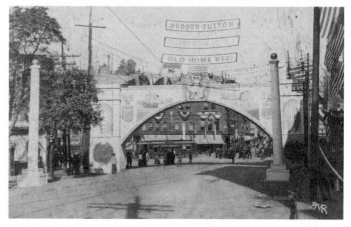

Getty Square in Yonkers, 1909
Photographic postcard,
3⅜ x 5½ in.
Hudson River Museum,
75.0.1482 f

accessible, it should be a place of renovation and inspiration for the toiling multitudes. Here should be the people's countryside for the common recreation.[40]

This interlocking relationship between upriver and downriver, city and country, was a new dimension in which the Hudson became not only a highway for commerce and transportation but also a haven in an overcrowded and increasingly urban world. Now the preservation of the Hudson and its riverscape was essential, a necessary antidote to the excesses of modern life. This celebration introduced a new Hudson, unveiled by Governor Hughes in his Palisades Interstate Park dedication speech calling for conservation.

On Tuesday, September 29, the *Half Moon* and the *Clermont* moved upriver to Yonkers and on to Tarrytown, followed two days later by the Naval Parade, which left New York City at 9:30 a.m. and steamed to Newburgh, triggering a series of local celebrations and rowing and canoe races, were part of the aquatic competitions of the celebration.

Yonkers Ceremonies: Living Flag in Front of High School
In *Hudson-Fulton Commission Report*, 1909

Yonkers welcomed about twenty Historical Floats from the New York City parade and seventy-five Iroquois who accompanied the "Indian" floats on October 3. They were housed on barges in the Hudson that accompanied the floats up the river and provided sleeping quarters for "sqwas and paposis."[41] The largest crowds outside the city gathered in Yonkers, swelled by contingents from Eastchester, Mount Vernon, and New Rochelle. Two thousand schoolchildren in red, white, and blue costumes formed a human flag—one of the most popular 1909 events repeated in many river communities. Yonkers participated in the very popular old home week initiative and invited former residents to return to their town. Getty Square was decorated with a Deweyesque arch and illuminated in ways that were described as "exciting and memorable."[42] Special interdenominational religious ceremonies, another common event, were held in all the churches of the city.

On Tuesday, October 5, the parade of floats moved to Hastings, Dobbs Ferry, Irvington, Tarrytown, and North Tarrytown. Events in Hastings are representative of the response of many river towns and villages. A local citizens' committee consisting of the village fathers and benefactors organized the celebration, working closely with the Lower Hudson Committee. They greeted

Dudley Lawrence
as Lewis Morris and
Arthur Lawrence as
Frederick Philipse,
Westchester Historical
Pageant, 1909
Bronxville Public
Library, Reproduction
image courtesy
Westchester County
Historical Society,
M-502

Dais of the Bronxville Westchester Historical Pageant, 1909. Governor Charles
Evans Hughes at center, William V.D. Lawrence is second from left.
Bronxville Public Library, Reproduction image courtesy Westchester County
Historical Society, M-470

Parade for Kaiser Wilhelm's son at Briarcliff Manor, 1909
Briarcliff Manor, Scarborough Historical Society, Reproduction image
courtesy Westchester County Historical Society, M-2205

the *Half Moon* and the *Clermont*, saluted the naval flotilla, and on October 5 launched their own parade, including 500 schoolchildren. Three of the 21 Historical Floats that arrived from Yonkers were to be manned by Hastings residents. The local parade included representatives from a wide range of civic organizations and preceded the procession of floats. The afternoon was filled with a series of public addresses. Hastings also dedicated a park to the memory of Robert Fulton, next to the village library, in November 1909.[43]

As the celebration moved north into the region of the upper Hudson, the river became the focus suggesting how much more directly and experientially connected to the Hudson the people of the region were. New York City's celebration had turned inward and away from the river, far more interested in honoring the founding and development of Manhattan and the emergence of the great metropolis.

For Newburgh's citizens the key event was the 1709 settlement of German Lutherans from the Rhenish Palatinate under the leadership of Reverend Joshua Kokerthal, who named the town Quassic. They escaped from persecution, received a patent, cultivated the land, and built a community. They overcame suffering and privation and "with God's help" and their own spirit of

Newburgh Ceremonies: Arrival of Naval Parade, October 1, 1909
In *Hudson-Fulton Commission Report*, 1909
Fordham University Library, Bronx, New York

industriousness and resourcefulness, they prospered. The 1909 event marked the birth of the city and is in keeping with the theme of pluralism reiterated throughout the celebration. Newburg also laid claim to its revolutionary credentials based on the Hasbrouck House, the longest-serving headquarters of George Washington, a site featured in speeches and local festivities. The visit of the fleet and the evening fireworks attracted over 30,000 people to the city. Old home week and the human flag, now mainstays of the celebration, were also very popular.[44]

The *New York Times* reported on events in Poughkeepsie:

The appearance of the fleet was greeted with a salute of twenty-one guns from Kaal Rock, and this was answered by the booming of cannon on the warships. Simultaneously began a long-continued blowing of whistles and sirens, and a ringing of all the church bells in the city, while from a stone quarry six miles down the river came the rumble of 500 blasts arranged for the occasion.

The first tap of the fire alarm, which was the signal of the fleet's arrival here, brought thousands of people to the river front, and the shores were lined by the time the ships came to anchor.[45]

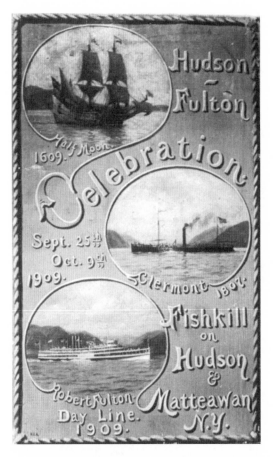

WILLIAM E. NORTON (1843–1916)
"Half Moon," "Claremont," and "Robert Fulton," 1909
Oil on canvas, 20⅛ x 12⅛ in.
Hudson River Museum, Gift of William Krais, 42.99

The Hudson River Day Line probably commissioned this program cover art because it features the steamboat *Robert Fulton*, which they launched earlier that year. Fishkill-on-Hudson and Matteawan were 17th-century villages that became part of Beacon four years later.

C. MORTIMER
Cartoon of the Poughkeepsie Hudson-Fulton Celebration, 1909
Ink on paper, 13½ x 20 in.
Franklin D. Roosevelt Presidential Library and Museum, Hyde Park, New York, 42.207.1

MRS. BROOKFIELD VAN RENSSELAER

"For Flavor and Mildness I've never found a cigarette that compares with Camel"

Mrs. Van Rensselaer finds America gayer and more stimulating than Europe. "If I'm tired from the exhilarating American pace," she says, "smoking a Camel gives me a 'lift'—a feeling of renewed energy, and I'm all ready to go on to the next thing." Camels release your latent energy in a safe way.

At home or abroad, Mrs. Brookfield Van Rensselaer smokes Camels. "Once you've enjoyed Camel's full, mild flavor, it is terribly hard to smoke any other cigarette," she says. "I can't bear a strong cigarette—that is why I smoke Camels." Camel spends millions more every year for finer, more expensive tobaccos than you get in any other popular brand. Camels are milder!

AMONG THE MANY DISTINGUISHED WOMEN WHO PREFER CAMEL'S COSTLIER TOBACCOS:

MRS. NICHOLAS BIDDLE, *Philadelphia*
MISS MARY BYRD, *Richmond*
MRS. POWELL CABOT, *Boston*
MRS. THOMAS M. CARNEGIE, JR., *New York*
MRS. J. GARDNER COOLIDGE, II, *Boston*
MRS. ERNEST DU PONT, JR., *Wilmington*
MRS. HENRY EIELD, *Chicago*
MRS. JAMES RUSSELL LOWELL, *New York*
MRS. POTTER D'ORSAY PALMER, *Chicago*

Mrs. Van Rensselaer at Palma de Mallorca. She says: "Americans abroad are tremendously loyal to Camels. They never affect my nerves. I can smoke as many Camels as I want and never be nervous or jumpy." Camel's costlier tobaccos *do* make a difference!

Camels are Milder!...made from finer, more expensive tobaccos ...Turkish and Domestic...than any other popular brand

© 1935, R. J. Reynolds Tobacco Co., Winston-Salem, N. C.

October 1935 Good Housekeeping

Good Housekeeping magazine advertisement, *"Mrs. Brookfield Van Rensselaer Smokes Camels,"* October 1935, Hudson River Museum

Attributed to JOHN WATSON
(1685–1768)
Mrs. Kilaen Van Rensselaer,
ca. 1730
Oil on canvas, 50 x 41½ in.
The New-York Historical
Society, Bequest of Waldron
Phoenix Belnap, Jr., 1950.242

From the eighteenth century
to World War II, "Old Dutch"
families continued to play an
aspirational role in society.

Illustrative of the ways river communities linked Hudson-Fulton to the re-juvenation of local history is Poughkeepsie's "Old Home Week," inviting her sons and daughters to return and renew old acquaintances and see how "your old home city has improved." The Old Home Week Committee mailed out 100,000 booklets, secured special railroad rates, and reserved rooms for its returning native sons.

In public speeches President Taylor of Vassar credited the Dutch with New York's cosmopolitanism, largess, and liberality while Henry S. Van Duzen, President of the Poughkeepsie Holland Society, reminded his audience of the Dutch institutions of freedom of worship and free schools that had taken root here. He noted that

when we look back, it is not only the Dutch energy, and Dutch strength, and Dutch force to which we are indebted in this nation but the Dutch Hospi-tality which first received the Pilgrims, or Puritans from England. When they came here they were clothed with liberality and it was that spirit that was that strong in the original settlers in New England, those that landed in Plymouth Rock, that has been potent in all the great achievement of this nation.[46]

Holland Societies throughout the state were active in organizing and participating in the Celebration.

Governor Hughes noted in a banquet speech that evening:

Every community is now searching its early records and studying its history that it may know more surely of what it may be proud; and there is no community along this river but has reason for gratification at the part its sons have played from time to time in the development of this commonwealth and of the nation to which the prosperity of this commonwealth has so close a relation.[47]

At the Esopus light, a fleet of Cornell tugs from Kingston met the naval parade while hundreds on shore cheered. Colonel Arthur MacArthur from Scotland marveled at "the amalgamation of nationalities." He argued that perhaps those who'd come down the river to meet and greet those coming up the river formed the antipodes of the notable Hudson and embodied the spirit of those who joined hands with Hudson and Fulton to make the river celebration memorable.[48]

In Catskill, Hughes reiterated the event's educational goals:

One object of this Celebration is to stimulate the patriotic pride of our people; to bring to the attention of our young men and women, of our boys and girls, the interesting history of the country. It is the desire of all that as a result of the Celebration, the leading events in our history should be better known; the struggles of the early days better appreciated; and that we may be equipped to meet the exigencies of the present and to solve the problems of the future.[49]

In Albany on October 8 the Dutch roots were recalled by the indefatigable governor, who reminded New Yorkers,

You Dutch—and I am a good deal Dutch myself—are proud to-night of the contribution made in the early days by the Netherlanders and which you still make. For there never was a finer vindication of human rights against tyranny than that which preceded the great commercial development of the Netherlands, which sent Hudson upon his voyage of discovery.[50]

In a lengthy response, His Excellency Jonkheer J. Loudon, Minister of the Netherlands, noted that one can find

UNKNOWN PHOTOGRAPHER
Purchase of Manhattan/Hudson-Fulton Parade, Pleasant Plains, N.Y., 1909
Albumen print postcard, 3½ x 5⅓ in.
Staten Island Historical Society

This float was likely part of the Great Children's Festival that took place
Friday, October 1, 1909, on Staten Island.

. . . in Holland the institutions based upon those ideas of freedom, of free
education and of a free church, which were so delightfully represented in
floats this afternoon—those school children—children of the free school
and church, a free church in a free State. Those institutions and many others
besides came from Holland, and I am proud to state this.[51]

It is right and fitting indeed that Hudson-Fulton Celebration should have
concluded with paeans to the Dutch and have publicly reconnected the river
valley to the Dutch moment in New York's history.

Governor Hughes, fatigued by the rigors of speechmaking, quipped that
if he should die he wanted the simple epitaph, "Sacred to the memory of
the Hudson-Fulton Celebration," a justified request given his perserverance
through these local ceremonies. He said he had discovered the Spirit of 1909 in
Poughkeepsie "gathered in effective symbolism—the immigrant, the student,
the working man, and the veteran of the civil war." The celebration was a great
embrace of diversity of class and ethnicity, which he hoped would be deepened. He believed it would reconnect citizens with neglected local history and
bind diverse Americans to place and country.[52]

Sextette learn Dutch Folk Dances as taught on the Recreational Agencies Program in New York City, Photograph Record of WPA for the City of New York: Education and Recreation District, Album File, PR 002-209, 1938
The New-York Historical Society Library, 81606d

Dutch iconography continued to play a popular role in New York culture and architecture in the years after the 1909 Hudson-Fulton Celebration.

The Hudson-Fulton Celebration of 1909 was judged by most commentators a success, marked by large, well-behaved, and enthusiastic crowds and appreciative international visitors. *The History Teacher's Magazine* reported in November that New York City and State were richer after the celebration in historic monuments and commemorative tablets of constant educational value. They noted that "the city and state have been stirred to an extraordinary pitch of civic pride and civic activity and children have participated largely."[53] One could counter this enthusiastic evaluation by pointing to the exclusion of African Americans, the continued stereotyping of Native peoples, and the demise of the *Half Moon* and the *Clermont* despite the commission's promise to preserve them.

Beyond its importance to its contemporaries, the celebration is a rich historical source for understanding New York and the rise of the modern city, as well as the uses of history and the place of ethnicity, race, and class in creating cultural identity.

NOTES

1. David Glassberg, *American Historic Pageantry: The Uses of Tradition in the Early Twentieth Century* (Chapel Hill: University of North Carolina Press, 1990), 1-67. Michael Kammen, *Mystic Chords of Memory: The Transformation of Tradition in American Culture* (New York: Vintage, 1993), 93-282.

2. John Bodnar, *Remaking America Public Memory: Commemoration and Patriotism in the Twentieth Century* (Princeton: Princeton University Press, 1992).

3. Marjorie P. Balge, "The Dewey Arch: Sculpture or Architecture," *Archive of American Art Journal* 23, no. 34 (1983): 2-6.

4. Brooks McNamara, *Day of Jubilee: The Great Public Celebrations in New York, 1788-1909* (New Brunswick: Rutgers University Press, 1997).

5. Randall Mason, "Memory Infrastructure: Preservation, Improvement and Landscape in New York City, 1898–1925" (Ph.D. diss., Columbia University, 1999), 86-87. Also Max Page and Randall Mason, *Giving Preservation a History* (New York: Routledge, 2004), 3-18, 131-162.

6. *Official Minutes of The Hudson-Fulton Celebration*, 2 vols. (New York: J. B. Lyon, 1911), 16-18.

7. Clifton Hood, "Journeying to 'Old New York': Elite New Yorkers and Their Invention of the Idealized City in the Late Nineteenth and Early Twentieth Centuries," *Journal of Urban History* 26, no. 6 (September 2002): 709.

8. Annette Stott, *Holland Mania: The Unknown Dutch Period in American Art and Culture* (Woodstock, N.Y.: Overlook Press, 1998), 78-120.

9. Edward Hagman Hall, *The Hudson-Fulton Celebration, 1909, The Fourth Annual Report of the Hudson-Fulton Celebration Commission to the Legislature of the State of New York*, 2 vols. (New York: J. B. Lyon, 1910) (H-FC hereafter) I:336. This is the official report of the commission and needs to be approached with a critical eye. The *Official Minutes of The Hudson-Fulton Celebration* in two volumes, published in 1911 (New York: J. B. Lyon), provide additional details about the organization of the events and the commission's relationship with city and state officials and various participating groups. Hall, a newspaper reporter and writer, served as secretary for the American Scenic and Historic Preservation Society and the commission.

10. Russell Shorto, *The Island at the Center of the World* (New York: Vintage, 2005).

11. H-FC I:4-5.

12. H-FC I:6-7.

13. Margaret Werry, "'The Greatest Show on Earth': Political Spectacle, Spectacular Politics, and the American Pacific," *Theater Journal* 57, no. 3 (2005): 374. James R. Reckner, *Teddy Roosevelt's Great White Fleet* (Annapolis, Md.: Naval Institute Press, 2001).

14. Alice Crary Sutcliffe, *Robert Fulton and the* Clermont (New York: The Century Co., 1909), preface.

15. David Nye, "Republicanism and the Electrical Sublime," *American Transcendental Quarterly*, 4, no. 3 (September 1990), 189.

16. Ibid., 192.

17. H-FC I; James Tobin, *To Conquer the Air* (New York: Simon & Schuster, 2003), 344-357.

18. Moses King, *New York: The Metropolis of the American Continent, The Foremost City of the World* (Albany: J. B. Lyon, 1910). King describes New York of 1906 as the American Cosmopolis. See James Huneker, *The New Cosmopolis* (New York: Charles Scribner's Sons, 1915), 3-180.

19. *Historical Pageant: Hudson-Fulton Celebration, September 25 to October 9, 1909* (New York: Redfield Brothers, 1909).

20. H-FC I:287.

21. H-FC I:274-313.

22. Alessandro Lorini, *Ritual of Race: American Public Culture and the Search for Racial Democracy* (Charlottesville: University Press of Virginia, 1999), 208-217.

23. H-FC I:448.

24. Hood, "Journeying to 'Old New York,'" 705-707.

25. Lincoln Diamant, *Hoopla on the Hudson: An Intimate View of New York's Great 1909 Hudson-Fulton Celebration* (Fleischmanns, N.Y.: Purple Mountain Press, 2003). Contains the dispatches of Rudolf Diament, father of the author and correspondent for Nieuwe Rotterdamsche Courant from September 2 to October 2, 1909.

26. Gustav Kobbe, *The Hudson-Fulton Celebration MCMIX* (New York Society of Iconophiles, 1910), 43. A good supplement to Diament is the coverage in *The New York Times*.

27. H-FC I:362.

28. Carrie Tirado Bramen, "The Urban Picturesque and the Spectacle of Americanization," *American Quarterly* 52, no. 3 (2000): 446-447.

29. H-FC I:507.

30. H-FC I:413-414; *New York Times*, September 28, 1909.

31. H-FC I:417.

32. *Scientific American* 98, no. 15 (April 11, 1908).

33. *New York Times*, February 25, 1908.

34. The Riverdale section of the Bronx was annexed in 1894 and incorporated into Greater New York in 1898.

35. The terms "downriver" and "upriver" will be used to distinguish New York City from the river communities north up to Albany. City and country, city and suburb, town and country, and lower and upper did not provide a clear or sufficiently discriminating division.

36. Johnson, *Picturesque Hudson* plus other histories. The plethora of publications the celebration instigated examples.

37. Blanche McManus, *How the Dutch Came to Manhattan* (New York: E. R. Herrick & Co., 1897).

38. H-FC I:397-401.

39. H-FC I:401-402.

40. H-FC I:402-403.

41. H-FC II:891-894.

42. H-FC II:909-923.

43. Jennifer Stern, "The Hudson-Fulton Celebration of 1909," *Hasting Historian* 30, no. 4 (Fall 2000).

44. H-FC II:930-938; *The Newburg News*, Anniversary Edition, July 7, 1959. Philip Otterness, *Becoming German: The 1709 Palatine Migration to New York* (Ithaca and London: Cornell University Press, 2004).

45. *New York Times*, October 4, 1909.

46. H-FC II:958-959.

47. HF-C II:952.

48. H-FC II:981.

49. HF-C II:991.

50. HF-C II:1034.

51. HF-C II:1040.

52. H-FC II:950-952.

53. *The History Teacher's Magazine* 1, no. 3 (November 1909): 55.

11

Franklin Roosevelt's "Dutchness"

AT HOME IN THE HUDSON VALLEY

CYNTHIA KOCH

All that is within me cries out to go back to my home on the Hudson River.[1]

DUTCH HERITAGE

Only three American presidents have been of Dutch heritage: Martin Van Buren (1782–1862), Theodore Roosevelt (1858–1919), and Theodore's younger cousin Franklin (1882–1945). Van Buren was descended from Cornelis Maessen Van Buren, who arrived in Albany in 1631. Martin Van Buren's father was a tavern keeper and farmer in Kinderhook, New York; the future president grew up speaking Dutch, which remained his first language throughout his life. Despite Van Buren's strong connections to his Dutch ancestry, it is the two Roosevelt presidents who are today most closely associated in the public's mind with the Dutch roots of the Hudson Valley.

Theodore and Franklin Roosevelt were both descended from Claes Martenszen van Rosenvelt, who, with his wife Jannetje Samuel-Thomas, is said to have settled in New Amsterdam in about 1650.[2] They had a son Nicholas, a prosperous miller who in turn had two sons—Jacobus, who was the ancestor of Franklin; and Johannes, from whom Theodore and his niece Eleanor, the First Lady, were descended. Claes and his wife were said to have emigrated from the village Oud-Vossameer, in the province of Zeeland, in the southwest of the Netherlands. The name Roosevelt apparently derives from the name of the farm on which they lived, which must have had a "field of roses." That is, Claes was the son of Martin (Martenszen) from (von) rose field (rosenfeld).[3] Its similarity to the name Rosenfelt gave rise in the 1930s to speculation that the Roosevelt family was originally Jewish. FDR settled the point in 1935 when he answered the question thus: "In the dim distant past they may have been Jews or Catholics or Protestants. What I am more interested in is whether they were good citizens and believers in God."[4]

Later generations of Roosevelts in America made their fortunes as merchants and traders. FDR's immediate ancestors prospered in the sugar refining business in the West Indies. His great-great-grandfather Isaac (1726–1794) fought in the American Revolution, served as an early New York State senator, voted in the state convention that ratified the U.S. Constitution and, with Alexander Hamilton, founded the Bank of New York.

The Roosevelt ancestor,
Claes Martenzen van Rosenvelt,
circa 1649, in a portrait painted in
Europe prior to his emigration
from the Netherlands.
Franklin D. Roosevelt Presidential
Library and Museum, Hyde Park,
New York, 50-70 1

By then the Roosevelts had become part of the city's old Knickerbocker elite—quiet, staid, and private. But Theodore and Franklin were more Dutch in name than parentage. As biographer Frank Freidel has pointed out, each was more fully English than Dutch. "Theodore, a fifth cousin to Franklin, was less than a quarter Dutch; Franklin had only a trifling percentage of Dutch ancestry." But both were proud of their Dutch names and family.[5]

FDR's great-grandfather James (1760–1847) followed his father as a sugar refiner and banker; he was also the first Roosevelt to settle in the Hudson River Valley. In 1818 he bought a substantial tract of land on the river north of Poughkeepsie where he built a large home, Mount Hope, and settled in as a country squire. His reclusive son Isaac (1790–1863), Franklin's grandfather, lived with his parents until, at the age of thirty-seven, he surprised everyone by marrying their young neighbor Mary Rebecca Aspinwall, from a wealthy shipping family with New England roots dating back to the *Mayflower*.[6] Isaac and Mary Roosevelt built a home, Rosedale, near Mount Hope on the Hudson River.[7]

Isaac Roosevelt (1726–1794),
FDR's great-great grandfather
Photograph after the undated
painting by Gilbert Stuart
that hangs in Springwood,
the Roosevelt family home at
Hyde Park, New York.
Franklin D. Roosevelt Presidential
Library and Museum, Hyde Park,
New York, 48-22 3641(1)

Born in 1828, James Roosevelt, FDR's father, graduated from Harvard Law School and was admitted to the New York Bar. His grandfather James left his namesake most of his estate, including Mount Hope and a fashionable New York City townhouse. FDR's father was now wealthy enough to devote himself to managing his investments and live the life of a Hudson Valley aristocrat. In 1853, he married Rebecca Brien Howland, a daughter of his mother's first cousin and heiress to another shipping fortune. The next year James Roosevelt Roosevelt (Rosy), the president's half-brother, was born. An era ended—and another began—when Mount Hope burned to the ground in 1865, and James purchased the neglected estate of a railroad executive a few miles north in Hyde Park. This would become Springwood, Franklin Roosevelt's beloved life-long home on the Hudson River.

Rebecca died in 1876, and in 1880 James remarried the beautiful Sara Delano, a daughter of Warren Delano II and Catherine Robbins (Lyman) Delano. Like the Aspinwalls and the Howlands, they came from old New England seafar-ing stock—socially prominent and immensely wealthy. Warren Delano II had

FDR's father, James Roosevelt, 1880
New York, New York, 1880
Photograph
Franklin D. Roosevelt Presidential
Library and Museum, Hyde Park,
New York, 47-96 2775

made and lost two fortunes in the China trade (first tea and later opium) before settling in at the highest rank of the New York shipping trade.[8] The Delanos lived at Algonac, an Italianate villa designed by Andrew Jackson Downing in Newburgh, across the river from the Roosevelts. Sara's ancestry included seven members of the original *Mayflower* Pilgrims. Her paternal ancestor Phillippe de lay Noye was reputedly the first French Huguenot to set foot on American soil, arriving in Plymouth in 1621.

Sara was extremely proud of this illustrious heritage and made sure that her son understood it as well. Her brother (FDR's uncle) Frederick Delano presented the young Franklin with *Ancestral Tablets* at age two, on which he subsequently traced in his genealogy.[9] Pride in the Dutch ancestry also surfaced; the family's two sloops, for example, were both named *The Half Moon*. As a sophomore at Harvard University, Franklin wrote his thesis on the history of the Roosevelt family before the American Revolution. He dutifully recounted the marriages and other historical lore about the various generations and branches of the Roosevelt family, concluding: "As regards the marriages of the Roosevelts, the first three were, as was natural in a Dutch colony with Dutch-descended women. After the third generation on the marriages were for the most part with those of English descent, but Dutch marriages occurred even then, as the best New York families were still Dutch."[10]

Sara Delano Roosevelt, circa 1880
Franklin D. Roosevelt Presidential
Library and Museum, Hyde Park,
New York, 47-96 2835

THE DUTCH, THE AMERICANS, AND HOLLAND MANIA

Franklin Roosevelt wrote this thesis when he was nineteen. His father had died
the year before after a lengthy illness and Franklin had become his formidable
mother's sole focus of attention. Sara Delano Roosevelt took an apartment in
Boston to be close to her son and guide his active social life while he was at
Harvard. His distant "cousin" Theodore Roosevelt had just ascended to the
presidency, and a phenomenon convincingly identified by historian Annette
Stott as "Holland Mania" was sweeping the land.[11]

This social and cultural fascination with things Dutch seems to have developed in the years following the 1876 Centennial and in the wake of sev-

eral popular histories of the Dutch Republic that interpreted the beginnings of modern American democracy in the Low Countries' overthrow of the forces of the Holy Roman Empire during the Eighty Years War, which ended in 1648.[12] Newly reminded of the lessons of the War for Independence, many in the United States turned away from their traditional ties to England with its monarchy and saw in the Dutch a middle-class democracy that valued religious freedom, hard work, and egalitarianism. The Netherlands Holland [Holland is a single province] was a Protestant republic that had thrown off its Roman Catholic royal oppressor; its people's reputation for religious tolerance and intellectual freedom, combined with the wealth and glory of their mercantile civilization—especially as seen in the art of the Dutch masters—only added to their appeal for Americans.[13]

Nineteenth-century Americans who admired the Dutch found it easy to overlook that the wealth of the great Dutch merchants derived from the African slave trade and brutal colonization in Asia and South America. Instead, they saw antecedents for their own burgeoning middle-class society. Even better, as a source for American cultural identity, the Netherlands' worldwide empire augured well—this being the era of Manifest Destiny—for an eventual empire for the United States.[14]

Holland Mania expressed itself in numerous ways. Affluent Americans traveled to the Netherlands, commissioned Dutch and Flemish revival architecture, amassed collections of Dutch masters, and supported the work of

Theodore Roosevelt in his White House study, c. 1905.
Franklin D. Roosevelt Presidential Library and Museum, Hyde Park, New York, 74-20(609)

hundreds of American artists in Holland, who developed a cottage industry in painting views of the Dutch people and landscape. The art of the Golden Age in the Netherlands became familiar to many Americans as wealthy industrialists donated their collections and founded the great art museums.[15]

The celebration of small-town life and neighborliness was also very much a part of Holland Mania. Those Dutch festivals and the paintings of windmills and canals all harkened back to a sentimentalized preindustrial Holland where time seemed to have stopped.[16] This was an era of rapid change in American society. Railroads, manufacturing, the telegraph and telephone, and the influx of Roman Catholic immigrants from Eastern and Central Europe to work in the new industries threatened to destroy the rural lifestyle that many Americans yearned for and equated with a simpler, more virtuous time—the time when their republic was founded by tight communities of modest tradesmen and yeoman farmers who were Protestants of northern European ancestry.

With Theodore Roosevelt as president from 1901 through early 1909, the nation even had a Dutch American leader. After leaving the presidency in 1909,

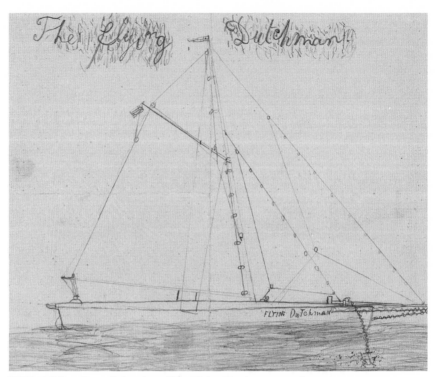

FDR's childhood pencil drawing of *The Flying Dutchman* at anchor.
Franklin D. Roosevelt Presidential Library and Museum, Hyde Park, New York,
MO 82.8.5.

TR made a trip to Holland, visiting Delft and paying homage to the statue of William the Silent, the Protestant martyr of Dutch independence. He acknowledged his Dutch heritage with pride, evoking the popular sentiments of the day: "I come from a great free Republic to the home of my forefathers, of which it may be said, that they were among the very first, to establish freedom as we now understand the word."[17]

The most popular evocation of the Dutch in America, of course, had come from Washington Irving's 1809 *History of New York*. Knickerbocker's humorous view of the Dutch and Dutch Americans was repeated as fact in textbooks and guidebooks of the early nineteenth century. An 1840 travel guide advised that the people of New York have "the temper of the early settlers of the state, the Dutch, [which] is still observable in numbers of its present inhabitants, as exhibited in the passion for gain, in economy, diligence, neatness, and a plodding industry."[18] Even Eleanor Roosevelt, more Dutch herself than her husband, had this to say about a sculpture of the young Franklin Roosevelt: "This apparently pliable youth had strength and Dutch obstinacy in his make-up."[19]

LEIGH HUNT (1858–1937)
Half Moon and Clermont on the Hudson, 1909
Etching
Franklin D. Roosevelt Presidential Library and Museum, Hyde Park,
New York, 41.3.775b

This etching commemorates the Hudson-Fulton Celebration of 1909.
The centennial of Robert Fulton's first commercial steamboat (1807)
was celebrated along with the tricentennial of Henry Hudson's voyage.
From the president's personal collection.

FDR'S "DUTCHNESS"

It was in this milieu that Franklin Roosevelt engaged with his own heritage—
on his father's side from one of the oldest and most admired Knickerbocker
families in New York; on his mother's side from a family rooted in the nation's
early New England seafaring history. Like Theodore Roosevelt, he joined the
Holland Society, the hereditary genealogical society of male descendants of
early New Amsterdamers, maintaining a membership throughout his life. He
conspicuously did not seek membership in the comparable Sons of the Revolution or Society of Colonial Wars, for which he would have qualified.[20] He
preserved the Dutch family relics of the first Roosevelts in America, even as he
treasured his mother's family mementoes from the China trade and nurtured
a lifelong love of the sea and the navy.

FDR exemplified the gentleman's interest in public-spirited celebrations of
historical events that were popular in the early twentieth century. In 1909 he

Eleanor and Franklin Roosevelt, at far right, hosting the Dutchess County
Historical Society's fall "pilgrimage" to the Roosevelt home, Springwood, in 1927.
Franklin D. Roosevelt Presidential Library and Museum, Hyde Park, New York,
48-22 3837(28)

Left to right: John G. Mylod, Helen W. Reynolds, and William Platt Adams,
President of the Society. Helen Wilkinson Reynolds was FDR's advisor and
collaborator on many historical projects.

served—along with 805 other members of the New York and Hudson Valley
gentry—as a member of the Hudson-Fulton Celebration Commission.[21] He
was very young at the time (just two years out of law school) with a growing
family and political ambitions, even as he labored as a beginning attorney at
the New York City firm of Carter, Ledyard, and Milburn. He served on the
Public Health and Convenience Committee, conveying the recommendations
of Miss Eleanor Blodgett, chair of the Executive Committee of the New York
Chapter of the Red Cross, to the larger commission of influential men (no
women served directly on the commission).[22]

FDR also became a founding member (in 1914) of the Dutchess County
Historical Society, and his papers are rich in correspondence with members.
Later, in planning his presidential library, FDR would set aside one room to
be used as the headquarters for this society. From 1926 to 1931, when he was

Franklin D. Roosevelt Memorial Library, Hyde Park, New York, c. 1948
Postcard
Franklin D. Roosevelt Presidential Library and Museum, Hyde Park, New York, Doc 08-25

most active in historical affairs, he held an appointment as local historian of the Town of Hyde Park. His most important accomplishment was publication in 1928 of the *Records of the Town of Hyde Park, 1821–1875*. He also urged that all descendants of early settlers be canvassed for their knowledge of early history.[23]

FDR also took great pride in his own collections—of books, naval and maritime prints and paintings, ship models, and memorabilia that encompassed Hudson Valley and Dutch colonial themes.[24] In his presidential library (built in 1940–41), the original museum galleries displayed an eclectic mix of Hudson Valley memorabilia along with his ship models, presidential gifts, and other collections. The president's art collection included works that reflect distinctly Dutch themes by American artists Charles P. Gruppe, J. Gari Melcher, and John Sartain, who had practiced in the Netherlands during the Holland Mania.[25]

The presidential library holds 885 titles on the Hudson Valley alone, and in his very extensive collection on world and American history are volumes by John Lothrop Motley, whose historical works on the Dutch Republic did much to excite Holland Mania.[26] FDR's affection for things Dutch included

Dutch colonial architecture and decoration. He installed a matched set of antique Dutch tiles around the fireplace in his study in the presidential library [the library not the study is the reference point for the Hudson River Dutch style], which was itself designed according to FDR's instruction in the "Hudson River Dutch style." In planning the library he described what he saw as the "salient characteristics" of that style: extreme simplicity of exterior (and interior); small and few windows and large wall surfaces; steep pitched roofs; and simple porches.[27]

But Roosevelt's engagement with Dutch colonial history is more profound than his collecting, historical, and genealogical interests. His political career began when he was elected New York state senator in 1910. He then went to Washington to serve as Woodrow Wilson's assistant secretary of the navy for seven years, resigning at the comparatively young age of thirty-eight to run for vice president on the Democratic ticket in 1920 (the last election he would ever lose). He seemed primed for greatness, but his political career nearly ended in 1921 when he suffered a devastating attack of infantile paralysis (polio) that rendered him paraplegic. FDR spent much of the next decade seeking cures and undergoing rehabilitation in the vain hope that he might regain the use of his legs.

During this period he had time to devote to quieter pastimes that his previous busy lifestyle had precluded. In 1924 he began two writing projects—a screenplay on John Paul Jones and a history of the United States. Neither came to fruition, but in his fragmentary history, Roosevelt set forth his thoughts on the simple foundational stories of America. To him Henry Hudson's "discovery" of the Hudson River, for example, seemed nonsensical.[28] "What a ridiculous assumption to teach that Henry Hudson in 1609 was the first to enter the river that bears his name; or that Chesapeake Bay was first seen by the Virginia colonists in 1607; or that the Pilgrims were the first to see Cape Cod in 1620." In accord with his time in ignoring the native inhabitants, he argued that Spanish and French traders were just as likely to have been the "first" to exploit the resources of the East Coast of North America, but due to illiteracy, death at sea, or the compulsion to keep secret profitable contacts with the natives, they had never laid claims that were recorded by history.

His disregard for the significance of Henry Hudson notwithstanding, FDR's interest in Dutch heritage was sincere and substantial when it came to the Dutch colonial architecture of the Hudson River Valley. In 1923 he urged the Holland Society to sponsor publication of two volumes documenting this vanishing heritage in historical narrative, photographs, and old prints. His appeal was successful and he eventually became chairman of the Publication Committee.[29] It would take more than a dozen years to complete the two volumes—

The John Brinckerhoff house, built 1738 in Swartwoutville, with its stone exterior, adds the picturesque curved roofline over the porch to the basic form FDR found so appealing. From Helen Wilkinson Reynolds, *Dutch Houses in the Hudson Valley* (New York: Payson and Clarke Ltd., 1929), Plate 114
Franklin D. Roosevelt Presidential Library and Museum, Hyde Park, New York

Dutch Houses in the Hudson Valley Before 1776 and *Pre-Revolutionary Dutch Houses and Families in Northern New Jersey and Southern New York.*[30] FDR advised and provided moral support to the project photographer and writers (most importantly working with Helen Wilkinson Reynolds, who became his lifelong friend and advisor on Dutchess County history), and negotiated with publishers.[31] He contributed the introductions to both volumes. The first, written in 1928, provides an important perspective on FDR's thoughts on Dutch heritage.

> That which has interested me in this survey even more than the collection of architectural data has been the information as to the manners and customs of the settlers of the valley of the Hudson, which has been afforded by an examination of the houses the people lived in. . . . One fact that stands out clearly . . . is the mode of life of the first settlers of New Netherland and of their immediate descendants was extremely simple, a statement which is true not only of the smaller landowners but of large grants. From high to low their lives were the lives of pioneers, lives of hardship, of privation and often of danger.[32]

Val-Kill Stone Cottage, as it appeared in 1930, replicates the
simplest form of early Dutch houses.
Franklin D. Roosevelt Presidential Library and Museum, Hyde Park,
New York, 58-246

Here was a recurring theme for Roosevelt—the value of early history as a
lesson on endurance and eventual triumph over hardship. It was a lesson that
provided hope, and may have helped him personally as he struggled to reclaim
his life from the paralysis that rendered his legs useless. A decade later he conveyed this lesson to the nation and eventually the world.

FDR also noticed something else about the early Dutch houses:

I have been impressed also with another thought that comes from an examination of the locations of these old houses. . . . A large number of them are
found in cosy [sic] places, away from the highway, down behind a hill, snug-
gling as it were into a perfect small setting, happy in their isolation. There is
less of the New England community influence, more independence.[33]

For Roosevelt simplicity, independence, cozy isolation, and self-sufficiency
were hallmarks of the Dutch in New York. In 1928, these seemed commend-
able characteristics; the dangers of international isolationism were not yet
apparent.

FDR also continued to adhere to ideas from the Holland Mania, as he explained to the Holland Society in 1935: "The influence of New Netherland [sic]

on the whole Colonial period of our history, which culminated in the War for Independence, has not as yet been fully recognized. It was an influence which made itself felt in all of the other twelve Colonies, and it is an influence which manifests itself today in almost every part of our Union of States." For Roosevelt the early Dutch represented "a quality of endurance against great odds—a quality of quiet determination to conquer obstacles of nature and obstacles of man."[34]

Although a dedicated member of the Holland Society, it was not "firsts" that interested FDR, and he did not aspire to a superior status derived from a distinguished lineage. Independent thinker that he was, Roosevelt loved history and architecture for their value to contemporary life. And in them, during his long years of struggle against paralysis, he found useful lessons of endurance and optimism in the heroics of everyday life. He would use those lessons a few years later to lift the spirits of a people crippled by the Great Depression.

FDR's love of the simplicity of Dutch colonial architecture was such that he used it as the model for several Roosevelt family buildings whose construction he oversaw.[35] The first was Val-Kill cottage, built in 1925 as a retreat for Eleanor Roosevelt and her friends Marion Dickerman and Nancy Cook. With another partner, Caroline O'Day, the women founded Val-Kill Industries nearby, a furniture and handcrafts workshop to employ local youth. Miss O'Day's cousin Henry J. Toombs, who was at the time a draftsman for New York City architects McKim, Mead, and White, was soon brought on board for what would be his first architectural commission and the beginning of a long collaboration with FDR.[36] Val-Kill cottage was built as a close adaptation (on the exterior) of an eighteenth-century Dutch cottage, whose form was approved by FDR's collaborator on the Dutch houses book, Helen Wilkinson Reynolds.[37] Eventually the Dutch colonial historical model would dominate in FDR's most personal building projects—his presidential library and his retirement retreat, Top Cottage.[38] FDR chose a style of architecture that for

Top Cottage, as restored in 2001, reflects FDR's love of the sloped porch, simple form, and stone architecture.
Franklin D. Roosevelt Presidential Library and Museum, Hyde Park, New York, Slide 51

many Americans was synonymous with domesticity and simple, democratic values—as well as a "cosy," practical, and unpretentious lifestyle.

Harold Eberlein, who published a popular and classic study of colonial American architecture in 1915—a copy of which is in FDR's personal library—found colonial Dutch architecture uniquely suited to the needs of modern Americans. He "considered the Dutch style as the best model for American domestic architecture" and "accepted the common characterization of the Dutch people as unassuming, home-loving, and democratic."[39] In his 1924 volume *The Manors and Historic Homes of the Hudson Valley* (also in FDR's library), he wrote: "Most of the houses built along . . . the river . . . were substantial but unpretentious. . . . They possessed a charm of a very pronounced type and they were rich in the homelike domestic quality that is too often lost."[40] This attractiveness of the Dutch colonial was so ingrained that *Wallace's Farmer*, the farmers' journal published by the Iowa Republican family of Henry A. Wallace (later FDR's secretary of agriculture and second vice president), printed plans by William Draper Brincklkoe for "a Farm Home of the Dutch-colonial type." The writer pointed out that the gambrel roof reflected a common type of barn roof beloved by "Peter Stuyvesant and the rest of those practical old Dutchmen," making it the ideal image for a modern American farmhouse.[41]

DUTCHNESS IN THE PRESIDENCY

Four times FDR was sworn in as president, each time on an old Dutch family Bible, printed in Amsterdam in 1686. He always opened it to this passage: "And now abideth faith, hope and charity, these three; but greatest of these is charity."[42] Underscoring the importance of this Bible, he sat for a photograph with it just days before his first inauguration on March 4, 1933. But by the time Franklin Roosevelt was elected president, the national passion for all things Dutch had run its course. World War I destroyed sentimental ideas of a pre-industrial Europe, and some saw the Dutch as too close to the Germans for comfort.[43]

A generation later the Dutch suffered conquest at the hands of the Nazis, and there was no confusing the Dutch with the Deutsch. In December 1939, in the months leading up to the widely anticipated German onslaught, FDR wrote to Queen Wilhelmina of the Netherlands offering to send a cruiser to transport the queen's daughter, Princess Juliana, and her young daughters to safety in the White House or his Hyde Park home. As for the queen herself, he said, "You, my good friend, I know will want to stick by the ship."[44] After the Netherlands fell, Wilhelmina established a government-in-exile in London and sent the princess and her daughters to Canada (because the United States was not yet an Allied nation) to escape the relentless London bombardment.[45]

Franklin Delano Roosevelt, a few days before his first inauguration, in his study
in Hyde Park reading the old Dutch Bible on which he was to take the oath of office.
Franklin D. Roosevelt Presidential Library and Museum, Hyde Park, New York,
80-118(443)

The princess and her family became frequent guests of the Roosevelts in Washington and Hyde Park.[46] Finally in 1942, with the United States in the war,
Queen Wilhelmina herself took a respite from London, visiting her daughter
in her summer residence in Lee, Massachusetts, not far from Hyde Park. The
Roosevelts visited them there and the royal family visited Hyde Park.[47] FDR's
sympathy for the Dutch also meant that he was much easier on them about
their Indonesian empire after the war—less adamantly opposed to their return to power than he was to British and French resumption of their colonial
empires.[48]

But on the surface Roosevelt's affection for the Dutch and his Dutch heritage played a relatively minor—and somewhat predictable—role in his public
persona. He did not, for example, refer to his Dutch background frequently
in his public addresses. When he did it was often paired with his Scottish
heritage[49] (derived from his mother through her mother, Catherine Robbins
Lyman Delano) to strengthen messages about thrift and practicality: "When

Princess Wilhelmina, Artotype by
Edward Bierstadt, New York, in the *Year
Book of the Holland Society of New-York*,
1888–1889, opp. p. 112
Hudson River Museum, Gift of the
Dutchess County Historical Society,
2008

we are making up the budget down in Washington, every department of the
Government wants to have a little bit more money, as you can well imagine.
When the President of the United States starts in to pare the budget and cut
it down, the favorite expression is that it is my old Dutch blood which cuts it
down."[50] ER and FDR sometimes referred to "getting his Dutch up"—meaning
"simmering" anger.[51]

In informal remarks before the Roosevelt Home Club, a group of supporters in Hyde Park, he urged approval for construction of new schools—much of
the cost to be funded by federal agencies—and used the stereotype to remind
people that he was no spendthrift: "That perhaps is the old Dutch coming out
in me or maybe it is the old Scotch Irish coming out in me; but, anyway, I
think most people in this town agree that we have to do something to give the
children of this town, from almost every part of the town, better educational
facilities."[52] A few years later, when speaking at the TVA's Chickamauga Dam

Wilhelmina, Queen of the Netherlands, in June 1942 while visiting her family summering in Lee, Massachusetts. Franklin D. Roosevelt Presidential Library and Museum, Hyde Park, New York, 48-22 3753(5)

near Chattanooga, Tennessee, he used the same allusion to describe the beneficial effects in dollars and cents of investment in flood control. "Being of a practical turn of mind—some people say I am part Scotch and part Dutch and therefore ought to have a practical turn of mind—I asked for figures relating to losses [from flooding and erosion] and figures to show the cost of stopping these losses."[53] Thus he was able to lightheartedly set forth a very sophisticated cost-benefit analysis.

When he was closer to home in the Hudson Valley, FDR referred at greater length to his Dutch background, but still he typecast it for political effect. For example, in a 1944 election eve address in Poughkeepsie, New York:

You can see I am pure Hudson River when you come down to it—that my mother's family came from Newburgh—but up in Kingston—well, there was an old boy in 1660 who went up there from New York City. He was

Franklin D. Roosevelt Presidential Library and Museum, Hyde Park, New York, 48-22 3711(114)

The dedication of the post office in Rhinebeck, New York on May 1, 1939 attracted a huge crowd, due to the presence of Danish royalty. FDR is shown speaking with (seated left to right): Princess Ingrid of Denmark; Eleanor Roosevelt; and Sara D. Roosevelt, the President's mother.

young, and I guess he was rather Dutch—with the old stubborn qualities. [He is referring here to Nicholas Roosevelt, the progenitor of both TR and FDR.] About that time the Indians attacked Kingston, and he became a member of the militia that rolled the Indians back. And I think that it is for that reason, perhaps, that I am interested and have been all my life—though not in uniform—in military and naval affairs. It comes from the old Dutch boy in 1660 who belonged to the militia.[54]

He then went on to discuss more contemporary military matters. By today's standards it might seem hackneyed, but Roosevelt's use of stereotypes allowed him to tackle sensitive—even confrontational—issues with a lightheartedness that softened the tough messages he was conveying.

As president, Roosevelt strongly influenced the design for post offices, schools, and other federal construction projects throughout the Hudson Valley and the United States.[55] In the Hudson Valley, they were built of stone—some in Dutch colonial style and others as replicas of historically significant eighteenth-century buildings that had vanished from the landscape. His words at the dedication of the Rhinebeck, New York, post office describe what he thought of the Dutch colonial style and the use of stone.

> We are seeking to follow the type of architecture which is good in the sense that it does not of necessity follow the whims of the moment but seeks an artistry that ought to be good, as far as we can tell, for all time to come. And we are trying to adapt the design to the historical background of the locality and to use, insofar as possible, the materials which are indigenous to the locality itself. Hence, the fieldstone for Dutchess County. Hence, the efforts during the past few years in Federal buildings in the Hudson River Valley to use fieldstone and to copy the early Dutch architecture which was so essentially sound besides being very attractive to the eye.[56]

FDR insisted that the new post office in Rhinebeck should be a re-creation of the Kip-Beekman-Hermance house, an early eighteenth-century farmstead that had been lost to fire at the turn of the twentieth century. While Roosevelt's motives were clearly close to his heart, he justified the reconstruction by exaggerating the importance of the vanished house as a relic of America's Revolutionary past. He claimed it was important to replicate this house because it was the first house occupied by a European settler in Dutchess County, because George Washington used it as a headquarters, and because it was where Washington took the oath of office as president. Of course all of this was classic Roosevelt hyperbole.[57] But FDR knew the importance of a sense of a shared past and the importance Americans placed on "firsts," and he was not above using historical platitudes—or even inaccuracies—to accomplish what he considered to be a higher purpose. In this case it was the re-creation of common links to an earlier time and place—when Americans had encountered great obstacles and overcome them. He used his personal heritage and experience to provide the link between then and now.

> Half a century ago . . . a small boy was often driven through the town of Rhinebeck by his father and mother. . . . On those drives . . . he passed a number of old stone houses, most of them with long, sloping roofs; and he was told that they had been built by the early settlers nearly two centuries before.[58]

As conveyed to his listeners, Roosevelt's memory of those early settlers was personal and a tangible connection to the present. His ancestry was their ancestry and their hometown was his.

Because through one line of my ancestry I am descended from the early Beekmans who settled Rhinebeck, and because on the Roosevelt side my great-great-grandfather lived in Rhinebeck for some time during the period of the Revolution and was not only a member of the State Senate, as his great-great-grandson was, but also a member of the Dutchess County Militia, I have a claim to kinship with this town that is second only to the town of Hyde Park.[59]

Ever building human connections—between past and present, neighbors near and far, the president and the people—Roosevelt insisted that other stone buildings built by the federal government in the Hudson Valley be re-creations of historically significant vanished buildings in their various locales: the house of Dr. John Bard, grandson of the original English settler, for the Hyde Park post office (after the failure to locate a suitable sketch of Jacobus Stoutenburgh's house, which was the earliest Dutch stone house in the village); the stone 1809 Dutchess County Court House (whose predecessor on the site hosted New York's ratification of the U.S. Constitution) for the Poughkeepsie post office; and the Brouwer-Mesier house—an FDR-approved Dutch colonial model associated with Dutchess County's own "Tea Party," an attack by Revolutionary rebels on its Loyalist owner and his slaves in 1777—for the post office in Wappingers Falls.[60] Schools in Hyde Park and post offices in Ellenville and Beacon were history lessons also, imaginative composites of familiar colonial revival forms rendered in FDR's favorite building material—stone.

In other parts of the country, post offices were built in Spanish colonial, federal, and other styles, reflecting the president's interest in using historical models appropriate to different regions.[61] To him it was important to emphasize the *connection* between the people and their past, and thus highlight a source for drawing social and human lessons.

HOME AND FAMILY: THE POWER OF A DUTCH IDEA

The architectural historian Witold Rybczynski describes the seventeenth-century Dutch as the originators of the modern idea of home as a place of comfort, refuge, and privacy for the nuclear family. This was itself a new idea: the Dutch were prosperous enough and urban enough to begin to establish workplaces separate from the home, and thus homes, no matter how modest, became associated with the family's identity. Compared to the "big houses" of other European cities of the time, where family members, tenants, servants, apprentices, and employees lived together,[62] the Dutch house began to take on the characteristics that Franklin Roosevelt observed in the Dutch houses of the Hudson Valley—cozy and independent.[63] These qualities suggest broader

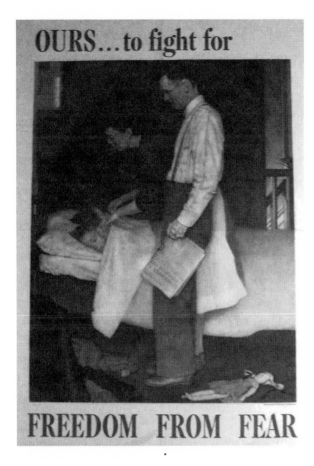

OURS... to fight for

FREEDOM FROM FEAR

War Bond poster based on Norman Rockwell's painting, *Freedom from Fear*, Office of War Information Poster No. 46, 1943.
Franklin D. Roosevelt Presidential Library and Museum, Hyde Park, New York, 2005-13-40-8

American values of the family itself. FDR used the part of the Dutch stereotype that had to do with home-loving domesticity to draw people closer to him and his home in the Hudson River Valley as a metaphor for home everywhere. This association between the Dutch and home—whether it derived from Dutch master paintings of cozy interiors or stone cottages "snuggled" against a hillside—led FDR to connect people everywhere to his home through his Dutchness.

Not surprisingly, the home as dwelling place and the family itself were largely interchangeable. As Rybczynski wrote, "The Dutch loved their homes . . . . 'Home' brought together the meanings of house and of household, of dwelling and of refuge, of ownership and affection. 'Home' meant the house, but also everything that was in it, as well as the people, and the sense of satisfaction and contentment that all these conveyed."[64]

By the 1930s in America, this idea of "home" that had begun some three centuries earlier in the Netherlands was well established among all social classes, native born and immigrant alike.[65] But in the midst of the Great Depression, homes were threatened everywhere. One out of four workers was unemployed. Millions lost their homes as mortgaged houses and farms fell into default.[66] Home, that old Dutch idea, this most fundamental institution synonymous with independence, autonomy, and refuge, even with the family itself, was in peril.

During World War II, magazines, newsreels, and government films and posters played upon these ideas of home to engender support for the war effort, sell war bonds, or simply reinforce patriotic ideals so essential to morale. Norman Rockwell's popular paintings of Roosevelt's Four Freedoms—symbolized by a neighbor speaking at a town meeting (Freedom of Speech and Expression), young and old in church together (Freedom of Worship), a family celebrating Thanksgiving together (Freedom from Want), and parents serenely admiring the security of their children in their beds (Freedom from Fear)—were a powerful statement of the association of home and family with fundamental ideas about American democracy.[67]

Throughout FDR's long presidency, Hyde Park, Dutchess County,[68] and the Hudson River Valley—and sometimes Warm Springs, Georgia—became familiar as a sort of national "home." He saw his job not as one of introducing America—and eventually the world—to his home in Dutchess County, but rather as helping people to understand that a little bit of Dutchess County (that is, "home") connects people everywhere. "Dutchess County has spread all over the United States; and the influence of the fine old stock that we have raised here is being felt in our American citizenship in every part of the country."[69] He made this pronouncement in 1933, but throughout his presidency FDR "proved" the truth in this idea again and again.

During the 1930s, he told his Hyde Park supporters a story about impoverished Dutchess County farmers who had left the Hudson Valley in the 1850s to become settlers in the Kansas territory, abandoning their homes and farms on one week's notice. Making the contemporary and personal connection, and proving once again that the people of Dutchess County could be found everywhere, he told his neighbors, "When I go through the United States, west of the Mississippi, there is hardly a State that I go into on any trip, that somebody does not come up to me and say, 'Mr. President, do you know a family back in Dutchess County named so-and-so?' And I say, 'Why, yes, I have heard the name.' And then they say, 'Why, she was my grandmother' or 'He was my grandfather.'"

FDR was expressing his fundamental political philosophy—the civic kinship of all Americans as neighbors. Speaking in Texas in 1938, he used the concept of neighborly connections to talk about policy, this time about the importance of a national farm program: "Not only does the cotton in Texas have a definite relationship to cotton in Georgia, but cotton in the South and

Springwood, the Roosevelt home in Hyde Park, circa 1933
Franklin D. Roosevelt Presidential Library and Museum, Hyde Park, New York, 56-343

Southwest is clearly connected with the economics of the wheat grower in the Dakotas, the cattleman of Wyoming and the potato grower of Maine. When one has a poor year, his lack of prosperity hits all of the others. When one is prosperous, all the others are helped."[70]

The patrician from Dutchess County became the man from Everywhere—everybody's friend and neighbor. As in Iowa: "And so my friends—this is not a prepared speech—I just want to talk to you as one neighbor to another. I don't pretend to be a farmer; I happen to be by profession a lawyer. But I have farmed the best part of my life, up on the Hudson River and down in the state of Georgia, so I do know about some of the problems of agriculture in the United States."[71]

Roosevelt stressed that everybody's homes were connected—their futures and their fortunes intertwined—as neighbors. His most memorable use of this metaphor, of course, is the 1940 press conference when he extended it internationally, calling upon Americans to adopt Lend-Lease to aid the beleaguered British: "Suppose my neighbor's home catches fire, and I have a length of garden hose. . . . If he can take my garden hose and connect it up with his hydrant, I may help him to put out his fire."[72]

In September of that year, with many still holding out against involvement, FDR reminded Americans that his own home—and by extension theirs—was among those places threatened by a false sense of security. With an eye, no

Roosevelt addressing a church fair at the invitation of the Ladies Aid Society of the
Plattekill Dutch Reformed Church, Mt. Marion, New York, July 5, 1937
Franklin D. Roosevelt Presidential Library and Museum, Hyde Park, New York,
48-22 3868(631)

doubt, on the isolationist strongholds in the Midwest, he addressed a national
conference of civic organizations with this stern warning in the guise of re-
minding everybody of what they already knew—in a sense taking them into
his confidence: "A good many people were startled when I said that planes
from Mexico could cause a certain amount of damage in Omaha, St. Louis,
and Kansas City, and that probably that section of the Middle West would be
more dangerous to live in, in case of attacks, than Dutchess County, N.Y."[73]

His warnings were often couched in the same friendly neighborliness that
drew upon his friends and neighbors in the Hudson Valley as idealized exem-
plars of the kind of spirit of cooperative preparedness he hoped to instill in
Americans across the land. In this parable from 1941, an ordinary Dutchess
County man served as FDR's Everyman, an example of the way an American
could "do his part" by performing useful public service in whatever capacity he
could: "I got a letter the other day from a driver of a school bus up in Dutchess
County, 52 years old, who wanted to do something. Well, he is taking kiddies
to school every morning and taking them back every night. Somebody has to

do it, and he is performing useful service at the present time. . . . He ought to be satisfied. He is really doing something."[74]

Even as he relied upon his Hudson Valley neighbors to provide (metaphorical) explanations of political actions and policies, FDR also urged those who actually *were* his Hudson Valley neighbors to broaden their sense of community connectedness. The message was strongest when he was dealing not just with neighbors, but also with those who shared his long lineage. And so Mrs. Myer, a Hudson Valley neighbor—and a fellow descendant of America's founders—piqued his interest (and perhaps his ire) ,with this invitation, "We are a plain, pioneer American family, who for eight generations have lived in our Hudson Valley home and tilled the same acres that we wrested from the wilderness. . . . We have been quiet, self-sustaining citizens for 227 years. Our service during the Revolution . . . is unparalleled as we gave eighteen sons to the service, not counting any of the daughters' children who are unrecorded. Since we helped then to make July Fourth possible, would it be so unsuitable for our President to grant us a favor on this Fourth of July?"

FDR could not resist confronting the sense of entitlement embedded in her words. He attended her gathering, seizing an opportunity to spread his message of national community: "Mrs. Myer referred to her family's being a pioneer family today after 227 years and she is absolutely right! Some of our neighbors who are out on the Great Plains and on the Pacific Coast think of themselves as pioneers. I claim that we, after 227 years in the Hudson Valley, are just as much pioneers as they are."[75] The same message was delivered to a national convention of the Daughters of the American Revolution in 1938.

It so happens, through no fault of my own, that I am descended from a number of people who came over in the *Mayflower*. More than that, every one of my ancestors on both sides—and when you go back four generations or five generations it means thirty-two or sixty-four of them—every single one of them, without exception, was in this land in 1776. . . . Remember always that all of us, and you and I especially, are descended from immigrants and revolutionists.[76]

Even as he would suffer no pretensions to high rank, he expected high standards of civic responsibility—which meant, hearkening back to the Bible passage upon which he took the oath of office,[77] understanding that a purpose of government was to help those who could not help themselves.

Members of the Roosevelt family were equally as important as the Hudson Valley or the home in Hyde Park to modeling this sense of "Dutch" civic connectedness, especially during the war. The couple's four sons all served in America's military; their daughter Anna lived at the White House in 1944–45

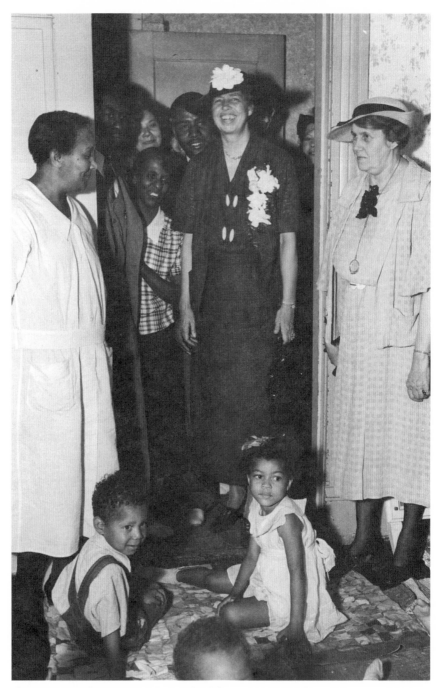

Eleanor Roosevelt at a WPA nursery school for
African American children, Des Moines, Iowa, June 8, 1936
Franklin D. Roosevelt Presidential Library and Museum,
Hyde Park, New York, 64-141

while her husband served overseas on a military-government assignment. Roosevelt himself registered for the "old man's draft" in 1942, when all men between ages forty-two and sixty-four were required to make themselves available for service.

Eleanor Roosevelt's tireless travels speaking in support of community organizations, young people, education, working people, and civil rights convinced people that the First Lady was indeed their friend and neighbor. Beginning in December 1935, her daily column, "My Day," (which was widely syndicated in newspapers across the country) provided millions of Americans a window into the Roosevelt presidency. She gave all Americans an access to the Roosevelt family that helped build a sense of kinship with the broader family of Americans struggling to make ends meet or facing fears of an impending war. In her popular Sunday evening radio program, Mrs. Roosevelt spoke directly and intimately to the American people in their living rooms; it was her voice on Sunday evening, December 7, 1941, speaking as a mother who shared the fears of all mothers, that first reassured Americans in the face of the Japanese attack on Pearl Harbor and other American bases in the Pacific. In summer 1943 she made a grueling 25,000-mile tour of combat troops serving in the South Pacific and upon her return urged all Americans to put aside prejudice and consider them all as family: "In a nation such as ours, every man who fights for us is in some way *our* man. His parents may be of any race or religion, but if that man dies, he dies side by side with all of his buddies. And if your heart is with any man, it must be with all. *All the men are our men.*"[78]

The Roosevelts returned to Hyde Park to vote in every election. And on every election, FDR addressed the nation from Springwood. Always these messages evoked the image of home—the home of the Roosevelts connected to the homes of Americans. As in this 1940 message with war against democracy raging in Europe:

> As I sit here tonight with my own family, I think of all the other American families—millions of families all through the land—sitting in their own homes. They have eaten their supper in peace, they will be able to sleep in their homes tonight in peace. Tomorrow they will be free to go out to live their ordinary lives in peace—free to say and do what they wish, free to worship as they please. Tomorrow, of all days, they will be free to choose their own leaders who, when that choice has been made, become in turn only the instruments to carry out the will of all the people.[79]

Four years later the country was at war. This time the family of neighbors—and the American family—truly stretched around the world. And everyone knew that Franklin and Eleanor's sons, like theirs, were on the front lines. "As

President Roosevelt is shown making his final radio broadcast of the 1936 campaign
from the study in his Hyde Park home, November 2, 1936
Franklin D. Roosevelt Presidential Library and Museum, Hyde Park, New York, 60-248

we sit quietly this evening in our home at Hyde Park, our thoughts, like those
of millions of other Americans, are most deeply concerned with the well-being
of all of our American fighting men. We are thinking of our own sons—all of
them far away from home—and of our neighbors' sons and the sons of our
friends."[80]

By this time FDR's home on the Hudson River was familiar to most Americans. Through three terms as president, it had become a familiar second
"home" for many Americans, and even for people around the world—so much
so that in 1945 Hyde Park was seriously considered as the location for the headquarters of the new United Nations.[81] Dutchess County—as the Roosevelts'
home—could be "home" for everybody, everywhere in the world. And when
FDR died, as my own father said, "It was like losing your own father."

Franklin and Eleanor Roosevelt on the south lawn of Springwood, overlooking the
Hudson River Valley, August 16, 1933
Franklin D. Roosevelt Presidential Library and Museum, Hyde Park, New York, 62-53

WHEN THE PEOPLE HEARD their "Dutch" president speak from his home to theirs, perhaps subconsciously they remembered those old Dutch ideas of cozy domesticity, industriousness, practicality, middle-class prosperity, tolerance, community, and (most of all) independence—the sort of independence that is fought for and won, whether in a war against a foreign tyrant, the tycoons of Wall Street, or the guns of totalitarianism. FDR reminded Americans that they were neighbors, family after all, and they were facing their hardships together an defense of their homes, their freedom, their independence, their autonomy, their sense of satisfaction and contentment with life, all of which could only be achieved in unity with one another. Some say this idea is Dutch in origin; it was then (and remains) the most powerful of ideas.

ACKNOWLEDGMENTS

This chapter could not have been completed without the efforts of many who helped me. Supervisory Archivist Robert Clark, Archivist Alycia Vivona, and Archives Specialist Karen Anson provided indispensable guidance, fact-checking, editing, and photo assistance. The Roosevelt Library's curator, Herman Eberhardt, and deputy director, Lynn Bassanese, read the manuscript and helped me focus my ideas. Allida Black reviewed what I had to say about Eleanor Roosevelt. My friend J. Garry Clifford gave the manuscript a very close reading and made innumerable improvements to the text and suggestions about sources previously unknown to me. And, my husband, Eliot Werner, is my most loyal editor. Thank you one and all.

NOTES

1. The President Announces He Will Accept a Nomination for a Fourth Term, Exchange of Letters Between the President and Robert E. Hannegan, July 11, 1944, *The Public Papers and Addresses of Franklin D. Roosevelt*, Samuel I. Rosenman, ed., vol. 13 (New York: Harper and Brothers, 1950), 197.

2. Theodore Roosevelt, *Autobiography* 1, as quoted in Jean Edward Smith, *FDR* (New York: Random House, 2007), 3.

3. Hendrik Willem van Loon, "Roosevelt Alias Geldersman," 4. FDR Library, PPF 2259, August 11, 1937. This article was intended for *Redbook* magazine, but there is no evidence that it was ever published.

4. A Letter on the Religion of the President's Ancestors, FDR to Philip Slomovitz, March 7, 1935, *The Public Papers and Addresses of Franklin D. Roosevelt*, vol. 4 (New York: Random House, 1938), 96.

5. Frank Freidel, "The Dutchness of the Roosevelts," in *A Bilateral Bicentennial: A History of Dutch-American Relations, 1782–1982*, ed. J. W. Schults Nordholdt and Robert P. Swierenga (New York: Octagon Books, 1982), 149.

6. Smith, *FDR*, 4. I am indebted principally to Smith for the recounting of early family history as set forth here. Other important sources for understanding FDR's early life are Frank Freidel, *Franklin D. Roosevelt: A Rendezvous with History* (Boston: Little, Brown, 1990) and Geoffrey C. Ward, *Before the Trumpet: Young Franklin Roosevelt* (New York: Harper and Row, 1985).

7. Smith, *FDR*, 5.

8. In 1862 Warren Delano brought his family to live with him in China. Sara celebrated

her eighth birthday on board the clipper ship the *Surprise*. Her four-month voyage and the two years that followed remained the source of family pride, legend, and countless stories of sea and the mysterious East that she recounted to her son.

9. Franklin D. Roosevelt, "The Roosevelt Family in New Amsterdam before the Revolution," December 1901, FDRL, Family, Business and Personal Affairs, Harvard College Notes and Papers. In noting the use of the word "virile," reader J. Garry Clifford reminds us that this was the era of Theodore Roosevelt, when "virility, however defined, was popular" (personal communication).

10. Annette Stott, *Holland Mania: The Unknown Dutch Period in American Art and Culture* (Woodstock, N.Y.: Overlook Press, 1998).

11. Stott dedicates a chapter to this subject, "Rewriting American History." John Lothrop Motley's *The Rise of the Dutch Republic* (1855) and *History of the United Netherlands* (1867) were highly popular treatments of the Dutch struggle for independence against the hated Spanish Catholic Hapsburgs. According to Stott, in *The Puritan in Holland, England and America: An Introduction to American History* (1892), Douglas Campbell built upon Motley and introduced the idea of the Dutch as progenitors of the American system of government. It took the popularizing work of William Elliot Griffis, a Dutch Reformed clergyman, who "wrote eight books and dozens of pamphlets and articles, gave innumerable lectures and sermons, and organized clubs around the country to study Dutch influence and erect commemorative plaques in the Netherlands" (85), to really establish the idea of the Dutch origins of American democracy.

12. During the Eighty Years War, the United Provinces of the Netherlands—a Protestant republic of representatives elected from the seven provinces that made up the northern Low Countries—united in defense against their common enemy, Spain, seat of the Roman Catholic Holy Roman Empire. Through the extraordinarily profitable Dutch East and West India companies, which were granted monopolies over trade in Asia, Africa, and the Americas, the Dutch developed a mercantile empire of vast wealth and influence. Led by an aristocracy of city merchants rather than the feudal lords of other countries, every Dutch city and province had its own government and a great deal of autonomy. Amsterdam became a leading city of Europe, a world center for capital and finance. The first stock market, developed by French-speaking Walloons, was established in Rotterdam and soon thereafter in Amsterdam. Holland, one of the seven provinces, became the richest and most urbanized region of Europe. With business and trade—rather than religion or royal succession—a priority in politics, the Dutch Protestants became known for their tolerance. High levels of immigration were encouraged to fuel the burgeoning economy, drawing people from across the Continent in search of work and religious freedom. Among them were Portuguese and German Jews, French (Huguenots) and Flemish Protestants, and—before they embarked for New England—the English Pilgrims of Massachusetts Bay.

13. The seventeenth century also saw a flourishing of the arts and learning as well as commerce and came to be known as the Golden Age in the Netherlands. Émigré philosophers René Descartes, John Locke, and Baruch Spinoza (born in Amsterdam to Portuguese Jewish parents) all found the tolerant and prosperous social climate conducive to their work. The Dutch master artists—among them Rembrandt van Rijn, Frans Hals, Johannes Vermeer, Meindert Hobbema, and Jacob van Ruysdael—and the so-called "little Dutch masters," who specialized in small-scale domestic genre scenes, still lifes, and landscapes, recorded for all time the Netherlanders' worldview: exquisite portraits of the burgher class; genre paintings of interiors, landscapes, seascapes; and paintings of farmers and the working class.

14. Stott, *Holland Mania*, 10.

15. Stott, *Holland Mania*, 22–23.

16. In chapter 2 of *Holland Mania*, Stott describes the towns of Volendam and Laren as particularly popular locations for American painters in search of an old-fashioned Dutch picturesqueness.

17. Quoted in Stott, *Holland Mania*, 251. The reference to the William the Silent homage is on 38.

18. Charles A. Goodrich, *The Universal Traveller Designed to Introduce Readers at Home to An Acquaintance with the Arts, Customs, and Manners of the Principal Modern Nations on the Globe* (New York: P. Canfield, 1840), 23.

19. Eleanor Roosevelt, *This Is My Story*, quoted in Olin Dows, *Franklin Roosevelt at Hyde Park* (New York: American Artists Group, 1949), 81.

20. FDRL, Family, Business, and Personal Affairs, Memberships folder, contains the following memberships at different points throughout FDR's life. In 1923–24 and 1933 he resigned from a great many clubs for obvious reasons. American Museum of Natural History (life member), Century Club, New-York Historical Society, Hudson River Ice Yacht Club, Harvard Club, New York Society Library, Hudson Valley Federated Chamber of Commerce, Civitan Club of New York, American Antiquarian Society, Holland Society, Men's Club of St. James Church, Racquet and Tennis Club, Dutchess County Society in the City of New York, Club of Odd Volumes, New York Press Club, Adirondack Mountain Club, Navy League of the United States, Society of Iconophiles, New York Agricultural Society.

21. There were 212 charter members of the commission, which grew to 805 by the time of the celebration, September 25–October 11, 1909. In the county of New York, more than 3,000 participated in the Citizens Committee. The celebration was an immense affair, with a budget of "slightly more than $1 million," funded jointly by the State and City of New York and private contributions (12 cited below). Among the activities: full-scale replicas of the *Half Moon* and the *Clermont* sailed to communities between New York and Albany. There were military, naval, and carnival parades, "Illuminations and Pyrotechnics," a children's festival, "Art, Historical and Science Exhibits" in museums, a celebration dinner in New York with dignitaries from around the world, celebration dinners and public festivals in all the principal river towns, and the installation of markers and monuments up and down the Hudson. The most lasting accomplishment was the creation of the Palisades International Park Commission. The Hudson-Fulton Commission's activities are recorded in a two-volume beautifully published report, *The Hudson-Fulton Celebration, 1909*, ed. Edward Hagman Hall (Albany: J. B. Lyon for the State of New York, 1910).

22. Letter, FDR to John R. Eustis, Secretary, Public Health and Convenience Committee, Hudson-Fulton Celebration Commission, August 13, 1909, FDRL, Family, Business and Personal Affairs, Hudson-Fulton Celebration Commission, Public Health and Convenience Committee folder.

23. Hyde Park Matters, Correspondence About Local History, FDRL, Family, Business and Personal Affairs.

24. He was also a well-known stamp collector. The collection numbered 1.2 million stamps at the time of his death, when it was sold to benefit his estate according to his instruction.

25. Annette Stott's research in Dutch archives identified more than 400 American artists who registered for copy permits at Dutch museums, had memberships in artists' organizations, took lessons, or were listed in the guest registers of hotels frequented by visiting artists. See Stott, *Holland Mania*, appendix. The following artists from her research are represented in Roosevelt's collection: Charles P. Gruppe, pencil sketch of a small sailboat (MO 56.343); Leigh Hunt, etchings of the *Half Moon* (41.3.75a & b); J. Gari Melchers, black and white photogravure of "The Pilots"; John Sartain, a group of 16 prints of engravings of maritime, landscape, and genre scenes.

26. John Lothrop Motley, *History of the United Netherlands, from the Death of William the Silent to the Twelve Year's Truce, 1609* (New York: Harper, 1888); Motley, *The Correspondence of John Lothrop Motley*, ed. George William Curtis (New York: Harper and Brothers, 1889).

27. As quoted and paraphrased from correspondence between FDR and Henry J. Toombs in "The Franklin D. Roosevelt Library Historic Structure Report 2002," prepared by John G. Waite Associates, Architects (Albany: GSA, National Capitol Region), 4.

28. FDR, "History of the U.S.," FDRL, 1924, Family, Business and Personal Affairs, Writing and Statement File. Instead he set forth an argument that surely the Spanish and French in their marauding for riches had laid anchor in these northern harbors, but failed for any number of reasons to record their visits.

29. Letter, FDR to Frederic R. Keator, May 3, 1923, FDRL, Family, Business and Personal Affairs, Holland Society folder; Franklin D. Roosevelt, "Preserve the Pictures of Old Landmarks," *De Halve Maen* 1, no. 3 (April 1923).

30. Helen Wilkinson Reynolds, *Dutch Houses in the Hudson Valley Before 1776*, introduction by Franklin D. Roosevelt (New York: Payson and Clarke for the Holland Society of New York, 1929) and Rosalie Fellows Bailey, *Pre-Revolutionary Dutch Houses and Families in Northern New Jersey and Southern New York*, introduction by Franklin D. Roosevelt (New York: William Morrow for the Holland Society of New York, 1936).

31. Holland Society Correspondence, FDRL, Family, Business and Personal Affairs, Holland Society folder.

32. Reynolds, *Dutch Houses in the Hudson Valley*, introduction.

33. Reynolds, *Dutch Houses in the Hudson Valley*, introduction.

34. A Telephoned Greeting to the Holland Society of New York, January 17, 1935, *Public Papers*, vol. 4, 42. A different version of this address was prepared by the State Department at the request of Stephen Early. Roosevelt rewrote it to deliver a much more personal statement. See Memorandum, Stephen Early to Richard Southgate, January 17, 193[5], FDRL, PPF 484.

35. William B. Rhoads, "Franklin D. Roosevelt and Dutch Colonial Architecture," *New York History* (October 1978):430–464, remains the most important source on this subject. I have relied on it extensively.

36. Rhoads, "Franklin D. Roosevelt," 437–438, describes how FDR's ideas dominated the young architect's prerogatives, including a heated argument over the inclusion of an arched window in Val-Kill cottage, which was favored by Toombs and his clients but rejected by FDR as too "Italian" for a proper Dutch colonial design. More than a decade later, Toombs and FDR got into trouble with Frank Lloyd Wright's son John Lloyd Wright, when the plans for Top Cottage were published in *Life* magazine (October 31, 1938) with the inscription "Franklin D. Roosevelt, Architect and Henry Toombs, Associate," as quoted in Rhoads, "Franklin D. Roosevelt," 463–464. Soon after Val-Kill, FDR and Toombs collaborated on the James Roosevelt Memorial Library, built for the Town of Hyde Park. It was built in stone in a Georgian style. The story of the selection of Caroline O'Day's cousin, Henry J. Toombs, as architect is told in John G. Waite Associates, Architecture, *The President as Architect: Franklin D. Roosevelt's Top Cottage*, (Albany, N.Y.: Mt. Ida Press, 2001), 19.

37. Rhoads, "Franklin D. Roosevelt," 438.

38. Toombs designed Top Cottage with significant involvement by FDR. Toombs started the presidential library design, but the project was completed by Louis A. Simon, chief architect for the Treasury Department (see Rhoads, "Franklin D. Roosevelt," 436–439, 456–457).

39. Stott, *Holland Mania*, 172.

40. Harold Donald Eberlein, *The Manors and Historic Homes of the Hudson Valley* (Philadelphia: J. B. Lippincott, 1924), viii–ix.

41. Stott, *Holland Mania*, 172–173.

42. St. Paul's First Epistle to the Corinthians, 13th chapter, last verse.

43. Personal conversation with Cornelis van Minnen at the Roosevelt Institute Four Freedoms Ceremony, November 6, 2007. And, of course, there has long been confusion in Americans' minds between those of Dutch descent and the Pennsylvania Dutch, the group of Germans from the Palatinate and other southwestern German regions who settled in Pennsylvania in the seventeenth century. Germans from the Palatinate region also came to the heart of the Hudson Valley. Arriving in the very early eighteenth century, they eventually settled in and around Rhinebeck.

44. Quoted in Frank Freidel, "The Dutchness of the Roosevelts," in J. W. Schulte Nordholt and Robert P. Swierenga, eds., *A Bilateral Bicentennial: A History of Dutch-American Relations, 1782–1982* (New York: Octagon Books, 1982), 161.

45. They could not come to the United States, which was still a neutral nation, because only in an Allied country could Juliana with certainty ascend to the throne in the event of her mother's death. Freidel, "Dutchness of the Roosevelts," 162. Freidel recounts the warm relationship between the White House and the Dutch royal family on 161–163.

46. The Roosevelts often provided respite for exiled royalty during the war. Besides the Dutch royal family, the Roosevelts also often hosted Crown Princess Martha and Crown Prince Olav of Norway in both Hyde Park and the White House. They were visited by George II, King of Greece and Crown Prince Paul; Zita, former Empress of Austria (she was deposed during World War I and found refuge in Belgium, but she fled to America when Belgium was overrun by the Nazis); Charlotte, Grand Duchess of Luxembourg; and King Peter of Yugoslavia.

47. Correspondence detailing their relationship is found in FDRL, OF 246, Netherlands and PSF, Netherlands. I relied on Frank Freidel, "The Dutchness of the Roosevelts," 161–165, for the narrative of the relationship between the Roosevelts and the Dutch royal family.

48. J. Garry Clifford, personal communication, e-mail, March 11, 2008.

49. The descent is described in "Scott and Roosevelt," *The Weekly Scotsman*, February 21, 1942, which describes how FDR shares an ancestor, the Outlaw of Murray Hill, with Sir Walter Scott. FDR's Scottie dog Fala was named for the Outlaw of Murray Hill, who obtained from James Earl of Douglas a charter "terrarum de Fala" in 1321. See "President Roosevelt Link With Scotland" in *The Scotsman*, March 12, 1941.

50. Rear-Platform Extemporaneous Remarks at Grand Rapids, Michigan, October 15, 1936, *The Public Papers and Addresses of Franklin D. Roosevelt,* vol. 5 (New York: Random House, 1938), 489. He also opened these remarks with the comment "So many of the good people here are descended from the same old Holland stock as I."

51. Suggested by J. Garry Clifford, personal communication, March 11, 2008; confirmed by Curtis Roosevelt, e-mail, April 2, 2008.

52. Informal, Extemporaneous Remarks Before the Roosevelt Home Club, Hyde Park, New York, August 27, 1938, *The Public Papers and Addresses of Franklin D. Roosevelt*, vol. 7 (New York: Macmillan, 1941), 505. The Hyde Park School Board had met at Springwood in June 1938 and agreed to apply for a Public Works Administration grant for the construction of three new schools, serving a new consolidated school district. The voters approved the consolidation and by November contracts had been let. The three schools were dedicated on October 5, 1940. Roosevelt's contribution was an insistence on stone construction, which he stated at the dedication was mostly from "our famous stone walls" serving as a reminder of early settlers. Address at the Dedication of Three New Schools in the Town of Hyde Park, October 5, 1940, *The Public Papers and Addresses of Franklin D. Roosevelt*, vol. 9 (New York: Macmillan, 1941), 454.

53. "This Is a Demonstration of What a Democracy at Work Can Do," Address at Chicka-

mauga Dam Celebration, Near Chattanooga, Tennessee, September 2, 1940, *Public Papers*, vol. 9, 361.

54. Informal, Extemporaneous Remarks at Poughkeepsie, New York, November 6, 1944, *Public Papers*, vol. 13, 408–409.

55. For a complete treatment of this subject, see Rhoads, "Franklin D. Roosevelt," which is the most important source on this subject.

56. 70 Address at the Dedication of the New Post Office in Rhinebeck, New York, vol. 8, May 1, 1939, *Public Papers*, vol. 8, 303.

57. Helen Wilkinson Reynolds disapproved of the idea of re-creating the Kip-Beekman-Hermance house because of substantial alterations in the eighteenth century. Rhoads, "Franklin D. Roosevelt," 445–446.

58. Address at the Dedication of the New Post Office in Rhinebeck, *Public Papers*, 301.

59. Ibid., 301–302.

60. See Rhoads, "Franklin D. Roosevelt," 442, for the Poughkeepsie post office model and 453-54 for the Hyde Park post office. He describes the use of the Brouwer-Mesier house as an architectural model, 451–452. The history of the house is outlined in Harold Donaldson Eberlein and Cortlandt Van Dyke Hubbard, *Historic Houses of the Hudson Valley* (New York: Architectural Book Publishing Co., for the Hudson River Conservation Society, 1942), 68.

61. "Local tradition has been observed as far as possible. . . . Most of the materials used were obtained, as far as possible, from the State in which the project was located." *Public Buildings: A Survey Of Architecture Of Projects Constructed By Federal And Other Governmental Bodies Between The Years 1933 and 1939* by C. W. Short and R. Stanley Brown, Public Works Administration (Government Printing Office, 1939), xiv. See also http://www.postmarks.org/photos/ for a listing with photos of American post offices, many from the New Deal.

62. Witold Rybczynski, *Home: A Short History of an Idea* (New York: Viking Penguin, 1986), 59.

63. Reynolds, *Dutch Houses*, introduction.

64. Rybczynski, *Home*, 61–62.

65. Tamara K. Hareven, "Home and Family in Historical Perspective," in *Home: A Place in the World*, ed. Arien Mack (New York: New York University Press, 1993), 256.

66. David M. Kennedy, *Freedom from Fear: The American People in Depression and War, 1929–1945* (New York: Oxford University Press, 1999), 163.

67. Roosevelt's famous "Four Freedoms Speech" was delivered on January 6, 1941, in his annual message to Congress: "In the future days, which we seek to make secure, we look forward to a world founded upon four essential human freedoms. The first is freedom of speech and expression—everywhere in the world. The second is freedom of every person to worship God in his own way—everywhere in the world. The third is freedom from want—which, translated into world terms, means economic understandings which will secure to every nation a healthy peacetime life for its inhabitants—everywhere in the world. The fourth is freedom from fear—which, translated into world terms, means a world-wide reduction of armaments to such a point and in such a thorough fashion that no nation will be in a position to commit an act of physical aggression against any neighbor—anywhere in the world." Norman Rockwell painted four paintings illustrating the Four Freedoms, which appeared as magazine covers of the *Saturday Evening Post* at the height of the war (February 20–March 13, 1943).

68. Although it seems logical, and may well have been widely understood to be the case, the name Dutchess County does not refer to Dutchness. After the English gained control of the Hudson Valley in 1664, they established the twelve original counties of New York. The

county was named in 1683 by the English for the Duchess of York, Maria Beatrice D'Este (later to become Queen Mary). The "t" in Dutchess is an archaic spelling.

69. "The Golden Rule in Government," An Extemporaneous Address at Vassar College, Poughkeepsie, New York, August 26, 1933, *Public Papers and Addresses of Franklin D. Roosevelt*, vol. 2, 338.

70. Extemporaneous Remarks, Fort Worth, Texas, July 10, 1938, *Public Papers*, vol. 7, 447.

71. Rear-Platform Extemporaneous Remarks, Oelwein, Iowa, October 9, 1936, *Public Papers*, vol. 5, 415.

72. The Seven Hundred and Second Press Conference, December 17, 1940, *Public Papers*, vol. 9, 607.

73. Extemporaneous Remarks to Representatives of National Civic Organizations on Consumer Problems, Washington, D.C., August 2, 1940, *Public Papers*, vol. 9, 324.

74. The Seven Hundred and Nineteenth Press Conference (Excerpts), February 18, 1941, *Public Papers and Addresses of Franklin D. Roosevelt,* ed. Samuel I. Rosenman, vol. 10 (New York: Harper and Brothers, 1950), 25.

75. Informal, Extemporaneous Remarks at Mt. Marion, N.Y., July 5, 1937, *Public Papers*, vol. 6, 290.

76. "All of Us, and You and I Especially, Are Descended from Immigrants and Revolutionists," Extemporaneous Remarks Before the Daughters of the American Revolution, Washington, D.C., April 21, 1938, *Public Papers*, vol. 7, 259.

77. "And now abideth faith, hope and charity, these three; but greatest of these is charity." St. Paul's First Epistle to the Corinthians, 13th chapter, last verse.

78. Eleanor Roosevelt, "Mrs. Roosevelt Reports," Paramount News (newsreel), circa September 1942.

79. Final Radio Speech of the 1940 Presidential Campaign, Hyde Park, New York, "Democracy is Not Just a Word, to Be Shouted at Political Rallies and Then Put Back into the Dictionary After Election Day," November 4, 1940, *Public Papers*, vol. 9, 554.

80. "Our Task is Now to Face the Future as a Militant and a United People," Radio Address at Hyde Park, New York, November 6, 1944, *Public Papers*, vol. 13, 410.

81. There was a very serious effort on the part of an organization based in Hyde Park to secure the location for the United Nations headquarters. A letter from Congressman Jay LeFevre to President Harry Truman endorsed the idea: "I am strongly in favor of this selection and I believe that you will agree with me that there is no other spot in the United States that has quite the historical as well as the sentimental appeal as Hyde Park, not only to Americans but to the world at large." Harry S. Truman Library, letter, U.S. Representative Jay Le Fevre to President Harry S. Truman, October 22, 1945. The matter was put to rest when Truman responded through his secretary that he would leave the decision to Secretary of State Stettinius. Letter, Matthew J. Connelly, to LeFevre, October 25, 1945. www.trumanlibrary.org/whistlestop/study_collections/un/large /documents/index.php.

Displaying the Dutch

12

THE DYCKMAN FARMHOUSE MUSEUM
AND THE DUTCH COLONIAL REVIVAL

LAURA M. CHMIELEWSKI

In the summer of 1916, New Yorkers welcomed a new early American house museum. The Dyckman House, built by the descendants of one of New York's oldest Dutch families, had been saved from demolition and was now open to the general public. This lone relic of Manhattan's farming days was, according to Bashford Dean, one of the museum's creators, "happily, . . . for posterity . . . an excellent specimen of its kind."[1] New York City Parks Commissioner Cabot Ward agreed: at the museum's dedication ceremony, he praised the house for perpetuating "the memory of a noble era in our history."[2] In recognizing the Dyckman House's place in history, both men connected the modest Dutch structure to a heroic American past.

That this building survived at all was nothing short of extraordinary. For decades, the old house at 204th Street and Broadway had weathered the storms of urban development and neglect. Its orchards were plowed under to make way for apartment houses. New IRT subway lines ran under its foundation and made the house tremble. The portents for its survival had not been good. Yet three converging trends of the early twentieth century—the efforts launched by genealogical and historical groups to save landmark structures, the increasingly aggressive efforts to professionalize American museums, and a renewed interest in all things Dutch colonial—made this Dutch American landmark an attractive candidate for preservation. The Dyckman House emerged as a proud relic of a bygone New York, in which the city's character and the dignity of early American Dutch life were jointly celebrated.

To the modern museum-going public, this lofty, celebratory approach to New York's early Dutch seems appropriate. In 1916, however, celebrating these roots was a fairly recent trend. Some elements of nineteenth-century American popular culture had satirized the Dutch and denigrated their contributions to the city's growth and prosperity. Instead of being viewed as an alternative colonial system to the English settlement of New England, the Chesapeake, or even New York itself, the Dutch of New Amsterdam fell into the margins. Nineteenth-century stereotypes portrayed them as a population that lacked

"Restored" Dyckman House c. 1916
Photograph in the Reginald Pelham Bolton Scrapbook
Dyckman Farmhouse Museum, New York, New York

the discipline (as demonstrated by their girths) and the whiggish foresight (seen in their attachment to their own European traditions) of the more aggressive, praiseworthy English.

The creators of the Dyckman House Museum, however, rejected this perception of the Dutch as inept colonizers by applying new museological methods and historical theories to their interpretation. In part, these grew out of the Colonial Revival movement of the late nineteenth and early twentieth centuries, which used period artifacts and historic structures to illustrate the dignity of early American life. This attractive vision served Dyckman House's creators well, providing the framework on which they could build a story of early Dutch American achievement. The aforementioned Bashford Dean, who with his brother-in-law, Alexander McMillan Welch, restored and created the period rooms, wrote a substantial visitor's guide, *The Dyckman House Museum and Park*, to impart the message. This compelling artifact reveals the Colonial Revival mindset at work. The museum's creators wanted visitors to admire the spirit and foresight of the house's founders and to correct persistent myths about the early American Dutch. Helped along by new museological theories and applications, Dean and Welch made the Dyckman House Museum a showcase for a more sophisticated and dignified understanding of what it meant to be Dutch in early America.

THE HOUSE THAT DYCKMAN BUILT

The Dyckman House Museum—now known as the Dyckman Farmhouse Museum—still stands at the intersection of Broadway and 204th Street in Manhattan's now-northernmost neighborhood, Inwood.[3] Manhattanites jokingly refer to Inwood, once considered part of Kingsbridge, and its adjacent neighborhoods as "upstate Manhattan." Toward the end of the nineteenth century, this was practically a statement of fact. The subway line that would make the area accessible to the city had yet to be built, and the neighborhood's low density and open spaces resembled the leafy suburbs of nearby Bronx and Westchester.[4] Inwood clung to farming, grazing, and tourism long after the rest of the island, on which it depended for its prosperity, had become thoroughly industrialized.

The neighborhood was poised for transition, however, spurred on by economic growth to the south and the well-established farming communities to the north. By 1868, its stretch of Broadway was an active conduit for cattle headed to lower Manhattan markets.[5] Their noises, droppings, and often-uncouth drovers were an important reason the Dyckmans, an old and land-rich New York family, sold the farmhouse in the 1850s in pursuit of more pleasant surroundings. After all, they were no longer farmers. The developing city led to new opportunities for its citizens, and the Dyckmans, like other upwardly mobile families, abandoned farming and pursued different professions. The last Dyckman to live in the house, Isaac Michael, did not need a profession at all. Selling family land gave him a significant income for life, and he devoted his time to the gentlemanly pursuits of improving his properties and philanthropy.[6]

This was quite a contrast to the working lives of his ancestors, who relied on the fertility of the Kingsbridge property to make their lives comfortable. The first Dyckman in America was Jan, a native Westphalian who came to New Amsterdam in 1661.[7] The house he built, which predated the Dyckman House, sheltered three generations. His descendants remained and prospered—until local and imperial politics intruded on their lives. Jan's grandson William, builder of what was to become the Dyckman House Museum, was farming and raising a large family with his wife when hostilities with Britain forced them to flee to Westchester. All four of William's sons eventually fought as patriots; two lost their lives.[8]

The Dyckmans had the good fortune to side with the winners in the colonies' conflict with Britain, but the short-term consequences of their choices

meant severe losses for the family. When they returned to Manhattan at war's end, they found almost every part of their farm destroyed. Orchards were stripped bare; animals were stolen, lost, or eaten; and the family house, which probably sheltered British officers during the occupation, had burned to the ground.

William's resolve to rebuild resulted in the Dyckman House that exists today. Far different from the mid-nineteenth-century home it became, the original building was designed to be a useful structure, with plenty of spaces to fulfill the most basic needs of a late eighteenth-century household—work and shelter. After William's untimely death in 1787, the house eventually passed to a surviving son, Jacobus, who already had 11 children.[9] The postrevolutionary Dyckman property eventually encompassed 400 acres, worked by family

ARNULE BANDEL
Sketch of Dyckman House (built by William Dyckman, c. 1784), c. 1835
Pencil on paper, 17 x 10 in.
Dyckman Farmhouse Museum, New York, New York

members and as many as seven slaves.[10] Jacobus's large family made do with basic living spaces: no indoor staircase linked the basement kitchen with the rest of the house, and a large open loft provided sleeping quarters for children of both sexes.[11]

Jacobus presided over a transitional generation of Dyckmans. His sons were free to consider careers outside of farming. Two of them, Jacob and James, attended Columbia and, though they died young, had had promising careers in medicine and law. When Jacobus died in 1832, the property passed to two younger sons, Isaac and Michael.[12] Neither married, and as they grew older, they brought the son of their sister, Hannah Dyckman Smith, to live with them. In exchange for his labor and companionship, James Frederick Dyckman Smith became sole heir to the Dyckman Inwood properties. There was a catch, however—the boy needed to change his surname to Dyckman. Smith did one better by changing his first name to Isaac Michael, an affectionate tribute to the uncles who raised him like a son.

Isaac Michael Dyckman's devotion to his uncles came with a handsome payoff. Within a decade of inheriting the Dyckman property, he had sold much of it.[13] With the proceeds, he built a large Queen Anne–style house, named Mon Désir, near what is now Columbia University's Baker Field. He had married a distant cousin, Fannie Blackwell Brown, in 1867, and had two daughters. It was these children, Mary Alice and Fannie Fredericka Dyckman, who later memorialized their family through the Dyckman House Museum.

The experiences of the various Dyckman generations were typical for an

early Dutch American family. They retained their ethnically Dutch surname but otherwise adapted to their anglicized world. Their responses to adversity and opportunity smacked of both idealism and pragmatism. They saw opportunities to improve their status and seized them. They were practical and unsentimental about their land. They were stuck neither in time nor in place but, with much of the rest of the new nation, moved forward into the postrevolutionary and later industrializing world. In these essentials, the early American Dutch Dyckmans were far from retrograde relics of old peasant Europe, sharing more commonalities with their ethnically English neighbors and most other Euro-American contemporaries than differences.

THE DUTCH LOSE THEIR DIGNITY:
BETWEEN SATIRE AND HISTORY

Had it not been for the various popular interpretations of "Old New York" that became a minor literary genre in the nineteenth century, the Dyckman family story would have squared with a conventional American narrative of loss, restoration, and upward mobility in the wake of the American Revolution. But Dutch culture was perceived to cleave more closely to the peasant

UNKNOWN PHOTOGRAPHER
Fannie Blackwell Brown Dyckman
(Mrs. Isaac Michael Dyckman),
date unknown
Photograph, 10½ x 7½ in.
Dyckman Farmhouse Museum,
New York, New York

folkways of the Old World than anglicized colonial culture did. Therefore, it fell squarely into well-established literary traditions—stemming from Chaucer and even before—that satirized the religious practices, superstitions, and work habits (or lack thereof) of European peasants. In the new nation's search for a national mythology, the Dutch provided a convenient bridge between the colorful challenges of the New World and the long-established literary conventions of the Old World. These elements came together in the early nineteenth century in Washington Irving's work, which cast a long shadow on perceptions of Dutch Americans that prevailed for decades.

Irving's *Knickerbocker's History of New York* is a satirical account of the early Dutch bumbling through the American wilderness. In contrast to the English, Dutch colonizers were presumed to lack the lofty motivations of religion or philosophy. As described by Irving's fictional narrator, Diedrich Knickerbocker, their needs were more basic and modest and their mode of colonization decidedly less aggressive. In Irving's hands, they were also very silly. *Knickerbocker's History of New York* was actually a mild indictment of Jeffersonian politics, of which Irving, an old Federalist, disapproved.[14] Yet the author's use of historical figures such as Walter Van Twiller, William Kieft, Olaff Van

UNKNOWN ARTIST
Kingsbridge Road Near Dykemans [sic] Farm, c. 1866
Lithograph, 7¾ x 8¼ in.
Dyckman Farmhouse Museum, New York, New York

Cortlandt, and Peter Stuyvesant anchored the work in New York City's actual history, leading some readers to believe it was a narrative of authentic historical events. Three "distinctively Dutch" behaviors in particular—smoking, overeating, and an unwillingness to act on anything that was not geared toward a better smoke or a better meal—arise repeatedly. In Irving's hands, Olaff Van Kortlandt spent his days "crammed and almost choked with good eating and good nature."[15] Similarly gluttonous, "Wouter" Van Twiller did little more than sleep and eat.[16] William Kieft and Peter Stuyvesant were more physically active—yet similarly lacking in prudence, judgment, and self-control. These tropes carried over into Irving's other works, like "The Legend of Sleepy Hollow" and "Rip Van Winkle." Even in a serious biography, *The Life of George Washington*, Irving's Dutch fail to measure up to the demands of more farsighted Anglo-Americans. In Irving's retelling, young George falls hard for

Mary Philipse, niece of the wealthy Hudson Valley landowner Adolph. Mary's retrograde Dutchness, however, keeps her from taking the visionary Anglo-Virginian suitor very seriously.[17]

Irving-inspired visions of early Dutch New Yorkers are prevalent in a later popular nineteenth-century literary trope: "olden time," "crooked little," or "little old" New York.[18] Many New Yorkers were disconcerted by the city's astonishingly rapid industrial and population growth. Their concerns inspired of a new group of writers, called "patrician historians," to celebrate "Old New York" and its perceived eccentricities.[19] One of these was Thomas Janvier, whose *In Old New York* (1894) illustrates the durability of Irving's comic vision.[20] Lamenting the drive to streamline Manhattan streets, Janvier muses that the Dutch, "in the slave-dealing and piratical days of New York, when life here had a flavor of romance in it," would have planned their urban spaces with a good deal more "dash and spirit."[21] Untroubled by the ugly downside of this romantic vision, Janvier delighted in a haphazard world of the colonial Dutch that was governed by the senses.[22] To the patricians, the Dutch built canals not for moving people and goods but for their smell, which reminded them of the homes they had left in Europe. Canals also provided good places for smoking pipes and viewing "round, squat" sailors unloading goods from equally round, squat shallops—goods that, no doubt, contributed to the roundness and squatness of the Dutch themselves.[23]

Other historians attempted not to discredit Irving's work but to integrate it into serious historical analysis. Chief among these was Alice Morse Earle, a respected antiquarian of early American domestic life. Earle's books celebrate early American material culture and feature innovative, humanizing readings of the artifactual record. One book, *The Sabbath in Puritan New England* (1891), challenged prevailing Victorian notions that early New Englanders were cold, humorless zealots. Her popular *Home Life in Colonial Days* presented early American women as hearty helpmeets rather than submissive housewives.[24] Earle's *Colonial Days in Old New York,* however, draws heavily on Irving as a source and, as a result, is far less nuanced. Like others before her, Earle focuses on the quaint, comforting, and often lampoonable elements of Dutch life. In her treatment, Dutch men are portly, yet prone to cavorting; Dutch women are highly moral, decorous, and sensible, yet terrible gossips and neurotic housekeepers.[25] For all Dutch colonists, full stomachs, storerooms, and pipes were top priorities.[26] *Colonial Days in Old New York* frequently credits Irving's *Knickerbocker's History* as a source.[27] Given the importance of Earle's work to the creation of new house museums in the late nineteenth and early twentieth centuries, its propensity to pass on old chestnuts in new shells was highly problematic.

JOHN QUIDOR (1801–1881)
The Return of Rip Van Winkle, 1849
Oil on canvas, 39¾ x 49¹³⁄₁₆ in.
National Gallery of Art, Washington, D.C., Andrew W. Mellon Collection 1942.8.10
Image courtesy of the Board of Trustees, National Gallery of Art, Washington, D.C.

Washington Irving's creative impulses and love of folklore and mythology led him to draw on regional legends and colorful historical characters. But his playful blurring of lines between history and fiction led to confusion about the actual experiences of New Yorkers of Dutch origin, and perhaps even discouraged others from digging more carefully into the historical record. As a result, as Edwin G. Burrows notes, "too many New Yorkers would for too long accept [Irving's] affectionate mythmaking as authentic history."[28]

THE COLONIAL REVIVAL MAKES ITS MARK

The tide toward a dignified popular concept of early Dutch American life began to turn with the late nineteenth-century movement known as the Colonial Revival. Though fundamentally an inchoate collection of ideas about the

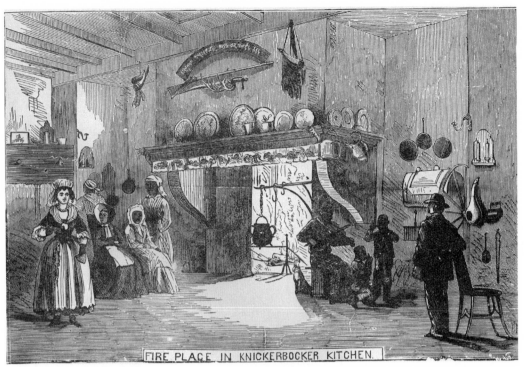

FIRE PLACE IN KNICKERBOCKER KITCHEN.

'Knickerbocker Kitchen' a panel featured in Metropolitan Sanitary Fair,
In Frank Leslie, *The Soldier in Our Civil War* (New York, Bryan, Taylor & Co.,
1893), pp. 344–345.
Hudson River Museum

intrinsic decency of early American life, it influenced museums, decorative
arts, architecture, and literature. The roots of this movement were planted during the Civil War, with Sanitary Fairs that featured exhibits of early American
artifacts (more commonly and provocatively termed "relics") as well as "colonial kitchen" re-creations.[29] Such displays were designed to raise money for the
Union cause, but they also illustrated the common bonds Americans shared
and the importance of women's work in challenging times.[30] Among the exhibits at New York's Metropolitan Sanitary Fair was the "Knickerbocker Kitchen,"
which featured all the stereotypically Dutch elements: stockpiled food, cozy
furniture, and unconventionally quaint architectural elements, including a
jambless fireplace surrounded by Dutch tiles.

A decade later, the Philadelphia Centennial Exposition expanded these
highly popular exhibits into full-scale colonial "homesteads," which featured
costumed interpreters preparing and serving food of "Ye Olden Time."[31] Encouraged by these sites, patriotic and genealogical organizations, and displays
of historical pageantry, Americans were by the 1890s founding house museums

HOWARD PYLE (1853–1911)
*Along the Canal in Old
Manhattan*, 1893
Oil on board, 18 x 11½ in.
Illustration for Thomas A. Janvier,
"The Evolution of New York,"
Harper's New Monthly, May 1893.
Also reproduced in Thomas A.
Janvier, *In Old New York* (New
York: Harper & Brothers, 1894).
Brandywine River Museum,
Gift of Mr. and Mrs. Howard P.
Brokaw (2007.11.6)

at the rate of two per annum.[32] Many museums were dedicated to instilling patriotism in their visitors. They were interpreted to illustrate the importance of distinctly American virtues—thrift, industry, hard work, and the importance of family—to both native and foreign-born Americans. They also showed the transcendence of good quality and good taste, influencing home decorating for even those of modest means for decades to come.[33]

Modern scholars often criticize Colonial Revivalism's pleasantly sanitized view of early American life. But the movement did spur serious interest in preserving historic structures and interiors. As it developed, it also prodded historians, preservationists, and enthusiasts to consider not just the differences but the similarities shared by seemingly disparate settlers. For the defenders of the long-derided Dutch, the challenge was to demonstrate that the Dutch colonial experience was as quintessentially American, with all the pride and dignity that term connoted, as anyone else's.

Fortunately, Colonial Revivalism coincided with renewed American interest in the Netherlands itself. This movement, termed "Holland Mania" by historian Annette Stott, created a penchant for all things Dutch and strongly influenced American visual and decorative arts between 1880 and 1920. Holland Mania focused on the Golden Age of the Netherlands—the Protestant Republic that threw off Spanish rule and Catholicism and, in its place, created a long-lived republic that foreshadowed America. This fascination with all things Dutch eventually included contemporary homes.[34] By extension, Dutch American structures became objects of cultural interest and inspired exhibits of Dutch life.

During the course of a few short decades, Holland Mania helped transform the colonial Dutch from overfed bumpkins and pinched eccentrics to frugal tastemakers and defenders of distinctly American Protestant values. The very magazines that had reinforced the popular notion of the Dutch as crass and vulgar now celebrated them. Edward Bok, the editor of *Ladies Home Journal*, argued that America's roots were, more than anything, Dutch. He laid out his argument in a 1903 article, "The Mother of America": "The men who founded New York were not Englishmen, but largely Hollanders: the Puritans who settled Plymouth had lived twelve years in Holland: . . . that New Jersey, as well as New York, was settled by the Dutch West India Company: . . . that William Penn, the founder of Pennsylvania, came of a Dutch mother."[35]

Both Colonial Revivalism and Holland Mania served another function by suggesting models for grappling with one of America's great contemporary cultural challenges: mass immigration from Europe and the fundamental changes it brought to the nation. Even the most earnest reformers admitted that their chances of converting newcomers from their own religions and customs were slim. Reformers could, however, promote models of ethnic assimilation that resonated with new Americans. The Dutch model of cultural pride joined with successful assimilation found in Colonial Revivalism and Holland Mania proved particularly useful. As Theodore Roosevelt noted, the Dutch "possessed the faculty of becoming good American citizens, completely Americanized in heart and mind. . . . The history of our Dutch ancestors, and of the part they have played in America, . . . has a direct bearing upon one of the greatest questions of the present day, the assimilation of the masses of our foreign-born citizens."[36] New Americans would do well to follow the Dutch as an example.

ORSON LOWELL (1871–1956)
"Father Knickerbocker making
good Americans of the Children
of All Nationalities," cover
illustration for City History
Club *Annual Report*, New York,
1897–98

Popular culture played a role in transmitting these new values to immigrants. Magazines advised working people and English-reading immigrants to replace crude Victorian-style knock-off furniture with simpler, "honest" colonial pieces and portraits of George Washington that "the workingman" would find uplifting.[37] Reformers founded clubs to introduce immigrant children to American history. One of these, the City History Club, was created in 1896 as a "kindergarten of citizenship." Its emblem was "Father Knickerbocker," a friendly Dutch schoolmaster modeled on Irving's Diedrich Knickerbocker. The cover of the club's 1897/98 *Annual Report* shows Father Knickerbocker leading a group of ethnic children in a dance around the seal of the City of New York.[38]

As institutions open to the general public, house museums became tools of cultural change, harnessing early American values propounded by Colonial Revivalism to impart their message. Leading the way in developing new museums were women's genealogical societies. Elite women of old family often had both the means and the incentive to preserve and interpret the nation's early history. Groups like the National Society of Colonial Dames assumed important roles in establishing house museums nationwide. As Jane Nylander notes, these societies were comprised of women who "often had family connections to people considered worthy of commemoration."[39] Spurred by patriotism and pride in family, they hoped to encourage immigrants to aspire toward assimilation, as their own ancestors had done.

These groups also enjoyed the thrill of preserving America's past. In the last decades of the nineteenth century and well into the twentieth, women's genealogical societies worked hard to maintain control over their aesthetic vision. The New York chapter of the National Society of Colonial Dames took charge of the Van Cortlandt House, the imposing Bronx country home of an elite, thoroughly anglicized family of Dutch origins. Members had interpreted the original 1897 museum, but by 1913, the story needed revision. This time, the Dames engaged a noted preservationist, Norman Isham, to reinterpret the interior.[40] When Isham's ideas conflicted with their own, however, the Dames retained the power of the purse to ensure that things were done their way. A case in point is the Dutch Chamber on the museum's second floor. Isham had several suggestions for interpreting this room, but the Dames independently decided on a period *kamer* (chamber) of a "typical" middle-class Dutch home in seventeenth-century New Amsterdam. Isham protested, but the Dames pushed back. In the end, he gave way and implemented the design.[41] The resulting space is the epitome of Dutch American tropes influenced by both the Colonial Revival and Holland Mania. It features snug cabinet beds, a jambless fireplace with Dutch tiles and cooking implements, and several pieces of sturdy, darkly stained furniture.[42] The room has an air of sober dignity, propriety, and economic success, which connects it to the basic philosophical principles of the Colonial Revival. Though they shared some obvious connections, the would-be inhabitants of this room were a far cry from the colonial Dutch who sprang from Washington Irving's imagination.

THE DEVELOPMENT OF THE DYCKMAN LEGACY

Like other women of their class and lineage, Isaac Michael's daughters, Mary Alice Dyckman Dean and Fannie Fredericka Dyckman Welch, were involved in numerous historical, patriotic, and genealogical societies. Unlike their peers at Van Cortlandt House Museum, however, they do not appear to have actively engaged with interpreting their own ancestral home. Even the idea to preserve the house came from elsewhere, specifically John and Winifred Judge, two other historically minded New Yorkers who purchased the Dyckman House around 1913 with an eye on restoration.[43] Working with the city, the Judges

left: Dutch Chamber, Van Cortland House, current installation,
as it was reinstalled during the early 1960s, under consultation with
Abbott Lowell Cummings
Van Cortlandt House Museum/The National Society of Colonial Dames
in the State of New York

right: Dutch Room, Van Cortlandt House, installation created by the
Colonial Dames to represent a typical seventeenth-century all-purpose
room in a New Amsterdam dwelling, c. 1918
Photographic postcard
Van Cortlandt House Museum/The National Society of Colonial Dames
in the State of New York

Dutch Room, Van Cortlandt House, original installation created by the
Colonial Dames to represent a typical seventeenth-century all-purpose room
in a New Amsterdam dwelling, c. 1918
Photograph
Van Cortlandt House Museum/The National Society of Colonial Dames
in the State of New York

hoped to move the house to the newly created Isham Park and turn it over
to the Daughters of the American Revolution for interpretation and management.[44] Thus Dyckman would have followed the trajectory of Van Cortlandt
House Museum: donation to the city and partnership with a women's genealogical society. But when Winifred Judge died unexpectedly in 1914, the project fell apart. It was then that the Dyckman sisters stepped in, purchasing the
house and surrounding half acre in 1915 and keeping alive the idea for a city
museum and park.

The challenge they faced was turning the shabby old house into something
the city actually wanted. Remaking such a decrepit space into a museum was
a daunting task, especially since the Daughters of the Revolution lost interest.
Fortunately, Mary Alice was married to Bashford Dean, one of the nation's
preeminent museum professionals. Fannie Fredericka was married to Alexander McMillan Welch, a preeminent architect. Between them, Dean and Welch
steered the museum into existence. They turned the tools of their trades—in

UNKNOWN PHOTOGRAPHER
Mary Alice Dyckman Dean, Fannie Fredericka Dyckman Welch,
and Alexander McMillan Welch, 1930s
Photograph, black and white gelatin print, 8¾ x 6¾ in.
Dyckman Farmhouse Museum, New York, New York

The Old Dyckman House To Be Presented to City: Quaint Homestead, Last of Its Kind on Manhattan Island, Will Be Transferred to Isham Park and Turned Into a Museum. In *The New York Times*, November 16, 1913

DR. BASHFORD DEAN (1867–1928), C. 1890
Photograph
In Carl Leavitt Hubbs, "History of Ichthyology in the United States after 1850," *Copeia*, American Society of Ichthyologists and Herpetologists 1 (1) (January 1964): 42–60.

this case, the most modern curatorial and architectural knowledge available—to restoring and interpreting the Dyckman House.

By the early twentieth century, it was not unusual for men to take a strong hand in house museum development. Women had for decades taken leadership roles in these sites, but Dyckman House's development coincided with the professionalization of museology, which encouraged specialized study, implemented new standards, and marginalized nonprofessional women.[45] As a result, the well-heeled female colonial and family history enthusiasts who preserved so many institutions were largely relegated to less prestigious parts in day-to-day management, special programs, guiding tours, and fund raising.

Historic fabric was assessed using newly emerging "scientific" methods, which were tools squarely in the hands of men.

Still, the Dyckman sisters' husbands were, by early twentieth-century standards, exceptionally well qualified for the task at hand. Alexander McMillan Welch graduated from Columbia's School of Architecture and the École des Beaux Arts in Paris.[46] Specializing in domestic architecture, he attracted prestigious clients, among whom were the Duke family. Their mansion on Eighty-second Street and Fifth Avenue still stands.

Bashford Dean was, like his wife, a descendant of Dutch New Amsterdamers. A brilliant man, he had by twenty-three earned a Ph.D. from Columbia. The following year, he was teaching biology there. But Dean's true interests lay elsewhere. At the beginning of the twentieth century, museology was still an evolving field, which allowed the multitalented Dean to pursue multiple professional roles in seemingly unconnected fields. He was trained as a metallurgist and geologist, yet he learned enough about ichthyology to become curator of fishes at the American Museum of Natural History. Close study of another field, arms and armaments, led to another prestigious appointment, as curator of armor at the Metropolitan Museum of Art, a position he held simultaneously with his Museum of Natural History job until 1915. To a modern observer, Dean's highly varied career seems thoroughly improbable. But in the first decades of the twentieth century, American museums were working toward professionalizing their staffs and differentiating positions, separating curatorial concerns from connoisseurship ones. In this milieu, Dean excelled. His achievements as a curator earned him respect throughout the museum world. As one admirer noted, "No one was better fitted to show that an expert's prestige and authority have little to do with his salary."[47]

Clearly Dean knew his way around American museums. Yet he had never interpreted a house museum or, for that matter, a history museum of any kind. The Dyckman challenge was fresh territory. The available literature on early American life was steeped in Colonial Revivalism, and it was to these theories that Dean and Alexander Welch turned for guidance in re-creating Dyckman House's historic interiors. In the process, they articulated a vision of the Dutch colonial experience that moved away from old stereotypes and harnessed the pan-colonial dignity espoused by Colonial Revivalism.

Dean and Welch left a clear record of what they wanted visitors to learn from their visit to the Dyckman House Museum. Their visitor's guide, *Dyckman House Museum and Park,* published in 1916, records one effort to popularize changing perceptions of early Dutch settlers, challenging the old stereotypes of the nineteenth century in favor of the more flattering ones of Colonial

BASHFORD DEAN (1867–1928)
and ALEXANDER MCMILLAN
WELCH (1869–1943)
Cover, *The Dyckman House
Park and Museum 1783–1916*,
New York City, 1916
Dyckman Farmhouse Museum,
New York, New York

Revivalism. The inviting cover image sets the tone: an iconic Dutch door, with the upper half ajar, beckons the reader to enter the world of Dutch New York.

Upon entering the Dyckman House Museum, the visitor was presented with an amalgam of quaintness, practicality, and ambition. Dean's nine period rooms spanned three floors and were arranged to display "the indoor surroundings of a well-to-do family about the year 1800."[48] Dutch origins notwithstanding, the museum was designed to join an established cadre of historic houses that demonstrated what early American life *should* have been like—regardless of the origins of the house's builders.[49]

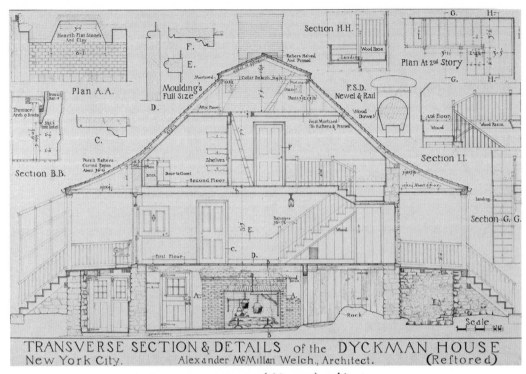

TRANSVERSE SECTION & DETAILS of the DYCKMAN HOUSE
New York City.   Alexander McMillan Welch., Architect.   (Restored)

ALEXANDER MCMILLAN WELCH (1869–1943), architect
Transverse Section & Details of the Dyckman House (Restored), n.d.
Black ink on paper, 29½ x 43⅛ in.
Avery Architectural and Fine Arts Library, Columbia University

In *Dyckman House Museum and Park*, there is little about Dyckman House that speaks of intrinsic "Dutchness." The entrance to the cellar is "in the ancient Dutch fashion." The case clock in the parlor is described as tall and Dutch. The family's Dutch Bible (a genuine artifact, printed in the Netherlands and still on display) sits in a place of honor in the parlor. Dutch tiles surround one fireplace. Dutch doors complete with "curious hinges and latches" and shutters with crescent moon cutouts decorate the exterior.[50] And in an uncharacteristically stereotypical passage, Dean and Welch muse that the owner of the Dyckman House (Jacobus Dyckman in the original period of interpretation), "might have long sat on this wide front porch, settled comfortably in a deep slat-back-armchair, . . . and [watched] lazily through the rings of smoke from a long-stemmed pipe the post-rider as he passed the thirteenth milestone, which was nearly in front of the old house."[51] But here the old Dutch tropes of picturesque inactivity end. Instead, the interior reflects a place of constant work. In contrast to earlier stereotypes, the Dyckman House Museum demonstrated thrift, industry, good taste, comfort, and patriotism—all cornerstone Colonial Revival beliefs about the nature of early American life.

As the curator of the period rooms, Bashford Dean strove to return furnishings that had once been in the house to their circa 1800 locations. To do this, he culled antiques and decorative objects from Dyckman relatives.[52] Though the styles of these objects spanned Queen Anne to Greek Revival, together they enhanced a sense of age and dignified comfort. Dean's assertion that he returned the furniture to its proper place is difficult to verify. He was operating under the Colonial Revival notion that rooms in early American houses all had distinct purposes,[53] but in a late eighteenth-century farmhouse like Dyckman, all rooms would have been flexible spaces. In addition, the museum project began almost seventy years after the Dyckmans moved out. Family members who might have remembered the layout were either very old or dead, and written reminiscences were scant. Dean's sources, then, were contemporary books on early American life and other house museums themselves. Colonial Revivalism informed both.

The Dyckman House Museum's floors, walls, and window treatments were among the most distinctly Colonial Revival elements. Rag carpets and sheer curtains and valances decorated floors and walls. Fancy woodwork was extended throughout the house, as were mantles too ornate to be authentic. Surfaces that had been finished long after 1800 were left intact, as were the circa-1840 walls that created five chambers out of the once-open loft on the "bedroom floor." In early America, textiles were scarce, and woodwork uncommon in practical dwellings. Yet Colonial Revivalism saw both as important hallmarks of domestic comfort and upward mobility, which meant they appeared in most interpretations of early American life. Whole rooms were distinctly Colonial Revival. Both the parlor and the dining room were late innovations to early American domestic architecture, and a modest structure like a farmhouse would not have had them in 1800.[54] These rooms in the Dyckman House, however, showed off family treasures of silver, china, and well-made, fashionable furnishings. The dining room's sideboard was for Dean and Welch "still in a place of honor, bearing family Sheffield and cut class."[55] As scholar Jacquetta Haley notes, the family would have, in all likelihood, still been recovering from the depredations of seven years of war and, of course, the death of the family patriarch, William.[56] The parlor, with Dean's symmetrically arranged furniture, silver, and import porcelain, was also far too grand for the people the Dyckmans actually were—though certainly consistent with other Colonial Revival house museums.

The upstairs bedrooms were portrayed as a cozy warren for women and children. Also rich with textiles, these spaces featured Franklin stoves, which "brought heat more economically into the room" to warm new generations of Dyckman babies, who were "thoroughly rocked" in a heavy wooden cradle by

UNKNOWN PHOTOGRAPHER
Dyckman House Dining Room, original installation created
by the Colonial Dames, c. 1916
Photographic postcard, 3½ x 5½ in.
Dyckman Farmhouse Museum, New York, New York

Dyckman House Southeast Bedroom, original installation
created by the Colonial Dames, c. 1916
Photographic postcard, 3½ x 5½ in.
Dyckman Farmhouse Museum, New York, New York

UNKNOWN PHOTOGRAPHER
Dyckman House Summer Kitchen, original installation created
by the Colonial Dames, c. 1916
Photographic postcard, 3½ x 5½ in.
Dyckman Farmhouse Museum, New York, New York

practical mothers in heavy caps and nightgowns.[57] Next door, a schoolroom
showed where these children would begin their lives of learning or, if they
were girls, work samplers "with patient fingers."[58] Once out of the classroom,
they would be free to wander a pretty ornamental garden, complete with gravel
paths and boxwood parterres.[59]

Consistent with new museology, both Dyckman House's kitchens were
veritable "museums of cooking implements," which underscored not only the
ingenuity and hard work of early American life but also the talents and tastes
of the cook/hostess.[60] Both kitchens were designed to impress visitors with
their practicality. In addition to providing cooking space for the family, the
winter kitchen helped heat the house in cold weather. The summer kitchen, in
an adjoining wing, served the opposite function. Aside from the presence of
a waffle iron and the Dutch oven, items identified by Alice Earle as present in
most colonial houses, little else displayed in these rooms spoke of the intrinsic
"Dutchness" of the Dyckmans—even in their eating habits.

The first interpretation of the Dyckman House Museum told the stories
of the individuals who lived, worked, and visited there. These too represent a
retreat from the old stereotypes. For one thing, the Dyckman men worked—
hard. Dean and Welch assert that Jacobus Dyckman in particular was "widely

known for his clear judgment and effective methods" and became "the court of last appeal in local matters," even for local elites like Eliza Jumel and Elizabeth Schuyler Hamilton.[61] Education was also important. One of the five upstairs chambers (which was subdivided long after the turn of the century) was interpreted as "Isaac Michael Dyckman's Study," a place for a young heir of great expectations to learn from a tutor the works of Cicero and Jefferson and prepare for a life of civic engagement.[62] This was not the Brom Bones approach to learning that Ichabod Crane encounters in the lower Hudson Valley. Other anonymous males defied the stereotype too. According to the visitor's guide, neighborhood men relaxed in the Dyckman dining room to share news in the style of Rip Van Winkle's neighbors, talking of "the duel of Burr and Hamilton, or of the *Clermont* puffing up the Hudson River, or of Decatur's African pirates."[63] But these were stolen moments compared to the work life of Dyckman's industrious inhabitants. In addition, their knowledge of global events demonstrated that these men were well-informed citizens of the new republic.

Directly below Isaac Michael Dyckman's study was the relic room, a space that still underscores the Dyckmans' connections to the great people and events of American history. This exhibit was the brainchild of Reginald Pelham Bolton, a local historian and amateur archaeologist with an unbounded enthusiasm for northern Manhattan's history. Bolton's numerous excavations, which took place in the first few decades of the twentieth century on what had once been Dyckman land, yielded a rich archaeological record of the region's inhabitants. The relic room he set up at Dyckman House was based on similar exhibit spaces that first appeared in the Sanitary Fairs.[64] In in were some of Bolton's best finds, including tools of warfare (musket stocks, grapeshot, bar shot, shell fragments) and household and personal objects (knives, buttons, coins, and pottery fragments). This fragmentary evidence presented for Dean and Welch another opportunity to confirm the refinement of the Dyckmans: "[the porcelain and pottery fragments] show, by the way, not a little artistic merit . . . it is from the examination of this material that one sees clearly that the early people of the neighborhood were fond of good things and chose them intelligently."[65]

Bolton was also responsible for one of the site's most unusual artifacts. When he found the remains of a British cantonment on the side of a nearby hill, he brought the excavated floor and hearth of an officer's shelter to the Dyckman House Museum property in 1916.[66] There he reassembled the pieces, filling in with new materials to re-create a revolutionary-era Hessian hut. If visitors to the site were unclear about its importance to the greater story of American history, the hut drilled home that the property and its inhabitants had an important link to larger events. In addition, the hut underscored the property's years of military occupation and its happy rebirth after.

Bolton is an interesting figure in and of himself. Like his contemporaries, he believed that his work at the old Dyckman site was a valuable tool for imparting proper values to young Americans. Dyckman House Museum should educate "our youngest citizens . . . [with a] living history of honest and upright life."[67] Judging from the number of immigrant children that the New York History Club brought through the museum's doors, the message certainly met with an audience.[68]

House museums inspired by Colonial Revival ideas celebrated great men and their deeds. They also celebrated domesticity.[69] It should therefore come as no surprise that, while individual men stand out in the Dyckman House interpretation, the women are lumped together, nameless and voiceless. According to Dean and Welch, these Dyckman women performed admirably as helpmeets, mothers, hostesses, and housewives. The authors urged visitors to envision women devoting their waking hours to an array of home industries, including soap and candle making, baking, spinning and weaving, and raising barnyard fowl.[70] "How many to-day, for example, even those of us who pride ourselves on our housekeeping and cookery, could go into one of the old kitchens of the present house and make use of apparatus there?" Dean and Welch asked. In all likelihood, new arrivals from Europe and elsewhere probably could, but for native-born visitors now used to domestic conveniences, the Dyckman House taught valuable lessons in the virtues of difficult housework.

The Colonial Revival movement preserved conventional nineteenth-century views of gender, for the women achievers of the Dyckman House go about their work with anonymous cheer. The lone exception is Jemima Dyckman, who is described as huddling in a wing chair, safe from drafts and comfortably close to the heat, enjoying the comforts of her bedchamber. The seemingly enfeebled Jemima stands in stark contrast to her dashing loyalist relative, States Morris Dyckman, whose story is also told through the object record of the museum. States Morris Dyckman was William Dyckman's nephew. A fervent loyalist, he served as a clerk for the British Army's Quartermaster General in New York. In 1779, he moved to London and spent the next ten years amassing a tidy fortune, spending most of it on luxury items. States Morris was by all accounts a handsome and charming rogue—quite opposite in temperament to the values that Dyckman Museum's interpreters attached to the early American character. Yet his taste in personal items—exhibited in a room called the office—fit well with their interpretation of the family's overall upward mobility. States's story added to Dyckman House a bit of color and dash—and a real, tangible link to the shifting alliances of the revolutionary generation.

"Outsiders" to the Dyckman's family circle did not fare as well. Federal census records show the Dyckmans owned seven slaves in 1790. By 1810, there were two on the property, as well as two free people of color, one of whom was a woman named Hannah. Nothing more is known about her, but in *Dyckman House Museum and Park,* Dean's description of "black Hannah" relies on stereotypes directly out of contemporary racist literature and theater. According to "tradition," the authors note, Hannah had "a bright-colored headgear, face black as ebony, temper decidedly irregular, and a strong leaning toward a corncob pipe."[71] Dean and Welch's "Old Hannah" contrasts sharply with the "Knickerbocker Kitchen" exhibit of the 1867 New York Metropolitan Fair. That period room's two Africans are depicted as industrious, "respectable people of color."[72] As Patricia West notes, "'people of color' [during the Civil War era were] deemed worthy of defending and deserving of freedom if in their place."[73] Racist and condescending in its own right, this display at least assumed that American blacks should receive care and concern. With her outlandish headgear and unpredictable character, Dean's "Old Hannah" was meant to incur laughter or ridicule, not compassion. Dean and Welch's harsh treatment of her mirrored the consistent degradation of African Americans since the nation's "retreat from Reconstruction" in 1876. Other parts of *Dyckman House Museum and Park* describe the human remains of blacks and Indians with cool anthropological detachment, noting that "various odds and ends of aboriginal life" were frequently excavated in the area, along with the bones of dogs.[74] The authors had done their part to redeem New York's colonial Dutch from crude stereotypes. Unfortunately in this case, they reinforced others.

But Dean and Welch were most concerned with using the Dyckman House

ALEXANDER MCMILLAN WELCH
(1869–1943), architect, E. Eldon Deane,
delineator
The 'Dyckman House' of to-day 1917, 1917
Watercolor on paper, mounted on board
with "before" rendering in decorative mat,
image: 16 x 22 in., mat: 38⅜ x 26¼ in.
Avery Architectural and Fine Arts Library,
Columbia University

Philipsburg Manor, early view of
restoration and costumed guides,
c. 1950s
Photograph
Historic Hudson Valley, Tarrytown,
New York

In the foreground: the mill pond,
dam, and bridge. In the background:
the water-powered grist mill and the
Manor House.

Museum to help correct stereotypes of the Dutch. Though many of their assumptions were firmly rooted in the general Colonial Revival romanticism of their day, they did strive to present to the public an image of early American Dutch life that was sober, refined, dignified, industrious, and aesthetically pleasing. They made clear that the historical inhabitants of the Dyckman House were not the stout, overindulging burghers of Irving's imagination. Instead, they were people of their time, taking the best from contemporary culture and retaining the elements of their Dutch heritage that enriched their identities and gave them pleasure.

The Colonial Revival presented a picture of America that was all of a piece. Ethnicities, regions, and economic status varied, but early Americans were kindred spirits in fundamentals. The interpreters of the Dyckman House Museum helped ensure that New York's early Dutch Americans were integrated into this larger panorama.

NOTES

1. Bashford Dean and Alexander McMillan Welch, *The Dyckman House Park and Museum* (hereafter *DHMP*), 2nd ed. (New York: The Gilliss Press, 1917), 8. I would like to thank Angelo Angelis, Carol Berkin, Edwin Burrows, Laura Jean Carpenter, Susan de Vries, Herman Eberhardt, Kate Hallgren, Mark Sgambettera, and Iris Towers for their insights into this topic and their thoughtful readings of all or part of this text.

2. *The New York Times*, July 12, 1916.

3. Dyckman Farmhouse Museum is today part of the Historic House Trust of New York City, a consortium of twenty-two historic houses located in city parks. Inwood claimed this distinction only after Marble Hill was separated from the island by the creation of the Hudson River Shipping Canal in 1895. Marble Hill was then attached, via landfill, to the Bronx. "Marble Hill," in *Encyclopedia of New York City*, ed. Kenneth Jackson (New Haven: Yale University Press, 1995), 726-27.

4. The IRT line came through Inwood in 1906. Jackson, *Encyclopedia of New York City*, 597.

5. Jackson, *Encyclopedia of New York City*, 597.

6. *The New York Times*, May 11, 1899.

7. H. Dorothea Romer and Helen B. Hartman, *Jan Dyckman and His Descendants* (New York: J. A. Thompson, 1981), 4.

8. Romer and Hartman, *Jan Dyckman*, 71.

9. Romer and Hartman, *Jan Dyckman*, 32.

10. Federal Census of 1790. Qtd. in Romer and Hartman, *Jan Dyckman*, 71.

11. Jacquetta M. Haley, "Furnishings Plan: The Dyckman House" (September 2002), *Collections of the Dyckman Farmhouse Museum*, 6.

12. Romer and Hartman, *Jan Dyckman*, 71.

13. Haley, *Collections of the Dyckman Farmhouse Museum*, 7.

14. Andrew Burstein, *The Original Knickerbocker: The Life of Washington Irving* (New York: Basic Books, 2007), 81.

15. Irving, *Knickerbocker History of New York*, Vol. I (1809), 126.

16. Irving, *Knickerbocker History of New York*, Vol. I, 93. Qtd. in Burstein, *The Original Knickerbocker*, 77.

17. Irving did not need to embellish the story's final factual twist: the loyalist Morrises were forced to abandon their northern Manhattan estate, which Washington later commandeered for his headquarters during the fall of 1776. Karal Ann Marling, *George Washington Slept Here: Colonial Revivals and American Culture, 1876-1986* (Cambridge, Mass.: Harvard University Press, 1988), 145.

18. Clifton Hood, "Journeying to 'Old New York': Elite New Yorkers and Their Invention of an Idealized City History in the Late Nineteenth and Early Twentieth Centuries," *Journal of Urban History* 28 (6) (September 2002): 703.

19. Hood, "Journeying to 'Old New York,'" *passim*.

20. I am indebted to Edwin Burrows for this insight. Personal correspondence, April 24, 2008.

21. Thomas Janvier, *In Old New York* (New York: St. Martin's Press, 2000), xviii.

22. Janvier, *In Old New York*, 6.

23. Janvier, *In Old New York*, 8-11.

24. Patricia West, *Domesticating History: The Political Origins of American's House Museums* (Washington, D.C.: Smithsonian, 1999), 72.

25. Alice Morse Earle, *Colonial Days in Old New York* (New York: Scribner's, 1899), 150, 167.

26. This last comment has a strong ring of truth: an English clergyman named Wolley, who served as chaplain to Fort James, referred to the Dutch as 'obstinate and incessant smokers." Qtd. in Earle, 4.

27. Earle, *Colonial Days in Old New York,* 168.

28. Burrows and Wallace, *Gotham: A History of New York City to 1898* (New York: Oxford, 1999), 419.

29. West, *Domesticating History,* 40.

30. West, *Domesticating History,* 40

31. West, *Domesticating History,* 42.

32. West, *Domesticating History,* 42.

33. West, *Domesticating History,* 80; Haley, *Collections of the Dyckman Farmhouse Museum,* 12.

34. Annette Stott, *Holland Mania: The Unknown Dutch Period of American Art and Culture* (Woodstock, N.Y.: Overlook Press, 1998), 12.

35. Edward Bok, "The Mother of America," *Ladies Home Journal* 20 (October 1903): 16. Qtd. in Stott, *Holland Mania,* 78.

36. Qtd. in Stott, *Holland Mania,* 95.

37. Berthe Lynde Holden, "Tenement Furnishings," *House Beautiful* (April 1900):307-313. Qtd. in West, *Domesticating History,* 80.

38. William B. Rhoads, "The Colonial Revival and the Americanization of Immigrants," in *The Colonial Revival in America,* ed. Alan Axelrod (New York: Norton, 1985), 342.

39. Jane C. Nylander, "Treasure Houses of the Colonial Dames," *The Magazine Antiques* (July 2007):70.

40. http://www.vancortlandthouse.org/Significant_dates_in_history_of_.htm.

41. Personal correspondence with Laura Carpenter, Executive Director, Van Cortlandt House Museum, Bronx, New York, April–May 2008. I am indebted to Ms. Carpenter sharing her thoughts on this episode.

42. http://www.vancortlandthouse.org/The%20Dutch%20Chamber.htm.

43. *The New York Times,* November 16, 1913.

44. *The New York Times,* November 16, 1913.

45. For details of this transformation, see West, *Domesticating History,* 94-99.

46. *The New York Times,* September 25, 1943.

47. *The New York Times,* December 12, 1928.

48. *DHMP,* 35.

49. Haley, *Collections of the Dyckman Farmhouse Museum,* 13.

50. *DHMP,* 40.

51. *DHMP,* 31.

52. Haley, *Collections of the Dyckman Farmhouse Museum,* 15.

53. Haley, *Collections of the Dyckman Farmhouse Museum,* 55.

54. Haley, *Collections of the Dyckman Farmhouse Museum,* 26.

55. *DHMP,* 40.

56. Haley, *Collections of the Dyckman Farmhouse Museum,* 26.

57. *DHMP,* 41.

58. *DHMP,* 41.

59. Lee Dassler and Shirley Hibbard, *Historic Structures Report, Dyckman House,* The Center for Preservation Research, Graduate School of Architecture, Planning and Preservation, Columbia University, July 24, 1991, 66.

60. Haley, *Collections of the Dyckman Farmhouse Museum,* 103.

61. *DHMP,* 26.

62. *DHMP*, 39.

63. *DHMP*, 39.

64. West, *Domesticating History,* 40.

65. *DHMP*, 41.

66. *DHMP*, 17.

67. Qtd. in Rhoads, "The Colonial Revival and the Americanization of Immigrants," 342.

68. Rhoads, "The Colonial Revival and the Americanization of Immigrants," 342.

69. West, *Domesticating History,* 40.

70. *DHMP*, 36-38.

71. *DHMP*, 35.

72. Qtd. in West, *Domesticating History,* 41.

73. West, *Domesticating History,* 41

74. *DHMP*, 15-16.

Philipsburg Manor "Dutchiana"
Photograph of early costumed guides,
wearing Dutch headdresses and shoes,
c. 1950s
Photograph
Historic Hudson Valley, Tarrytown, NY

In 1951, the Rockefeller family began
another major effort to preserve the region's
landmarks of Dutch colonial history.

CONCLUSION 2009 – What Does Dutch Heritage Mean Today?

JOSEPH SQUILLANTE, b. 1949
Half-Moon at Yonkers Pier, 2008
Photograph, pigment print, 16 x 24 in.
Courtesy of the artist

The Dutch Legacy in America

13

DAVID WILLIAM VOORHEES

"I mention this spot with all possible laud," Washington Irving wrote of Sleepy Hollow in New York's Westchester County, "for it is in such little retired Dutch valleys, found here and there embosomed in the Great State of New York, that population, manners, and customs remain fixed; while the great torrent of migration and improvement, which is making such incessant changes in other parts of this restless country, sweeps by them unobserved."[1] Thus Irving, along with his contemporaries James Kirke Paulding and James Fenimore Cooper, popularized during the first decades of the nineteenth century a romantic literary vision of a bucolic Dutch culture slumbering in niches along the shores of the Hudson River Valley.[2] Although the culture so charmingly stereotyped by these writers was indeed the product of the initial European occupation of the region by the Dutch Republic two centuries earlier, it was not static. Rather, it was the result of a long evolutionary development. Indeed, the golden age of "Dutch culture" in the Hudson Valley was not during its four decades under Dutch administration but in the eighteenth century under English rule.

The reasons for Dutch cultural tenacity in the Hudson River Valley are complex. The official Dutch presence in North America lasted a mere forty years, from 1624 until 1664, with an interregnum of fifteen months in 1673–74. Moreover, the ethnic Dutch never formed a majority of the population even in that period.[3] Nonetheless, a Dutch imprint is found not only in place names and the political geography of the region but also in cultural patterns that persisted into the twentieth century. Dutch political traditions, particularly the guarantee of freedom of conscience and concepts of republican government, came to influence the wider development of American political theory. America's modern party system had its origins in Dutch political disputes. And seventeenth-century Dutch culture left a lasting impress in regional folklore, language, religion, cuisine, and material culture that eventually found their way into mainstream American culture.

THE LEGACY OF A DUTCH POLITICAL GEOGRAPHY

The most noticeable legacy of the Dutch is in the political geography of the mid-Atlantic states. At the time that West India Company Director-General

N. C. WYETH (1882–1945)
Hendrik Hudson (with map of the Hudson River), 1926
Charcoal and gouache on paper
46⅞ x 27⅝ in.
Brandywine River Museum, Bequest of Carolyn Wyeth, 1996

JACQUES GÉRARD MILBERT (1766–1840)
Maison du Gouverneur Hollandais a Albani, Etats-Unis (View in Albany,
House of the First Dutch Governors), 1828
Lithograph from *Itineraire pittoresque du fleuve Hudson et des parties laterales
de l'Amerique du Nord, d'apres les dessins originaux pris sur les lieux.*
5¼ x 8 in.
Hudson River Museum, Gift of Mr. Ernest Weidhaas, 70.106.6.2

Petrus Stuyvesant surrendered Fort Amsterdam on Manhattan to an English
invasion force in September 1664, New Netherland contained about nine thousand inhabitants, with two major towns, New Amsterdam (New York City)
and Beverwijck (Albany); sixteen villages; and a number of smaller settlements
scattered over a vast territory extending from the Delaware to the Connecticut
rivers and northward into the Mohawk River Valley. The change in regimes
was not catastrophic for most of the residents. The terms of capitulation guaranteed the Dutch their customary rights of property, inheritance, and religious
practice. Through the widespread influence of Dutch cartographers, Dutch
place names, such as Brooklyn, Staten Island, Catskill, Harlem, and Kinderhook, had become widely accepted and remained in use.[4] New Netherlanders,
now New Yorkers, continued to view their spatial environment through Dutch
eyes long after the English conquest. The English guarantee in 1664 of their

property and inheritance rights, and re-patenting of their town charters, confirmed that the political geography that the Dutch had established throughout the region would remain in place.

Among the attributes that the Dutch established in the Hudson Valley region are the ingrained traditions of diversity and localism. In the seventeenth century, the Dutch Republic was not a commonwealth but, as English diplomat Sir William Temple noted in 1672, "a confederacy of Seven Sovereign Provinces, united together for their common and mutual defense, without any dependence one upon the other."[5] Neither cultural nor commercial nor ethnic unity bound the seven provinces together as much as their successful rebellion against the Spanish Habsburg regime and resulting federation for military protection. Ethnic diversity was a key characteristic of the Dutch Republic. The impressive economic growth of the cities in the western provinces of Holland and Zeeland drew enormous numbers of immigrants. By 1625 one third of Amsterdam's population was of foreign derivation; students of English migration note that more English emigrated to Holland than to New England.[6] The result was that an ethnically diverse commercial interest dominated these cities and their overseas enterprises.

The Dutch West India Company's settlement of New Netherland reflected this heterogeneous society. As in Holland, the company's directors allowed various nationalities to settle and form communities under its auspices. By the time of the English conquest, New Netherland's population reflected metropolitan Dutch culture. Dutch, German, Scandinavian, English, French, Swiss, Irish, and Scots created a complex, if not always harmonious patchwork of neighborhoods and communities coexisting in unity. As historian Alice Kenney wrote, "The foundation for this unity [in the Hudson Valley] was an unspoken agreement shared by the Dutch people to respect in each other the same loyalty to communal privileges and local customs that they claimed for themselves."[7]

In early modern Holland, towns dominated the countryside, and merchant oligarchies dominated the towns. The Dutch brought this tradition of urban culture with them to the New World. The West India Company's grant of local governing rights to Beverwijck (Albany) in 1652 and municipal rights to New Amsterdam (New York City) in 1653, as well as the various town charters granted by the company's directors, resulted in the re-creation of a society familiar in the Old World. As a result, the province of New York became unique among the American colonies for having two competing urban centers dominating the hinterlands. Under the English, New York City and Albany retained their Dutch forms of government, and no new changes were immediately introduced into the political administration except the adoption of English titles for public offices: mayor for *burgomaster*, sheriff for *schout*, and alderman for *schepen*. Because the English allowed the Dutch in New York to retain their customs and English imperial administration from London remained distant, the transition to English political culture was gradual. With New York's incorporation into the English mercantile world, the city's urban cultures flourished, albeit in Dutch fashion.

As new communities became established and matured, they maintained an independent corporate identity along the lines of the early modern Dutch town. This is most evident in the lack of provincewide cooperation and shifting loyalties during periods of political crisis. When in 1664 the threat of English invasion was imminent, Stuyvesant's attempts to get them to unite for their defense was met with "a general discontent and unwillingness to assist in defending the place."[8] After the 1673 Dutch recapture of New York, Dutch governor Anthony Colve frequently arbitrated between contentious communities.[9] Thomas S. Wermouth writes that eighteenth-century Hudson River Valley communities "had relatively few reservations about using their power to protect their corporate standing, whether from outsiders or, more routinely, to maintain the social order within the community."[10]

New Yorkers' localism reflected Dutch traditions, where loyalties were foremost to the home community rather than to a national entity. The land-grant policies of James, as duke and king, ironically reinforced the Dutchness of New York's political geography. In the Dutch Republic, multiple jurisdictions overlapped among provinces, towns, and manorial estates. James's establishment of counties in 1683 and of manors with political privileges in 1685 followed a pattern familiar to the republic's political division into duchies, counties, and lordships—the latter a jurisdictional form that had been introduced into New Netherland with the patroonship in 1629 but had, except for Rensselaerswijck, ultimately failed prior to 1664 due to the expense of maintaining private colonies.[11] The larger manorial patents included Rensselaerswijck, established in 1629 and re-patented in 1685; Livingston Manor (1686); Philipsburgh Manor (1696); and Cortlandt Manor (1697). These grants, which gave their owners jurisdictional rights within their properties, concentrated much of the best arable land in the Hudson River Valley in the hands of a few mercantile families, who, in Dutch regent fashion, derived their wealth from trade and continued to maintain their primary residences in the urban centers.[12]

Outside towns and manorial holdings, the English conquest had little impact on rural communities, except for the requirement that farmers secure new patents for their land. The English royal government left a considerable amount of autonomy to New York's villages and farming hamlets, a situation similar to that in the republic, where government was decentralized. The

Duke's Laws of 1665, written originally for New York's English communities, only gradually expanded provincewide. Moreover, they contained a number of Dutch features, including toleration in leaving the religious character of a community up to that community and plural nomination and partial retirement in public offices. The imposition of the English form of town government in the Hudson Valley after 1675 thus did not represent a complete break with Dutch traditions. As late as the American Revolution, villages were said to continue to follow "modes peculiar to the Hollanders."[13] The consequence was a tangled web of governments, traditions, and jurisdictions in New York, which, as in the republic, complicated decision making and resulted in intercommunal bickering that persists into the twenty-first century.[14]

The political geography that the Dutch established in the mid-Atlantic region four centuries ago thus continued to inform New York and eastern New Jersey and the lower counties of Pennsylvania (the present-day state of Delaware) for centuries. As in the Netherlands, the region surrounding New York Bay and the Hudson River Valley presents a contrasting pattern of closely settled and compact urban communities, scattered villages and market towns, and, at least well into the nineteenth century, sparsely settled manorial lands. If New York City and Albany replicated the urbanized culture of the western Dutch provinces of Holland and Zeeland, much of the rural Hudson Valley echoed the republic's eastern provinces, once dominated by manorial estates and market villages. American visitors to the Netherlands were often struck by the similarity of the two regions despite their vast topographical differences. "As we approached Amsterdam it almost seemed like the approach to the upper end of New York when coming in on the railroad," wrote one traveler in 1888.[15] But it was the diversity of the Dutch political geography of New Netherland that would have the most long-lasting impact upon the future of America.

DUTCH CULTURAL EXPANSION

Scholars amply demonstrate that the Dutch in the Hudson and Mohawk valleys, on western Long Island, and in New Jersey formed a key cultural area in preindustrial America.[16] But what exactly do we mean by a "Dutch" culture in English America? In his masterful history of New Netherland, Jaap Jacobs suggests that the "culture of the Dutch under English rule was cut off from patria and went its own way."[17] There is no doubt that there was great regional variation among New Jersey, Long Island, and the Hudson and Mohawk valleys. Yet, as noted above, fundamental Netherlandic traditions continued to inform these cultures well into the nineteenth century. Although the spoken Dutch language in New York and New Jersey was by 1689 "as different" from contemporary Holland's Dutch "as from the Dutch of 1614" and rapidly evolving into *de Taal* (American Dutch) with its regional dialects known as "Albany" and "Jersey" Dutch, evidence suggests that all New Yorkers continued to look to the republic's urban centers, notably Amsterdam and Rotterdam, for news, fashion, and ideas for generations after the English conquest.[18]

The Hudson Valley's communities, whether trading or agricultural, had been founded as part of the commercial expansion of the Dutch Republic at the beginning of the seventeenth century and developed within this commercial world. Flourishing trade, both legal and illegal, continued between Holland, the wider Dutch colonial world, and New York long after 1664 and effectively evaded England's attempts to restrict it with various Navigation Acts. After 1675, the major change in New York–Netherlands trade was that the city of Rotterdam supplanted Amsterdam as the major Dutch port for New York merchants. Nonetheless, as late as 1756, when the British Parliament passed an act to stem the flow of smuggled goods on Dutch vessels into America, it created a crisis in New York.[19] Although imports of Dutch manufactured goods declined throughout the eighteenth century in relation to the import of English manufactured goods, Dutch exporters adjusted by developing markets for new products, such as porcelains, paper, and gin.[20] As a result, New York merchants had continuous contact with Dutch metropolitan centers throughout the colonial period.

The Dutch Reformed Church, which remained under the auspices of the Classis of Amsterdam until 1754, is seen as the central institution in maintaining a Dutch identity in the New World.[21] What is particularly surprising in the postconquest period, however, is the rapid growth of that denomination among all ethnic groups. Whereas at the time of the English takeover of New Netherland in 1664, only three Dutch Reformed dominies oversaw 11 congregations, by 1780, and despite the Anglican Church's favored position after 1693 and the establishment of the Anglican Society for the Propagation of the Gospel in Foreign Parts in 1701, the number of Dutch Reformed congregations in the middle colonies soared to 127.[22] Because the Reformed Church was the central, and often the only, public institution in many New York and New Jersey communities, its influence was much wider than simply among its communicants.[23] Reformed theology provided a common bond and ideological framework for the colonists.

The 1764 call by the New York City Dutch Reformed Church of Archibald Laidlie, who could preach in English as well as in Dutch, to be its pastor is often cited as an indicator of the decline of the Dutch language in the middle colonies. However, it resulted in widespread protests and appeals to the public authorities.[24] Although the pro-Dutch-language party eventually lost in New York City, it was not until 1787 that the Long Island Reformed consistory called a dominie who could preach in English. The switch was even slower in rural areas. Martinus Schoonmaker, for example, continued to conduct his Midwood, Long Island services solely in Dutch until his death in 1824, while the last service in Dutch in the Tappan, New York Reformed Church was in 1835.[25]

The church's use of Dutch reinforced it as the primary language in private affairs. So pervasive was it in eighteenth-century New York and New Jersey that in 1730 New York City printer William Bradford was compelled to publish a Dutch–English dictionary, "whereby the Low-Dutch inhabitants of North America may (in a short time) learn to spell, read, understand and speak proper English. And . . . the English may also learn to spell, read, understand and write Low-Dutch."[26] As late as 1866, the wife of the Dutch consul-general to New York City noted, "it is a fact that one out of ten people [in the city] will be able to understand you although it is not our civilized Dutch that they speak."[27] Dutch *courants*, literally modern newspapers, and *mercuriuses*, somewhat akin to news magazines, circulated in the region well into the eighteenth century.[28] Such writings, Willem Frijhof writes, "testify not so much to the intensity or the frequency of communications across the ocean as to a sense of community founded on a common language, a common religion, and a common culture."[29] The result was a widespread bonding between New Yorkers and the Netherlands. As New Jersey governor William Livingston wrote to Baron van der Cappellen in the Netherlands in 1778, "From my affection for *het Vaderland* (political considerations apart) I could wish for a friendly connection between the *old & the new Netherlands*, being by parentage at least three quarters of a Dutchman myself."[30]

The influence of the Dutch language on the mid-Atlantic dialect is still found, according to Dutch scholar Hendrick Edelman, in the distinctive New York and New Jersey accents as well as in words and phrases peculiar to the region.[31] The oft-ridiculed New York pronunciation of Long Island, with a harsh "g," is one example. Moreover, a large number of regional words and phrases are based on Dutch origins: "cranky," "-kil" (for creek), "stoop," "hook" (a point of land), and "scow" are a few among them. H. L. Mencken's study of Hudson Valley English in the 1920s includes "hay-barrack," a corruption of *hooiberg*, and the use of "bush" for "backcountry" with the still common Hudson Valley designation of poor country people as "bushwhackers." Others, such as "cruller," "coleslaw," "cookie," "pancake," "pit" (as in "peach pit"), "waffle," "boss," and "Santa Claus" have made their way into standard American English.[32]

Customs brought to New Netherland by the Dutch also remained entrenched in the mid-Atlantic region for generations. The gift of a silver spoon to commemorate the birth of a child and of a spoon rack as a wedding gift are two.[33] Other customs merged with those of other nationalities to create distinctly American holidays. Sint Maarten's Eve, or Beggar's Day, when on the eleventh of November children went from house to house wearing masks and carrying lanterns while begging for gifts of sweets and fruit, eventually merged with the Irish-Celtic celebration of All Saints Eve on October 31 into the modern American Halloween. More commonly known is the creation of the American Christmas character of Santa Claus from the Dutch legend of Sinter Klaas.[34] Pancakes, waffles, bread with butter, pretzels, cookies, whole grains with milk for breakfast, and coleslaw are also among the foodways introduced by the Dutch that have become mainstays among Americans.[35]

Few material objects, however, more aptly express the survival of Dutch culture than the Hudson Valley's vernacular architecture. In 1744, Dr. Alexander Hamilton of Annapolis, Maryland, found the houses of New York City "compact and regular, and in general higher built, most of them after the Dutch model, with their gable ends fronting the street."[36] Swedish naturalist Pehr Kalm noted in 1749 that most of the houses of Albany were "built in the old way with the gable end towards the street."[37] Richard Smith in 1769 found the buildings of Schenectady in the "old Dutch taste."[38]

Architectural historians note that the bent system, two principal posts connected by a girder, or tie beam, is a defining characteristic of Dutch vernacular architecture in the New World, and, despite variations in building materials and changing architectural tastes, was found throughout the region until the development of the balloon frame in the mid-nineteenth century. High ceilings on the first stories of buildings, sometimes 10 to 12 feet high, and large windows are other characteristics. Other architectural features with a Netherlandic ancestry, once common throughout the region, such as cupboard beds, jambless fireplaces, wall anchors, and brick tumbling, disappeared in the early nineteenth century, but the basic underlying structure remained based on Dutch prototypes.[39] Moreover, architectural historians are now debating if the changeover to more "modern" styles in eighteenth-century New York was not also derived directly from the Netherlands. For example, architectural histories reveal that, beginning in the 1680s, architects in the republic were the first Europeans to widely accept the sash window and that the stepped gable had largely disappeared from new constructions by the 1660s. Perhaps, then, New York builders continued to be influenced by and adapt contemporary models in the republic. By the late seventeenth century, according to architectural historian Juliette Roding, Dutch and English architecture were virtually indistinguishable, "because both the Dutch and English architects of the period to a great extent used the same architectural treaties and visual models."[40]

TRADITIONAL LIBERTIES

In the Dutch Republic, ancient privileges and traditional liberties acquired by communities as corporate rights resulted in decentralization and factionalism. The settlers brought these traditions with them to the New World. They are most evident in New Yorkers' and Jerseyite's opposition to centralizing tendencies in governmental authority and jealous guarding of the prerogatives granted to them in their local town charters. The colonial competition between Albany and Schenectady over the fur-trade monopoly, between New York City and Albany over the export-trade monopoly, and between New York City and upriver communities over the flour-bolting monopoly are a few such examples. Monopolies, however, were favored when they contributed to the order and stability of the local corporate community as a whole. Opposition arose when they were found to benefit an individual at the expense of the community. Individual rights and liberties were tied to the corporate welfare and manifested in the concept of toleration.[41] The paradoxical nature of rural New York and New Jersey, simultaneously insular and parochial while socially liberal and tolerant, is a legacy of the Dutch influence, which continues to set the region apart.

Within New York's communities, special-interest groups coalesced in Dutch fashion to pursue common goals. Individual rights were defended through the acquisition of communal privileges. The medieval Dutch trade guilds, for example, regulated and promoted specific craft interests. Although the guild system never formally developed in New Netherland, beginning in the 1670s, New York's bakers, boatmen, butchers, cartmen, coopers, shoemakers, and tanners combined to protect their collective rights.[42] Special interests thus became a fixture in eighteenth-century New York politics, which, because of the localized concerns of each group, fractured the promotion of a larger provincewide interest before the English crown.[43]

Another legacy of the Dutch is the concept of freedom of conscience as a component of a healthy society. In the Dutch Republic, this principle was enshrined in the 1579 Union of Utrecht, which grew to be seen as the republic's basic constitutional document. Article 13 specifically states that "each person shall remain free, especially in his religion, and that no one shall be persecuted or investigated because of their religion."[44] Although this guarantee applied only to private beliefs and not to public worship, its embodiment as a cornerstone in the foundation of their state makes the Dutch truly unique.

THE DUTCH POLITICAL LEGACY

The traditional liberties that the Dutch brought to the New World were incorporated into the complexities of the political institutions they also introduced.

In early modern Holland, where towns dominated the countryside, the surest avenue to property ownership and its attendant prestige was through mercantile pursuits.[45] In 1679, Dutch traveler Jasper Danckaerts noted that New Yorkers seemed to be "almost all traders."[46] As an individual acquired wealth through trade, he was elevated in the community's standing. One indication of the status of merchants is their prominence as church elders and deacons and their appointment as magistrates and to militia commands.[47] The result was the emergence of a middle-class (*burgerlijke*) urban patrician class that gained social and political hegemony after 1664. This followed the pattern of the Dutch Republic, where a small group of regent families gained control over civic offices. As in the republic, colonial New York's urban and provincial offices became dominated by a handful of interrelated mercantile families whose lifestyle remained comfortably middle class.[48]

In the Dutch Republic, political factionalism emerged from conflicts within the Regent class. In a similar fashion, after 1675 the close-knit kinship network that formed New York's mercantile elite—which included Bayards, Cuylers, Gouverneurs, Kierstedes, Leislers, Loockermans, Schuylers, Staatses, Stuyvesants, and Van Cortlandts—began to feud, fracture, and coalesce into opposing camps.[49] Like European factional leaders, New York's political leaders came from an elite intrafamilial network in which cousins, brothers, and in-laws vied for public opinion and royal favor.

In the seventeenth century, the Dutch Republic's body politic split into two factions. On one side were the supporters of the office of *raadpensionaris*, the principal representative of the town regents, loosely identified as the *Staatsfactie*. Opposing them were the Orangists, supporters of the office of *stadholder* or provincial military commander-in-chief, traditionally held by a prince of Orange. In their protracted disputes, New York political interests aligned with those in the republic, according to theology. In the Netherlands, Orangists and *Staatsgezinde* took opposing sides in the doctrinal conflict between the followers of Utrecht University professor Gisbertus Voetius, who stressed moral precision and the need for a personal conversion to Christ, and the followers of Leiden University professor Johannes Cocceius, who espoused a more liberal covenant theology. By the last third of the century this controversy colored every aspect of the republic's political life and provided the ideological glue for factional disputes in colonial New York.[50]

The 1676 controversy over domine Nicholas van Rensselaer is illustrative. James, Duke of York, had appointed Van Rensselaer, ordained an Anglican, to the Albany Reformed pulpit. This outraged the Reformed Dutch, who held to the rule from the Synod of Dort that a minister must be ordained in the Reformed Church and called by the congregation. The controversy came to

SOLON H. BORGLUM (1868–1922)
Jacob Leisler Memorial, 1913
Reproduction image courtesy Westchester County Historical Society, H-968

Since no portrait of Leisler exists, this statue in New Rochelle is largely imaginary, presenting a heroic figure dressed in a long cloak and a Dutch beaver hat and carrying a large staff.

a head when in July 1676 Jacob Leisler, a New York City Reformed Church deacon, circulated a four-point gloss criticizing a sermon by Van Rensselaer on original sin. The theological dispute, which followed current doctrinal divisions in the republic's Reformed Church, nearly tore the colony apart until brought to an end by the command of the governor.[51] Tensions reemerged in the 1680s, when Voetian-inspired pietist movements swept through New York's Reformed and Lutheran congregations, despite opposition by the province's more urbane dominies and ministers.[52] Factional rivalries increased as the Duke of York, now King James II, implemented centralizing governmental policies and patronized a small group of New York merchants with offices and other perquisites. Orangist populist and antirepublican ideology emanating from Rotterdam, which had become the primary focus for New York's Continental trade, further inflamed the population. Paralleling popular support for the House of Orange in the Netherlands, Orangism and anti-Catholicism became a rallying cry for the opposition to Stuart policies in New York, while New York's Anglicizing Dutch elite was increasingly portrayed in terms of Holland's regents.

The 1689 event known as Leisler's Rebellion shows the continuing influence of Dutch political culture in New York. In November 1688, William, prince of Orange, *stadholder* of Holland and Zeeland, and son-in-law and nephew of England's King James II, invaded England with a force of 21,000 men. The subsequent Glorious Revolution, which replaced the Roman Catholic King James with the Protestant William III and his wife, James's daughter, Mary, on the English throne, set off rebellions in the American colonies. Revolt broke out in New York at the beginning of May 1689 on Long Island's east end, when the towns of Suffolk County, following Boston's example, overthrew James II's government. Rebellion spread across Long Island and up the Hudson River Valley, where mobs ousted James's appointees and chose others to replace them. In pattern, the New York and east Jersey uprisings bear similarities to the 1672 Orangist uprisings in the Netherlands, when mobs forced numerous towns to replace their magistrates with Voetian-Orangists.[53]

This is most evident in the central role taken by the militias. A peculiar characteristic of colonial New York was the prominence in public affairs of the local militia company, or burgher guard. In the Low Countries, citizens' militias, the *schutterijen*, traditionally played a pivotal role in civic life. In the medieval Netherlands, civilian military units, created to maintain order within the towns, would be employed in military tasks outside the city walls during times of crisis. But they acquired a more ceremonial role and active political capacity as the guardians of traditional liberties under the republic.[54] Likewise, the New York militia company served a more social and potent political role rather than that of a defensive unit. Indeed, the English mocked the New York militia companies as a burlesque of militarism.[55] Yet attempts by English governors to diminish their autonomy through patronage in the appointment of officers were perceived by New Yorkers throughout the colonial period as a threat to traditional governmental balances.[56]

In June 1689, the rebellious New York militia captains organized themselves as a Council of War and called for a meeting of representatives from New York and eastern New Jersey to oversee the government. In doing so, they followed Dutch political structure, in which fundamental law, natural rights, representative institutions, and popular sovereignty were important. The convention's election of senior militia captain and wealthy merchant Jacob Leisler as commander of the fort and, in August, as commander-in-chief of the province thus followed Dutch precedents. In the republic, when ruling elites in the Netherlands were discredited, their loss of legitimacy caused a demand for change in office holders and restoration of the corporate rights of the local community. The convention's election of Leisler as commander-in-chief fell within the Dutch political tradition of finding a leader to balance the power of the magistrates.[57] Drawing on Dutch populist ideology, Leislerians sought to restore the traditional balances in the government by reclaiming the corporate rights of the people, abolishing monopolies, demanding no taxation without representation and the right of the people to bear arms unrestricted, and devolving governmental authority to local communities.

The republic's political divisions continued to influence New York politics into the eighteenth century. In the 1720s, mercantile and agrarian interests hardened. A faction led by the Morris and Livingston families, known as the Country Party, supported Dutch Reformed and Presbyterian interests and reflected Orangist ideology; an opposing faction of mostly Anglican mercantile and manorial families including DeLanceys, Schuylers, Philipses, and Van Cortlandts, known as the Court Party, reflected the interests of the Dutch regent class. In Dutch fashion, elites with fluid allegiances dominated. The two parties, supplemented by lesser factions throughout the province, disagreed on economic, constitutional, and religious issues, and the establishment of a college, today Columbia University.[58]

New Yorkers clearly saw their political alignments in terms of those in the Republic. When Robert Livingston called Leislerians "butter boxes and boors" or Leislerians termed their opponents "grandees" and "Cocceians," they were using commonplace Dutch political labels. Seeing New York's factionalism as an extension of Dutch politics, one Leislerian pamphleteer reflected that the opposition had "scap'd being Dewitted by a sufficiently provoked People." The reference was to the brutal 1672 murders of Holland *raadpensionaris* Jan de Witt and his brother Cornelis by an Orangist mob in The Hague.[59]

The continuing impact of Dutch events upon New York politics is seen in the wake of the Dutch Revolution of 1747, which placed Willem IV of Orange as *stadholder* in all seven provinces. At the time, the Dutch turned out an enormous literature looking back to the traditional balances of good government and the corporate rights of the people. Historian James Tanis convincingly argues that during the English imperial crisis of the 1740s and 1750s, New Yorkers and Jerseyites followed this example and again looked to their Dutch traditions. Citing numerous New York and New Jersey Dutch Reformed and Presbyterian sermons, he writes that "the Dutch example became an important symbol for the colonists at the time of the Albany Congress in 1754."

For the population of the middle colonies, then, the sixteenth-century Dutch revolt against Spain and the actions of William III during the 1688 Glorious Revolution served as the "paradigm" of "union and independence."[60] As an illustration, in the 1750s, American Dutch-language almanacs republished the 1581 Act of Abjuration, by which the republic had declared independence from Spain, and the 1579 Union of Utrecht, the republic's basic federalizing document.[61] Indeed, Thomas Jefferson's 1776 Declaration of Independence so closely follows the Act of Abjuration in construction that some scholars suggest that the act served as Jefferson's model, and the influence of the Dutch Republic's body politic as developed under the Union of Utrecht on the Articles of Confederation and the U.S. Constitution has been long suggested.[62] Most important, out of the Dutch tradition of party factionalism and special interests emerged the modern American political party system, which was introduced by Martin Van Buren, a descendant of one of the early settlers of the patroonship of Rennselaerswijck, in the creation of New York State and, later, the National Democratic Party organization.[63]

CONCLUSION

For those familiar with Dutch history and society, the persistence of Dutch culture in New York and New Jersey seems self-evident. From place and family names to folklore to material culture and cuisine, this presence is still very much alive in the region. New York inherited unfettered commerce, freedom of conscience, the concept of toleration, and a republican political culture from the Dutch. The complex political alliances and intrafamilial feuds among New York's interrelated patrician families, the Presbyterian–Anglican rivalry, and the contest between commercial and landed interests all reflected political alignments in the republic. The concept of individual liberties protected through corporate rights left a strong tradition in New York and subsequently the national government, as seen in the influence of special interests on the shaping of governmental policies. But to best understand Dutch culture in New York and its legacy in America, I suggest regarding it not in the light of an increasingly distant "Golden Age" or the mythical stereotypes of Washington Irving's sleepy villages, but as a contemporary component of the dynamic and ever-changing culture of the Netherlands.

NOTES

1. Washington Irving, *The Sketch Book of Geoffrey Crayon Gent.* (1820; reprint, New York and London: Penguin, 1981), 331.

2. Wayne Franklin, "Cooper and New York's Dutch Heritage," James Fenimore Cooper Society Miscellaneous Papers, No. 5 (Oneonta, N.Y., 1994).

3. David Steven Cohen, "How Dutch Were the Dutch of New Netherland?" *New York History* 62 (January 1981): 43-60.

4. Benjamin Schmidt, *Innocence Abroad: The Dutch Imagination and the New World, 1570-1670* (Cambridge, Eng. and New York: Cambridge University Press, 2001), 315-320.

5. Sir William Temple, *Observations Upon the United Provinces of the Netherlands* (London, 1672), 94-95.

6. Simon Hart, *Geschrift en Getal: Een keuze uit de demografisch-, economisch- en sociaal-historische studien op grond van Amsterdamse en Zaanse archivalia, 1600-1800* (Dordrecht: Holland Historical Society, 1976), 115-181; Jonathan Israel, *The Dutch Republic: Its Rise Greatness and Fall 1477-1806* (Oxford and New York: Oxford University Press, 1995), 622, 626-627; T. H. Breen and Stephen Forster, "Moving to the New World: The Character of Early Massachusetts Immigration," *William and Mary Quarterly*, 3rd series, 30, no. 2 (April 1973): 189-222.

7. Alice P. Kenney, *Stubborn for Liberty the Dutch in New York* (Syracuse, N.Y.: Syracuse University Press, 1975), 2-3, 174-174, 188-189.

8. "Report of the Surrender of New Netherland," Edmund B. O'Callaghan, ed., *Documents Relative to the Colonial History of the State of New York*, 15 vols. (Albany, N.Y., 1853-85), 2:36 (hereafter cited as *NYCD*). See also "Remonstrance of the People of New Netherland" and "Answer of the Honorable Peter Stuyvesant," 2:248-250; 444-445.

9. "Minutes of Council," 1673-1674, *NYCD*, 2:675 (Willemstadt [Albany] vs. Schenectady); 712 (Jamaica vs. Huntington); 714, 730 (Bergen vs. the surrounding communities); 722-723 (Woodbridge vs. Piscataway).

10. Thomas S. Wemurth, *Rip Van Winkle's Neighbors: The Transformation of Rural Society in the Hudson River Valley, 1720-1850* (Albany: State University of New York Press, 2001), 27.

11. Maarten Prak, *The Dutch Republic in the Seventeenth Century: The Golden Age*, trans. Diane Webb (Cambridge: Cambridge University Press, 2005), 131-132; Jaap Jacobs, *New Netherland: A Dutch Colony in Seventeenth-Century America* (Leiden and Boston: Brill, 2005), 114.

12. Sung Bok Kim, *Landlords and Tenants in Colonial New York Manorial Society, 1664-1775* (Chapel Hill: University of North Carolina Press, 1978).

13. William Smith, *The History of the Late Province of New-York, From its Discovery, to the Appointment of Governor Colden, in 1762*, ed. Michael Kammen, 2 vols. (New Haven: Yale University Press, 1972), 1:327-328.

14. Patricia U. Bonomi, *A Factious People: Politics and Society in Colonial New York* (New York and London: Columbia University Press, 1971), 279-286.

15. Sheldon T. Viele, "Narrative of The Visit of the Holland Society to the Netherlands," Holland Society *Yearbook* 1888 (New York: Holland Society of New York, 1888).

16 Donald W. Meinig, *The Shaping of America: A Geographical Perspective on 500 Years of American History, vol. 1—Atlantic America, 1492-1800* (New Haven and London: Yale University Press, 1986).

17. Jacobs, *New Netherland*, 481.

18. H. L. Mencken, *The American Language: An Inquiry Into the Development of English in the United States* (New York: Knopf, 1921), 416; quote from Mrs. M. P. Ferris, intro., *Dutch Nursery Rhymes of Colonial Times* (New York, 1890), n.p.

19. Cathy Matson, *Merchants and Empire: Trading in Colonial New York* (Baltimore and London: Johns Hopkins University Press, 1998), 147-149, 271-273, 298-299.

20. Walter H. Salzmann, *A Market to Explore: A History of Public-Private Partnership in the Promotion of Trade and Investment Between the Netherlands and the United States* (Amsterdam: The Netherlands Chamber of Commerce in the United States, Six Art Promotion bv, 1994), 35.

21. Firth Haring Fabend, "The Synod of Dort and the Persistence of Dutchness in Nineteenth-Century New York and New Jersey," *New York History* 77 (July 1996): 273-300; Fabend, "New Light on New Netherland's Legacy to the Religious Culture of New York and New Jersey," *de Halve Maen* 73 (Fall 2000): 51-55; Fabend, *Zion on the Hudson: Dutch New York and New Jersey in the Age of Revivals* (New Brunswick, N.J.: Rutgers University Press, 2000), 214; Fabend, "Church and State, Hand in Hand: Compassionate Calvinism in New Netherland," *de Halve Maen* 75 (Spring 2002): 3-8; Joyce D. Goodfriend, "The Social Dimensions of Congregational Life in Colonial New York City," *William and Mary Quarterly*, 3rd series, 46 (April 1989): 252-278.

22. Edwin Scott Gaustad, *Historical Atlas of Religion in America*, rev. ed. (New York: Harper & Row, 1976), 3-4.

23. Willem Frederik (Eric) Nooter, "Between Heaven and Earth: Church and Society in Pre-Revolutionary Flatbush, Long Island" (Ph.D. diss., Vrije Universiteit te Amsterdam, 1994).

24. Michael Kammen, *Colonial New York: A History* (New York: Charles Scribner's Sons, 1975), 237; Alexander J. Wall, "The Controversy in the Dutch Church in New York Concerning Preaching in English, 1754-1768," *New-York Historical Society Quarterly* 12 (July 1928): 38-58.

25. Gerald de Jong, *The Dutch in America 1690-1974* (Boston: Twayne, 1974), 105-106. Fabend, *Zion on the Hudson*, 71-72, 213-214.

26. Hendrik Edelman, *Dutch-American Bibliography 1693-1794: A Descriptive Catalog of Dutch-Language Books, Pamphlets and Almanacs Printed in America* (Nieuwkoop, Neth.: DeGraaf, 1974), 39.

27. De Jong, *The Dutch in America 1690-1974*, 106.

28. See, for example, Jacob Melyn to Abraham Gouverneur, October 1691, Melyn Letter Book, n.p., American Antiquarian Society, Worcester, Mass.

29. Willem Frijhoff, "New Views on the Dutch Period in New York," *de Halve Maen* 71 (Summer 1998): 23.

30. *The Papers of William Livingston, Volume 2: July 1777–December 1778*, ed. Carl E. Prince and Dennis P. Ryan (Trenton: New Jersey Historical Commission, 1979), 491.

31. Edelman, *Dutch-American Bibliography 1693-1794*, 12.

32. William H. Carpenter, "Dutch Contributions to the Vocabulary of English in Amer-

ica: Dutch Remainders in New York State," *Modern Philology* 6, no. 1 (July 1908): 53-68; Mencken, *The American Language*, 54.

33. Kenney, *Stubborn for Liberty*, 84; Roderic H. Blackburn and Ruth Piwonka, *Remembrance of Patria: Dutch Arts and Culture in Colonial America, 1609-1776* (Albany, N.Y.: Albany Institute of History and Art, 1988), 159-161, 277.

34. Esther Singleton, *Dutch New York* (New York: Dodd Mead, 1909), 308-309; Charlotte Wilcoxen, *Seventeenth-Century Albany: A Dutch Profile*, rev. ed. (Albany, N.Y.: Albany Institute of History and Art, 1984), 120-122.

35. Peter G. Rose, *The Sensible Cook: Dutch Foodways in the Old and the New World* (Syracuse, N.Y.: Syracuse University Press, 1989), 35.

36. Alexander Hamilton, *Hamilton's Itinerarium: Being a Narrative of a Journey from Annapolis, Maryland Through Delaware, Pennsylvania, New York, New Jersey, Connecticut, Rhode Island, Massachusetts and New Hampshire from May to September, 1744*, ed. Albert Bushnell Hart (St. Louis: William K. Bixby, 1907), 13, 51.

37. Pehr (Peter) Kalm, *Travels in North America—Adolph B. Benson, The America of 1750, Peter Kalm's Travels in North America: The English Version of 1770*, rev. and ed. Adolph B. Benson, 2 vols. (New York: Dover, 1966), 1:341.

38. Richard Smith, *A Tour of Four Great Rivers, the Hudson, Mohawk, Susquehanna and Delaware in 1769, Being the Journal of Richard Smith of Burlington, New Jersey*, ed. Francis W. Halsey (New York: Charles Scribner's Sons, 1906).

39. Jeroen van der Hurk, "The Architecture of New Netherland Revisited," in *Building Environments: Perspectives in Vernacular Architecture 10*, ed. Kenneth A. Breisch and Alison K. Hoagland (Knoxville: University of Tennessee Press, 2005), 133-152; John Stevens, *Dutch Vernacular Architecture in North America, 1640-1840* (West Hurley, N.Y.: Society for the Preservation of Hudson Valley Vernacular Architecture, 2005).

40. J. G. Roding, "North Sea Coasts, an Architectural Unity?," in *The North Sea and Culture (1550-1800)*, ed. Juliette Roding and Lex Heerma van Voss (Larenseweg, Neth.: Uitgeverij Verloren, 1996), 97.

41. Matson, *Merchants and Empire*, 102-103.

42. Allan Tully, *Forming American Politics: Ideals, Interests, and Institutions in Colonial New York and Pennsylvania* (Baltimore: Johns Hopkins University Press, 1994); Simon Middleton, *From Privileges to Rights: Work and Politics in Colonial New York City* (Philadelphia: University of Pennsylvania Press, 2006), chapter 2.

43. Allison Gilbert Olson, *Making the Empire Work: London and American Interest Groups, 1690-1790* (Cambridge, Mass.: Harvard University Press, 1992), 72-73.

44. A. Th. Van Deursen, "Between Unity and Independence: The Application of the Union as a Fundamental Law," *The Low Countries History Yearbook* 14 (1981): 50-65. The text of the Union of Utrecht is in E. H. Kossman and A. F. Mellink, eds., *Texts Concerning the Revolt of the Netherlands* (Cambridge, Eng., and New York: Cambridge University Press, 1974), 165-173.

45. Fernand Braudel, *The Mediterranean and the Mediterranean World in the Age of Philip II*, trans. Siân Reynolds (New York: Harper & Row, 1976), 1:277-278.

46. Henry C. Murphy, ed. and trans., *Journal of A Voyage to New York and a Tour in Several of the American Colonies in 1679-1680, by Jasper Dankers and Peter Sluyter of Wiewerd in Friesland* (Brooklyn: Long Island Historical Society, 1867), 79.

47. For the prominence of merchants see Beverly McAnear, "Politics in Provincial New York 1689-1761" (Ph.D. diss., Stanford University, 1935), 1:69-71; Thomas J. Archdeacon, *New York City 1664-1710* (Ithaca, N.Y.: Cornell University Press, 1976), 58-77; Joyce Goodfriend, *Before the Melting Pot: Society and Culture in Colonial New York, 1664-1730* (Princeton: Princeton University Press, 1992).

48. For the development of oligarchies in New York see Alice P. Kenney, *The Gansevoorts of Albany: Dutch Patricians in the Upper Hudson Valley* (Syracuse, N.Y.: Syracuse University Press, 1969), particularly the introduction.

49. For family connections see William Brouwer Bogardus, *Dear 'Cousin': A Chartered Genealogy of the descendants of Anneke Jans Bogardus (1605-1663) to the 5th Generation— and of her sister, Marritje Jans* (Wilmington, Ohio: Anneke Jans and Everardus Bogardus Descendants Association, 1996), esp. charts on pages 53-124. For one view of the division among the elite see Firth Haring Fabend, "'According to Holland Custome': Jacob Leisler and the Loockermans Estate Feud," *de Halve Maen* 67 (Spring 1994): 1-8.

50. *Journal of Jasper Danckaerts*, x-xii.

51. Lawrence H. Leder, "The Unorthodox Domine: Nicholas Van Rensselaer," *New York History* 35 (April 1954): 166-176.

52. James Tanis, "Reformed Pietism in Colonial America," in *Continental Pietism and Early American Christianity*, ed. F. Ernest Stoeffler (Grand Rapids, Mich.: William B. Eerdmans, 1976), 34-73; Martin H. Prozesky, "The Emergence of Dutch Pietism," *Journal of Ecclesiastical History* 28, no. 1 (January 1977): 29-37.

53. Charles Howard McCormick, *Leisler's Rebellion* (New York: Garland Press, 1989); A. F. Salomons, "De rol van de Amsterdamse burgerbeweging in de wetsverzetting van 1672," *Bijdragen en Mededelingen betreffende de Geschiedenis der Nederlanden* 106 (1991): 198-219.

54. Paul Knevel, *Burgers in het geweer: De schutterijen in Holland, 1550-1700* (Hilversum, Neth.: Hist. Verlag Holland/Verloren, 1994); J. C. Grayson, "The Civic Militia in the County of Holland, 1560-81. Politics and Public Order in the Dutch Revolt," *Bijdragen en Mededelingen betreffende de Geschiedenis der Nederlanden* 95 (1980): 35-63.

55. Donna Merwick, *Possessing Albany, 1630-1710: The Dutch and English Experiences* (Cambridge and New York: Cambridge University Press, 1990), 273.

56. Bonomi, *A Factious People*, 158-159.

57. Martin van Gelderen, *The Political Thought of the Dutch Revolt 1555-1590* (Cambridge, Eng.: Cambridge University Press, 1992), 286.

58. Kammen, *Colonial New York*, 203-206.

59. For the use of "butter boxes and boors" see Robert Livingston, "A Satyr Upon the Times" (1702) in *The Glorious Revolution in America: Documents on the Colonial Crisis of 1689*, ed. Michael G. Hall, Lawrence H. Leder, and Michael G. Kammen (Chapel Hill: University of North Carolina Press, 1964), 133-134; for "Cocceian" see *NYCD* 3:751-754.

60. James Tanis, "The American Dutch, Their Church, and the Revolution," in *A Bilateral Bicentennial: A History of Dutch-American Relations, 1782-1982*, ed. J. W. Schulte Nordholdt and Robert P. Swierenga (Amsterdam: Meulenhoff, and New York: Octagon Books, 1982), 116.

61. *De AMERICAANSE Almanak, Voo't Jaar na Christi geboorte* 1754 (New York); Edelman, *Dutch-American Bibliography*, 56. English texts of the Union of Utrecht and Act of Abjuration are in Kossman and Mellink, eds., *Texts Concerning the Revolt of the Netherlands*, 166-173, 216-228.

62. James R. Tanis, "The Dutch-American Connection: The Impact of the Dutch Example on American Constitutional Beginnings," in Stephen L. Schechter and Richard B. Bernstein, eds., *New York and the Union: Contributions to the American Constitutional Experience*, ed. Stephen L. Schechter and Richard B. Bernstein (Albany: New York State Commission on the Bicentennial of the United States Constitution, 1990), 22-28; Stephen E. Lucas, "The Plakkaat van Verlatine: A Neglected Model for the American Declaration of Independence," in *Connecting Cultures: The Netherlands in Five Centuries of Transatlantic Exchange*, ed. Rosemarijn Hoefte and Johanna C. Kardux (Amsterdam: Vrij University, 1994), 187-207.

63. Kenney, *Stubborn for Liberty*, 266-267.

Contributors and Index

GUY GILLETTE
Celebration of 300th anniversary of the first settlement
of New Netherlands pioneers at Oude Dorp, 1962
Staten Island, NY
Photograph, 11 x 14 in.
Hudson River Museum, 2007.08

Contributor Biographies

Contributing Editor and Co-Curator of the Exhibition

Roger Panetta is a Visiting Professor of History and Curator of the Hudson River Collection at Fordham University. He is also Adjunct Curator for History at the Hudson River Museum and Affiliated Faculty member of the Beacon Institute for the Study of Rivers and Estuaries. He was the contributing editor of *Westchester: The American Suburb*, published by Fordham University Press, and coauthor of *The Hudson: An Illustrated Guide to the Living River*, published by Rutgers University Press. He has published numerous articles on the history of Sing Sing Prison, the American suburbs, and the process of oral history. He received the Cultural Heritage Award from the Lower Hudson Conference in 2006.

Co-Curators of the Exhibition and Contributing Essayists

Bartholomew F. Bland is the Curator of Exhibitions at the Hudson River Museum, where he co-curated *Westchester: The American Suburb*, and was a contributor to the companion book published by Fordham University Press. His survey exhibitions and their accompanying catalogues for the museum include *Red Grooms: In the Studio*; *Whitfield Lovell: All Things in Time*; and *Got Cow? Cattle in American Art*. In previous positions he organized interpretive projects for the Staten Island Museum at the Snug Harbor Cultural Center and the Flagler Museum in Palm Beach. He is coauthor of the book *Merry Wives and Others: A History of Domestic Humor Writing*.

Laura Vookles is the Chief Curator of Collections at the Hudson River Museum, where she has worked for twenty-four years. She co-curated and wrote catalogue essays for *The Old Croton Aqueduct: Rural Resources Meet Urban Needs*; *Next Stop Westchester! People and the Railroad*; *Bedazzled: Costume Embellishments of the Early Twentieth Century*; and *Westchester: The American Suburb*. She has completed numerous furnishing, conservation, and interpretation projects for Glenview, an 1877 historic house at the museum.

Foreword

Michael Botwinick is Director of the Hudson River Museum. He was previously Director of the Brooklyn Museum and the Corcoran Gallery of Art, Assistant Director of the Philadelphia Museum of Art, and Assistant Curator-in-Chief of the Metropolitan Museum of Art. Among the exhibitions he has organized are *The Great East River Bridge*; *Africa in Antiquity: The Arts of Ancient Nubia and the Sudan*; and *The American Renaissance 1876–1917*.

Introduction

Russell Shorto is the author of *The Island at the Center of the World*, which chronicles the Dutch colony of New Netherland and its legacy in New York and American history. His most recent book is *Descartes' Bones*. He is a contributing writer at the *New York Times Magazine* and the director of the John Adams Institute in Amsterdam. He lives in Amsterdam.

Contributors

Laura M. Chmielewski earned a Ph.D. in American history from the City University of New York. She teaches Atlantic world, early American, and public history at Purchase College, SUNY. Her areas of specialization include social history, religious history, and material culture. Chmielewski is also the author of the forthcoming book *The Spice of Popery: Converging Christianities on an Early American Frontier*. Before joining Purchase, she worked for more than a decade at area museums and nonprofit organizations, including the Historic House Trust of New York City, Fordham University, and Thirteen/WNET.

Firth Haring Fabend in an independent historian whose subject is the Dutch in America. She holds a Ph.D. from New York University and is the author of *A Dutch Family in the Middle Colonies, 1660–1800,* and *Zion on the Hudson: Dutch New York and New Jersey in the Age of Revivals,* both published by Rutgers University Press. She has published many essays and articles on the Dutch in New Netherland and after, as well as a historical poem in book form, *A Catch of Grandmothers,* and a historical novel, *Land So Fair,* set in the Hudson Valley in the eighteenth century, with flashbacks to New Netherland.

Cynthia M. Koch is Director of the Franklin D. Roosevelt Presidential Library and Museum in Hyde Park, New York. Previously she was Associate Director of the Penn National Commission on Society, Culture and Community, a research group at the University of Pennsylvania for which she supervised research and published "The Contest for American Culture: A Leadership Case Study on the NEA and NEH Funding Crisis" in the commission's online journal. Her dissertation appeared in part as "Teaching Patriotism: Private Virtue for the Public Good in the Early Republic" in *Bonds of Affection: Americans Define Their Patriotism*. She has published in numerous publications and holds her Ph.D. and M.A. in American civilization from the University of Pennsylvania.

Phillip Lopate is primarily known as an essayist: his personal essays have been collected in *Bachelorhood, Against Joie de Vivre,* and *Portrait of My Body*, and in a book of selected writings entitled *Getting Personal*. He is the editor of *The Art of the Personal Essay* and *Writing New York: From Washington Irving to the Present,* and has written extensively about New York City, for instance in *Waterfront: A Journey Around Manhattan*. His most recent books are *Two Marriages* (novellas) and *Notes on Sontag*. He is a professor at Columbia University, School of the Arts, and lives in Brooklyn with his wife and daughter.

Dennis J. Maika holds a Ph.D. in history from New York University; his dissertation was awarded the Hendricks Manuscript Prize. He is a Fellow of the Holland Society of New York, the New Netherland Institute, and the New York Academy of History, and a member of the International Seminar on the History of the Atlantic World (Harvard University). As a historian of colonial New York, he has published numerous articles and essays and has served as a consultant for local history and education projects. He currently teaches American history and psychology at Fox Lane High School in Bedford, New York.

Ruth Piwonka is an independent scholar in Columbia County, New York. She has co-authored *A Visible Heritage: Columbia County; New York: A History in Art and Architecture*; and *Remembrance of Patria: Dutch Arts and Culture in Colonial America, 1609–1776* with Roderic H. Blackburn. She has published numerous articles on Dutch material culture and regional architecture.

Oliver Rink is a professor of history at California State University at Bakersfield. He is the author of *Holland on the Hudson: An Economic and Social History of Dutch New York*, winner of the New Netherland Project's Hendricks Prize, and coauthor of *The Empire State: A History of New York*, a History Book Club selection. He has also published numerous articles on Dutch New York.

Sean E. Sawyer received a Ph.D. in architectural history from Columbia University, where he is currently the chief administrator of the Department of History. He is also an adjunct assistant professor at Parsons/The New School Master's Program in the History of Decorative Arts and Design at the Cooper-Hewitt Museum. From 2001 to 2007 he was the Executive Director of the Wyckoff House and Association, where he lectured extensively on Dutch American architecture and museum management. He is a founding organizer of *5 Dutch Days 5 Boroughs: Dutch Art and Culture Past and Present*, an annual celebration of Dutch art and culture across New York City.

William A. Starna is professor of anthropology emeritus at the State University of New York, College at Oneonta. He has published widely on the Iroquoian and Algonquian Indian populations of the eastern United States and Canada, in addition to contemporary state–federal–Indian relations. He and Charles T. Gehring are editors of Adriaen van der Donck's *A Description of New Netherland*, translated by Diederik Willem Goedhuys (University of Nebraska Press, 2008).

David William Voorhees earned a Ph.D. from New York University. He is Director of the Papers of Jacob Leisler Project at New York University and managing editor of *de Halve Maen*, a quarterly scholarly journal devoted to New Netherland studies. His published works include *The Holland Society: A Centennial History 1885–1985* (1985), *Records of the Reformed Protestant Church in Flatbush, Kings County, New York, Volume 1: 1677–1720* (1998), and numerous articles on the Dutch in post-Conquest New York.

Index

Page locators in *italic* refer to illustrations in text.

Adventures of Ichabod and Mr. Toad, The, 194
Aertse, Elbert, 58
African American history, 125
Africans. *See also* slavery
    Atlantic creoles, 49
    Cartagena, Nicholas, 49–51
    Domingo, Francisco (Frank), 51
    Marramita, 51
Afro-Dutch culture, 125
agrarian presence in New Netherland, 97
Albany, city planning, 95
Alexander, Henry, *The 'Half Moon,' 306*
All-purpose room, Jan Martense Schenck House, 103
All-purpose room, John DeWint House, Tappan,
    Rockland County, New York, *110*
Along the Canal in Old Manhattan (Pyle), *388*
American Bible Society, 150
American Protestantism, 153
American Sunday School Union, 146
American Tract Society, 150
Amsterdam, 286
Amsterdam, Holland, 281–82
anchor-bent houses, 98
Anglicization of architecture, 109
animal skins, economy and, 7
Anniversary Week, 150
Anthony Van Corlear, The Trumpeter of New
    Amsterdam (Pyle), *212*
Antony Van Corlear Brought into the Presence of Peter
    Stuyvesant (Quidor), *236, 237*
architecture, 420
    anchor-bent houses, 98
    Anglicization of, 109
    Bailey, Rosalie Fellows, 120–21
    Bull house, 121, *122*
    churches, 110–11
    Daniel Winne house, 126–27
    Day, Frank Miles, 118
    demolition of structures, 124
    dugout shelters, 94
    Dutch colonial house, 121
    Dutch doors, 109
    Dutch Renaissance revival, 117–20
    Eberlein, Harold, 354

Embury, Aymar II, 121–23
English, adaptation of, 106–7
farmhouses
    bedrooms, 109
    casement windows, 109
    central hall, 108
    Dyckman, 124
    Embury, Aymar II, 121–23
    fireplaces, 109
    gambrel roof, 108, 121
    groote kamer (best room), 108
    New Netherland, 98
floor plans, evolution of, 99
Georgian style, 104, 105
Gibson, Robert W., 117
H-bent houses, 98–99
Holland Mania, 120
home as place of comfort, refuge, and privacy,
    360–62
Hubbard house, 124
Irving, Washington and, 112–14
jambless hearth, 101
Johannes Decker house, 99
kruiskozijn, 103
multiple entry doors, 99, 101
New Amsterdam History Center, 126
New World Dutch barn, 99, 124
Rensselaerswyck manor, 126–27
revival of Dutch-inspired, 116
Reynolds, Helen WIlkinson, 120–21
roof forms, 101
Roosevelt, Franklin Delano and, 350–51, 353–54
surviving structures, 124
Tubby, William B., 117
urban, development of, 117
Vleeshal, 117
West End Collegiate Church and School, 117
windows, 101, 103
Wyckhoff house, 98–99
Wyckoff Farmhouse Museum, 126
Armchair, 174
Arrival of Stuyvesant in New Amsterdam (Pyle), *x*
Aspinwall, Mary Rebecca, marriage to Isaac
    Roosevelt, 340
aspiring inventories, 181
At Home-Marken-Holland, 283

Atlantic creoles, 49
Attack on House of Adriean Van Der Donck, 2

Bacon, Edgar Mayhew, *Stone Farmhouse, 234*
Bailey, Rosalie Fellows, 93, 120–21
Balldridge, Adam, 50
Bancker, Elizabeth, estate inventory, 173
Bandel, Arnule, *Sketch of Dyckman House, 381*
Barbadian slaves, 52
Baronial Order of the Magna Carta, 262
*Battle Scene from Knickerbocker's History of New York,
    A* (Quidor), *243, 244–45*
Baur, John I. H., rediscovery of John Quidor's work,
    227
beaver, Fort Orange, 83
beaver hats, 10
Belgii Novi, Angliae Novae et Partis Virginiae (Map of
    New Netherland, New England, and parts of
    Virginia), *4*
Bencke & Scott, *"Dis von don't count"* (Joseph
    Jefferson as Rip Van Winkle), *220*
Bensell, George, *Rip Van Winkle, 218*
Berckheyde, Gerrit Adriaensz, *The Dam and the
    Damrak, Amsterdam, 12*
Bergen County Historical Society, 100
Bertholf, Reverend Guiliam, 140
    travel between churches, 140
beverstivers, value of, 27
Beverwijck, development of, 96–97
Beverwyck, material culture, 170–71
Bible
    Staten-Bijbel, 144
    translation into Dutch, 144
The Bible, The Best Book, 147
Bierstadt, Albert, *Discovery of the Hudson River, ix*
black labor, 57–58
Blakelock, Ralph Albert, 228
Bland, Bartholomew, 2
Blauvelts, 120
Bodnar, John, celebrations, 301
Bok, Edward, 389
    Ladies Home Journal, 155
Borglum, Solon H., *Jacob Leisler Memorial, 422*
*Bradbury's Golden Shower of S.S. Melodies: A New
    Collection of Hymns and Tunes for the
    Sabbath School, 148*
Brinkerhoff-Christie-Paulison Homestead, *138*
Broadway Tabernacle, 150
Bronck, Jonas, 161–67
Bronck, Pieter, property belonging to Jonas, 162

Browere, Alburtus Del Orient
    *Recruiting Peter Stuyvesant's Army for the
        Recapture of Fort Casimir, 244, 245*
    Rip in the Mountains, 219
Brown, Fannie Blackwell, 381, *383*
Bull house, 121, *122*
Burrows, Edwin, Irving's Dutchman character, viii

Calvinism, 151
Campbell-Christie House, *100*
Canons of Dort, 144
capstocken, 179
Carleton, Sir Dudley, 16
Carson, 181–82
Cartagena, Nicholas, 49–51
*Cartoon of the Poughkeepsie Hudson-Fulton
    Celebration 1909, 331*
*Cartouche detail depicting Indians engaged in hunting,
    preparing food and other details, 78*
Cartouche with African figures and animals, *41*
Castello Plan, 95–96
Castello Plan, c 1665 (Adams), *95*
Castor gras, 22
Celebration of 300th anniversary at Oude Dorp
    (Gillette), *431*
celebrations, 301, 302–3
Centennial, 343–44
*The Centennial—An Old Fashioned Wind-Mill,
    Agricultural Hall, 265*
chairs
    Hudson Valley Queen Anne, 183, 185
    York, 183
Chicago World's Fair, 302
Children of Marken-Holland, 280
chocolate cups and saucers, *180*
Christian Intelligencer, 146
    Colored Camp Meeting at Tarrytown, 148–49
Christianity, Kongolese slaves and, 45–48
Christmas, 153
Christopher Billop house, 101
Church, F. S., *The New England Kitchen at the
    Centennial Exhibition, 261*
churches
    architecture, 110–11
    Colored Camp Meeting at Tarrytown, 148–49
    evangelical age, 147
    fervor of meetings, 148–49
    Finney, Reverend Charles Grandison, 147–48
    group prayer, 148
    Jesus as "feeling" savior, 153

New Measures, 147–48
origins, 139
personal testimonies, 148
Second Great Awakening, 147
Cinderella (Woodbury), *284*
city planning
Albany, 95
Beverwijck, 96–97
Castello Plan, 95
New Amsterdam, 95, 96
New York, 95
Civil War, 155
claims filed before notaries, 12
class, forks and, 181–82
classifying inventories, 180–81
Classis of Amsterdam, American Church's separation
from, 110
cleanliness, 171
estate inventory, Bancker, Elizabeth, 173
Cocceius, Johannes, 421
Coeymans House, 103
Cohen, David, agrarian settlers, 97
Colonial Dames of America, 262, 293
Colonial Revival, 386–91
colonists
Nieu Nederlandt ship, 17
Walloons, 17–18
West India Company contradictions and, 29
comforter of the sick, 139
common property, 76
communal ownership of land, 75
competition for slaves, 41
Congo (map), 42
conservatism of material culture, 182–83
Cooper, James Fenimore, 111
Couple with a Globe (Dommer), *5*
Cozzens, Frederick, *'Half Moon' and 'Clermont' in
Hudson River, New York, 1909, 311*
Cradle, 170
Cross-section of Stuyvesant Pear Tree, 263
Crucifix, early 17th century, *48*
cultural expansion, 416–19
cultural retention, 151
customs
forks and, 181–82
remaining, 418–19

*Dais of the Bronxville Westchester Historical Pageant
1909, 328*
The Dam and Damrak, Amsterdam (Berckheyde), *12*

Damen, Jan Jansen, estate inventory, 168, 170
Danckaerts, Jasper, 421
Daniel Coutant workshop, 185
Daniel Winne house, 126–27
Darley, Felix Octavius Carr
"Rip Van Winkle," *201, 202, 203, 204*
Scene from *Knickerbocker's History of New York,
189, 192, 193*
Daughters of Holland Dames, 290–91
Daughters of the American Revolution, 293
Daughters of the Cincinnati, 293
Daughters of the Revolution, 293
Davidts, Kit, estate inventory, 171
Day, Frank Miles, 118
de lay Noye, Phillippe, 342
de Rasieres, Isaack, 23, 26
de Saint-Mémin, Charles Balthazar Julien Fevret,
*View of the City and Harbour of New York,
xii*
de Victoria, Francisco, on land ownership, 79
Dean, Bashford, 377, 378, 393, 395–96
debts, estate inventory and, van Marcken, Jan
Gerritsz, 173
decent inventories, 181
Delano, Frederick (FDR's uncle), 342
Delano, Sara, *343*
marriage to James Roosevelt, 341
Delaware Bay, 13
garrison, 20
Delaware Indians. *See* Lenape
Delftware, *172*
Deming, Edwin Willard, *Peter Minuit Buying
Manhattan Island from the Indians, 79*
Dempsey, Lavinia, 290
Dewey Arch, *304*
Diagram of Dutch-American anchor-bent framing, 116
"Dis von don't count" (Bencke & Scott), Joseph
Jefferson as Rip Van Winkle, *220*
discovery
the Nineteen, 16–17
ownership and, 17
Discovery of the Hudson River (Bierstadt), *ix*
Doctrine of Discovery, 79
Dodge, Cleveland H., 323
Domingo, Francisco (Frank), 51
Dominic Johannes Weeckstein, 142
Dommer, Lambert, *Couple with a Globe, 5*
*Dudley Lawrence as Lewis Morris and Arthur
Lawrence as Frederick Philipse, Westchester
Historical Pageant, 1909, 328*

dugout shelters, 94
Duke's Laws of 1665, 416
Dutch
    contributions to history, vii
    Nazis and, 354
    population increase, 85–86
    settlements, expansion, 85–86
    word origins, vii
Dutch, Circle of (Teniers), *164*
Dutch Americans, intermarriage, 114–15
Dutch and Indians Trading Goods (Pyle), *8*
Dutch children postcard, *282*
Dutch Citizens in a Crowd (Ogden), *198*
Dutch colonial house, 121
The Dutch Colonial House (Embury), 121
Dutch colonial revival, 94
Dutch costumes, postcard, *258*
Dutch culture, survival of, 251
Dutch Domestic Furniture (Ogden), *199*
Dutch doors, 109
Dutch explorers, existing economy in Hudson Valley,
    7
Dutch Girls Parading, 1909, 320
Dutch heritage, celebrations of, 262, 264–66. *See also*
    Hudson-Fulton Celebration of 1909
Dutch Mill Restaurant, Yorktown, 309
Dutch Old Master artists, 266
Dutch Reformed Church
    Dutch identity and, 417
    New York City Dutch Reformed Church, decline
        of language and, 417
    Philipse, Frederick, 46
    Pinkster celebration, 47
    segregation in, 47
    slaves' membership, 46–47
Dutch Reformed Church, Albany, New York, *138*
Dutch Renaissance revival, 93–94, 117–20
Dutch Revolution of 1747, 425
Dutch seal ring, *162*
"Dutch Traders in New Netherlands," *86*
*Dutch Vernacular Architecture in North America
    1640–1830, 99*
Dutch Women Immigrants at Ellis Island, *308*
Dutchess County Historical Society, 348–49
Dutchman character, Washington Irving, viii
Dyckman, Fannie Fredericka, 381, 391, 394
Dyckman, Fanny Blackwell Brown, 383
Dyckman, Isaac, 381
Dyckman, Isaac Michael, 381
Dyckman, Jacobus, 380–81

Dyckman, Jan, 379
Dyckman, Mary Alice, 381, 391, *394*
Dyckman, Michael, 381
Dyckman, William, 379–81
Dyckman farmhouse, 124, 379–80
    Kingsbridge Road Near Dykemans Farm, 384
    Portrait of Jacob Dyckman, 380
Dyckman House
    Daughters of the American Revolution, 393
    Dean, Mary Alice Dyckman Dean, 391, *394*
    development of Dyckman legacy, 391–405
    The 'Dyckman House' of to-day, 405
    opening of, 377
    rebuilt, 380
    "Restored" Dyckman House, *378*
    Smith, Hannah Dyckman, 381
    Smith, James Frederick Dyckman, 381
    Welch, Fannie Fredericka Dyckman, 391, *394*
Dyckman House Museum, 393–403
    Dyckman House Dining Room, *400*
    The Dyckman House Museum and Park, 378
    The Dyckman House Park and Museum cover, *397*
    Dyckman House Parlor, *404*
    Dyckman House Southeast Bedroom, *400*
    Dyckman House Summer Kitchen, *401*

Earle, Alice Morse, on Washington Irving, 385
Eberlein, Harold, Dutch architecture, 354
economy, early
    animal skins, 7
    Dutch explorers and, 7
    furs, 7, 8, 11
    leather, 7
    material culture, 176
    trade, 10–11
The Edict of William the Testy Against Tobacco
    (Quidor), 250, *252*
Eendracht (ship), 25
Eights, James, *North Pearl Street—West Side from
    Maiden Lane North as it was in 1814, 105*
elite inventories, 181
Elizabeth, Charlotte, *147*
Embarkation from Comminipaw (Quidor), 248, 249,
    251
Embury, Aymar II, 121–23
English, Reformed Church and, 140
English rights to North American seaboard, 16
Erie Canal, opening of, 109
Esopus Wars, 87
estate inventory. *See also* material culture

Bancker, Elizabeth, 173
Bronck, Jonas, 162–67
classifying, 180–81
Damen Jan Jansen, 168, 170
Davidts, Kit, 171
debts and, van Marcken, Jan Gerritsz, 173
Philipse, Adolphe, *56*, 179–80
Quick, Willem, 167
Schut, Jan Willemsen, 167
Steenwyck, Cornelis, 177, 179
van Rensselaer, Nicholas, 177
ethnic diversity, 414
etiquette, 180
Europeans, population growth, 29
exploration, merchants' rights, 12

Fabend, Firth, 2
family coherence, 151–52
Fannie Fredericka Dyckman and Mary Alice Dyckman (Loop), *393*
farmhouses
    bedrooms, 109
    casement windows, 109
    central hall, 108
    Dutch colonial house, 121
    Dutch doors, 109
    Dyckman, 124
    Embury, Aymar II, 121–23
    evolution of, 114–15
    fireplaces, 109
    gambrel roof, 108
    groote kamer (best room), 108
    last generation of, 114
    New Netherland, 98
    transformation, English design and, 106
farming, immigrants, 115–16
fashion
    furs and, 8
    lifestyle influence, 180
"Father Knickerbocker making good Americans of the Children of All Nationalities," *390*
Fine Arts Museum Amsterdam, *278*
Finney, Reverend Charles Grandison, 147–49
fire destruction of Dutch remnants in New York City, 202
firearms, introduction of, 10
fish as currency, 27
Float No. 11: Title Car, Dutch Period, *315*
Float No. 12: The Half Moon, *316*
florin, stability of, 27

forks, 181–82
Fort Amsterdam, development, 95
Fort Nassau, 21
Fort New Amsterdam, 21
Fort Orange, 20
    development, 95
    material culture, 170–71
    trade house established, 82
Founders and Patriots of America, 293
Four Freedoms, FDR and, 362
Franklin and Eleanor Roosevelt on the south lawn of Springwood, overlooking the Hudson River Valley, *369*
Franklin D. Roosevelt Memorial Library, Hyde Park, New York, *349*
Franklin D. Roosevelt Presidential Library and Museum, Hyde Park, New York, *358*
Freedoms and Exemptions, 24–25, 80
Friendly Sons of Saint Patrick of New York, The, 259
Fulton, Robert, biographies, 313–14
Fulton Centennial Celebration Committee, establishment, 303–4
fur trade, 11
    agricultural support communities, 20
    beaver hats, 10
    as cash crop of lower Hudson estuary, 21
    changes in, 21
    decline of beaver population, 25
    economy and, 7
    fashion and, 8
    Native Americans and, 22
    New Netherland Company, 13
    Patroonship Plan, 24
    profit potential, 22–23
    profits, 25
    Provisional Orders, 19

"The Geneological Craze," 292
George Van Siclen, 272
Georgian style, 104, 105
Getty Square in Yonkers, 1909, *326*
Gibson, Robert W., 117
Gillette, Guy, Celebration of 300th anniversary at Oude Dorp, *431*
Glimpse of the Court of Honor, A, *303*
Glorious Revolution, 140
Good Housekeeping magazine advertisement, "*Mrs. Brookfield Van Rensselaer Smokes Camels*," *299*, *333*
Governors Island, 20

"Great Negro Plot," 55
Gregory, Eliot, 292–93
groote kamer (best room), 108
Grotius, Hugo, on property, 76, 77
Grumet, Robert, 81
guilders, stability of, 27
Gunston Hall study, 181–82

H-bent houses, 98–99
half-freedom of slaves, 38
The 'Half-Moon' (Alexander), 306
*'Half-Moon' and 'Clermont' in Hudson River,
    New York, 1909* (Cozzens), 311
Half Moon and Clermont on the Hudson (Hunt),
    347
The 'Half Moon' at Yonkers, 1909, 326
"Half Moon," "Claremont," and "Robert Fulton," 1909
    (Norton), 331
The Half Moon Ramming the Clermont, 312
*The 'Half Moon' (with Hudson River Day Line steamer
    Hendrick Hudson)* (Ogden), 313
Hamilton, Alexander, 159
Hardenbroeck, Margaret (Philipse), 38
Harper's Weekly, on architecture, 118–19
Hartgers, Joost, *t' Fort nieuw Amsterdam op
    de Manhatans* (The Hartgers View of
    Manhattan c. 1626), 85
Harvey, George, 112
hats, pelts for, 22
Hazlitt, William, 191–92, 194
Headless Horseman in Pursuit of Ichabod Crane
    (Jenkins), 230
The Headless Horseman Pursuing Ichabod Crane
    (Quidor), 229
Heath, William, *Peter Stuyvesant's Army Entering
    New Amsterdam*, 211
Heidelberg Catechism, 146
Hendrik Hudson (with map of the Hudson River)
    (Wyeth), 412
*Henrik Hudson Entering New York Harbor, September
    11, 1609* (Moran), 74
"Henry Hudson got many furs from the Indians . . ."
    (Shrader), 22
Henry Hudson Memorial Bridge, 323
*"Here they used to sit in the shade through a long
    lazy summer's day"* (Wyeth), 240
heritage societies
    founding of, 262
    pilgrimages, 258
    social culture and, 259

Het West Indisch Huys (West India Company House),
    30
Hill, Spuyten Duyvil, 323–24
*Historic Philipse Manor Hall decorated for the
    Hudson-Fulton Celebration in Yonkers, 1909*,
    325
*History of New York from the Beginning of the World
    to the End of the Dutch Dynasty, A* (Irving),
    111, 227
Hoagland-Durling farm, 126
Holland
    Amsterdam, 281–82
    featured in *New York Times*, 266
    Marken, 279, 281
    travel to, 269–71
Holland, John Joseph, A View of Broad Street, Wall
    Street and the City Hall, New York, New
    York, 104
Holland Mania, 120, 344–46, 389
    Roosevelt, Franklin Delano and, 352–53
Holland Society Chair of the Memorial Committee,
    290
Holland Society of New York, 120
    1888 trip to Holland, 257, 271–93
        Amsterdam, 281–83
        George Van Siclen, 272, 288
        Marken, 279–81
        Procession in Leiden, 288
        Third of October Society, 288
    Israels, Lehman, 283, 285, 287
    Roosevelt, Franklin Delano, 120, 347–48
    Roosevelt, Theodore, 269–70
    scholarly pursuits, 271
    social culture and, 259
    social pursuits, 271
    Van Duyn, Dr. John, 273, 274
Holland Trust, George Van Siclen and, 289–90
home, idea of, 360–62
Home Life in Colonial Days (Earle), 385
households, in New Netherland, 161–75
Howland, Rebecca Brien, marriage to James
    Roosevelt, 341
Hubbard house, 124
Hudson, Henry, biographies, 313
Hudson-Fulton Celebration of 1909, 301–2
    Albany, 334
    attendance, 317
    Carnival Parade, 319–20
    Cartoon of the Poughkeepsie Hudson-Fulton
        Celebration 1909, 331

Catskill, 334
celebration beginning, 311–12
civics lesson of, 309–10
Clermont, 312–13, 314, 326
commercial, rejection of, 306–7
conclusion, 335
cultural centers and, 316–17
day of prayer and reflection, 314–15
Dobbs Ferry, 327, 329
Dodge, Cleveland H., 323
Dutch Girls Parading, 320
early planning, 311
Festival at Mulberry Bend, 321
Float No. 11: Title Car, Dutch Period, 315
Float No. 12: The Half Moon, 316
Fulton Centennial Celebration Committee, 303–4
German societies, 315
Half Moon, 312–13, 326
Half Moon, Hudson-Fulton 1909, 335
"Half Moon," "Claremont," and "Robert Fulton,"
     1909 (Norton), *331*
Hastings, 327, 329
Henry Hudson Memorial Bridge, 323
Henry Hudson Monument, 322–23
Historic Philipse Manor Hall decorated for the
     Hudson-Fulton Celebration in Yonkers,
     1909, 325
Historical Parade, 315
historical societies and, 316–17
Hudson Tri-Centennial Commission, 304
Inaugural Naval Parade, 311–12, 314, 326
Irvington, 327, 329
Maquette for the Henry Hudson Monument, 1909,
     321
military parade, 318–19
Model for Hudson Fulton Monument (Konti), *318*
monuments and, 317
museums and, 316–17
New York City and, 305–6
Newburgh, 329–30
Newburgh Ceremonies: Arrival of Naval Parade,
     October 1, 1909, 330
North Tarrytown, 327, 329
official program, *302*
Old New York, 307–8
Palisades Interstate Park, 324–25
Parade in Getty Square at McKenzie Building, *324*
postcard, *310*
Poughkeepsie, 333–34
primary schools and, 320–21

race and, 317
schoolchildren and, 316
second week proposed, 324
statutes and, 317
Tarrytown, 327, 329
Yonkers celebration, 326–27
Hudson-Fulton-Champlain quadricentennial, 1
Hudson-Fulton Commission, membership, 304
Hudson-Fulton Postcard with Schedule of Events, 307
Hudson-Fulton Poster Postcard, 305
Hudson Memorial Monument, Riverside Drive, New
     York, 1910–1920, 322
Hudson River, preservation of, Charles E. Hughes
     and, 325–26
Hudson River Museum, Westchester Year of History
     displays, 3
Hudson Tri-Centennial Commission, 304
Hudson Valley Queen Anne chair, 183, 185
Hughes, Charles E., 325
Huguenot Society of American, 262
Hunt, Leigh, *Half Moon and Clermont on the Hudson,*
     347

Ichabod Crane at a Ball at Van Tassel's Mansion
     (Quidor), *231, 235*
Ichabod Crane Flying from the Headless Horseman
     (Quidor), *226*
Ichabod Crane Romancing (Keller), *233*
immoveable property, 161
In Old New York (Janvier), 385
Indians
     fur trade and, 22
     land
          access to, 78
          acquisition of by Dutch, 80–84
          relationship with, 73–75
          social structure and, 78
          usufructuary privilege, 78
     settlements, shifting, 80
     trade and, 22
     wampum and, 26
inflation, 27–28
Irving, Washington, viii
     as amateur folklorist, 201–2
     American amnesia as theme, 202
     architecture, 112–14
     attraction to Dutch, 201–2
     Author's Apology, 215–19
     Bracebridge Hall, 191
     comedy, language and, 208

Irving, Washington *(continued)*
    Crayon, Geoffrey, 196
    democracy, 212
    Dutch maidens' petticoat length, 235
    Dutchman character, viii
    Dutchness of New York, 137
    Esopus Dutch Tour, 137
    essayist, 191
    European audience, 191
    expatriates and, 200–201
    exterior view of house, *112*
    fantasy of old New York, 206
    father and, 199
    as first professional writer, 191
    historical analysis, 385
    A History of New York, 194–95, 346
    A History of New York from the Beginning of the
        World to the End of the Dutch Dynasty,
        111, 195, 227
        apology to readers, 209–10
        creation myths and, 207–208
        epigrams, 208
        historical events, 214
        layout of Manhattan streets, 214
        relationship to readers, 209
        revisions by author, *220*
        on Stuyvesant, Peter, 209
        as wild history, 214
    history-writing, political satire and, 213–14
    Kieft, William, death of, 209
    Knickerbocker, Diedrich, 196–97, 227
        being in on the joke, 208
        doctrine of progress, 211
        inner exile, 199
        New Amsterdam, 207–8
        reasons for writing history, 197–98
    Knickerbocker tales, 112
    Knickerbocker's History of New York, viii, 383
    The Life of George Washington, 384
    Mcdowell, Tremaine, 215
    new viewpoint, *220*
    New York literati and, 212
    the patriarch of American literature, 221
    Quidor, John and, 223–24
    "Rip Van Winkle," 194
    Salmagundi, 207
    Scott, Sir Walter and, 112
    as secular rationalist, 194
    The Sketch Book of Geoffrey Crayon, Gent., 191
    sleep and, 202–3

Sleepy Hollow, reasons for choosing, 203
Stuyvesant, Peter, Kieft, William and, 213
Sunnyside (home), 112–14
sympathy for the poor, 212
Tales of a Traveler, 191
"The Legend of Sleepy Hollow," 112, 194, *200*
    Ichabod's horse, 227–28
travel writer, 191
Van Buren, Martin and, 137
Williams, Stanley, 215
Isaac Michael Dyckman (Ritchie), 382
Isidore Konti and crew installing his Hudson Fulton
    Monument, Yonkers, 1924, 319
The Island at the Center of the World (Shorto), 1, 125,
    309
Israels, Josef, *A Ray of Sunshine, 268*
Israels, Lehman, 283, 285, 287

Jacob Leisler Memorial, *422*
jambless hearth, 101
Jan Martense Schenck house, 101
    modernization, 123
Janvier, Thomas, *In Old New York,* 385
Jarvis, John Wesley, 224
Jenkins, George Washington Allston, *Headless*
    Horseman in Pursuit of Ichabod Crane, 230,
    231–232
Jerome C. Bull House, *122*
Jersey Dutch, 154
Johannes Decker house, 99, *100*
John Brinckerhoff house, *351*
joint-stock companies, 17
Jonker's land, 1
Jurriaens, Teuntje, 162

Kammen, Michael, 207
kapstock (cloak rack), 173
kas/kassen, 183, 185
kast, *184*
Keller, Arthur Ignatius, *Ichabod Crane Romancing,*
    233, 234
kerck stooff (church stove), 173
Kieft, Willem, 383
    war, 86–87
Kikongo terminology, Kongolese Christians and,
    45–46
Kingsbridge Road Near Dykemans Farm, 384
kinship networks, 152
Knickerbocker, Diedrich, 196–97, 227
    being in on the joke, 208

inner exile, 199
    New Amsterdam, 207–8
    reasons for writing history, 197–98
Knickerbocker Holiday, *197*
Knickerbocker Holiday, 196
Knickerbocker's Kitchen, A (Quidor), 251, *254*
'Knickerbocker Kitchen' *a panel featured in*
    Metropolitan Sanitary Fair, 387
Knickerbocker Tea Party, A (Quidor), 251, *253*
Knickerbocker's History of New York (Irving), viii
Koch, Cynthia, 3
kolff (golf club), 173
Kongolese slaves, 39, 41–42, 44
    Christian names, 53
    Christianity and, 45
        Christian symbols, 47–48
        Kikongo terminology, 45–46
    religion of, 46
    skills learned, 44
Konti, Isidore, Model for Hudson Fulton Monument,
    318
kruiskozijn, 103
Kunz, Dr. George Frederick, World's Fair proposal,
    301

Ladies Home Journal, 155
Laidlie, Archibald, 144
Lamb, Charles, 191
land
    acquiring, 79
    boundaries, 79–80
    communal ownership, 75
    Doctrine of Discovery and, 79
    Indians
        access to, 78
        acquisition of by Dutch, 80–84
    Indians' relationship with, 73–75
        social structure and, 78
        usufructuary privilege, 78
    Mahican, purchase of, 83
    ownership, 75
    rights of, 75
    selling, trading goods and, 83
    shifting settlements, 80
    trade and, 83
    use right, 75
Landing of Henrik Hudson (Weir), 75
language, 143–44, 151, 182–83
    Canons of Dort, 144
    decline of, 417
        influence of, 418
        Jersey Dutch, 154
        Post-Acta, 144
        Reformed Church, 146
        sacredness of Dutch, 144
        Staten-Bijbel, 144
        Synod of Dort, 144
        translation of Bible into Dutch, 144
leather, economy and, 7
Leendert Bronck house, 99, *100*
"The Legend of Sleepy Hollow," 194, *195, 200*
        artistic expressions of Ichabod's meeting Headless
            Horseman, 227
        Ichabod's horse, 227–28
Leisler, Jacob, 423; memorial, *422*
Leisler's Rebellion, 140, 423
Lenape, 7
Lennox, Charlotte, on Dutch cleanliness during
        childbirth, 171–72
lepelbort (spoon rack), 173
Leyendecker, J. C., *Young Dutch Girl—Study, 292*
lidded jars, *172*
The Life of George Washington (Irving), 384–85
Livingston, John Henry, 144
Livingston, Robert, 424–25
localism, 415
Long Island, population growth of Europeans, 29
Loop, Henry A., *Fannie Fredericka Dyckman and*
        Mary Alice Dyckman, 393
Lopate, Philip, 2
Loudon, Jonkheer J., Hudson-Fulton Celebration of
        1909, 308–9
Lutherans, Reformed Church and, 140

Mahicans
    land, purchase of, 83
    war with Mohawks, 21
Maika, Dennis, 2
Maison du Gouverneur Hollandais a Albani Etats-
        Unis (View in Albany, House of the First
        Dutch Governors) (Milbert), *413*
maize, as currency, 27
Manhattan
    de Rasieres, Isaack on, 23
    early growth, xi
    layout of streets, 214
    purchase of, 21, 80
    "upstate Manhattan," 379
    urbanization and, 116
    van Wassenaer, Nicholaes on, 23

manners, 180
    forks and, 181–82
Manor House of the Philipsburg Upper Mills with
        tulip bed, *115*
manorial system, 23
maps
    Belgii Novi, Angliae Novae et Partis Virginiae
            (Map of New Netherland, New England
            and parts of Virginia), *4*
    The Castello Plan c. 1665, *95*
    Central Europe, including The Netherlands, *259*
    Congo, 42
    *New Netherland, Which is Now Called New York
            and New England and Part of Virginia, 77*
    Philipsburg Manor, *40*
Maquette for the Henry Hudson Monument, 1909, 321
Margaret Philipse (Wollaston), *37*
Marken, Holland, 279, 281
Marken Bedroom (Penfield), *281*
Marken-Holland, 280
markets, Wallabout Bay, 115
marrying patterns, Reformed clergy, 151
Mary Philipse (Wollaston), *62*
master/slave relationship, 35
    naming practices and, 58
    Philipse, Adolph, 57
    Philipse, Frederick, 51–52
    Philipse, Frederick II, 57
material culture, 175–76. *See also* estate inventory
    armchair, *174*
    Beverwyck, 170–71
    capstocken, 179
    chairs
            Hudson Valley Queen Anne, 183, 185
            York, 183
    chocolate cups and saucers, *180*
    conservatism of, 182–83
    cradle, *170*
    economy, 176
    forks, 181–82
    Fort Orange, 170–71
    immoveable property, 161
    kapstock (cloak rack), 173
    kas/kassen, 183, 185
    kast, *184*
    kerck stooff (church stove), 173
    kolff (golf club), 173
    lepelbort (spoon rack), 173
    lidded jars, *172*
    moveable property, 161

pair of candlesticks, *181*
platter with armorial decoration representing the
        province of Overysel, *175*
salt cellar, *176*
sconce, *178*
seal ring, *162*
spoon rack, *169*
spoons, 182
stoelen, *177*
tric-trac table, 173
two-handled cup, *179*
wall clock with nautical scenes, *166*
Matteson, Tompkins H., *Santa's Workshop*, 260
May, Cornelis Jacobsz, *Nieu Nederlandt* (ship), 19
McChesney, James, 185
Melchers, Julius Garibaldi, *The Pilots*, 344
*Memorial to Henry Hudson: The Arrival of the Halve
        Moon* stained glass, 289
Men Smoking, 164
mercantile pursuits, 421
metal items, 10–11
Milbert, Jacques Gérard, *Maison du Gouverneur
        Hollandais a Albani Etats-Unis* (View
        in Albany, House of the First Dutch
        Governors), *413*
militias, 423–24
Miller, William Rickarby, *The Mill Pond, Sleepy
        Hollow*, 229; *Old Dutch Church at Sleepy
        Hollow*, 45
Milne, Reverend John, commentary on Dutch family
        in 1744, 159–61
Minuit, Pieter, 21
Model for Hudson Fulton Monument (Konti), *318*
modern travel industry, 267, 269
Mohawks, war with Mahicans, 21
The Money Diggers (Quidor), *235*
Montanus, Arnoldus, *Novum Amsterodamum* (New
        Amsterdam) as it looked in 1651, *28*
Moran, Edward, *Henrik Hudson Entering the New
        York Harbor, September 11, 1609, 74*
Mortimer, C., Cartoon of the Poughkeepsie Hudson-
        Fulton Celebration 1909, *331*
Mossell, Thijs, 50
moveable property, 161
Mrs. Kilaen Van Rensselaer (Watson), *299, 333*
Munsee, sale of land to Dutch, 81–82
murder of family by slaves, 38

naming practices with slaves, 58, 59, 61
National Daughters of the American Revolution, 262

National Society of New England Women, 292
National Society of the Colonial Dames of America, 262
Native Americans. *See* Indians
Netherlands
    citizens' trade restrictions, 14
    tours to, 257–58
New Amsterdam
    development of, 96
    planning, 95
New Amsterdam, a Small Town in New Holland in North America, on the Island of Manhattan (Schenk), *18*
New Amsterdam History Center, 126
New Brunswick Theological Seminary, 146, 151
New England Kitchen at the Centennial Exhibition (Church), *261*
New England Society in the City of New York, 259
New Measures, 147–48
    Reformed Dutch Church and, 149
New Netherland, ix
    agrarian presence, 97
    agrarian settlers, 97
    architecture, 1609, 94–103
    boundaries, 12–13
    Dutch households in, 161–75
    farmhouses, 98
    Freedoms and Exemptions, 24–25
    naming, 12
    New World Dutch barn, 99
    population growth of Europeans, 29
    tobacco, 164–65
New Netherland, Which is Now Called New York and New England and Part of Virginia, 77
New Netherland Company
    competition, elimination of, 13
    extension of patent, 13
    formation of, 12
    Fort Nassau, 21
    fur trade, 13
    May, Cornelis Jacobsz, 19–20
    private traders, 16
New Salem development, 123
New World Dutch barn, 94, 99
    increase in interest, 124
New York City
    boroughs, newly consolidated, 305
    city planning, 95
    conspiracy to destroy city, slave uprising, 55–57

fires in 1741, 55
    as immigrant center of colonies, xi
    as largest city in United States, 305
    robberies in 1741, 55
    slave importation rates, 57
    as spectacle, 305–6
    as world city, 321
New York City Slave Auction (Pyle), *49*
"The New York Conspiracy," 55
Newburgh Ceremonies: Arrival of Naval Parade, October 1, 1909, 330
Nieu Nederlandt (ship)
    colonists and, 17
    May, Cornelis Jacobsz, 19–20
North American animals, *11*
North Pearl Street—West Side from Maiden Lane North as it was in 1814 (Eights), *105*
Norton, William E., *"Half Moon," "Claremont," and "Robert Fulton," 1909, 331*
Noten (Nut Island), 20
Novi Belgii Novaeque Angliae (New Netherland and New England), *xi*
Novum Amsterodamum (New Amsterdam) as it looked in 1651 (Montanus), *28*
Nzinga, João I, baptism of, 45

Office of the Overseer, Philipsburg Manor, *61*
Officer and Laughing Girl (Vermeer), *9*
Official Program of the Hudson-Fulton Celebration 1909, *302*
Ogden, Henry A.
    Dutch Citizens in a Crowd, 198
    Dutch Domestic Furniture, 199
Ogden, Henry Alexander, *The 'Half Moon' (with Hudson River Day Line steamer Hendrick Hudson), 313*
Ogsbury Barn, 103
Old Dutch Church, Sleepy Hollow, *94*
Old Dutch Church, Tarrytown, *141*
Old Dutch Church at Phillipsburg
    building of, dam washout, 44
    processional order, 47
Old Dutch Church at Sleepy Hollow (Miller), *45*
old-fashioned inventories, 181
Old Man Scaling Fish (Van Brekelenkam), *160*
Old Master artists, 266
Old New York, 385
The Old Pear-Tree Planted by Governor Stuyvesant, 263
Old Queen's (Queens College), *143*

The Opening of the National Synod at Dordrecht, the Netherlands, November 13, 1618, 145
Orangists, 421
Oranje Boom (ship), 20

Pach Bros., Joseph Jefferson as Rip Van Winkle, *221*
pair of candlesticks, seventeenth century, *181*
Palisades Interstate Park, 324–25
Panetta, Roger, 2
Parade for Kaiser Wilhelm's son at Briarcliff Manor 1909, *329*
Parade in Getty Square at McKenzie Building during Hudson-Fulton Celebration 1909, *324*
patents for land, 415–16
Patroonship Plan, 23–25
Paulding, James Kirke, 111
Peach War, 87
Penfield, Edward, *Marken Bedroom, 281; Windmills, 264*
Pentecost celebration, 47
Perkins, George W., 324–25
personal knife and fork set, 182
Peter Minuit Buying Manhattan Island from the Indians (Deming), *79*
Peter Stuyvesant and the Cobbler (Quidor), *248*
Peter Stuyvesant Watching Festivities on the Battery (Quidor), *246, 247*
Peter Stuyvesant's Army Entering New Amsterdam (Heath), *211*
Peter Stuyvesant's Voyage Up the Hudson River (Quidor), *248, 249*
petticoat length, Washington Irving and, 235
Philadelphia Centennial Exposition, 387
Philipsburg
    Old Dutch Church, building of, dam washout, 44
    slaves
        ethnicities of, 52
        reasons for purchasing, 60
Philipsburg Manor
    from the air, *43*
    "Dutchiana," *408*
    early view of restoration and costumed guides, *405*
    Pinkster Festival, *125*
    reinterpretation, 125
Philipse, Adolph, 39, 56–60
Philipse, Adolphe, 179–80, 182
Philipse, Catherine, 58–59
Philipse, Frederick, 38
    as active slave trader, 38–39
    Dutch Reformed religion, 46

Last Will and Testament of, 52–55
master/slave relationship, 51–52
slaves
    Cartagena, Nicholas, 49–51
    Domingo, Francisco (Frank), 51
    Madagascar, 49
    Marramita, 51
    perception of people enslaved, 44
    runaway slave, 35
Philipse, Frederick II, 39
    master/slave relationship, 57
    slaves, 59–60, 63
Philipse, Frederick III, 38
    slaves, sale of, 59–60
Philipse, Mary, *62*
Philipse family, slaves and, 39
Philipse Manor Hall, bicentennial, 264, *266*
Phillipsburg Manor Garden, *43*
Piece of Wampum, 25
Pieter Bronck house, *100*
Pieter Claesen Wyckoff House (Wyckoff Farmhouse Museum), 116
The Pilots (Melchers), *344*
Pinkster celebration, 47, 125–26
    Philipsburg Manor Festival, *125*
Piwonka, Ruth, 2
platter with armorial decoration representing the province of Overysel, *175*
political divisions, 424
political factionalism, 421
political geography, legacy of, 411–16
political legacy, 420–21, 423–25
population growth, 29, 83
Portrait of Adolphus Philipse, 36
Portrait of Adriaen Van Der Donck (Vanderwelden), *76*
Portrait of Ann Stuyvesant (Wyeth), *291*
Portrait of Jacob Dyckman, 380
Post-Acta, 144
postcards
    Dutch children, 282
    Dutch costumes, 261
    Getty Square in Yonkers, 1909, 326
    The 'Half Moon' at Yonkers, 1909, 326
    Hudson-Fulton Celebration 1909, *310*
    Hudson-Fulton Postcard with Schedule of Events, 307
    Hudson-Fulton Poster Postcard, 305
Poughkeepsie, Hudson-Fulton Celebration 1909, 333–34

President Roosevelt making his final radio broadcast of the 1936 campaign from the study in his Hyde Park home, *368*

presidents with Dutch heritage, 339

Princess Juliana, Roosevelt, Franklin Delano and, 354–55

Princess Wilhelmina, 287, *356*

private traders, 16

Procession in Leiden, *288*

Proposed Coat-of-Arms for New Amsterdam, New Netherlands, 19

Protestant Holy Week, 150

Provisional Orders, 18–19

public property, 78

Purchase of Manhattan/Hudson-Fulton Parade, Pleasant Plains, N.Y., 335

Purchase of White Plains, 81

Pyle, Howard
    Along the Canal in Old Manhattan, 388
    Anthony Van Corlear, The Trumpeter of New Amsterdam, 212
    Arrival of Stuyvesant in New Amsterdam, x
    Dutch and Indians Trading Goods, 8
    New York City Slave Auction, 22, 49
    Slaves at Jamestown Being Unloaded from a Dutch Man-of-War, 15

Queen Wilhelmina, *357*
    Roosevelt, Franklin Delano and, 355

Queens College, 143

Quick, Willem, estate inventory, 167

Quidor, John, 223
    Antony Van Corlear Brought into the Presence of Peter Stuyvesant, 237
    artistic maturity of, 225
    A Battle Scene from Knickerbocker's History of New York, 243, 244–45
    The Edict of William the Testy Against Tobacco, 250, 252
    Embarkation from Communipaw, 248, 249, 251
    The Headless Horseman Pursuing Ichabod Crane, 228, 229, 230–31
    historical information, 224
    A History of New York (Irving), 243–44
    Ichabod Crane at a Ball at Van Tassel's Mansion, 231, 232–33, 235
    Ichabod Crane Flying from the Headless Horseman, 226
    Irving, Washington and, 223–24
    tales of Dutch New York, 225

John Baur's rediscovery of work, 227
    Keift, William, in paintings, 250
    A Knickerbocker Tea Party, 251, 253
    Knickerbockers and, 225, 227
    A Knickerbocker's Kitchen, 251, 254
    laziness of Irving's Dutch, 239
    The Money Diggers, 234, 235
    move to Illinois, 225
    Peter Stuyvesant and the Cobbler, 248
    Peter Stuyvesant Watching Festivities on the Battery, 246, 247
    Peter Stuyvesant's Voyage Up the Hudson River, 248, 249
    The Return of Rip Van Winkle, 239, 241, 241–42, 386
    "Rip Van Winkle," as favored source, 227
    Rip Van Winkle and, 253–54
    Rip Van Winkle and His Companions at the Inn Door of Nicholas Vedder, 237, 238
    stereotypes of Dutch, 223
    Stuyvesant, Peter, appearing in paintings, 246–49
    Tavern Scene, 242, 242–43
    "The Legend of Sleepy Hollow"
        as favored source, 227
        Ichabod meeting Headless Horseman, 226, 227
        Ichabod's horse, 227–28
    Tom Walker's Flight, 232
    The Vigilant Stuyvesant's Wall Street Gate, 245, 246
    Voyage to Hellgate from Cummunipaw, 249, 250
    Wolfert's Will, 234, 236
    Wyeth, N. C. and, 239

raadpensionaris, 421

Raritan River valley, 97

Ray of Sunshine, A (Israels), *268*

Recruiting Peter Stuyvesant's Army for the Recapture of Fort Casimir (Browere), *244, 245*

Reformed Church in America, 137, 155

Reformed Church of Tappan, *91, 141*

Reformed Dutch Church, 137
    American Protestantism and, 153
    American Sunday School Union, 146
    Amsterdam Classis, 140, 143
    Canons of Dort, 144
    change to Reformed Church in America, 155
    Christian Intelligencer, 146
    Coetus, 143

Reformed Dutch Church (continued)
    Conferentie, 143
    conservatives and, 143
    and the corner of Wall Street and Main Street,
        Kingston, New York c. 1916, 158
    disapproval of Finney, 149
    Dutch American culture and, 150
    English and, 140
    Glorious Revolution, 140
    growth of, 150
    Jesus as "feeling" savior, 153
    language, 146
        translation of bible into Dutch, 144
    Leisler's Rebellion, 140
    Lutherans and, 140
    modernization of, 150
    New Measures and, 149
    organization, Bertholf, Reverend Guiliam,
        140
    origins, 140
    as outpost of Dutch country, 154
    Post-Acta, 144
    progressives and, 140, 143
    shortage of ministers, 140
    society's modernizing influences, 146
    States Bible and, 146
    Sunday school, 146
    Synod of Dort, 144
Reformed Dutch Church, Fishkill, New York,
    157
Reformed Protestant Dutch Church, 139
religion
    Dutch Reformed religion, 46
        Pinkster celebration, 47
        segregation and, 47
    of Kongolese slaves, 46
    Old Dutch Church, processional order, 47
    omens, 46
    Roman Catholicism, fear of conspiracy, 46
    slaves, Dutch Reformed Church, 46–47
    Tappan Reformed Church, segregation in, 47
Rensselaerswyck manor, 126–27
Residence of E.S.F. Arnold, M.D. (Reformed
    Church), 154
"Restored" Dyckman House c. 1916, 378
The Return of Rip Van Winkle (Quidor), 239, 241,
    241–42, 386
Reynolds, Helen Wilkinson, 120–21
rights of land, 75
rights of merchants to explore, 12

Rink, Oliver, 2
Rip in the Mountains (Browere), 219
Rip Van Winkle, 194
    Blakelock, Ralph Albert, 228
    cover illustration (Wyeth), 205
    Groups of Statuary by John Rogers, 215
    illustrations from (Wyeth), 206
    as played by Joseph Jefferson, 216, 217
    set of drawings (Darley), 201, 202, 203, 204
    transition of Dutch culture, 237
Rip Van Winkle and His Companions at the Inn Door
    of Nicholas Vedder (Quidor), 237, 238
Rip Van Winkle (Bensell), 218
Rip Van Winkle (Pach Bros), Joseph Jefferson as,
    221
Rip Van Winkle Returned (Rogers), 214
Ritchie, A. H., Isaac Michael Dyckman, 382
Rockland County, New York, 97
Rodriquez, Jan, 50
Rogers, John
    Groups of Statuary ("Rip Van Winkle"), 215
    Rip Van Winkle Returned, 214
Roman Catholicism
    fear of conspiracy, 46
    Kongolese slaves and, 45
Rondout valley, 97
roof forms, 101
Roosevelt, Eleanor
    Eleanor Roosevelt and Franklin Roosevelt
        hosting the Dutchess County History
        Society fall "pilgrimage" to Roosevelt
        home, 348
    elections, 367
    on Franklin Roosevelt, 346
    "My Day," 367
    at WPA nursery school for African American
        children, Des Moines, Iowa, 366
Roosevelt, Franklin Delano, 3
    childhood pencil drawing of The Flying
        Dutchman at anchor, 346
    civic responsibility, 365
    collections, 349
    connection of homes, 363
    Dutch ancestry, 339–40
    Dutch colonial architecture, 350–51, 353–54
        re-creating in buildings, 359–60
    Dutch colonial history and, 350
    on Dutch colonial style and use of stone, 359
    Dutch family Bible, 354, 355
    Dutchess County Historical Society, 348–49

Eleanor Roosevelt and Franklin Roosevelt
hosting the Dutchess County History
Society fall "pilgrimage" to Roosevelt
home, *348*
Eleanor Roosevelt on, 346
elections, 367
Four Freedoms, 362
Franklin and Eleanor on the south lawn of
Springwood, *369*
Franklin D. Roosevelt Memorial Library, Hyde
Park, New York, *349*
Franklin D. Roosevelt Presidential Library and
Museum, Hyde Park, New York, *358*
getting his Dutch up, 356
Holland Mania and, 343–44, 352–53
Holland Society, 120, 347–48
Hudson River home, 368, 370
The John Brinckerhoff house, *351*
lessons of history, 352
making final radio broadcast of 1936 campaign
from study in his Hyde Park home, *368*
Mrs. Myer, 365
offer to transport Princess Juliana to U.S. during
WWII, 354
post office design, 358
presidential library, 349–50
Princess Juliana and, 354–55
Queen Wilhelmina and, 355
references to Dutch heritage, 356–58
Roosevelt addressing a church fair at the
invitation of the Ladies Aid Society of
the Plattekill Dutch Reformed Church,
364
school design, 358
Scottish heritage, 355
Springwood, *363*
thesis on history of Roosevelt family, 342
Top Cottage, *353*
Val-Kill Stone Cottage, *352*
writing projects, 350
Roosevelt, Isaac, 341
Roosevelt, James
FDR's father, marriage to Sara Delano, 341
FDR's half-brother, 341
Roosevelt, Sara Delano, *343*
Roosevelt, Theodore
Dutch ancestry, 339–40
Holland Society and, 269–70
Theodore Roosevelt in his White House Study, *345*
trip to Holland, 346

Roosevelt family
history of, 339–40
Jewish background, 339
Roosevelt Home Club, 356
Ruijter (ship), capture of, 20
Rutgers College, 146, 151
Rutgers University, 143
Rybczynski, Witold, Dutch as originators of idea as
home as place of comfort, 360

The Sabbath in Puritan New England (Earle), 385
Saint David's Society of the State of New York, 259
Saint George's Society of New York, 259
Saint Nicholas Society, 259
Saint Nicholas (Weir), *260*
salt cellar, early eighteenth century, *176*
Santa's Workshop (Matteson), 260
satirizing of Dutch, 382–85
Sawyer, Sean, 2
Scene from *Knickerbocker's History of New York*
(Darley), *189, 192, 193*
Schaats, Bartholomew, two-handled cup, *179*
Schenk, Peter, *New Amsterdam, a Small Town in New
Holland in North America, on the Island of
Manhattan,* 18
Schut, Jan Willemsen, estate inventory, 167
sconce, early eighteenth century, *178*
Scott, Sir Walter, 112
Scudder, Reverend John, 151
Second Great Awakening, 147
segregation of slaves and whites, 48
settlements, shifting, 80
sewant, 26–27
sewantstivers, value of, 27
*Sextette learn Dutch Folk Dances as taught on the
Recreational Agencies Program in New York
City,* 336
Shorto, Russell, *The Island at the Center of the World,*
125, 309
Simple Rhymes for Little Children, 148
Sketch of Dyckman House (Bandel), *381*
slavery, 2. *See also* Africans
African burial ground, 48
ages of slaves, 54–55
Barbadian slaves, 52
blacks banished from colony, 56
blacks burned at stake, 56
blacks hanged, 56
Cartagena, Nicholas, 49–51
competition for slaves, 41

slavery *(continued)*
    Domingo, Francisco (Frank), 51
    ethnicities of Philipsburg's, 52
    half-freedom, 38
    importance of in colonial North, 38
    importation rates in New York City, 57
    Kongolese slaves, 39, 41–42, 44, 53
    Marramita, 51
    master/slave relationship, 35, 51–52
    murder of family by slaves, 38
    naming of slaves, 59, 61
    naming practices and, 58
    New York City Slave Auction (Pyle), 49
    Philipse, Adolph, 56–58
    Philipse, Catherine, 58–59
    Philipse, Frederick, 35, 52–54
    Philipse, Frederick and, 39
    segregation, 48
    slave burial ground, 48
    slave insurrection in New York City, 38
    slaves in Dutch Reformed Church, 46–47
    slaves in Tappan Reformed Church, 47
    Upper Mills area, 39
    uprising in New York City, 55–57
    West India Company slaves, 38
Slaves at Jamestown Being Unloaded from a Dutch
    Man-of-War (Pyle), 15
Sleepy Hollow, 195
Smith, Hannah Dyckman, 381
Smith, James Frederick Dyckman, 381
Sneek, Zeilvereeniging, *From Yearbook of the Holland*
    Society of New York, 285
social life, 151–52
Society of Mayflower Descendants, 293
Society of the Daughters of Holland Dames, 120,
    290
Sons of the American Revolution, 293
spoon rack, *169*
spoon rack (*lepelbort*), *173*
spoons, 182
Springwood, Roosevelt home in Hyde Park, *363*
Staatsfactie, 421
Staatsgezinde, 421
stadholder, 421
Starna, William, 2
state government, relocation of, 109
Staten-Bijbel (States Bible), 144, 146
States General, rights of merchants to explore, 12
Steenwyck, Cornelis, 176, 177, 179
stereotypes of Dutch, John Quidor and, 223

Stevens, John, 99
stoelen, 177
Stone Farmhouse (Bacon), 234
Storck, Abraham, *View of the IJ Before Amsterdam*,
    13
Stott, Annette, Holland Mania, 120, 257
Stuyvesant, Peter
    Kieft, William and, 213
    pear tree
        cross-section, *263*
        destruction, 262
        lithograph, *263*
        stereograph, *264*
Stuyvesant, Petrus, 175
Sunday school, 146
Suydham, Reverend J. H., 300th anniversary
    proposal, 301
Synod of Dort, 144
    Calvinism of, 151
    departures from, 153
    The Opening of the National Synod at Dordrecht,
        the Netherlands, November 13, 1618, 145

t' Fort nieuw Amsterdam op de Manhatens (The
    Hartgers View of Manhattan c 1626),
    Hartgers, *85*
Tappan Reformed Church, segregation in, 47
Tavern Scene (Quidor), *242,* 242–43
tea, cultural impact of, 252–53
Teniers II, David, *Dutch, Circle of, 164*
textiles
    Bronck, Jonas, 165, 167
    Vernu, Jacob, 167
Theodore Roosevelt in his White House Study,
    345
Third of October Society, 288
Thorpe, Thomas Bangs, student of John Quidor,
    224
Tile Picture of a Painting by Franz Hals, 267
timber as currency, 27
tobacco
    as currency, 27
    raising, New Netherland, 164–65
tolerance
    origin of concept, ix
    Shorto on, 1
Top Cottage, *353*
trade, 10–11. *See also* WIC (West India Company)
    English rights to North American seaboard, 16
    Fort Orange, 83

furs, 11
    metal items, 10–11
    Native Americans and, 22
    selling land and, 83
    wampum, 83
traditional liberties, 420
transatlantic cable, 269
translation of Bible into Dutch, 144
Transverse Section & Details of the Dyckman House,
    398
travel industry, 267, 269
travel to Holland, 267, 269–71
tric-trac table, 173
Tubby, William B., 117
Twelve Year Truce (Spain), expiration of, 13
two-handled cup (Schaats), 179

Upper Mills, slaves, 39, 41–42
urbanization, Manhattan and, 116
use right of land, 75
usufructuary privilege, 78

Val-Kill Stone Cottage, 352
van Brekelenkam, Quiringh Gerritsz, Old Man
    Scaling Fish, 160
Van Buren, Cornelis Maessen, 339
Van Buren, Martin, 339
    Irving, Washington and, 137
Van Cortlandt, Frederick, 105–6
van Cortlandt, Maria, 160
Van Cortlandt, Olaff, 383
van Cortlandt, Stephanus, 160
Van Cortlandt House Museum
    Dutch Chamber, 392
    Dutch Room, 392
Van Cortlandt Mansion, 105–6, 107
van Crieckenbeeck, Daniel, 21
van Curler, Arent, 175
van der Donck, Adriaen, 1, 175
    Description of New Netherland, 75–76
    Jonker's land, 1
Van Duyn, Dr. John, 274, 277
Van Houten, Teunis, 140
van Marcken, Jan Gerritsz, estate inventory, debts
    and, 173
van Rensselaer, Kiliaen, 160
van Rensselaer, Nicholas, 176–77, 421, 423
van Rosenvelt, Claes Martenszen, 339, 340
Van Twiller, Walter, 383
Van Voorhees, 120

van Wassenaer, Nicholaes, on Manhattan, 23
Vanderwelden, Theo, Portrait of Adriaen Van Der
    Donck, 76
Veile, Sheldon, 285
Verhulst, Willem, 20–21
    acquisition of Indian lands, 80
Vermeer, Johannes, Officer and Laughing Girl, 9
Vernu, Jacob, textiles, 167
View of Amsterdam (Loots), viii
View of Dutch Colonial style house, 123
View of Broad Street, Wall Street and the City Hall,
    New York, New York (Holland), 104
View of the City and Harbour of New York (de Saint-
    Mémin), xii
View of the IJ Before Amsterdam (Storck), 13
The Vigilant Stuyvesant's Wall Street Gate (Quidor),
    245, 246
Vleeshal, 117
Voetius, Gisbertus, 421
Vookles, Laura, 2
Voorhees, David, 4
Voyage to Hellgate from Cummunipaw (Quidor), 249,
    250

wall clock with nautical scenes, 166
Wallabout Market, 117
    stalls, 118
    tower, 118
Wallkill valley, 97
Walloons, 17–18
wampum, 26, 83
war
    Esopus Wars, 87
    Kieft, Willem, 86–87
    Peach War, 87
War Bond poster based on Norman Rockwell's
    painting Freedom from Fear, 361
war-making ability, firearms, introduction, 10
Washington's Head-quarters, Newburgh, N.Y. (Weir),
    111
Water Street-Zaandam, Holland, 279
waterway crowding in early 1660s, 29–31
Watson, John, Mrs. Kilaen Van Rensselaer, 299, 333
weathercock, 156
weather vane or weathercock from The Reformed
    Church of Tappan, New York, installed by
    1788, 156
Weir, Robert W.
    Saint Nicholas, 260
    Washington's Head-quarters, Newburgh, N.Y., 111

Welch, Alexander McMillan, 396
    The 'Dyckman House' of to-day, 405
    Transverse Section & Details of the Dyckman
        House, *398*
West End Collegiate Church and School, 117
West End Collegiate Church and School complex, *119*
West India Company. *See* WIC (West India
    Company)
    church origins, 139
    colonists contradictions and, 29
    comforter of the sick, 139
    slaves, 38
    ziekentrooster, 139
Westchester Historical Pageant, *328*
Westchester Year of History displays, *3*
WIC (West India Company)
    administration of, 14–15, 16
    de Rasieres, Isaack, 23
        wampum and, 26
    founding of, 14
    inflation and, 27
    monopoly, 22–23
        dropping monopolistic privileges, 28–29
    Netherlands citizens' restrictions, 14
    the Nineteen, 14, 16–17
    trade restrictions, 14
    war with Spain, 14
Wier, Robert W., *Landing of Henrik Hudson, 75*
wilden (savages), 31
Wiltwyck, 97
Windmills (Penfield), 264
With Roosevelt Through Holland, 269
*Wm. H. Crane as Peter Stuyvesant Governor of New
    Amsterdam, 212*

Wolfert's Will (Quidor), *236*
Wollaston, John
    Margaret Philipse, 37
    Mary Philipse, 62
Woodbury, Marcia Oakes, *Cinderella, 284*
World's Columbian Exposition, 302
Wyckoff, Abraham, renovated farmhouse, 114
Wyckoff Durling Barn Education Center at Wyckoff
    Farmhouse Museum, *126*
Wyckoff Farmhouse Museum
    African presence, 126
    The Pieter Claesen Wyckoff House, 116
Wyckoff Farmhouse Museum and Historic House
    Trust, 126
Wyckoff House, architecture, 98–99
Wyckoffs, 120
Wyeth, N. C.
    cover illustrations for *Rip Van Winkle, 205*
    *Hendrik Hudson (with map of the Hudson River),
        412*
    "Here they used to sit in the shade through a long
        lazy summer's day," *240*
    Portrait of Ann Stuyvesant, 291
    Quidor, John and, 239

Yearbook of the Holland Society of New York (Sneek),
    285
Yonkers, 1
York chairs, 183
Young Dutch Girl—Study (Leyendecker), *292*

ziekentrooster, 139